# INTERNATIONAL COMMUNISM AND
## WORLD REVOLUTION

# INTERNATIONAL COMMUNISM AND WORLD REVOLUTION

## HISTORY & METHODS

by

## GÜNTHER NOLLAU

*With a Foreword by*

## LEONARD SCHAPIRO

FREDERICK A. PRAEGER, *Publishers*
NEW YORK

*This English edition is a translation of the improved and expanded text of*
Die Internationale: Wurzeln und Erscheinungsformen des Pro-
letarischen Internationalismus (*Verlag für Politik und Wirtschaft,*
Cologne). *The translation was made by* VICTOR ANDERSEN.

BOOKS THAT MATTER

Published in the United States of America in 1961 by Frederick A.
Praeger, Inc., Publishers, 64 University Place, New York 3, N.Y.
Library of Congress Catalog Card Number: 61-10515

PRINTED IN GREAT BRITAIN

# FOREWORD

IT will soon be a hundred years since the International
Working Men's Association was founded at a big meeting in
St Martin's Hall in London on 28 September 1864. Since
then the short-lived First International, as it became known,
has been succeeded by a Second and yet by a Third or Communist International which, in turn, was dissolved in 1943.
Both the First and Second Internationals foundered, as so
many other attempts at international co-operation have
foundered, on the nationalist aspirations and interests of the
units which composed them. The Third Communist International, founded by Lenin some time after the October
revolution which put the Bolsheviks in power, differed from its
predecessors in that it included a strong disciplined central
organization. But if the earlier bodies failed because of excess of
nationalism, Lenin's creature failed because of excess of
centralism: what had been proclaimed at the outset as an
association of equals soon became little more than a network of
agencies dominated by Moscow, to whose policy interest the
Communist parties throughout the world were firmly subordinated. Of internationalism there remained no trace. So
solid was this control by Moscow that by 1943 it was possible
for the Soviet Union to dissolve the Third International without in the slightest impairing its hold over the Communist
parties of the world—so long as Stalin was alive—if exception
be made for the momentous assertion of its independence by
the Communist party of Yugoslavia in 1948. Indeed, the Third
International as an organization had become a cipher long
before its demise. The reality which survived it was the strictly
controlled network of obedient agencies which Stalin had
created, for the effective operation of which in the interests of
Soviet foreign policy or intelligence work the organizational
control of the Communist party in Moscow was fully adequate.
In this sense, the demise of the Third International, like that of
its two predecessors, was also in some measure due to an excess
of nationalism.

The death of Stalin brought new problems. When once the
dictator was gone and his reputation was shattered by the

v

revelations made by his successor in 1956, here and there in the Communist parties signs of long-forgotten independence began to appear. The emergence of China as a major Communist power revealed the fact that this new Communist state, which, like Yugoslavia, owed comparatively little to Soviet efforts for its existence, was not prepared to accept without question either the ideological or the organizational leadership of Moscow. The Soviet Union itself was also learning from experience that a network of foreign agencies lightly camouflaged as independent Communist parties was not necessarily the best method of advancing world Communism. The problem of resolving national aims and world revolution which defeated Marx in the infancy of the movement is still baffling those who claim to be his disciples today.

Such are the bare facts of a highly intricate and complicated story which is not only a fascinating aspect of contemporary history, but is still of vital importance in understanding contemporary events. The documentation of the international revolutionary movement is immense. There is first of all a great mass of reports of congresses and meetings, and of authoritative texts. There is further a vast literature of memoirs of one kind and another by participants in the movement, many of whom have in the course of its turbulent history ended outside its ranks. A great deal of information on the movement is to be found in the general literature of diplomatic history, since the history of international relations has for long been interwoven with the world revolutionary aims of the Soviet Union. International Communism has been discussed at length in numerous books—praised, attacked, analysed, defended or condemned. Serious monographs have been devoted by scholars to certain of its phases. Yet until Dr Nollau's book appeared in Germany in 1959 no single work, so far as I am aware, had ever attempted to present a complete picture in short compass of the whole movement—from its beginning until the present day.

Dr Nollau's work has been well received by scholars and in my opinion deservedly so. It is well known that it is no easy task to maintain standards of serious scholarship when writing about Communism. Yet it is just this that Dr Nollau seems to me to have achieved. In spite of the difficult task of compression which he has had to undertake in the interests of space, his account never loses in clarity. His assertions of fact are fully documented and his conjectures, where conjecture is unavoidable, are clearly indicated as such and the reader is led to the sources upon which the conjectures are based. He is critical of the sources which he has used and seems to me to have shown steady judgment in weighing the value of the evidence which is available. To have ignored all but official material would have been to give a picture which is completely unreal, and therefore valueless. To have attached equal weight to all secondary material, be it guesswork or gossip—as I am afraid some writers on Communism tend to do—would have meant giving an equally unreliable picture. Dr Nollau has with great judgment steered a sure course between the Scylla and Charybdis which await those who venture upon the seas of the history of Communism. The result is a reliable guide for any student of the world revolutionary movement, whether he wishes to make it the starting-point for his own deeper researches or to accept it as another man's honest summary of events.

Myself a lawyer, I like to think that it is Dr Nollau's legal training which has enabled him to produce this admirable work of summary and analysis. Circumstances have not given him much chance to practise his chosen profession for long. For an advocate's profession, if he is honest, is hardly compatible with dictatorship, as Dr Nollau found both under the Nazis and later in Dresden under the dictatorship of the Communists. He is now working in the Civil Service in Bonn. I hope his duties will not prevent him from continuing his work in the field of the history of Communism.

LEONARD SCHAPIRO

# CONTENTS

### Appendices

# PREFACE TO THE ENGLISH EDITION

I HAVE to thank the numerous friends and critics who were kind enough, following the request contained in the preface to the German edition, to offer suggestions for the improvement of my book. I have made use of these suggestions in preparing the English edition now offered to the reader. I have also tried not only to bring my work up to date but to amplify it by the addition of two new sections, "The Comintern and the Peoples of the East" and "The Soviets and the Chinese Party", as well as many new references to Communism in Asia.

The present book carries the story up to the Third Party Conference of the Russian Workers' Party in June 1960 and to the Declaration of the twelve Communist parties issued on that occasion. The fact that the Moscow Declaration of November 1960 contained nothing fundamentally new made it all the easier to decide not to deal with it.

For their patient acceptance of my many demands for corrections and improvements, I must thank not only my translator, Victor Andersen, but also all the others who have so uncomplainingly borne with this onerous task.

G. NOLLAU

Cologne, *December 1960*

# PREFACE TO THE GERMAN EDITION

"The purpose of the enquiry we are about to undertake is to give us a correct understanding of what is, in order that we can better understand what will be."— Trotsky, *The Revolution Betrayed*.

I KNOW of no account of the origins and features of the collaboration between the parties of the working classes, and particularly none on the essential features of the Comintern and Cominform, written with the specific aim of revealing not only the realities behind the theses and resolutions of the Bolsheviks but also those underlying confused beliefs held by their opponents. This book is an attempt to provide such an account. It does not purport to be a history of the three Internationals. At the same time, I hope I have been able to bring out the salient features of the international collaboration between Communist parties. The collaboration between the Social Democratic parties has only been touched upon in so far as the roots of the Third International extend into the history of those parties.

"Proletarian internationalism" is the name the Bolsheviks give to the principles governing the political relationships between Bolshevik or similarly constituted parties and States. There is, I believe, another reason for regarding "proletarian internationalism" as a correct description of these principles. This is that the activities of the state-capitalistic, bureaucratic and imperialist functionary caste in the present-day Soviet Union can be called neither Socialist nor, in the original meaning of the word, Communist. Whether the Soviet efforts to enlist the working-class parties of the world into the service of the Soviet State, originating as far back as 1925, are an example of genuine internationalism, must be left to the judgment of the reader, who will find presented and commented on in this book a large number of facts throwing a less than favourable light on the behaviour of the Soviet leaders. In presenting these facts, however, it is not my intention to disparage the peoples who have the misfortune to live under Soviet rule.

I shall be grateful to anyone who can provide correction or amplification of my work.

G. NOLLAU

# Chapter I

## "PROLETARIAN INTERNATIONALISM"
## —WHAT IT WAS AND WHAT IT IS

THE Socialist working-class movement has possessed international features from its earliest days, and the content of this internationalism has been subject to the same fluctuations as the collaboration between the parties of the working class.

The call, "Workers of the World, Unite!", appeared in the Communist Manifesto and in the statutes of the League of Communists, the first international workers' association. The declared aim of this internationalism was the overthrow of the "bourgeoisie" in every country and the setting up of the rule of the proletariat. For Marx and Engels, the fathers of these ideas, it went without saying that all members of the League must enjoy equal rights.

Marx's draft statutes for the International Working Men's Association (the First International) embodied these same ideas on the international collaboration of the proletariat with the aim of overthrowing the bourgeoisie and the equality of rights of all members. The organization of the First International was loose in form; and the "General Council acting as an international agency" (p. 15) served mainly for the mutual exchange of information between the various national and local groups. The Second International had no statutes and no fixed organization, and there was not even an International Socialist Bureau until 1896. Questions of international proletarian collaboration were, it is true, discussed at the "International Socialist Congresses", but there is little indication that these discussions led to any results in the practical political sdhere. The First and Second Internationals failed because of a historically-rooted nationalism which, in the wars of 1870 and 1914, moved the masses, in spite of all these ideas of internationalism, to try to kill each other as good Frenchmen, Germans, Russians and so forth.

When the Third International, the Comintern, was founded, it was not only on the expressed basis of fidelity to the traditions of the First International: the principles of the First International—international solidarity, equality of rights for all members and international collaboration for the overthrow of the bourgeoisie—were even anchored in the Comintern statutes. The founders of the Comintern wanted to prevent the new organization from falling a victim to what appeared to them—and especially to Lenin—to be the cause of the failure of the Second International, namely its inability to take action. The *21 Conditions* accepted at the 2nd World Congress and the statutes of the Comintern made it possible for the Executive Committee (the ECCI) to make decisions which the Sections were bound to observe. The ECCI could intervene in the internal affairs of these parties and thus exercise a degree of authority far surpassing that of any of the organs of the previous Internationals. Moreover, the victory of the Bolsheviks in the October Revolution created a new situation in the sphere of proletarian internationalism. The proletarian internationalists had come into power in one country—in Russia. It now remained to be seen whether the power they now wielded would have the same pernicious effects as nationalism had had on the First and Second Internationals. At the 2nd World Congress, Lenin defined the concept of proletarian internationalism as follows:

> . . . proletarian internationalism demands firstly, that the interests of the proletarian struggle in one country be subordinated to the interests of the proletarian struggle on a world scale, and, secondly, that a nation which is achieving victory over the bourgeoisie be able and willing to make the greatest national sacrifice for the sake of overthrowing international capital.[1]

The delegates to the 2nd World Congress may have had the impression that Russia was making "the greatest national

[1] Lenin, *Selected Works* (two volumes), London, 1947, Vol. II, p. 657.

sacrifice for the overthrow of international capital" when, in August 1920, she vainly tried to press forward westwards across the Vistula, hoping to carry the Revolution into a "progressive" country by linking up with the German proletariat. As early as this, in spite of the formal equality of rights of the Russian party with other Sections of the International, there was unmistakable evidence that the authority of the Russian party had been steadily increasing ever since the foundation of the Comintern. The way the Russian party had achieved power was declared at the 2nd World Congress to be a model for others to follow. It was the only Communist party to govern a country. Moscow was the seat of the Comintern bureaucracy, in which Soviet functionaries were strongly represented from the beginning and in which, in the years that followed, they came to achieve a dominant position. In Moscow, too, all the World Congresses met. Thus even in Lenin's lifetime the influence of the CPSU in the Comintern was overwhelming. The 3rd World Congress in 1921 demonstrated that international Communist policies had already become dependent on internal developments within Russia.

At this date domestic reasons—the consequences of "War Communism",[1] the Workers' Opposition and the revolt at Kronstadt—made it impossible for the Russian party to undertake any revolutionary activity outside Russia. Only this can explain the fact that at the 3rd World Congress the Communist parties of the West allowed themselves to be diverted from their revolutionary aims to the struggle for the "vital necessities of life of the proletariat", that is to say, to economic questions. So the interests of world Communism were now subordinated to the demands and requirements of the Russian party.

Lenin believed that if the revolution were to triumph in even one of the "progressive" countries, Russia would soon cease to be the model, and would once more become a backward country. But when in 1924, contrary to the expectations of classical Marxism and the belief of Lenin, it seemed certain

---

[1]The term used by the Russian Communists to describe the incomplete Communist State which was all that could be achieved in the stormy years from 1918 to 1921.

that the revolution would not in the foreseeable future succeed
in the "progressive", i.e. in the Western industrial countries,
it was no longer Lenin who was at the helm. It was the three-
man team of Zinoviev, Kameniev and Stalin. Stalin began to
make his influence felt in the Comintern. He preached his
thesis of "Socialism in One Country" and violently attacked
Trotsky's revolutionary internationalism. At the 14th Party
Congress of the CPSU in 1925, Stalin demanded that the
proletariat of the Western countries should "defend our State
against imperialism". This laid the foundation for the subsequent dogma that the attitude towards the Soviet Union
constituted the test of proletarian internationalism.[1] A significant indication of the role of internationalism and of the part
allotted to the Sections of the Comintern, in spite of their
formal equality of rights, was the attenuation of the power of
the World Congress. Whereas this highest organ of the World
Communist Party was convened fairly regularly until the 5th
Congress in 1924, the 6th Congress did not take place until
1928. Stalin had prevented the Congress from meeting in the
meantime because the "left wing" opposition, Zinoviev and
Trotsky, who had always had a strong following in the Comintern, had not yet been disposed of. Even before the 5th Congress
—and thus while Lenin was still alive—the ECCI had begun to
take basic political decisions on its own authority (such as the
decision to begin the United Front policy) for which, according
to the statutes, authority lay with the World Congress. The less
often the World Congress met, the more the Executive Committee usurped its functions. The CPSU had such a dominating
position in the Executive Committee that it was by the votes of
the CPSU representatives that most questions were decided.
How these CPSU representatives were to vote was decided in
the Politbureau of the CPSU, in which, from 1925 onwards, the
personality of the Secretary-General, Stalin, became ever more
decisive. Stalin, who was concomitantly the most powerful
man in the Soviet State, openly declared that it was the duty of
the international proletariat to defend that State. In other
words, the international proletarian movement was transformed

[1]This development is described by R. N. Carew-Hunt in *A Guide to
Communist Jargon*, London, 1957, p. 128.

into an auxiliary force of the Soviet Union. Whenever it was deemed expedient to realign Soviet foreign policy, the Comintern and its Sections had not only to conform with the altered line, but also had to provide ideological justification for it. From the beginning of the bolshevization of the Communist parties in 1924, the selection of functionaries was made contingent on their devotion to the Soviet Union, although when opposition groups were being eliminated, this criterion was seldom employed openly, as opposed to other charges such as sectarianism or separationism. In the international field, too, the purges of 1936 to 1938 were a means of wiping out even potential opposition. Grave accusations, such as espionage or suspicion of being an enemy agent, were made the justification for the operations of the NKVD and the measures they took. The terror inspired by Stalin's rule also paralysed any impulse to independence amongst international Communists. The national party organizations experienced considerable difficulty when Soviet policy displayed such changes as that from the Popular Front policy to the Stalin-Hitler Pact. Since the end of the 1930s, when such changes of policy have occurred, it has become more difficult to persuade the rank-and-file members of the correctness of the Party line than to persuade the functionaries.

Stalin maintained his dominating position even after the dissolution of the Comintern in 1943. He further strengthened it when a new factor came into being in 1945, that of the Communist-controlled countries of Eastern Europe. These countries were incorporated, not only politically and economically, but also as regards their police forces and their secret services, into the Soviet domain, which at that time represented proletarian internationalism. International Communism was controlled and directed by the CPSU, and the founding of the Cominform in 1947 signified no change in that situation. The conflict with Yugoslavia led to the Cominform Bureau's being transferred from Belgrade to Bucharest. As a result of this development the Cominform became useless to the CPSU as an organ of control over Yugoslavia in its struggle for independence. Stalin had overstepped the mark in the Yugoslav question. In order to prevent any other country within his sphere of domination from following Yugoslavia's example, he adopted a policy of crushing every impulse to nationalism in the other East European countries.

The terrorism of the Stalin régime reached a new high point and was now quite openly carried into the international sphere. In the "People's Democracies" there began the trials of Kostoff, Rajk and Slansky, trials which ended with the destruction of this portion of the "fascist Tito clique" and of the "cosmopolites" and "Zionists". In order to lend emphasis to his meaning, Stalin openly proclaimed that the attitude to the Soviet Union constituted the only test of proletarian internationalism.

This is what proletarian internationalism *was*.

Present-day proletarian internationalism lacks the "iron logic" of Stalin's rule of terror. After Stalin's successors had broken the inordinate power of the secret police, they tried in May 1955 to make a contribution to the easing of tension in the "Socialist" camp by means of a settlement with Tito—no doubt with the intention of coaxing Yugoslavia back into the fold.

The results of the 20th Party Congress—the acceptance of individual roads to Socialism and the destruction of the Stalin cult—had far-reaching effects on international Communism. It is not necessary at this point to consider whether the Soviet leaders realized from the beginning that this would happen. The acceptance of individual roads to Socialism—intended by the Soviet leaders to be the bait to entice Yugoslavia to return to the Eastern bloc and utilized as a weapon in the attempt to bring about united working-class action in the countries of the free world—formed the basis for criticism of the Soviet system by Communist countries such as Poland, Hungary, China and Yugoslavia. Similar criticism of the system from within the international field was evoked when Khrushchev—apparently for reasons of international policy—condemned some of Stalin's crimes in his secret speech. The subsequent attempt to minimize Stalin's "mistakes" as consequences of the cult of personality showed that the probable results of Khrushchev's astonishing frankness were not appreciated until later. When such a tried and true Stalinist as Togliatti, the leader of one of the most powerful Communist parties in Europe, could speak of a polycentric system of Communism, it was a sign of the severity of the shock caused by the publication of the secret speech.

The events in Poland and Hungary in the autumn of 1956 were to a large extent the result of Stalin's repression of the national sentiments of the peoples of Eastern Europe and of the policies of Stalin's successors in allowing exponents of Stalinist policies such as Rakosi, Gerö, Berman and Rokossovski to continue their activities unhindered for so long. The brutal intervention in Hungary showed how little respect the Soviet leaders paid to the principles of proletarian internationalism that they themselves proclaimed—equality of rights, respect for the interests of all nations and non-intervention in the internal affairs of other countries.

The Soviet negotiations with Tito as early as the summer and autumn of 1956 showed that the Soviets were not disposed to grant to the East European countries they had helped to liberate a status comparable with that of Yugoslavia. The Russian views were at first only guardedly stated but were later made public in a stream of Soviet propaganda denying that relationships between "Socialist" countries could be put on the same footing as relationships between them and "capitalist" countries: a theory which allowed the intervention in Hungary to be interpreted as an act of "international solidarity". Under the influence of events, Yugoslavia, Poland and—though not quite to the same extent—China rejected these views as firmly as they rejected Moscow's attempt to persuade faithful satellites to suggest the formation of a new international organization. The solidarity of the world Communist movement was just as much affected by the new factor in the sphere of internationalism after 1945—the existence of the Communist-controlled states in Eastern Europe—as by the death of Stalin and the curtailment of the power of his secret police. When the leaders of Communist parties can no longer be summoned to Moscow and held there (as happened, for example, to Dimitroff as late as 1948); and even more, when it is possible for "deviationists" such as Gomulka to attain leading positions in Communist parties contrary to the will of the Central Committee of the CPSU, then the magnitude of the change becomes clear.

Ever since Stalin died and Yugoslavia managed to attain and hold on to its independence, the Soviet Union has been in the difficult position, as it was in Hungary in 1956, of having to use armed force to maintain its dominating position. This provides the clue to the present character of proletarian internationalism. It furnishes an ideological cloak for Soviet domination.[1] The Communist parties of the free world are used to support the power of the Soviet State and the rule of the bureaucratic functionaries.

This is what proletarian internationalism *is*.

[1]Milovan Djilas, *The New Class*, New York, 1957, p. 174.

# Chapter II

## THE ORIGINS

"Seventy-two years have gone by since the Communist Party announced its programme to the world in the form of a manifesto written by the greatest preceptors of the proletarian revolution, Karl Marx and Friedrich Engels."— *Manifesto of the Communist International to the Proletariat of the Entire World*, 6 March 1919.

### THE LEAGUE OF COMMUNISTS

THE roots of proletarian internationalism go back to the Socialist movement which developed at about the middle of the nineteenth century.

*The Manifesto of the Communist Party* of February 1848, in which Marx and Engels raised their cry, "Workers of the World, Unite!", was composed for the League of Communists. This League, which can be called the first international working-class movement, had developed out of the *Bund der Gerechten* (Federation of the Just), a confederation of German workers who had emigrated to Paris at the time of the Restoration. This *Bund der Gerechten* was already in contact with French revolutionary societies such as the *Société des Saisons*, led by Blanqui.[1]

Several of the active members of the *Bund der Gerechten*, for example Karl Schapper and Heinrich Bauer, had to flee to London as a result of their having taken part in an insurrection organized by the *Société des Saisons*, and it was to London that the centre of their activity was transferred. In 1847 the London group of the *Bund der Gerechten* addressed an appeal to Marx and Engels, who were at that time running a "Communist Correspondence Bureau" in Brussels, to join the *Bund*, and offered to put their programme into a manifesto, to be issued as a manifesto of the *Bund*.[2] Marx and Engels agreed, and in the summer

[1] F. Engels, *Zur Geschichte des "Bundes der Kommunisten"*, Appendix I to *Manifesto der Kommunistischen Partei*, Dietz-Verlag, Berlin, 1949, p. 35.

[2] Franz Mehring, *Einleitung zum 4. Abdruck der Enthüllungen über den Kommunistenprozess zu Köln*, Berlin, 1914.

of 1847 there took place in London the first congress of the
organization, which henceforth called itself the League of
Communists.[1] The first congress drew up statutes, which were
given final approval at the second congress in the same year.
The statutes provided for a legislative organ, the Congress,
which was to meet annually, and for the "Central Committee"
as the executive organ.[2] The lower formations were so be
"leading circles", "circles" and "communes". Regarding the
aims of the League, Article I stated:

> The aim of the League is the overthrow of the bourgeoisie,
> the establishment of the rule of the proletariat, the abolition
> of the bourgeois social order founded upon class antagonisms,
> and the inauguration of a new social order wherein there
> shall be neither classes nor private property.

Article 3 described all members as equal. The international
character of the League was emphasized by the device which
headed the statutes, "Workers of the World, Unite!"

The principal task of the second congress of 1847 was to
discuss the programme of the new League. The congress
agreed with the basic principles of the "critical Communism"
expounded by Marx, and Marx and Engels were commissioned
to work out the manifesto of the League.[3] Marx despatched his
*Manifesto of the Communist Party* to the Central Authority in
London in January 1848, only a few weeks before the French
February Revolution, and it was published in London in
February 1848. The *Communist Manifesto* had hardly any
influence on the outbreak of the 1848 revolution,[4] nor did it
achieve a wide circulation among European workers. According to August Bebel, the *Communist Manifesto* did not become
generally known until the end of the 1860s and the beginning
of the 1870s.[5]

[1]Engels, *op. cit.*, p. 66; Wermuth and Stieber (*Die Communisten-Ver-
schwörungen des neunzehnten Jahrhunderts*, Berlin, 1853, p. 53) believed that the
Communist League had its origin in the League of the Banished, founded
in Paris in 1834. Their error was revealed by Engels in writings which
appeared after the publication of their book. I have followed Engels on this
point.
    [2]Articles 21 and 30 of the statutes, which are reproduced as Appendix I
to this book.
    [3]Engels, *op. cit.*, p. 67.        [4]Wermuth and Stieber, *op. cit.*, p. 65.
    [5]Bebel, *Aus meinem Leben*, Stuttgart, 1914, Part I, p. 131.

The only sections of it which will be quoted here are those touching on the international aspect. The slogan, "Workers of the World, Unite!", was already featured on the cover of the first edition. It was also repeated in the final paragraph:

The Communists scorn to conceal their views and their intentions. They openly proclaim that their aims can only be attained by the overthrow by force of all existing orders of society. Let the ruling classes tremble before the Communist revolution! The proletariat have nothing to lose but their chains. They have the world to gain. Workers of the World, Unite!

This remained the slogan of the international working-class movement right up to the days of the Comintern.

On the international question, Section II of the Manifesto had this to say:

National differences and conflicts between peoples are already tending to disappear with the development of the bourgeoisie, freedom of trade, world markets, uniformity of industrial production and corresponding standards of living. Proletarian rule will cause them to disappear even more. United action, at least by civilized nations, is one of the first conditions for the liberation of the proletariat. To the extent that the exploitation of one individual by another is abolished, to that extent will the exploitation of one nation by another be abolished. The abolition of class distinction within a nation will mean the disappearance of the hostile attitude of nations one to another.

Section VI included these words:

Finally, Communists everywhere will work towards the linking up of the democratic parties of all countries and their understanding of one another.

The League did not confine itself to stressing the international character of the working-class movement in its statutes, but was also internationally active. Its members included Englishmen, Belgians, Hungarians, Poles and Germans. International meetings were held in London.[1] In the introduction to the *Manifesto of the Communist Party* it was stated that the Manifesto

[1] Franz Mehring, *Deutsche Sozialdemokratie*, Berlin 1878, p. 58.

had been published in English, French, German, Italian and Danish.

The *Bund der Gerechten* had been a clandestine society.[1] Although Engels declared[2] that the League, "at least for normal times of peace" had been transformed into a propaganda society, the statutes contained, along with democratic features, sections which made it possible to revive clandestine activity.[3] Examples were:

Article 2. Conditions of membership are:

......................................
......................................

(f) they shall not disclose any matters concerning the internal life of the League;

Article 4. All who enter the League shall assume special membership names.

Article 9. The communes are not to know one another or to carry on any correspondence with one another.

Article 42. Expelled or suspended members, and likewise all persons under suspicion should, for the sake of the League, be supervised and rendered harmless. Any machinations on the part of such individuals are to be instantly reported to the commune concerned.

The "times of peace" Engels had had in mind ended with the outbreak of the French February Revolution in 1848. In an attempt to extend this revolution to other countries in Europe, many of the émigrés returned to their homelands[4] and the League temporarily lost three-quarters of its membership.[5] League members tried to push forward the revolution in the Rhine States, in Hesse, Prussia and Saxony. Engels, Freiligrath and Marx acted as the editors of a newspaper, *Die Neue*

[1]Engels, *op. cit.*, p. 58, "The Clandestine League"; p. 66, "Time for Conspiracy".

[2]Engels, *op. cit.*, p. 66; also Franz Mehring, *Deutsche Sozialdemokratie*, Berlin, 1878, p. 58.

[3]That R. Meyer, on page 100 of his *Der Emanzipationskampf des vierten Standes* (Berlin 1874) called the League of Communists "a completely clandestine League" was probably due to the limited information available to him at that time.

[4]Wermuth and Stieber, *op. cit.*, p. 67.        [5]Engels, *op. cit.*, p. 70.

*Rheinische Zeitung*, in Cologne from 1 June 1848, and supported the interests of the working class in a manner which was in those days unique. Nevertheless, reports by William Wolff, Ernst Dronkes and Stefan Born to the Central Authority (Central Committee) in London made it clear that hardly any results worthy of note were achieved.[1] The failure of their efforts forced the revolutionaries to leave their homelands once more and by November 1849 most of the members of the former Central Authority (Central Committee) were back in London.[2] The revolution had been crushed. As is clear from his *Address to the League by the Central Authority* (Central Committee) Marx misjudged the situation and continued to expect revolutionary action in the future. He accordingly gave advice on how bourgeois democratic reforms could be given an added revolutionary complexion by attacks on private property and heavy taxation of capital.

The many trials of League members which took place in Germany at this period,[3] and particularly the Cologne Communist Trial, put an end to the work of the League of Communists. Within a few days of the pronouncement of sentences in the Cologne trial on 12 November 1852, the League accepted a proposal by Marx that it should also be dissolved in countries outside Germany.

### THE INTERNATIONAL WORKING MEN'S ASSOCIATION (THE FIRST INTERNATIONAL)

In the years that followed, only Karl Marx and a few of his associates such as Engels and Liebknecht, who were sharing his exile in London, still fostered the idea of international working-class solidarity. It was not until 1860 that circumstances made possible preparations for the founding of a new international workers' movement.[4]

---

[1] Franz Mehring, *Einleitung zum 4 Abdruck*, Berlin, 1914, reproduced in K. Marx's *Enthüllungen über den Kommunistenprozess zu Köln*, Dietz-Verlag, Berlin, 1952, pp. 158 ff.; also Wermuth and Stieber, *op. cit.*, p. 69, ". . . nevertheless, the Communist Party's activities in 1848 were in fact a fiasco . . .".

[2] Engels, *op. cit.*, p. 72.     [3] Wermuth and Stieber, *op. cit.*, pp. 121 ff.

[4] Th. Rothstein provides information in the years preceding the foundation of the First International in *Aus der Vorgeschichte der Internationale* in a supplement to the *Neue Zeit*, Stuttgart, 1913.

The years of high liberalism had brought English business-men enormous profits and wealth, whereas among large sections of the working population there were poverty and want. Child labour was accepted as normal.[1] The American Civil War (1861-65) gave rise to a scarcity of cotton in England, and this led to unemployment in the textile industry. The English manufacturers tended to support the Southern cause, while the sympathies of the workers were with the Northern States and their fight against slavery. In 1863 there were also, both in England and in France, workers' demonstrations in favour of the Poles, who had risen against Tsarist Russia. Deputations of French workers went to London and on 28 September 1864, on the occasion of one of these visits, workers of all nationalities assembled in St Martin's Hall. This marked the birth of the International Working Men's Association, which was called the First International. The meeting went on from a discussion of the Polish situation to consideration of the position of the working masses in the industrialized countries. A Committee was formed and was instructed to work out a programme and statutes for an international working men's union and to call a subsequent international congress to approve the programme and the statutes. The Committee included Frenchmen (le Lubez and Bosquet), Italians (Major Luigi Wolff, Mazzini's private secretary, and Ilama), a Pole (G. E. Holthorp), a Swiss (Nusperli), a number of Englishmen, including Odger, and the Germans Marx and Eccarius.[2]

The Italian members persuaded this General Council, as the Committee styled itself, to agree to ask Mazzini, the Italian revolutionary, who was at that time very popular in England, to work out a programme in the form of an inaugural address and statutes. Mazzini's draft programme showed that he was more concerned with political than with social problems. He rejected the class struggle, and his draft statutes envisaged a centrally-organized clandestine organization.[3] The General

[1]Karl Marx, *Inaugural Address to the International Working Men's Association:* Marx/Engels, *Ausgewählte Schriften*, Dietz-Verlag, Berlin, 1951, pp. 351 ff.

[2]R. Meyer, *op. cit.*, pp. 103 ff.; Mehring, *op. cit.*, p. 65. A complete list of the members of the Committee is given in William Z. Foster's *History of the Three Internationals*, New York, 1955, p. 49.

[3]R. Meyer, *op. cit.*, p. 104.

uncil rejected Mazzini's draft and gave the task to Marx. His inaugural address, like his Manifesto of 1848, ended with the words, "Workers of the World, Unite!" and was unanimously accepted by the General Council, together with his draft statutes. The international congress held at Geneva in 1866 confirmed the acceptance of Marx's draft.[1] The statutes included a demand that the working class bring about its own emancipation—this to be an international task—by taking over the means of production. Article 1 laid down that the purpose of the Association was to create a focal point for planned collaboration between the working-class movements of the various countries.

Article 3 laid down that an International Congress was to be held once a year. The task of the General Council was defined as follows:

> The Central Council shall form an international agency between the different co-operating associations, so that the working men in one country be constantly informed of the movements of their class in every other country; that an enquiry into the social state of the different countries of Europe be made simultaneously, and under a common direction; that the questions of general interest mooted in one society be ventilated by all, and that when immediate practical steps should be needed, as, for instance, in case of international quarrels, the action of the associated societies be simultaneous and uniform. Whenever it seems opportune, the General Council shall take the initiative of proposals to be laid before the different national or local societies. (Article 6.)

The Association was based on the assumption of the equality of rights of all its members, and declared:

> that this International Association and all societies and individuals adhering to it will acknowledge truth, justice and morality as the bases of their conduct towards each other, and towards all men, without regard to colour, creed or nationality; . . . No rights without duties, no duties without rights.

The classic exponents of Marxism, Marx and Engels, both

[1] R. Meyer, *op. cit.*, p. 109. The statutes are reproduced as Appendix II to this book.

co-founders of the First International, similarly deman
that all members should enjoy equal rights. On 29 April 187
speaking of the possibility that émigré Russians might be
permitted to occupy important posts in the Sections of the
International, Engels wrote to Marx:

> A capital piece of impudence, that in order to introduce
> unity into the European proletariat, it should be under
> Russian command! . . . with the excuse of the "principe
> internationale" they will insinuate themselves into every
> working-class movement, sneak into leading positions, bring
> into the Sections the private intrigues and squabbles in-
> separable from Russians—and then the General Council
> will have its hands full.[1]

The International Working Men's Association did hold its
annual congresses, but it soon became clear that it was not
likely that it would be able to fulfil its most important task,
that of preventing armed conflict between nations.

Not many members were as unhesitating in their belief in
cosmopolitan republicanism as Karl Marx. Some, such as
Wilhelm Liebknecht, may have come to support internationalism because of their dislike of Prussia. In 1865, after he had
been expelled from Prussia, Liebknecht was living in Leipzig,
where he found that many people fostered a violent hatred for
everything Prussian, a hatred felt not only by the extreme Right
but also by the Left.[2] In his own early days August Bebel was
influenced by Liebknecht's anti-Prussian views, as is clear from
his first speeches in the Reichstag.[3]

Many adherents were attracted to the Association by its
antipathy to nationalism. However, it turned out that the First
International was unequal to dealing with the clash between
national states which developed in 1870. The Congress held in
Brussels in 1868 was still recommending its members to down
tools immediately upon the outbreak of a war,[4] but when the
Franco-Prussian War broke out in 1870, it did no more than

---

[1] Karl Marx/Friedrich Engels, *Briefwechsel*, Vol. IV, Berlin 1950, pp.
375 ff., and Wolfgang Leonhard, *Kominform und Jugoslavien*, Belgrade, 1949,
p. 12.

[2] Mehring, *op. cit.*, p. 85.        [3] See also Bebel, *op. cit.*, Part I, p. 126.

[4] R. Meyer, *op. cit.*, p. 117.

Cᴄduce the members of the International Working Men's Association to publish a manifesto addressed to "the workers of all nations" and protesting against the war, declaring that this "dynastic" war was unjust and would only lead to "complete despotism on both sides of the Rhine".[1] The First Address made play with declarations of support by workers in Berlin, Chemnitz and Brunswick, but assurances such as "we shall never forget that the workers of every land are our friends and the despots of every country are our enemies", or "we solemnly swear that neither the blare of the trumpet nor the thunder of the cannon, neither victory nor defeat shall divert us from the common task of uniting the workers of every land", did nothing whatever to deter the warring "despots".

Still, when the vote was taken on the War Loan in the Reichstag on 21 July 1870, Wilhelm Liebknecht and August Bebel abstained from voting. Their statement, not made in a speech but only laid before the House in writing, said *inter alia*:

> As opponents in principle of every dynastic war, as Social Republicans and members of the International Working Men's Association, which opposes all oppressors irrespective of nationality and seeks to bind together the oppressed into one great band of brothers, we cannot declare, either directly or indirectly, in favour of the present war: and accordingly we abstain from voting.[2]

Liebknecht and Bebel voted against further military expenditure in the session of 26 November 1870, when they particularly expressed their opposition to the imminent annexation of Alsace-Lorraine. On 24 March 1872 both Liebknecht and Bebel were sentenced to two years' fortress confinement for their agitation against the war, the charge being "preparing to commit high treason against the State".

After the fall of Napoleon III, and at the suggestion of the General Council of the International, English workers began a campaign for the recognition of the French Republic. A

[1] Cf. the *First Address of the General Council on the Franco-Prussian War*, addressed to the members of the International Working Men's Association in Europe and the United States; and Marx/Engels, *Ausgewählte Schriften*, Vol. I, p. 458.

[2] August Bebel, *Aus meinem Leben*, Stuttgart, 1914, Part II, p. 179.

B

*Second Address* by the General Council on the Franco-Prussian War, dated 9 November 1870,[1] called on the Sections of the International Working Men's Association to "take positive action"; but in vain.

What the Addresses by the First International failed to achieve, namely the activation of the working masses, came about when the Paris Commune was proclaimed on 18 March 1871. This was in point of fact a single action confined to Paris, but it achieved international significance because of the fact that at that time Paris was beleaguered by the Germans. Since then there have been a number of similar situations, when there has been a change from a bourgeois to a proletarian revolution following on defeat in war. The French Government crushed the insurrection of the Commune with a severity which led to a heavy toll of human life.[2]

Although Lenin thought that the Paris Commune was the most magnificent example of a proletarian movement the nineteenth century ever saw,[3] the First International played little part,[4] even if some of the Frenchmen who participated were members of the Working Men's Association. One of these was Eugène Varlin, an anarchist and one of the founders of the International Working Men's Association, who was executed for being one of the members of the Commune.[5]

The Government of the Third Republic used the insurrection by the Paris Commune as an excuse to make it a penal offence

[1] Marx/Engels, *Ausgewählte Schriften*, Vol. I, pp. 463 ff.

[2] Edouard Dolléans, *Histoire du Movement Ouvrier*, Paris 1948, speaks in Vol. II, p. 13, of 100,000 dead.

[3] *Über die Pariser Kommune*, Berlin, 1946, p. 11.

[4] It is doubtful whether Marx had a "gigantic plan" to bring about social upheavals in various European countries, as R. Meyer thinks (*op. cit.*, Part I, p. 123). Meyer's opinion on this aspect obviously springs from his over-estimation of the influence of the International Working Men's Association. In fact, the lack of resolution of the Association was one of the causes of the mistrust of the French members towards the "German Jew", Marx (Cf. Meyer, *op. cit.*, Part II, pp. 613 and 718), which was later exploited by the supporters of Bakunin.

[5] Joll, *The Second International*, London, 1955, p. 27, note 2: also Marx/Engels, *op. cit.*, Vol. I, pp. 513–4: Mehring, *op. cit.*, pp. 67–8: R. Meyer, *op. cit.*, Part II, pp. 620, 632, 673, 690.

to be a member of the International,[1] and the Foreign Minister, Jules Favre, wrote round to the European Powers demanding rigorous measures against the Association. The punitive measures taken against it made impossible any further activity by the Association in France.[2] It told heavily against the standing of the First International that its part in the international conflict had been confined to making paper protests. The next congress could not be held until the autumn of 1872, when it met at The Hague. At this congress Marx, who had hitherto dominated the General Council, and with it the International, found himself faced with a powerful opposition led by Bakunin, a Russian. As an anarchist, Bakunin demanded the abolition of all classes, all forms of authority, all nationalities and all social inequality. Marx's omnipotent State of the future seemed to Bakunin to be the most reactionary picture possible.[3] Bakunin's anarchist demands appear utopian to us, although his vision of the omnipotent State of the future as postulated by Marx has assumed a form which, in the Soviet Union and some of the People's Democracies, is the very opposite of progressive —it is reactionary. The majority at the Hague Congress remained loyal to Marx. Bakunin and some of his followers were expelled from the International. In view of the repressive measures being taken in Europe, the seat of the General Council was transferred to New York,[4] which made any further activity by the First International in Europe practically impossible. The last congress, held in Geneva in 1873, was already little more than a gesture, and the First International was formally dissolved by a resolution passed in Philadelphia in July 1876.[5]

[1] Joll, *op. cit.*, p. 12. The Third Republic was at this time following in the footsteps of Napoleon III, who had before 1870 already had various members of the International prosecuted (*see* Meyer, *op. cit.*, Part I, p. 123, Part II, p. 591). The basis for the subsequent prosecutions was the French law against the International of 14 March 1872 (*see* Dr Zacher, *Die Rothe Internationale*, Berlin, 1884, p. 68).

[2] Cf. a letter by the Secretary of the General Council of the International Working Men's Association, John Hales, to *The Times* on 13 June 1871, also R. Meyer, *op. cit.*, p. 718.

[3] Franz Mehring, *Deutsche Socialdemokratie, op. cit.*, p. 128.

[4] William Z. Foster, *History of the Communist Party of the United States*, New York, 1952, p. 60.

[5] Joll, *The Second International*, London, 1955, p. 22.

## THE SECOND INTERNATIONAL

The International Socialist Congresses held in Geneva (1877) and Coire (1881), the International Trade Union Congresses in Paris (1883 and 1886), the Social Democratic Party Conference in St Gallen in 1887 and the London Trade Union Conference of 1888, which was also attended by French and Belgian Socialists, showed that in spite of the dissolution of the First International the working classes had not abandoned the idea of collaboration on the international plane. The celebrations of the 100th anniversary of the French Revolution seemed to call for the holding of the long-projected large-scale international Socialist assembly in Paris in 1889. Two international Socialist congresses met in Paris in that year, one composed of the *Possibilistes* of Paul Brousse, who were supported by the trade unions; and one composed of the adherents of Marx, led by Jules Guesde.[1] The Marxist congress was held in the Salle Pétrelle and was attended by some 400 delegates from 20 European countries and from America. Of these 221 were French and 81 were from Germany, in spite of the fact that the anti-Socialist laws against the Social Democrats were still in force.[2]

Among the German delegates were August Bebel, Wilhelm Liebknecht, Eduard Bernstein, Clara Zetkin and Karl Legien, who was to contribute to the collapse of the Kapp Putsch in 1920 by calling a general strike.[3] Other delegates of note were the Frenchmen Jules Guesde, Edouard Vaillant, and Charles Longuet (Marx's son-in-law), the Belgians Edouard Anseele and Emile Vandervelde, the Italian Andreas Costa, the Austrian Viktor Adler, the Dutchman Domela Nieuwenhuis and the Russian Georgi Plekhanov.

The meeting in the Salle Pétrelle may be regarded as the inaugural meeting of the Second, or Paris International.[4] Its outstanding characteristic was the strong French and German representation which was manifested in the handshake between the two presidents of the inaugural congress, Edouard Vaillant

[1]G. D. H. Cole, *The Second International*, London, 1956, Part I, pp. 7 ff.
[2]Joll, *op. cit.*, p. 36: Edouard Dolléans, *Histoire du Mouvement Ouvrier*, Paris, 1948, Vol. II, pp. 99 ff.
[3]Cole, *op. cit.*, Part I, p. 7.        [4]Joll, *op. cit.*, pp. 36–7.

and Wilhelm Liebknecht. The foundations of Franco-German Socialist solidarity seemed to have been laid.

The Second International had no statutes and no fixed organization. (An "International Socialist Bureau" was not created until seven years later, in 1896.[1]) Accordingly the Workers' International was mainly occupied in calling the international Socialist congresses. The rise of parliamentary democracy since the middle of the nineteenth century had given the working-class parties an increasing number of opportunities to enter parliaments. The demands they voiced make it clear that they were bent on making their social and political contribution to improving the situation of the working class. Internationalism continued to be the animating spirit of the workers' parties, but had scarcely any effect in the practical sphere.

### THE INTERNATIONAL SOCIALIST CONGRESSES

The resolution passed on the final day of the inaugural Congress of 1889 demanded the introduction of the eight-hour day and the organizing of international workers' demonstrations on 1 May 1890. In their demonstrations, however, the workers were to have regard to the particular circumstances optaining in their home countries. This clause was inserted into the resolution at the suggestion of the German Socialists, who were anxious to do nothing which might lead to a prolongation of the anti-Socialist laws due to expire in 1890. The way in which 1 May should be celebrated was also the main item on the agenda of the international congress held in Zurich in 1893. The Austrian Socialist leader, Viktor Adler, was in favour of laying down tools on May Day, while August Bebel reiterated that there could be no general stoppage of work in Germany on that day. Against the votes of the German delegates, a resolution was passed recommending that May Day should be celebrated by stopping work and by workers' demonstrations in favour of peace and the eight-hour day.[2]

The Anarchists rejected every form of State rule, whether

---

[1]Friedrich Adler, *Die Erneuerung der Internationale*, Vienna, 1919, p. 189.

[2]Joll, *op. cit.*, p. 53: Bernstein, *Zur Theorie und Geschichte des Sozialismus*, Berlin, 1940, Part II, p. 8.

bourgeois or proletarian, and preached the doctrine of "direct action". Their quarrel with the Marxists was the cause of the passing of a resolution at the Zurich Congress aimed at the expulsion of the Anarchists.[1] There were more violent disagreements at the London Congress in 1896, at which the Zurich resolution was finally confirmed.[2]

The London Congress dealt for the first time with the question of the attitude which Socialist parties should adopt towards one another in the event of war between capitalist states, a problem which was to assume overwhelming importance for the Second International in the years to come. At this stage, however, first place was taken by the differences between the Reformists and the Revisionists. It was no accident that in Germany these differences were theoretical in origin, whereas in France they were evoked by an actual political event, to wit the Socialist Deputy Alexandre Millerand's joining a bourgeois Cabinet as Minister of Trade. Millerand's step was possible because the bourgeois parliamentary system was such that Socialists could justifiably collaborate with it, for example, in the sphere of social reform.[3] This situation did not exist in Germany. There, the Reich Chancellor did not depend on a majority in the Reichstag, and the government only fell if the Chancellor lost the Kaiser's confidence.[4]

In spite of their increasing parliamentary strength, the German Social Democrats could never be anything but the Opposition. Nevertheless, they held fast to their policy of seeking to attain power by parliamentary means. One is forced to ask what their leaders thought would have happened if the Social Democrats had in fact been able to obtain a majority in parliament. Did they expect that the Kaiser, on whose confidence alone the Chancellor depended, would call on August Bebel to form a government? Could it still be called classical Marxism when the Social Democrats refused to leave the parliamentary road in spite of hard constitutional reality?

[1] Cole, *op. cit.*, Part I, p. 26.
[2] Cole, *op. cit.*, Part I, p. 28.
[3] Joll, *op. cit.*, pp. 77 ff.
[4] Articles 15 and 24 of the Reich Constitution of 1871 in *Dokumente der Deutschen Politik und Geschichte von 1848 bis zur Gegenwart*, Berlin, 1952, Vol. I, p. 206.

In contrast to this "reformist" attitude in practical politics, in the theoretical sphere the "revisionism" of Eduard Bernstein was countered with classical Marxist arguments. Bernstein had published a book in 1899, *The Preconditions for Socialism*, in which he had set his face against Marx's theory of surplus value and his belief in the impending collapse of the capitalist system.[1]

At the next international congress in Paris in 1900 the only item for discussion after the case of Millerand was Millerand's "reformism". The resolution drafted by Kautsky, the "pontiff of Socialism", approved the entry of a Socialist into a bourgeois Cabinet as a tactical measure on the road to power.[2] This congress also put into effect the resolution, passed at the London Congress in 1896, that an International Socialist Bureau should be created.

This Bureau was given two organs. One was an International Committee composed of delegates elected by the Sections of the International. The other was an inter-parliamentary commission to co-ordinate the policies of Socialists represented in the various national parliaments. The secretariat of the Bureau was to act on behalf of the International between congresses and to implement decisions taken by the congresses when they met.[3]

"Revisionism" was definitely rejected by a large majority at the Amsterdam Congress of 1904, as it had also been at the Social Democratic Congress in Dresden in 1903. Jean Jaurès, the brilliant speaker for the Opposition, told the German Social Democrats in Amsterdam:

Behind the rigidity of your theoretical formulas, which Comrade Kautsky will go on supplying you with until the end of his days, you are concealing your powerlessness from your own and from the international proletariat.[4]

The German Social Democrats were able to force through their policies in spite of the opposition of the other European Socialist parties in the International, and this was to prove to be to their own disadvantage. In the summer of 1914 it was

[1]Pp. 37 ff. of Bernstein's book.   [2]Cole, *op. cit.*, Part I, p. 40.
[3]Cole, *op. cit.*, Part I, pp. 44 ff.   [4]Joll, *op. cit.*, p. 103.

made plain that when Jaurès had said at the Amsterdam Congress that what burdened Europe and the world most was the political impotence of the German Social Democrats, he had not been mistaken. The course of subsequent events demonstrated that the German Socialists of those days lacked the clear perception of their own potential they would have had to have in order to be able to steer the International through the impending storm.

## THE CAUSES OF THE DECLINE OF THE SECOND INTERNATIONAL

The Russo-Japanese War and the Morocco crisis of 1905-06 were followed in 1907 by an international Socialist Congress, held in Stuttgart. Henceforward the fear of armed conflict between the European Powers loomed so large that the problem of the attitude of the Socialist parties in the event of such a conflict came to be the main question at this and all subsequent congresses. In the course of the discussions at Stuttgart,[1] Bebel felt that military and war questions had been "discussed and voted on so often already that it would now be sufficient simply to reaffirm the decisions already taken". The resolution proposed by Bebel in the name of the Executive Committee of the Social Democrats regarding the attitude of the Socialists on the outbreak of a war said:[2]

> If an outbreak of war appears imminent, the workers and their parliamentary representatives in the countries concerned must take all possible action to prevent the outbreak, using any means they consider the most effective. And if a war should still break out, they must take all steps to bring it to a speedy conclusion.

Rosa Luxemburg, Lenin and Martow tried to give this resolution some revolutionary stiffening. After discussions lasting for days, the following formulation of their proposal was unanimously accepted:[3]

> If an outbreak of war appears imminent, the workers and their parliamentary representatives in the countries con-

---

[1] Cf. *Internationaler Sozialisten-Kongress, Stuttgart 1907*, Berlin, 1907, pp. 81 ff.
[2] Cf. *Internationaler Sozialisten-Kongress, Stuttgart, 1907*, p. 86.
[3] *Ibid.*, p. 102, Lenin/Zinoviev, *Gegen den Strom*, Hamburg, 1921, p. 476.

cerned must do everything in their power to prevent war breaking out, using suitable measures which will naturally differ and increase according to the intensifying of the class struggle and the general political situation. If war should still break out, they must take all steps to bring it to a speedy conclusion and make every possible effort to exploit the economic and political crisis brought about by the war to rouse the people and thereby accelerate the downfall of the rule of the capitalist class.

Developments in the European situation kept alive discussion of this problem. The annexation of Bosnia and Herzegovina by Austria in 1908 and the naval arms race between England and Germany made it obvious that war between the European Powers was within the realm of probability. Accordingly the question of the attitude of the Socialist parties in the event of war was again on the agenda at the next international congress in Copenhagen in 1910. The French Socialist, Vaillant, and the English Labour Member of Parliament, Keir Hardie, put forward the view that the general strike should be considered as a means of defence by the working classes against war. The majority evaded giving a definite decision on this suggestion and remitted it to the next congress for consideration. The International Socialist Bureau was charged, in the event of war becoming imminent, with taking the necessary steps to unite the parties of the working classes in the countries concerned in order to protect them from the war.[1] The resolution contained no clear suggestions as to what steps the Bureau should take to fulfil this responsibility or what means the working-class parties were supposed to use in order to banish the threat of war.

In the summer of 1912 the outbreak of the first Balkan War forced the International to convene an international congress sooner than had been planned, for the next regular congress was not to have taken place until 1913, in Vienna. The Congress met in Basle in November 1912. In his speech, the Belgian trade union leader, Edouard Anseele, the Chairman of the Congress, exhorted Germany and France to forget their differences and called on England and Germany to put an end to the

[1] Joll, *op. cit.*, pp. 142 ff.

naval arms race and to abolish poverty and repression instead. He continued:

> The International is strong enough to use this tone of authority to those in power and, if necessary, to follow up words with action. Let us declare war on war! Peace to the world! Hurrah for the Workers' International![1]

The Basle Congress reaffirmed the resolutions passed in 1907 and 1910, and declared that it regarded the artificially nurtured arms race between Great Britain and Germany as the greatest threat to the peace of Europe. There was still no progress towards defining practical measures likely to prevent the outbreak of war between the European Powers or to bring to an end a conflict once it had broken out. The speeches made at Basle were characterized by an optimism and self-confidence that continued until the outbreak of the war in 1914. The confidence of the German Social Democrats in their own strength was founded on the consciousness that they had kept their end up against the power of the State during the period of the anti-Socialist laws in Germany; and it was reinforced by their increasing electoral gains since the laws were repealed in 1890. In the 1912 Reichstag elections the Social Democrats gained 4,500,000 votes and 110 seats as compared with 1,500,000 votes and 35 seats in 1890. Similar tendencies were manifesting themselves in other European countries. In France, one of the Socialist groups, the Section Française de l'Internationale Ouvrière (SFIO), alone gained so many supporters that in 1914 it won 1,400,000 votes and 103 seats in the Chamber. In Belgium, the workers' leaders had tried to compel the introduction of universal suffrage by means of a general strike. The self-confidence of the Socialist leaders was further strengthened by their certainty that, in spite of all the crises, the peace which had existed between the Great Powers of Europe since 1870 would be maintained—a wish which was fathered by the idea of preventing any impairment of the condition of the workers, which had been steadily improving since the middle of the nineteenth century.

This optimism on the part of the Socialists was paralleled in

[1]Joll, *op. cit.*, p. 154.

the optimism of the bourgeois, which was based on the philosophical and biological teachings of people such as Darwin and
Comte, and was encouraged by the speed of technological
progress in the nineteenth century. To factors such as the power
of governments and international differences, which might
have lessened their optimism, the Socialist leaders paid as
little attention as they paid to warning voices from their own
ranks. As early as 1891 the Dutch Anarchist Domela Nieuwenhuis had given a disagreeable warning that the German
comrades had no international Socialist feelings.[1] George
Bernard Shaw had referred to the difficult situation of the
Socialists under the German Kaiser and the much greater
freedom in England when he wrote to the London Congress in
1896 that the Germans, with their compact Social Democratic
majority in the Reichstag, were far in advance of the English,
but that Wilhelm Liebknecht was to go to prison (for *lèse-
majesté*) for making a speech that the Conservative Arthur
Balfour could have made with the approbation of the whole of
England.[2] At the 1907 Congress, Gustav Hervé had said in the
course of the debate on "Militarism and International Conflicts":[3]

> I am not unaware of the great services rendered by Marx,
> Engels, Lessalle, Kautsky, Bebel and also Eduard Bernstein
> (the only one who still has any courage)—not at all. But
> now you are only voting and counting machines (*laughter*)
> of a party with mandates and party funds. You want to
> conquer the world with the ballot-paper. But what I ask you
> is this—when German soldiers are sent off to restore the
> throne of the Russian Emperor—when Prussia and France
> fall upon the proletariat—what will you do then? Give me
> your answer, not metaphysically, not dialectically, but
> openly and clearly, practically and tactically. What will you
> do then?
>
> I was very much looking forward to a personal meeting
> with the German Social Democrats, whom for years I had
> only known, and dismissed with a shrug of the shoulders,
> from their quibbling, hair-splitting quarrels about the

[1] Joll, *op. cit.*, p. 70.
[2] Quoted by Joll, *op. cit.*, p. 76.
[3] Cf. *Internationaler Sozialisten-Kongress*, Stuttgart, 1907, pp. 84 ff.

interpretation of Karl Marx. Now I have seen them here, in the streets of Stuttgart—the German proletariat. My naïve illusions have been shattered. They are good, contented and well-fed bourgeois.

The grain of truth in remarks such as these has been just as little appreciated as the significance of national dissimilarities which, in spite of all proclamations on the power of the International, had their effects inside the Socialist camp itself. There were, for example, differences of opinion between the German Social Democrats and the Polish Socialists who lived in the Polish areas under Prussian occupation.[1] Another example was when, at the Zurich Congress of 1893, Domela Nieuwenhuis charged August Bebel with having expunged all trace of the misdeeds of his own bourgeoisie when it came to dealing with the old national enemy. French Socialists, too, gave an indication of the power represented by nationalism. Millerand, for example, the Socialist who joined a bourgeois cabinet, said:[2]

"We must never forget that we are at one and the same time internationalists, Frenchmen and patriots."

At the Stuttgart Congress, Jaurès had expressed in a brilliant formulation the view that the nation was the treasury of human genius and progress and that it would ill become the proletariat to smash these precious receptacles of human culture.[3] French Socialists supported demands for the return of Alsace-Lorraine, while the German Social Democrats maintained (as they continued to do right up to 1919) that this question must be decided by means of a plebiscite.

In the multi-racial state of Austro-Hungary, too, the Social Democrats were affected by the nationality problem. The Austrian Social Democrats were restrained in their efforts to maintain Social Democratic unity in the whole kingdom. The Czechs, on the other hand, brought their desire for their own trade unions, separate from the Austrians, before the International. They were turned down by the Copenhagen Congress

[1] Letter from August Bebel to Viktor Adler of 2 August 1910 in Viktor Adler's *Briefwechsel mit A. Bebel u. K. Kautsky*, Vienna, 1954, p. 506.

[2] See p. 22 above and Albert Orry, *Les Socialistes Indépendants*, Paris, 1911, pp. 28–9.

[3] *Internationaler Sozialisten-Kongress*, Stuttgart, 1907, p. 89.

in 1910, but they refused to accept the decision and formed a separate Czech Socialist party.[1]

In Germany there were increasing signs that in an emergency the Social Democrats would yield to the demands of the national State. Bebel had said in Stuttgart in 1907 that the means Hervé proposed for opposing war—mass strikes, desertion by reservists and open insurrection—were quite out of the question in Germany. In a speech in the Reichstag in the same year, Gustav Noske said that every German, regardless of party, recognized the necessity for national defence as a matter of course.[2] In 1913 a large majority of the Social Democrats, including Karl Liebknecht, voted in favour of new financial measures intended to provide, *inter alia*, for increased military expenditure.[3] For years before World War I there had been a steadily increasing opposition in the Social Democratic Party to the "mulish rejection" of the military budget. This tendency implied the abandonment of the principle so long preached by the Social Democrats, "not a man and not a penny for this system".[4] Only a minority, led by Rosa Luxemburg, repeated their question whether a revision of the Prussian system of three-class suffrage should be brought about by "direct action", i.e. mass strikes.[5] On this question Rosa Luxemburg could point to the success achieved by the use of the general strike in Belgium in the struggle for universal suffrage.

Regardless of these portents, the Social Democratic deputy, Eduard David, declared in the Reichstag on 3 December 1912:[6]

The masses used to let themselves be whipped up against each other and unresistingly herded into mass murder by those with a vested interest in war. But not any more. The

---

[1]Viktor Adler, *Briefwechsel mit A. Bebel u. K. Kautsky*, Vienna, 1954, pp. 507 ff.

[2]G. Noske, *Erlebtes aus Aufstieg und Niedergang einer Demokratie*, Offenbach, 1947, p. 27.

[3]Noske, *op. cit.*, p. 42.

[4]Joll, *op. cit.*, p. 146.

[5]Letter from Kautsky to V. Adler, dated 9 October 1913, in V. Adler, *op. cit.*, p. 583: Rosa Luxemburg's essay, published in 1906, *Massenstreik, Partei und Gewerkschaften* in: Rosa Luxemburg, *Ausgewählte Reden und Schriften*, Berlin, 1951, pp. 157 ff.

[6]Quoted by Rosa Luxemburg, *op. cit.*, p. 268.

masses will no longer submit to being the pliant tools and accomplices of any war interests.

Jaurès, who was not only an optimist but also a friend of the Germans, said in February 1914, "If the Kaiser were to begin a war, four million German Socialists would rise as one man and put him to death".[1] As late as 25 July 1914 the Social Democratic paper *Vorwärts* wrote:

> Not a single drop of the blood of a single German soldier must be sacrificed for the benefit of the war-hungry Austrian despots or for imperialist commercial interests. Comrades, we call on you to express in immediate mass demonstrations the unshakable will for peace of the class-conscious proletariat! Everywhere the cry must ring in the ears of despots— "We want no war! Down with war! Long live international solidarity!"

There was no need for demonstrations to prove the desire of the masses for peace. It was evident enough. All that was needed was to push forward the policies of the International. This could have been achieved by political action by the proletariat, but it was precisely the preparations for such action that the international congresses failed to define.

What happened in August 1914 is well known. There were no "masses" ready for action. The individual German, French and English workers complied with their mobilization orders. Not even a handful of Socialist leaders were ready to stand by the principles they had been proclaiming ever since 1890. On 4 August 1914 the Social Democrats in the Reichstag, including Karl Liebknecht, voted unanimously in favour of war credits. The French and Austrian Socialists did the same. Only in the Serbian parliament did two Socialist deputies vote against war credits, and in the Russian Duma the fourteen Social deputies—Bolsheviks and Mensheviks in agreement for once—abstained from voting.[2]

Before matters had progressed to this point, signifying the end of the Second International, the following had taken place. After the murder of the Austrian heir-apparent on 28 June the first few weeks passed over quietly enough, considering the

---

[1] See Maurice Lair, *Jaurès et l'Allemagne*, Paris, 1935, p. 222.
[2] Cf. Bernstein in *Archiv für Sozialwissenschaft*, 1915, pp. 304 ff.

circumstances. The leading personalities of the International left for their summer holidays,[1] in the course of which they were taken unawares by the Austrians' presentation of their ultimatum to the Serbs on 22 July 1914. The International Bureau thereupon summoned a meeting of the International for 29 July in Brussels. Delegates travelling to the meeting could already see the traffic congestion caused by the movement of military transports, but most of them still did not believe that war would come.[2] Hugo Haase (who had succeeded August Bebel as the leader of the German Social Democrats) and others sharply attacked the Austrian Government, but there was no discussion of what should be done to prevent war breaking out. The delegates made speeches explaining how powerfully their parties had demonstrated in favour of peace. (In Germany there were a number of Social Democratic mass meetings between 26 and 30 July 1914.) From Brussels, Jaurès issued a call for more mass demonstrations in France,[3] but these mass meeting did not deter governments from carrying on with their war preparations, nor did they persuade any reservists to refuse to do their military duty.

The very fact that the Brussels meeting resolved that a Congress of the International should be called for 9 August in Paris makes it clear that among the leaders of the International the optimists were still in the majority. Vandervelde has described how, as they were leaving Brussels, Jaurès told him that he thought it impossible that "things would not turn out all right".[4] By 31 July Jaurès was dead, shot by the young Raoul Villain, who evidently believed the charges by the French nationalist newspapers that Jaurès was a traitor. And although it is certain that nothing that Jaurès could have done would have changed the course of events, his death removed the ablest and most determined champion of collaboration between French and German Socialists, in token of which collaboration he and Haase had appeared arm-in-arm at the

[1]Viktor Adler, *Briefwechsel, op. cit.*, pp. 394 ff.
[2]Viktor Adler, *Vor dem Ausnahmegericht*, Berlin, 1919, pp. 16–17.
[3]See also Lenin, *Collected Works*, London, 1929–1942, Vol. 18, p. 419, note 52.
[4]Emile Vandervelde, *Jaurès*, Paris, 1929, p. 6.

Brussels demonstration as late as 29 July.[1] When Haase arrived back in Berlin on 31 July, German mobilization was imminent. The Social Democrats had to decide whether or not they would vote in favour of war credits. Opinions differed, and a decision was postponed. However, Hermann Müller was told to go to Paris, *via* Brussels, and to make one more attempt at working out a common plan of action with the French Socialists.[2] When Müller reached Paris in company with Camille Huysmans, the Secretary of the International, mobilization was already in full swing there. He tried to harmonize views on the question of war credits, but it was obvious that he was bound to fail. He could not say definitely how the Social Democratic members of the Reichstag would vote, simply because when he had left Berlin the Social Democrats had not yet reached agreement. His personal feeling that it was impossible that the Social Democrats would vote in favour of war credits was not a sufficient basis for common action, even if the French Socialists had been willing and able to adopt the same view. It now became clear how disastrous were the results of the failure of the international congresses, from the Stuttgart Congress to the Basle Congress, to define the means or to create an organization which would have enabled the international proletariat to avert an imperialist war. If the surging tide of nationalistic passions in fact left room for any such means, the Socialist leaders did not control them. So the reservists in France and Germany reported for military service, and in both countries the Socialists voted unanimously for war credits.

This was the end of the practical effectiveness of the Second International, whether the Socialist leaders admitted it or not.[3] After the occupation of Belgium by German troops, Camille Huysmans transferred the International Bureau to Holland.[4] The Socialist leaders of the embattled countries remained

[1]Joll, *op. cit.*, pp. 164 ff.; Bernstein, *Die Internationale und der Krieg*, in *Archiv für Sozialwissenschaft* 1915, p. 268; also A. Zevaes, *Jean Jaurès*, Paris, 1951, pp. 244 ff.

[2]Cf. Scheidemann, *Der Zusammenbruch*, Berlin 1921, pp. 12 ff.

[3]See Karl Kautsky, *Die Internationale und der Burgfrieden* in *Die Neue Zeit*, 1915, p. 18; also E. Bernstein, *Die Internationale der Arbeiterklasse und der europäische Krieg*.

[4]Bernstein, *Archiv für Sozialwissenschaft* 1915, p. 319.

almost totally inactive: the slogan "Make war on war" failed
to be translated into action.

Yet even during the first months of the war, outsiders of the
Second International were calling for the creation of a new
International, unencumbered by the mistakes of the past. On
1 November 1914 Lenin wrote in No. 33 of the *Social Democrat*:[1]

> Overwhelmed by opportunism, the Second International
> has died. Down with opportunism, and long live the Third
> International, purged not only of "deserters" . . . but also of
> opportunism! The Second International did its full share of
> useful preparatory work in the preliminary organization of
> the proletarian masses during the long "peaceful" epoch of
> most cruel capitalist slavery and most rapid capitalist
> progress in the last third of the nineteenth and in the begin-
> ning of the twentieth century. The Third International is
> confronted with the task of organizing the forces of the
> proletariat for a revolutionary onslaught on the capitalist
> governments, for civil war against the bourgeoisie of all
> countries, for political power, for the victory of Socialism.

The future was to show whether the Third International
would be able to "continue and complete the great work begun
by the first International Working Men's Association".

### THE LEFT-WING INTERNATIONALISTS IN WORLD WAR I

As early as 1905, as a result of his differences with the
Mensheviks, Lenin had not completely shared the optimism of
the Social Democrats who composed the Second International.
At the Stuttgart Congress of 1907 he had joined Rosa Luxemburg in demanding active steps to prevent war.[2] He had also
demanded that the crisis arising from the war should be
exploited for the overthrow of the "capitalist class rule", and
had managed to get the Congress resolution amended accordingly.[3] This apart, Lenin and his supporters made only a
modest contribution to the work of the Second International.
Apart from the Stuttgart discussions, Lenin appeared only at
the Copenhagen Congress in 1910 and played no significant

[1]Lenin, *Collected Works*, Vol. 18, p. 89.
[2]See p. 24 above.
[3]See *Internationaler Sozialisten-Kongress, Stuttgart 1907*, Vorwärts-Verlag,
Berlin, pp. 102 ff.

part in it. He took as little part in the Congress of Basle in November 1912 as he did in the meeting of the International Socialist Bureau in London in December 1913. Nor did he attend the All-Russian Unification Conference in July 1914, at which the leading personalities of the International made great efforts to heal the rift among the Russian Social Democrats, split by Lenin and his supporters at the Prague Party Conference in 1912. On this point Lenin knew that he and the Bolsheviks were opposed not only by the most important of the other Russian Socialist groups, but also by the leaders of the International.[1] This may have been one of the reasons which moved Lenin to take up a determined stand against the revival of the Second International after 1914.[2]

The collapse of the Second International on the outbreak of World War I and the attitude of the leading personalities in the first months of the war led Lenin to demand, in a manifesto of his party dated November 1914 and in many other contemporary publications, that a new International should be established and that the imperialistic war should be turned into a universal war against the bourgeoisie.[3] Lenin put these demands through the medium of the Bolshevik delegates to the first congress of International Socialists to take place after the outbreak of the war, but neither the International Women's Conference in Berne (26 to 28 March 1915), presided over by Clara Zetkin, nor the International Socialist Youth Congress (5 to 7 April 1915), under the chairmanship of Willi Münzenberg, provided a majority in favour of them.[4]

The most important international Socialist conference of the war years met at Zimmerwald, near Berne, from 5 to 8 September 1915. Here Lenin himself propounded his view that a new International should be established. None of the

---

[1] Cf. Zinoviev in *Dix Années de Lutte pour la révolution mondiale*, Paris, 1929, p. 193; and Borkenau, *European Communism*, London, 1953, p. 29, also Bertram D. Wolfe, *Three who made a revolution*, New York, 1948, p. 608.

[2] At this time, Marxist ideological reasons played just as great a part as a certain feeling of enmity towards the West, which Lenin felt as a Russian.

[3] See Lenin, *Collected Works*, London, 1929–1942, Vol. 18, pp. 74 ff.; Lenin and Zinoviev, *Gegen den Strom*, Hamburg, 1921, pp. 15, 20 ff.; B. Lazich, *Lénine et la III Internationale*, Paris, 1951, p. 25 with further references.

[4] Lazich, *op. cit.*, pp. 41 ff.

well-known leaders of the Second International took part in this conference or in the subsequent one at Kienthal in April 1916. Although most of the groups represented at Zimmerwald —mainly Italian, Swiss, German, Russian and Polish Socialists —took an unfavourable view of the Second International, Lenin could still not obtain a majority in favour of his proposal. At the same time, however, a sizeable minority, the *Internationalisten der Tat*, also referred to as the "Zimmerwald Left-Wing", supported his proposal to establish a new International.[1] This minority included, in addition to Lenin himself, Leo Trotsky; Grigori Zinoviev; Jan Bersin, a Latvian; Karl Radek, a Pole; the Swiss Franz Platten and, of the Germans, only Julian Borchardt.[2] In spite of this international support for Lenin it would probably be misleading to describe the Zimmerwald Conference as the first step on the road to the foundation of the Third International, since the elements which clamoured for the setting up of a new International were still in a minority. Even the left-wing German delegates representing the Gruppe Internationale rejected Lenin's proposals.[3]

Nevertheless the Conference was important inasmuch as it enabled Lenin not only to gain a hearing for his demands that the imperialist war should be turned into a civil war, but also to attract an appreciable number of adherents, something he had never been able to do before.[4] And although Lenin had no more success in finding a majority in favour of his ideas at the Kienthal Conference than he had had at Zimmerwald, it added considerably to his influence that a number of the German Socialists, whom Lenin and Zinoviev very much wanted to keep in the new International, voted with Lenin on the important question of the attitude to be adopted to-

[1]Lenin, *Selected Works*, Vol. II, pp. 43 ff.; also Hugh Seton-Watson, *The Pattern of Communist Revolution*, London, 1953, p. 51.

[2]Lazich, *op. cit.*, pp. 46 ff.; also Lenin/Zinoviev, *Gegen den Strom*, p. 286.

[3]Cf. A. Rosenberg, *A History of Bolshevism*, London, 1934, pp. 76–77; the German delegates were: Georg Ledebour, Adolf Hoffmann, Josef Herzfeld, Ernst Meyer, Bertha Thalheimer, Julian Borchardt (Ruth Fischer, *Stalin and German Communism*, Cambridge, Mass., 1948, p. 12, note 3).

[4]Lazich, *op. cit.*, p. 54; Lenin/Zinoviev, *Gegen den Strom*, p. 288, Part I, p. 9.

wards the International Socialist Bureau.[1] These followers of
Lenin were delegates of the Gruppe Internationale, which
had been in existence since the spring of 1915 and which was
later to give birth to the Spartakus League in January 1916.[2]
Still further left than the Gruppe Internationale was the
Bremer Linke, which was represented at Kienthal by Paul
Frölich. Frölich gave his unconditional support to Lenin's
demand that a new International should be set up.[3] Still
another of Lenin's supporters was Willi Münzenberg, who was
then living in Switzerland.[4]

In Germany Rosa Luxemburg took up Lenin's demands in a
political pamphlet, in which she severely criticized the in-
effectiveness of the German Social Democrats on the outbreak
of war.[5] At a clandestine meeting held in Karl Liebknecht's flat
on 1 January 1916, the Gruppe Internationale accepted Rosa
Luxemburg's *Theses on the Tasks of International Social Democracy*.[6]
In Thesis 12 it was stated that "since the Second International
had been unable to organize common action by the proletariat
of all countries, a new workers' International must be formed".[7]

Lenin renewed his demands on his return to Russia in April
1917.[8] In his *April Theses*[9] he said, "Our Party must not 'wait'"

[1]See Zinoviev's remark quoted by Lazich, *op. cit.*, p. 31; also Zinoviev in
*Vorbote*, No. 2, p. 58, quoted by Lazich, *op. cit.*, p. 64.
[2]Paul Frölich, *Rosa Luxemburg*, Hamburg, 1949, pp. 248 ff., and *Zur
Geschichte der KPD*, Berlin, 1954, pp. 16 ff.
[3]See O. K. Flechtheim, *Die KPD in der Weimarer Republik*, Offenbach,
1948, pp. 12 ff.
[4]See Ruth Fischer, *op. cit.*, p. 610.
[5]R. Luxemburg, *Ausgewählte Reden und Schriften*, Berlin 1951, pp. 258 ff.;
also S. Leonhard and E. Drahn, *Unterirdische Literatur in revolutionären
Deutschland während des Weltkrieges*, Berlin, 1920, pp. 21 ff.; Lenin/Zinoviev,
"Über die Juniusbroschüre" in *Gegen den Strom*, p. 415. Criticism of the
Junius Brochure was also made by Karl Radek in *In den Reihen der deutschen
Revolution 1909 bis 1919*, Munich, 1921, p. 347.
[6]Ruth Fischer, *op. cit.*, p. 13.
[7]Rosa Luxemburg, *op. cit.*, p. 398; also Rosa Luxemburg's leading article
in the one and only issue of the periodical *Die Internationale*, dated 15
April 1915; also S. Leonhard and E. Drahn, *op. cit.*, pp. 17 ff., and Frölich's
*Zur Geschichte der KPD*, Berlin, 1954, p. 18.
[8]The agreement covering the journey of Lenin and 31 other émigrés was
the result of negotiations between the Swiss Fritz Platten and the then
German Minister in Berne, Romberg, W. Münzenberg, *Die Dritte Front*,
Berlin, 1930, pp. 237 ff., also Z. A. B. Zeman, *Verbündete wider Willen* in *der
Monat*, Issue No. 120, pp. 17 ff.    [9]Cf. Thesis No. 10, Lenin, *op. cit.*, p. 10

but must immediately *found* a Third International", and "There is no other land on earth as free as Russia is *now*. Let us make use of this freedom . . . in a bold, honest, proletarian, Liebknecht way, *to found the Third International*. . . ."[1] Here Lenin was referring to Karl Liebknecht, whose father, Wilhelm Liebknecht, had been a member of the First International. Karl Liebknecht had been in open opposition to the war ever since the autumn of 1914 and had been active on behalf of the Spartakus League, which supported Lenin's ideas.

Liebknecht was a convinced internationalist, who gave renewed evidence of his attitude when he proclaimed from the balcony of the Imperial Palace in Berlin on 9 November 1918.[2] "We want to build the new order of the proletariat, an order of peace and happiness, with liberty for all our German brothers and for our brothers throughout the world. We extend our hands to them and call on them to complete the world revolution."

Karl Liebknecht also eulogized Socialism and world revolution in the last leading article he wrote for *The Red Flag* before he and Rosa Luxemburg were murdered on 15 January 1919 by members of the Garde-Kavallerie-Schützen-Division (Dismounted Cavalry Guard).[3]

The international aspect was also brought out in the programme of the Communist Party of Germany, which was founded in December 1919 and January 1920. Section D of this programme said:[4]

The immediate establishment of relations with our brother parties abroad in order to put the Socialist revolution on an international basis and to shape and secure peace by international fraternization and the revolutionary rousing of the masses.

[1] Lenin, *The Tasks of the Proletariat in Our Revolution, Selected Works*, Vol. II, p. 46.
[2] Ruth Fischer, *op. cit.*, p. 60.
[3] P. Frölich, *op. cit.*, p. 347; Dr Bernhard Weiss, *Polizei und Politik*, Berlin, 1928, p. 75; also E. J. Gumbel, *Vier Jahre politischer Mord*, Berlin-Fichtenau, 1922, pp. 10 ff., and Waldemar Erfurth, *Die Geschichte des Deutschen Generalstabes*, Göttingen, 1957, p. 26, and F. W. v. Oertzen, *Die Deutschen Freikorps 1918-1923*, pp. 276 ff. Wilhelm Pieck, now president of the "DDR", was arrested the same day. (For details, see Appendix III, p. 332.)
[4] *Zur Geschichte der KPD*, Berlin, 1954, p. 61.

Regarding the founding of the German Communist Party, Lenin wrote ". . . when the Spartakus League changed its name to 'The Communist Party of Germany', the foundation of the genuinely proletarian, genuinely international, genuinely revolutionary Third International, the Communist International, became a reality";[1] but in fact the German left-wing internationalists were at this time neither strong in numbers nor united in their views on whether the new International that Lenin meant ought to be established. Rosa Luxemburg in particular, in keeping with her theory of the revolutionary spontaneity of the masses, came to believe that the new International ought to represent a merging of powerful revolutionary mass parties, and should not have its starting point in small groups of professional revolutionaries, as envisaged by Lenin.[2]

[1] *Zur Geschichte der KPD*, p. 62.
[2] See Flechtheim, *op. cit.*, p. 27: also Borkenau, *The Communist International*, London, 1938, p. 87.

# Chapter III

## THE DEVELOPMENT OF THE COMMUNIST INTERNATIONAL[1]

"The Third International was for all practical purposes created in 1918, when the long struggle against opportunism and social chauvinism, particularly during the war years, had led to the creation of Communist parties in a number of countries."[2]

### THE FIRST WORLD CONGRESS

THE Third, the Communist International, or Comintern, was founded at the First World Congress, which opened in Moscow on 2 March 1919. The final constitution was promulgated at the 2nd World Congress in July and August of 1920.[3]

The length of the war and the deprivations and sacrifices it had brought about in every country had given rise to a change of heart, not only among the proletariat of Europe, but also among the bourgeoisie. Nationalistic feelings, so inflamed in 1914, had cooled down considerably. In Germany there had been mass strikes even in 1916 (for example, after the sentencing of Karl Liebknecht). In Berlin alone food shortages in April 1917 caused over 200,000 workers to go on strike.[4] The proletariat of Europe greeted the Russian revolution with

[1]In 1959, forty years after its foundation, tributes were paid to the Comintern at the conclusion of a crisis in proletarian internationalism (Cf. the periodical *Probleme des Friedens und des Sozialismus*, Prague, 1959, No. 2, p. 16, and Wilhelm Koenen in *Neues Deutschland*, East Berlin, 8 March 1959).

[2]See Lenin's essay, *Die Dritte Internationale und ihr Platz in der Geschichte* (The Third International and its Place in History), in No. 1 of the periodical *Die Kommunistische Internationale*, Berlin, 1919, p. 111.

[3]Beschluss des I. Weltkongresses in der Organisationsfrage in No. 1 of *Die Kommunistische Internationale*, Berlin, 1919, pp. 38 ff.

[4]O. K. Flechtheim, *op. cit.*, p. 25.

sympathy. Lenin's peace offer and the attitude of Trotsky, who, as leader of the Russian delegation at the peace negotiations in Brest-Litovsk, was pressing for the cessation of hostilities, made an impression on the war-weary workers of Europe. From January 1918 onwards there were mass strikes in Hungary, Austria and Germany.

It was not only in the nations faced with impending defeat that the forces of the Left Wing increased, for the same process was evident in France, Italy, England, the United States and Japan. Even in neutral Switzerland[1] there was a general strike in November 1918.

During 1918, Communist Parties were established in various countries of Europe; in August in Latvia and Finland, in November in Hungary and in December in Austria, Poland and Germany.[2] "The tide of revolution in Europe began to mount. . . . With the rising tide of the revolution Communist Parties came to the surface."[3] The Communist Party of the United States of America was formed on 1 April 1919 in Chicago. Twenty-five per cent of its members were immigrants from Russia—in fact the proportion of the members who came from Eastern Europe was 75 per cent. The most prominent leaders of the party in the early years were Louis C. Fraina and Charles E. Ruthenberg.[4]

Orthodox Marxist teaching led the Bolsheviks, with Lenin at their head, to believe that the revolution would not be confined to Russia but that, at least in the progressive countries, their victory was imminent, and that revolution would break out all over Europe. On this point Lenin's beliefs were the same as Rosa Luxemburg's[5] and they could both appeal to Marx and Engels, who had declared in their *Address to the League by the*

---

[1]See a report on the revolutionary movement in Switzerland in No. 1 of *Die Kommunistische Internationale* and Angelica Balabanova's *Erinnerungen und Erlebnisse*, Berlin, 1927, pp. 190 ff.

[2]B. Lazich, *op. cit.*, pp. 89 ff.

[3]*History of the Communist Party of the Soviet Union (Bolsheviks), Short Course*, London, 1943, p. 212.

[4]Theodore Draper, *The Roots of American Communism*, New York, 1957, pp. 181, 184, 190.

[5]P. Frölich, *op. cit.*, p. 296, quotes Warski.

*Central Authority*, which they wrote for the League of Communists in March 1850:[1]

> While the democratic petty bourgeois want to conclude the revolution as quickly as possible and to satisfy at most the foregoing demands, it is in our interest and is our task to make the revolution permanent, until all the more or less propertied classes have been stripped of their authority, the governing power is in the hands of the proletariat, and the association of the proletariat, not only in one country but in all the leading countries of the entire world, is so far advanced that competition between the proletariat of these countries has ceased and at least the vital means of production are concentrated in the hands of the proletariat.

Following the line laid down by Marx and Engels, Lenin said at the 7th Party Congress of the CPSU on 7 March 1918:

> When the Bolshevik Party tackled the job alone, took it entirely into its own hands, we were convinced that the revolution was maturing in all countries and that in the end —but not at the very beginning—no matter what difficulties we experienced, no matter what defeats were in store for us, the international Socialist revolution would come—because it is coming; would ripen—because it is ripening and will grow ripe. I repeat, our salvation from all these difficulties is an all-European revolution.[2]

In accordance with this conviction, Lenin urged that the workers should take advantage of the revolutionary impetus to form the Third International and thus further the cause of the international revolution.

At the end of January 1918 a conference of international Socialists was held in St Petersburg. This conference decided to call an international Socialist congress at which the member parties and organizations were to be urged to pledge themselves to carry through a revolutionary fight against their own governments and to support the Soviet government with all their power.[3] However, this congress never took place.

The Central Committee of the Russian Party rejected all

[1]Cf. p. 93 below and Marx/Engels, *Ausgewählte Schriften*, Berlin, 1951, Vol. I, p. 97.
[2]Lenin, *Selected Works*, London, 1947, Vol. II, p. 297.
[3]Trotsky, *Stalin*, London, 1947, p. 244.

attempts to revive the Second International.[1] For example,
they refused an invitation of the British Labour Party to an
international Socialist conference in Lausanne, as they also
refused to take part in a conference of European Social Democrats to be held in Paris or Berne in February 1919.[2] They
mockingly referred to Friedrich Adler's attempts to bring into
alignment the efforts of the old Second International and the
new Third International as the "International Two-and-a-half".

On their side, the Central Committee of the Russian Party
published in January 1919 the draft of a manifesto calling on
the proletariat of the whole world to unite in the Third International.[3] This manifesto was composed by Leo Trotsky[4] and
was quoted in his works while he was still living in the Soviet
Union.[5] Trotsky also delivered a speech on this Manifesto at
the First World Congress,[6] to which thirty-nine parties and
political groups of the Extreme Left were invited.[7]

Fifty-one Communists from thirty countries attended this
Congress, which opened on 2 March 1919 in Moscow. Of a
total of thirty-five votes, the Credentials Committee allotted
five each to the German and Russian Communist Parties,
five to the American Socialist Labour Party and five to the
French "Zimmerwald Left",[8] the rest being divided among the

[1]Lenin, *Selected Works*, Vol. II, pp. 731, 736; also Lazich, *op. cit.*, p. 90, and Joll, *op. cit.*, pp. 188 ff. The "International 2½" was amalgamated with the remnants of the old Second International to form a "Socialist Workers' International" at a congress in Hamburg, 21 April to 2 May 1923. See an article by Z. Leder in *Die Kommunistische Internationale*, 4th Year, No. 27, p. 47, and P. Frölich, *Die Internationale Einigungskongress in Hamburg*, *op. cit.*, 4th Year, No. 26, p. 39.

[2]D. Shub, *Lenin*, New York, 1948, pp. 342–343.

[3]*Der I. Kongress der Kommunistischen Internationale*, Hamburg, 1920, pp. 3 ff. (Vol. 1 of the Library of the Communist International).

[4]Cf. Zinoviev's remark on the final day of the 2nd World Congress in Vol. 22 of the Library of the Communist International, p. 666.

[5]Lazich, *op. cit.*, p. 91.

[6]*Der I. Kongress der Kommunistischen Internationale*, Hamburg, 1921, p. 3 (Vol. 3 of the Library of the Communist International).

[7]Cf. the invitation addressed to the KPD, reproduced in No. 1 of *Die Kommunistische Internationale*, Berlin, 1919, pp. 3 ff. According to Borkenau, in *European Communism*, the invitation was signed by Chicherin, then Peoples' Commissar for External Affairs, an indication of the naïveté with which State and Party business were intermingled in those days.

[8]*Die Kommunistische Internationale*, No. 1, p. 7.

smaller parties. The majority of the delegates were émigrés living in Russia, who, as a result of difficulties of communication caused by the intervention of the Western Powers, had very little connection with the parties in their native countries. One Frenchman, Jacques Sadoul, had in fact been a member of his country's military mission in Russia.[1] The only delegates who actually came from abroad were Hugo Eberlein (alias "Albert") for the German Communist Party,[2] Rutgers from the United States, Grimlund from Sweden, Stange from Norway, and Steinhardt (alias "Gruber") from Austria.

On the first two days of the Congress, the delegates reported on the situation of their own parties. The foundation of the new International was by no means a certainty. Before the conference began, Hugo Eberlein, the German representative, had explained to Lenin the views of Rosa Luxemburg and Leo Jogiches, who felt that the International would emerge from a revolutionary mass movement, which would take power in the countries of Europe.[3] For this reason Eberlein wanted the Conference's task to be confined to making preparations for the subsequent setting-up of the International at some later date.[4] At this time the German party enjoyed such prestige that when Eberlein refused to budge from his position, Lenin and Zinoviev did not insist on actually founding the International at this Congress. Not long afterwards, at the 8th Party Congress of the Russian Party, Zinoviev said:

> The Central Committee of our Party, after studying the situation, thought it was out of the question that we should found the Third International immediately. We also felt that at a time when the German Communists were opposed to it, and put the matter in the form of an ultimatum, we could not allow the slightest discord to enter into our relations with the German Spartakists.[5]

The situation changed when the Austrian delegate, Karl

[1]Lazich, *op. cit.*, p. 98; A. Balabanova, *op. cit.*, p. 225, and William H, Chamberlin, *The Russian Revolution 1917–1921*, London, 1935, Vol. I. p. 404.
[2]*Die Kommunistische Internationale*, No. 1, p. 7.
[3]See above, p. 38, and Borkenau, *European Communism*, p. 39.
[4]Hugo Eberlein in *Dix années de lutte pour la révolution mondiale*, pp. 300 ff.
[5]Quoted by Lazich, *op. cit.*, p. 109.

Steinhardt (alias "Gruber"),[1] arrived at the end of the second day and urgently pressed for the founding of the Third International. He was supported by the representatives of the Hungarian Communists, the Swedish left-wing Social Democrats, and by Christian Rakowsky, the delegate of the Balkan revolutionary Social Democrats. Eberlein stood by his view that it was too soon to establish the International, but now Zinoviev took a stand against Eberlein, and insisted that he was underestimating the mightiest factor in Europe, the Revolution. In the voting which followed, all the delegates except Eberlein voted for the immediate setting up of the International. Eberlein abstained from voting, but indicated the possibility that on his return to Germany the German Communists might agree to join the Third International.[2] (In the event the German Communist Party did pass a resolution to this effect, the first non-Russian party to do so.[3])

Although the 1st Congress decided that the promulgation of the final constitution of the Communist International should be left to the next Congress, various organs were elected immediately so that the Comintern could begin its work. An Executive Committee was created, to which "the Communist Parties of the most important countries"—Russia, Germany, German Austria, Hungary, the Balkan Confederation, Switzerland and Scandinavia—were each to send one delegate.[4] The intention was that the executive organ of the International should be located in Berlin, and Moscow was only chosen as its temporary home until a German soviet republic should be established.[5] Equally temporarily, and until the arrival of the representatives of the non-Russian parties, "the Comrades belonging to the country in which the Executive Committee is located" assumed "the burden of the work".[6] In fact, as the

---

[1]This, like other aliases indicated throughout this book, refers to a Party cover-name used in respect of Party affairs.

[2]Cf. *Die Kommunistische Internationale*, No. 1, 1919, p. 38.

[3]See O. K. Flechtheim, *op. cit.*, p. 57.

[4]Cf. *Beschluss des I. Weltkongresses der Kommunistischen Internationale* (2.–6. März 1919) in *der Organisationsfrage*, reproduced in *Die Kommunistische Internationale*, No. 1, pp. 38 ff.

[5]*Die Kommunistische Internationale*, No. 1, 1919, p. 38.

[6]*Ibid.*

future was to show, they took over not only the work of the International but also the power.

The outcome of the 1st World Congress was not only that it founded the International but also that it gave the Bolsheviks the opportunity, as Lenin himself said later,[1] to announce their principles to the world. These principles were laid down in the *Documents* of the 1st World Congress, which were worked out by the best brains in the Soviet party. These *Documents* were the *Guiding Principles of the International Communist Congress*, written by Bukharin, the *Theses on Bourgeois Democracy and Proletarian Dictatorship*, drafted by Lenin, and the *Manifesto of the Communist International to the Proletariat of the World*, composed by Trotsky. Despite the varying subjects of these *Documents*, they all contained the following basic ideas. The existing crisis could only be overcome by means of a proletarian revolution combined with the dictatorship of the proletariat; the national State had become too narrow to allow the development of the productive forces; in order to make the mutual assistance of the workers of the various countries a reality and in order to co-ordinate action by the proletariat, the proletariat must amalgamate into a genuine Communist International. The *Manifesto* closed with the call:

> Workers of the World! In the struggle against imperialist savagery, against monarchy, against the privileged estates, against the bourgeois State and bourgeois property, against all kinds and forms of social and national oppression—unite! Under the banner of the workers' soviets of the revolutionary struggle for power and the dictatorship of the proletariat —under the banner of the Third International; Workers of the World, Unite![2]

### THE SECOND WORLD CONGRESS
#### (*19 July–7 August 1920*)

Between the 1st and 2nd World Congresses the situation in the international sphere seemed to be developing favourably

---

[1] *Die Kommunistische Internationale*, No. 19, p. 94. Zinoviev said at the 6th Session of the 2nd World Congress that in March 1919 the Communist International had been nothing but a propaganda society (Vol. 22 of the Library of the Communist International, p. 237).

[2] *Der I. Kongress der Kommunistischen Internationale*, Hamburg, 1920, pp. 17–18 (Vol. 1 of the Library of the Communist International).

for the Comintern. In March 1919 a Soviet republic was formed in Hungary and on 7 April 1919 there followed the proclamation of a Soviet republic in Bavaria. In the first number of the Comintern periodical Zinoviev wrote:

> As we write these lines, the Third International already has as its main foundation three soviet republics—in Russia, in Hungary and in Bavaria; but nobody will be surprised if, when these lines come to be printed, we have not three but six or even more soviet republics. Old Europe is rushing towards revolution at breakneck speed. In a twelvemonth we shall already have begun to forget that there ever was a struggle for Communism in Europe, for in a year the whole of Europe will be Communist.[1]

Developments did not justify this optimism. The Bavarian soviet republic remained in existence only until 1 May 1919[2] and in Hungary the ruling Communists had to retire on 1 August of the same year.

Nevertheless the situation in several countries of Europe between the 1st and 2nd World Congresses was not unfavourable to revolution. Severe unrest persisted in Germany. The nationalistic Kapp putsch on the 13 March 1920 was stultified in three days by a general strike of the workers. Karl Legien, the leader of the German trades unions, demanded for the strikers a deciding voice in the formation of the government and in the shaping of economic, social and political conditions. He demanded that the participants in the putsch should be punished and that the Reichswehr should be purged of anti-republican and politically doubtful elements.[3] If the government suggested by Legien, the "Labour Coalition Government", had been formed and had included the Independent Social Democratic Party of Germany (USPD), that party would very likely not have strayed into the Comintern fold.

On 25 March 1920, the Executive Committee of the Comin-

[1] *Die Kommunistische Internationale*, No. 1, pp. 9 and 12.

[2] The Bavarian soviet republic was not founded by the Comintern, and even the KPD would have nothing to do with the founders, whom they referred to as "romantic fools". See Ruth Fischer, *op. cit.*, p. 102, and *Die Niederwerfung der Räteherrschaft in Bayern 1919*, published by the Kriegsgeschichtliche Forschungsanstalt des Heeres, Berlin, 1939, p. 15.

[3] Theodor Leipart, *Karl Legien*, Berlin, 1929, pp. 100 and 117.

tern declared in a call "To the Workers in Germany! To the Workers of the World!":

> The workers of every country are following with bated breath the heroic struggle of the glorious German workers. The working masses of the world cherish the German proletarian revolution that is awakening before our eyes.[1]

In Italy Communist influence had greatly increased. Of the socialist groups which had taken part in the November 1919 elections under a combined list, the most powerful were the Communists. It was symptomatic of the growth of revolutionary feeling among the Italian workers that out of five million votes cast, two million were for the combined list.[2] In June 1920, Lenin, the master of political tactics, launched his paper on *Left-Wing Communism, an Infantile Disorder*, in order to instruct his followers that under certain conditions penetration of the trades unions and participation in parliamentary activity were advisable. At the same time he laid down tactical manoeuvres designed to overcome a sectarian "left-wing" attitude,[3] "left-wing sectarians" having split the German

[1] Vol. 1 of the Library of the Communist International, p. 241.

[2] See Serrati's report to the 2nd World Congress in Vol. 21 of the Library of the Communist International, pp. 116 ff.

[3] Whenever mention is made in the following pages of a "left-wing" attitude or "left-wing" tactics or policies, the meaning intended is the classical position of the Communists, who regarded capitalism as the arch-enemy and the socialist revolution as their goal. This policy called on the members of the socialist or petty-bourgeois parties to join with the Communists and stigmatized the leaders of the other parties as lackeys of capitalism or imperialism. The *21 Conditions* of the 2nd World Congress contain a perfect example of "left-wing" tactics. A variation of left-wing tactics was demonstrated by the Communists from 1930–1934, when they redoubled their attacks on the right-wing democratic leaders and described the whole of the Social Democrats as "the arch-enemy". "Right-wing tactics" consist of temporary collaboration with elements occupying a position to the right of the Communists and can even include coalition with bourgeois parties. The theoretical basis for such "right-wing" tactical manoeuvres are contained in Lenin's *Left-Wing Communism*. The best-known example of right-wing tactics embracing collaboration with bourgeois forces was the Popular Front policy of the 1930s. Unlike left-wing tactics, the right-wing policy allows the main enemy to vary. While the Communists were co-operating with the Kuomintang in China, the arch-enemy was colonialism. During the Popular Front period it was fascism. The present-day "right-wing" policy sets up "American NATO policies" as the prime enemy. On the question of terminology, see John H. Kautsky, *Moscow and the Communist Party of India*, New York/London, 1956, pp. 6 ff. Kautsky calls one variation of right-wing tactics "neo-maoist".

Communist Party a short time before.[1] Regarding the international aspect, Lenin said in his *Left-Wing Communism* that all the basic features of the Bolshevist revolution were of international significance because of their effects upon other countries. In order to fulfil the international task—the overthrow of the bourgeoisie and the setting up of a soviet republic and the dictatorship of the proletariat—Lenin laid down that the first thing to establish must be the specifically national element in the conditions of each country.[2] As the next step, not only the Party but also the masses must be convinced that the only alternative to the dictatorship of the "extreme reactionaries", such as Kornilov in Russia in 1917 or Kapp in Germany, was the dictatorship of the proletariat. Lenin shared Zinoviev's exuberant optimism:[3]

> Communists should know that the future in any case belongs to them; therefore we can (and must) combine the most intense passion in the great revolutionary struggle with the coolest and most sober estimation of the frenzied ravings of the bourgeoisie. . . . But in all cases and in all countries Communism is becoming steeled and is spreading; its roots are so deep that persecution does not weaken it, does not debilitate it, but strengthens it.

In support of this, Lenin could point to the fact that an appreciable part of the extreme left-wing Independent Social Democratic Party of Germany (USPD) had decided to enter into negotiations with the Comintern.[4] This decision was particularly important for Lenin, for unlike the German Communist Party, which was still very weak, the USPD was a mass party. At this time large sections of the working classes of

[1] Ruth Fischer, *op. cit.*, p. 119. Lazich (*op. cit.*, p. 144) is mistaken in believing that the German Communist Party split after the 2nd World Congress. In April 1920 the Communist Workers' Party (KAPD) split off from the KPD (Spartakist League), whereas the split of the Independent Social Democratic Party (USPD) did not come about until after the 2nd World Congress, at the Party Conference in Halle in October 1920. The remnants of the KPD allied themselves with the "left-wing" section of the USPD at the "Amalgamation Party Conference", 4–7 December 1920, and formed the VKPD. See O. K. Flechtheim, *op. cit.*, p. 71.

[2] Lenin, *Selected Works*, Vol. II, pp. 571, 626 ff.

[3] *Ibid.*, p. 633.

[4] Flechtheim, *op. cit.*, p. 68.

Europe felt a friendship for the Comintern, as was demonstrated by the fact that not only a French group, the Longuetistes,[1] but also the English Independent Labour Party were considering affiliation to the Comintern.[2] Completely misunderstanding conditions in America, Zinoviev optimistically asked Emma Goldman, when she was on a visit to Moscow, how soon the revolution could be expected to start in the United States.[3]

In Russia, the Bolsheviks had won the civil war. What was even more important, the Red Army, after beating off Pilsudski's attack on Kiev, had been marching in the direction of Warsaw since 4 July 1920.[4] Their rapid advance strengthened the Bolsheviks' hopes that they would shortly be able to unite with the German proletariat, the "most advanced" in Europe.[5]

The invitations to the 2nd World Congress sent out by the Executive Committee said that the time had now come to organize the Communist proletariat and the all-out struggle for the Communist revolution;[6] which was an apt description of the task of the 2nd World Congress.

Travelling conditions were still very difficult, yet many more delegates arrived for this Congress than had attended the 1st Congress. Of 167 delegates entitled to vote, 124 represented Communist parties and 31 non-Communist parties, while 12 had been sent by youth associations.[7] Although the delegates had gathered in Moscow, they all travelled to Petrograd for the opening of the Congress, the first meeting taking place in

[1]So called after Jean Longuet, the grandson of Karl Marx.
[2]Lenin, *op. cit.*, Vol. II, p. 578, and Ruth Fischer, *op. cit.*, p. 135.
[3]Draper, *op. cit.*, p. 248.
[4]Leon Trotsky, *My Life*, London, 1930, pp. 389, ff.
[5]Cf. the message *To the Proletarian Men and Women of all Countries* adopted on the first day of the Congress, and which dealt in detail with the significance of the Polish question. (Vol. 22 of the Library of the Communist International, pp. 51 ff.) Rosenberg, *A History of Bolshevism*, p. 157, Stefan T. Possony, *A Century of Conflict*, Chicago, 1953, p. 116, and A. Barmine, *Memoirs of a Soviet Diplomat*, London, 1938, p. 100.
[6]Library of the Communist International, Hamburg, 1920, Vol. 1, pp. 287 ff. ("To all Communist Parties and groups, to all red trade unions, to all Communist women's organizations, all Communist youth organizations, all workers' associations based on Communism and to all upright working men.")
[7]Cf. Vol. 22 of the Library of the Communist International, p. 788.

C

Smolny, which had been the headquarters of the October Revolution. When Lenin entered the hall, the English and American delegates surrounded him, singing "For he's a jolly good fellow", an indication of the extent to which Western ideas could still find room in the International at this time.[1] The Congress fulfilled the tasks laid on it by the Executive Committee following thorough, as yet unfettered, discussion. Both Zinoviev as Chairman and Karl Radek as Secretary of the Executive Committee exercised a distinct influence on the course of the discussions. The part played by the Communists from countries outside Russia, including the German Communists, was considerably less than the part they had played at the 1st World Congress,[2] whereas both the authority of the CPSU and the prestige of Lenin had greatly increased. The deliberations of the Congress were governed by the ideas developed by Lenin in his *Left-Wing Communism*, in which he had opposed the outright rejection of compromise. The Congress gave him their support in the *Theses on the Basic Tasks of the Communist International*.[3] The German "Left" had occasioned this debate by their refusal to co-operate with the Trade Unions. In the debates during the Congress, the American Communist John Reed continued to express strong opposition to the new trade union thesis Lenin had laid down in *Left-Wing Communism*:

> We must be able . . . to agree to any sacrifice, and even—if need be—to resort to all sorts of stratagems, artifices, illegal methods, to evasions and subterfuges, only so as to get into the trade unions, to remain in them, and to carry on Communist work within them at all costs.[4]

In accordance with this, the Congress demanded in the

[1] Alfred Rosmer, *Moscou sous Lénine*, Paris, 1953, p. 96.

[2] At the Congress, opposition by the Germans had almost led to the postponement of the founding of the Comintern (Cf. above, p. 43).

[3] Lenin, *Selected Works*, Vol. II, p. 607, and Library of the Communist International, Vol. 22, p. 753.

[4] A classic example of the use of this thesis of Lenin's has been provided by Ignazio Silone, who has told how a special commission of the ECCI was one day discussing an ultimatum in which the Central Committee of the T.U.C. had threatened its local branches with expulsion if they supported the Communist-led minority. The representatives of the British Communist Party had explained that the Communist group would either have to leave

*Theses* that Communists should penetrate the trades unions.[1] In *Left-Wing Communism* Lenin recommended that legal activity should be combined with the illegal, and the Congress followed him in this, too. The *21 Conditions* laid on the member parties of the Comintern the duty of "creating at all costs parallel organizational machinery which, at the decisive moment, will come to the help of the Party in fulfilling its duty towards the revolution".[2] Lenin had also criticized the Second International in *Left-Wing Communism* because it had been incapable of creating a genuinely controlling central authority. The impotence of the International Socialist Bureau at the outbreak of the First World War was still very much in everyone's mind and the 2nd World Congress created in the Statutes of the Comintern the pre-conditions for a rigidly centralized organization capable of taking effective action.[3]

### THE TWENTY-ONE CONDITIONS AND THE STATUTES OF THE COMMUNIST INTERNATIONAL

The 2nd World Congress fulfilled its task of making the Comintern capable of action. It accepted the *21 Conditions* and approved the statutes, which were to become extremely important in the development of the Comintern, since it was they that enabled the Executive Committee to exercise a degree of power such as no organ of the previous International had even remotely possessed.[4] They contained the bases of the umlimited power that the Central Committee of the CPSU and the Soviet State Security Service were later to exercise

the trade union or dissolve itself. Ossip Piatnitski, on the other hand, suggested that the individual sections should submit to the ultimatum and then, in practice, do the exact opposite (see Silone's contribution to *The God that Failed*). Piatnitzki understood the meaning of the injunction to stay in the trade unions and carry on Communist work in them at all costs. See also Draper (*op. cit.*, p. 256), who correctly points out that it was characteristic of the 2nd World Congress that, in spite of his opposition in the trade union question, Reed could still be elected to membership of the ECCI.

[1] Lenin, *op. cit.*, Vol. II, p. 597, and Library of the Communist International, Vol. 22, p. 755.

[2] Lenin, *op. cit.*, Vol II, p. 629, and Library of the Communist International, Vol. 22, pp. 389–90.

[3] Lenin, *op. cit.*, p. 626; cf. above, p. 32.

[4] Cf. the *21 Conditions* reproduced on page 339, Appendix V.

over the Comintern, and they thus created what was to be an important contributory factor in the subsequent dissolution of the Comintern.

Zinoviev expounded the *Conditions* to the Congress. It was necessary, he said, to lay down certain conditions for entry into the International in order to prevent undesirable parties and groups getting into it. There was a danger that the Communist International might be diluted by vacillating and lukewarm centralist elements.[1] In order to prevent this, and to make it possible for undesirable elements to be excluded from the International, the Conditions were made to include the provisos that the Sections:

(a) must give the whole of their agitation and propaganda a Communist character and must shape them in accordance with the decisions of the Comintern (1st Condition);

(b) must remove all reformist elements and adherents of the parties of the Centre from all positions of responsibility, party organizations, editorial staffs, trade unions, and parliamentary parties (2nd Condition);[2]

(c) must acknowledge the complete break with reformism and the policies of the parties of the Centre and must advocate this break as widely as possible among the members (7th Condition);

(d) must ensure before entry that two-thirds of the members of their Central Committees and of the most important central bodies should consist of comrades who had publicly spoken in favour of entering the Communist International before the 2nd Congress of the Communist International (20th Condition).

These rules were directed against the groups represented by such prominent politicians as Kautsky, Hilferding, Turati, Longuet and MacDonald.[3] The most important organization of this type was the Independent Social Democratic Party of Germany (USPD), which at this time had 800,000 members. The question of whether their delegates should be admitted

---

[1] Library of the Communist International, Vol. 22, p. 388.

[2] The description "adherents of the Centre" was applied by the Bolsheviks to those belonging to the Social Democratic centre, whose chief exponent in Germany was Karl Kautsky.

[3] Cf. *Conditions*, No. 7, para 2.

to the 2nd Congress was discussed in detail and in the end four representatives of the USPD took part in the deliberations of the Congress in an advisory capacity.

The Section Française Internationale Ouvrière (SFIO) was represented by Marcel Cachin, Loudovic O. Frossard, Alfred Rosmer and Raymond Lefèbre, who also took part as advisers.[1]

The rules contained in the statutes accepted by the 2nd Congress remained in force until the dissolution of the Comintern. The new statutes issued by the 6th World Congress in 1928 amended certain parts of the wording, but the basic content of the Statutes of the 2nd Congress remained essentially unchanged.[2]

Para 1 of the statutes defined the purpose of the Comintern thus:

> The new International Workers' Association is created for the organizing of common action by the proletariat of the various countries towards one goal—the overthrow of capitalism, the setting up of the dictatorship of the proletariat and of an international soviet republic for the complete abolition of class and the realization of Socialism, the first stage of a Communist society.

The new International did not wish to be an association of independent parties but wanted to create a single world Communist Party. "The parties working in the individual countries shall attend merely as separate Sections (of the Comintern)."[3] This was the principle on which the Comintern was organized.[4]

The highest organ was the World Congress, which was to meet once every year.[5] During the twenty-four years of the Comintern's existence, however, the World Congress met only

[1] Library of the Communist International, Vol. 22, pp. 127 ff., and Jean Fréville, *Die Nacht endete in Tours*, Berlin, 1953, p. 88.

[2] In the following pages, accordingly, the statutes quoted will, unless otherwise stated, be in the version adopted by the 2nd World Congress (see Appendix IV, p. 334).

[3] Library of the Communist International, Vol. 22, p. 602.

[4] A detailed description of the way in which the organization of the Comintern developed is given in Chapter IV.

[5] Cf. Article 4 of the statutes of the Second Congress. According to Article 8 of the statutes of the Sixth Congress, the World Congress was to meet every two years.

seven times. The World Congress was supposed to decide changes of programme and the most important policy issues (para. 4 of the statutes). It also elected the Executive Committee, which governed the Comintern between congresses and which was answerable only to the World Congress (para. 5 of the statutes). The Executive Committee (the ECCI) consisted of five representatives of the country in which the Committee was based and one representative from each of the ten to thirteen most important Communist parties. Furthermore the Trades Unions section of the Comintern (the Profintern) and the Communist Youth International each had a representative in the ECCI.[1] The 2nd Congress approved the following list of non-Russian members of the ECCI:[2]

| | | |
|---|---|---|
| 1. | Meyer  (candidate: Levi) | —Germany |
| 2. | Rosmer | —France |
| 3. | Serrati | —Italy |
| 4. | Quelch | —England |
| 5. | Reed (Gurvich) | —America |
| 6. | Steinhardt | —Austria |
| 7. | Fries | —Sweden |
| 8. | Shablin | —Bulgaria |
| 9. | Milkich | —Yugoslavia |
| 10. | Rudnianski | —Hungary |
| 11. | Pak | —Far East |
| 12. | Sultan Zadeh | —Near East |
| 13. | Radek | —Poland |
| 14. | Janson | —Holland |
| 15. | Maring (Sneevliet) | —Java |
| 16. | Stuchka | —Latvia |
| 17. | Chakaya | —Georgia |
| 18. | Shatskin | —Turkey |
| 19. | Manner | —Finland |
| 20. | Gula | —Czechoslovakia. |

[1] Cf. Articles 8, 14 and 15 of the statutes (Appendix IV, p. 334).

[2] Library of the Communist International, Vol. 22, pp. 661 and 666. It is not apparent from the Comintern publications how the fact that the list contains the names of twenty non-Russian members alone was made compatible with Article 8 of the Statutes, which spoke of one representative from each of ten to thirteen parties.

Immediately on the return of the delegates to their home countries, the decisions taken at the 2nd World Congress began to have effects on their parties both organizationally and politically. Parties and groups in which some of the members were pressing for affiliation to the Third International were split on the question of whether the *21 Conditions* should be accepted or not. At their party conference in Halle in October 1920, the majority of the German USPD, inspired by a long and stirring speech by Zinoviev, voted in favour of affiliation to the Comintern.[1] In France (Party Congress of Tours) the seceding majority of the Section Française Internationale Ouvrière formed the Communist Party of France, whose first General Secretary was Loudovic O. Frossard.[2] In England there was no actual split, but smaller groups, which were willing to accept the decisions of the 2nd World Congress, amalgamated with the Communist Party of Great Britain. In Italy the *21 Conditions* were rejected by both Filippo Turati (the "right-wing Socialist") and Giacinto Serrati, a "centralist", who had already drawn attention to himself at the 2nd World Congress by his opposition to criticism directed against the leaders of his party.[3] The Italian Communist Party was formed from a minority of the old Socialist Party.[4] In America there was still, in addition to the Communist Party of America already referred to, the "United Communist Party", and both these groups were represented at the 2nd World Congress. The ECCI tried for months to get them united, and when all efforts at persuasion

[1]Grigori Zinoviev, *Die Weltrevolution und die III. Internationale*, Halle, 1920. The "Amalgamation Party Conference" was the 6th Party Conference of the KPD (Spartakist League) and at the same time the 1st Party Conference of the VKPD. The 6th, 7th and 8th Party Conferences were designated the 1st, 2nd and 3rd Party Conferences of the VKPD. (See Wilhelm Pieck, *Reden und Aufsätze*, Vol. I, Berlin, 1951, p. 50, note 1.) From the 9th Party Conference (April 1924) onwards the title VKPD no longer appeared.
[2]Walter Gérard, *Histoire du PCF*, Paris, 1948, pp. 39 ff., and *Die Kommunistische Internationale*, No. 16, p. 641; also Jean Fréville, *op. cit.*, pp. 100 ff. Frossard only remained in the French party until 1923. Manuilski paid a "Tribute" to him in *Die Kommunistische Internationale*, No. 24 (1923), p. 54.
[3]Library of the Communist International, Vol. 22, pp. 654.
[4]18th Party Conference of the Italian Socialist Party, held in Leghorn in January 1921. Borkenau, in *European Communism*, gives a detailed account of the development in other European countries. See also *Die Kommunistische Internationale*, No. 17, pp. 26 ff.

seemed to produce no result, threatened them both with expulsion. At last, in May 1921, months of negotiation brought about the formation of the "Communist Party of America".[1]

The 2nd World Congress defined the political target of the Communist parties as "wresting to themselves the power to destroy the bourgeois State and to set up a Communist society".[2] In the months following the 2nd World Congress, revolutionary sections of the Central European workers made efforts to realize this aim, and this led to violent and bitter struggles.

### THE INFLUENCE OF THE RUSSIAN COMMUNIST PARTY ON THE COMINTERN IN 1920

Like the 1st World Congress, the 2nd Congress chose Russia as the location of the Executive Committee.[3] The five representatives of the Russian party can be regarded as being reinforced by Radek, who appeared as No. 13 on the list, representing Poland, but who for years had been working for the Russian party (for example in Germany), plus the representatives of the Trades Union Section and the Youth International. Thus its voting strength alone gave the CPSU considerable influence in the ECCI.

In the course of the discussions on the Statutes, Zinoviev insisted that the delegates of the member parties must reside permanently at the seat of the ECCI, that is, in Moscow. When the German Communist Paul Levi suggested that plenary sessions of the ECCI should take place every three months, and that delegates need only attend for these, Zinoviev, followed by the Congress, rejected the suggestion.[4] Zinoviev argued that the Congress had the job of "building up an international General Staff of the militant proletariat". They were living in an age of revolutionary struggle, so that the ECCI must always be in a position to give instructions and to speak in the name of the International. For this reason it had been furnished with extensive authority—for example, authority to exclude a party

---

[1]Draper, *The Roots of American Communism*, p. 279.
[2]Manifesto of the 2nd World Congress, Library of the Communist International, Vol. 22, p. 741.
[3]Library of the Communist International, Vol. 22, p. 659.
[4]*Ibid.*, p. 596.

from the Comintern. It was in point of fact these reasons and
the still-vivid memory of the failure of the Socialist International Bureau which led to the acceptance of Zinoviev's
proposals.[1] Whatever happened, the 2nd World Congress, and
in particular the Russians, wanted to make a complete break
with the tradition of the Second International. The Bolsheviks
maintained that the Comintern was carrying on the tradition
of the First International,[2] but it is doubtful whether this claim
was justified in 1920. The First International had been based
on the equality of rights of all members,[3] and regarded itself
as nothing more than a central point for planned collaboration
between associations of workers belonging to the various
countries.[4] The General Council of the International Working
Men's Association, which had a position comparable to that of
the ECCI, functioned as "an international agency between the
different national and local groups belonging to the Association" (Article 6 of the statutes). The tradition of this modest
federation, based on the equality of rights of all its members,
and whose Central Council played only an intermediary role,
was not carried on by the Comintern, armed as it was with
dictatorial authority. The Comintern, constructed on the
principle of extreme centralization, demanded from the national
Communist parties, the Sections, that they should organize
themselves on the basis of democratic centralism.[5] This dependence of the "Sections" on the Comintern was most clearly
demonstrated when, in 1938, the Polish Communist Party, a
party with a long-standing revolutionary tradition, was
dissolved by a resolution approved by the ECCI. The formal
right to make such a decision was contained in para. 9 of the
statutes. The reason alleged at the time—that the ranks of the
party leadership had been extensively penetrated by hostile
agents—was based on "forged evidence provided by agents-
provocateurs, who were later unmasked", as was stated in 1956

[1]Cf. p. 32 above.
[2]See the preface to the statutes and Zinoviev's contribution to the
proceedings of 4 August 1920: Library of the Communist International,
Vol. 22, p. 593.
[3]Cf. p. 1 above.
[4]Cf. Article I of the statutes, Appendix IV.
[5]Cf. the 12th and 21st of the *Conditions*, Appendix V, p. 339.

by the Central Committees of the CPSU, the Polish United
Workers' Party and the Communist Parties of Italy, Bulgaria
and Finland.[1]

The influence exercised by the Russian party on the Comintern was much greater than was justified by the position it was
entitled to by the statutes and the number of its members in the
ECCI. It was the only Communist party which actually ruled
a state, and all World Congresses were held on its territory.
The way in which it had come to power was declared at the
2nd World Congress to be a model for the Comintern.[2] The
increasing influence of the party bureaucracy on life in Russia,
an influence which was to develop into the dictatorship of Stalin,
continually weakened the position of the non-Russian members
of the ECCI. The Russian party had taken an important first
step towards gaining a pre-eminent position in the Comintern
when they persuaded the 2nd World Congress to agree to their
having five representatives entitled to vote in the ECCI. Five
seats were awarded to the party of "the country in which the
ECCI was located" because "the main weight of the work of the
ECCI fell on it". The Dutch delegate, Wijnkoop, the *enfant
terrible* of the 2nd World Congress, said during the discussions
that the result of this clause would be that the ECCI would not
be an international executive committee but an expanded
Russian one.[3] He was right. Even during the period of the
Comintern's beginnings, the Russian party was exercising a
direct influence on the internal affairs of the ECCI, not even
working through its own representatives on the Committee.
Angelica Balabanova, for example, has related how Trotsky
suggested to her one day that she should stay in Moscow and
assume the position of Secretary of the ECCI. When she was
shortly afterwards informed that she had been nominated to be
the Secretary of the Comintern, it was not by the ECCI but
by the Central Committee of the CPSU.[4]

The Russian party's dominant position in the Comintern

[1] *Neues Deutschland*, the main organ of the SED, Berlin, 21 February
1956.

[2] Cf. Kabakchev's contribution to the proceedings of 4 August 1920,
Library of the Communist International, Vol 22, p. 572.

[3] Library of the Communist International, Vol. 22, p. 583.

[4] A. Balabanova, *op. cit.*, pp. 228–9.

was in accordance neither with the tradition of the First International nor yet with the intentions of the classical Marxists;[1] nor was it Lenin's intention that the Russian party should enjoy a permanent position of predominance.[2] In *Left-Wing Communism*, Lenin said that if the Revolution should prevail in even one of the advanced countries, then Russia would soon be no longer the model, but would once more become a backward country.[3] However, things did not develop as Lenin had expected. The soviet republics in Hungary and Bavaria lasted only a few months and the Bolsheviks' attempts at revolution failed to achieve success in any of the "progressive countries".

### THE COMINTERN AND THE PEOPLES OF THE EAST

The 2nd World Congress also dealt with the "National and Colonial Question", in preparation for which Lenin had drafted a number of theses.[4] All the delegates were agreed from the beginning that the struggle in the colonial and semi-colonial territories must be carried on against:

  (a) "the reactionary and medieval influence" of the priests, the Christian missions and similar elements, and
  (b) Pan-Islamism and the Pan-Asiatic movement.[5]

Lenin's proposal that for tactical reasons the Communists should support the "bourgeois-democratic liberation movements" in the colonial and semi-colonial territories met, however, with opposition from some delegates, who rigidly insisted that any movement standing to the right of the Communist parties must be attacked. The chief of those who failed to appreciate the value of Lenin's more flexible tactics was the Indian delegate Manabendra Nath Roy. Less antagonistic, but still critical, was the Persian delegate Sultan Zadeh. Roy was opposed to the idea of supporting bourgeois-democratic libera-

---

[1]Cf. the quotation from Engels at p. 16 above.
[2]*Selected Works*, Vol. II, pp. 571–572.
[3]Cf. Ruth Fischer, *op. cit.*, pp. 185–186, regarding Lenin's attitude—still unchanged in 1922—in the disagreement between Ernst Meyer and his demand for a German NEP and the German "left-wing", who rejected the demand.
[4]*Preliminary Draft of Theses on the National and Colonial Questions*, in Lenin, Selected Works, Vol. II, London, 1947, pp. 654 ff.
[5]No. 11 of the "Guiding Principles" in *Die Kommunistische Internationale*, Nr. 13, pp. 127 ff.

tion movements in the colonial and semi-colonial territories and demanded the development of purely Communist movements there.[1] Roy also rejected the view of the majority of the delegates that the revolution in Europe must be brought to completion before "the hour of liberation for the toilers of Asia" could sound. In his view, the revolution in Europe could only be successfully accomplished if the European capitalists were deprived by a revolution in Asia of the profits they drew from the semi-colonial countries. Therefore, he said, the Communist International had only one task—to foster the revolution in Asia.[2] Nonetheless Lenin pushed through his ideas on both points, although he did go some way to meet Roy's arguments by agreeing to recommend support for the "national-revolutionary" as opposed to the "bourgeois-democratic" liberation movements in the wording of the "Guiding Principles on the National and Colonial Question".[3]

In the 1920s it was primarily in respect of the Kuomintang that the Comintern seems to have applied Lenin's unorthodox policy in the Far East.[4] M. N. Roy, the Indian Comintern representative, did of course try to bring about collaboration between the national liberation movement and the Communists in India in 1923 and 1924, but without success. The first to develop and successfully to apply Lenin's teaching was Mao Tse-tung in his collaboration with the national bourgeoisie.[5]

Still, the ECCI of the Comintern did take some practical steps to foster the victory of the Communist cause. As early as 1 September 1920, even before the 2nd World Congress, a

[1] The distinction between "colonial" and "semi-colonial" territories originated with Lenin (see his *Imperialism, the Highest Stage of Capitalism*, published in 1917, Moscow-Leningrad, 1934, p. 76). Lenin regarded Persia and Turkey as semi-colonial countries.

[2] Allen S. Whiting, *Soviet Policies in China, 1917–1921*, pp. 51, 54.

[3] The German version of the Guiding Principles as adopted by the 2nd World Congress is reproduced in *Die Kommunistische Internationale*, No. 13 (1920), pp. 127 ff. The supplementary theses on p. 132 of this edition were erroneously printed in the form of M. N. Roy's original draft. The Communists did not notice the mistake until 1934 (see Whiting, *op. cit.*, pp. 56 and 295, note 33).

[4] See p. 100 below.

[5] See Robert Payne, *Mao Tse-tung*, London, 1951, p. 246, and John H. Kautsky, *Moscow and the Communist Party of India*, New York and London, 1956, pp. 6 ff., on basic points of Mao's policies.

"Congress of Peasants and Workers of Persia, Armenia and Turkey" was called in Baku. The purpose of the congress and the aim of Communist efforts in the Near East were thus described in the invitations sent out by the Executive Committee:

> Peasants and workers of the Near East. If you organize yourselves, if you arm yourselves, if you unite with the Red Russian peasants' and workers' army . . . then you will be able to deal with the English, French and American capitalists—you will be able to get rid of your oppressors and will have a chance to look after your own interests in alliance with the workers' republics of the world. Then the riches of your land will belong to you.
>
> On 1 September thousands of Persian, Turkish and Armenian peasants and workers must peacefully assemble for the liberation of the peoples of the Near East.[1]

This meeting became in the event the "1st Congress of the Eastern Peoples", which was attended by 1,891 delegates from 32 "nations of the East" from Morocco to Manchuria. According to the report Zinoviev made to the ECCI Plenum on 20 September 1920, two-thirds of the delegates were Communists; 235 Turks, 192 Persians, 157 Armenians and—something new in the political life of the East—44 women took part.[2] The Turkish delegates included the former War Minister of the Young Turks, Enver Pasha, who at that time was hoping to gather together Turkish forces to combat Kemal Pasha's régime.[3]

The Executive Committee of the Comintern sent to the Congress the Chairman of its presidium, Zinoviev, and two members, Karl Radek and Bela Kun. Delegates of the workers'

---

[1] Library of the Communist International, Vol. 1, Hamburg, 1920, pp. 367, 371.

[2] Jane Degras, *The Communist International 1919–1943*, Vol. I, London-New York-Toronto, 1956, p. 105; G. Lenczkowski, *Russia and the West in Iran*, Ithaca (New York), 1949, p. 6.

[3] Charles Warren Hostler, *Turkism and the Soviets*, London and New York, 1957, p. 154. Enver Pasha subsequently turned against the USSR in connection with his efforts to free Central Asiatic Turkish tribes from Soviet domination. He lost his life in the course of this struggle in August 1922 (Hostler, p. 155).

parties from the "imperialist" countries were Tom Quelch (Britain), Johannes Proost (Holland), John Reed (USA) and Alfred Rosmer (France).[1] The members of the Comintern élite made rousing speeches in an effort to kindle the faith of their audience in the irresistible world victory of Communism and to turn the hatred of the delegates against the Western imperialists—especially Great Britain—and against the exploiters within their own countries. Zinoviev did fulminate against Islam, but at the same time managed to whip up the assembled Moslems against British imperialism to such an extent that his call for a "holy war" was received with wild enthusiasm.[2]

Radek attacked "the shahs, emirs and khans", and Bela Kun whipped up his audience against the national bourgeoisie. In his speech Radek named Russia as the guarantor of the coming common victory:

> Soviet Russia was surrounded by enemies, but now she can produce weapons with which to arm the Indians, the Persian and Anatolian peasants—in fact all the oppressed—and lead them into the common battle and to victory.[3]

In the discussion, a delegate from Turkestan said that the Moslems would not desert the Soviets if the Soviets recognized the distinctive characteristics of the Eastern peoples and if the Soviet Government would translate their words into deeds and not simply leave them on paper. The West accused the Bolsheviks of being red imperialists. Let the Bolsheviks therefore get rid of their colonizers who worked in the guise of Communists.[4]

The only immediate result of the Congress was the formation of a "Council for Action and Propaganda" as an instrument in the common struggle of the Bolsheviks and the Eastern peoples. This council was to have a permanent presidium, including

[1]Rosmer, *Moscou sous Lénine*, pp. 125 ff.

[2]Louis Fischer, *The Soviets in World Affairs*, Vol. I, 1951, pp. 283 ff. Fischer probably got the details of the course of the congress from Karl Radek (*op. cit.*, p. ix).

[3]Degras, *op. cit.*, p. 105.

[4]Degras, *op. cit.*, p. 105, and Baymirza Hayit, *Turkestan im XX. Jahrhundert*, Darmstadt, 1956, p. 189.

two ECCI delegates, and was to meet in Baku at least four times a year. It was also to publish a newspaper in three languages. The council's task was to be to put out propaganda in the East and to unite local liberation movements.[1]

All the delegates were certainly united in one respect—in their hatred of Western, and especially British, imperialism. Nonetheless it is improbable that at this period, in 1920, many of the Moslem delegates were so free of traditional oriental concepts that they could find much enthusiasm for Zinoviev's rejection of Islamism and Radek's attacks on traditional Eastern forms of government. In attacking the national bourgeoisie of the Eastern peoples—and this, be it noted, without criticism from Zinoviev or Radek—Bela Kun was acting in contradiction of the "Guiding Principles (of the 2nd World Congress) on the National and Colonial Question", which had recommended collaboration with the "national bourgeoisie" as a result of Lenin's efforts.

The "holy war" to which the delegates to the "Congress of Eastern Peoples" had pledged themselves never took place. The "Council for Action and Propaganda" achieved nothing worthy of mention and only remained alive for some twelve months.[2] Russian national interests—including the desire to improve the disastrous economic situation by means of trade treaties with the capitalist countries—was already making it impossible to carry on with the Baku policy. Indeed, in the Anglo-Soviet Trade Agreement of March 1921 the Russians pledged themselves to stop their propaganda attacks on Britain.[3]

In the same year Soviet Russia concluded pacts of neutrality and friendship with Persia, Turkey and Afghanistan, and these pacts were renewed in 1927. However, this "armistice" did not prevent Reza Shah and Kemal Ataturk from taking drastic measures to cripple the activities of the banned Communist parties of their countries.[4]

---

[1]Degras, *op. cit.*, pp. 105–6.
[2]Stalin, *Marxism and the National and Colonial Question*, New York, n.d., p. 299, note 39.
[3]Louis Fischer, *op. cit.*, p. 296.
[4]George Lenczkowski, *op. cit.*, pp. 104 ff., and Walter Z. Laqueur, *Communism and Nationalism in the Middle East*, pp. 210 ff.

THE REVOLUTIONARY ADVANCE AND THE RUSSIAN CRISIS OF 1921

After the 2nd World Congress it proved impossible to maintain the onward march of the revolution, militarily, politically or economically.

Following on the successful foiling of the Polish attack on Kiev, Lenin, against the advice of Trotsky, ordered the Red Army to march westwards. On 15 August 1920, shortly after the end of the 2nd World Congress, the Russian forces suffered a heavy defeat outside Warsaw.[1] It was a contributory factor in this defeat that, in spite of an appeal to them, the Polish workers failed to pave the way for the Red Army by an insurrection to the extent the Communists had expected.[2] Old national rivalries weighed heavier than the attraction of revolutionary ideas. The Bolsheviks' hope that the Soviet troops would be able to join forces with the revolutionary German proletariat were not going to be realized within the foreseeable future. There followed reverses in Western Europe. Following large-scale strikes in Italy in 1920, Communist workers failed in their attempts to occupy factories and great estates. A general strike was also started in Czechoslovakia, but that too collapsed.[3]

In the meantime, the results of war and internecine strife led to a catastrophic situation for the Russian people.

The number of those who died between January 1918 and July 1920 as a result of undernourishment and epidemics has been estimated at seven million.[4] Zinoviev wrote at the time:

> The economic life of Russia has fallen into terrible decay as a result of four years of imperialist war and three years of civil war.[5]

[1]Leon Trotsky, *My Life*, p. 391 (also dealing with Stalin's part in the war against Poland); W. G. Krivitsky, *I Was Stalin's Agent*, London 1949, p. 48 and Dolléans, *op. cit.*, p. 340. This defeat was one of the important factors leading to the failure of the revolutionary efforts of the Comintern in its early years.

[2]R. Fischer, *Stalin and German Communism*, Cambridge, Mass., 1948, p. 136. Cf. also Heinz Neumann, *Der ultralinke Menschewismus*, Berlin, 1926, p. 23.

[3]A. Balabanova, *op. cit.*, p. 259, Library of the Communist International, Vol. 23, pp. 448 ff., also *Die Kommunistische Internationale*, No. 17 (1921), p. 240.

[4]Cf. Leonard Schapiro, *The Origin of the Communist Autocracy*, London, 1955, p. 216.

[5]Zinoviev, in *Die Kommunistische Internationale*, No. 17, p. 38.

Trotsky suggested that industrial productivity could be increased by the introduction of methods which had proved successful in the Red Army. He wanted to replace trade union bureaucracy by "fresh, creative forces from below", just as he had overcome the opposition of the party bureaucrats in the Army by the mass recruitment of Communists from among the workers. It was only in this sense that he spoke of "production democracy".[1] In reality, Trotsky openly demanded that production should be militarized and that compulsion should be employed. Lenin's views did not differ greatly from Trotsky's as far as the control of production was concerned, although they did differ in respect of the method. Lenin was more cautious, declaring that all trade union organs should be elected and not nominated. However, the selection of the leading officials should "take place under the overall control of the party".[2] Lenin managed to win over the entire Central Committee to his point of view, the Central Committee's position at the beginning of 1921 having been weakened not only as a result of the distressed condition of the Russian people but also because of the rise of the "Workers' Opposition". This "Workers' Opposition", a trade union movement, had originated in 1919 among proletarian trade unionists who at that time opposed the employment of bourgeois specialists in responsible positions in industry. In January 1921 the "Workers' Opposition", led by Alexander Shlyapnikov and Juri Lutovinov, demanded that control over industry should in future be exercised by a body to be elected by the trade unions. The trade union functionaries should also be elected by the members.[3] These demands were aimed at breaking the power of the Central Committee of the party over the trade unions. In 1921 the left-wing Communists who composed the "Workers' Opposition" were joined by Alexandra Kollontai.[4] She was an

[1] Cf. Leonard Schapiro, *op. cit.*, p. 278. Rosenberg in his *History of Bolshevism*, *op. cit.*, pp. 153 ff., misunderstood Trotsky's phrase as meaning a genuine democratization of production.

[2] Cf. Leonard Schapiro, *op. cit.*, p. 277 ff. (with further quotations).

[3] Cf. Leonard Schapiro, *op. cit.*, p. 285.

[4] She had joined the Russian Social Democratic Workers' Party in 1899, and had belonged to the Communists since 1915, being elected to their Central Committee in 1917 (Ruth Fischer, *Stalin and German Communism*, pp. 159–160).

outstanding speaker, who both criticized the government in respect of the trade union question and attacked the party bureaucrats not only for stifling initiative but also for the privileges they enjoyed. During the preparations for the 10th Party Congress she represented the views of the "Workers' Opposition" in a series of brilliant speeches and in a highly effective pamphlet.[1]

The "Workers' Opposition" and other oppositional forces tried to force through their proposals within the party.[2] Confident of the support of large sections of the discontented Russian people, they represented a considerable threat to the dictatorship of the bureaucrats in the Bolshevik party. At the 10th Party Congress in March 1921, Lenin, who wanted to maintain the centralist régime whatever happened, had a resolution drawn up, *On Party Unity*, threatening severe disciplinary measures for any attempt to form a separate group.[3] While Lenin was alive, however, no drastic action was taken against antagonistic Bolshevik functionaries. Even after the 10th Party Congress, for example, Alexandra Kollontai was still able to speak in favour of the views of the "Workers' Opposition" at the 3rd World Congress.[4]

In February 1922 twenty-two members of the "Workers' Opposition", led by Alexander Shlyapnikov, went so far as to present the ECCI with a declaration (the so-called Declaration of the Twenty-two), in which they asked for help against the abuse of power by the bureaucrats within the Russian party. The ECCI appointed a commission under the chairmanship of Vasil Kolaroff to examine the complaints, but the commission rejected the charges as unfounded.[5] However, the supporters

---

[1] Alexandra Kollontai, *Workers' Opposition in Russia*, London, n.d.

[2] On similar oppositional groups see Leonard Schapiro, *Origin*, pp. 253 ff.; R. Fischer, *Stalin and German Communism*, pp. 156–159; Susanne Leonhard, *Gestohlenes Leben*, pp. 790 ff. Rosmer also gives much information, particularly on Trotsky's standpoint (*Moscou sous Lénine*, pp. 164 ff.).

[3] This resolution is reproduced in Lenin, *Selected Works* (two volumes), Vol. II, pp. 679 ff. See also Lenin's speech, *Party Unity and the Anarcho-Syndicalist Deviation*, delivered at the 10th Party Congress, in Lenin, *Selected Works* (12 volumes), London, 1937, Vol. 9, pp. 123–130.

[4] Library of the Communist International, Vol. 23, pp. 776 ff.

[5] Cf. Alfred Rosmer, *Moscou sous Lénine*, Paris 1953, pp. 208 ff. and L. Schapiro, *op. cit.*, pp. 332 ff.

of the "Workers' Opposition" had friends in the International, and particularly within the German "Left", and Shlyapnikov and Lutovinov were able to inform these friends when they were sent to Berlin with trade missions following the 10th Party Congress.[1]

Even though Lenin stood fast in the face of the Opposition's attacks on the centralistic party bureaucracy, he still tried to alleviate the economic distress prevailing in Russia at that time by making certain concessions to capitalist economics in the shape of the N.E.P., the New Economic Policy. He also made efforts through Willi Münzenberg to have an international assistance programme started and September 1921 saw the beginning of the International Workers' Relief.[2]

Not all opposition groups were satisfied to deal with their demands by means of party discussions. The Russian Navy had been a breeding ground for revolutionary ideas ever since 1905; and in 1917 the sailors at Kronstadt had won themselves the reputation of being the nucleus of the Revolution. In 1921 there broke out in Kronstadt a revolt which had revolutionary-libertarian features. The demands of the sailors, in revolt against the party dictatorship, were raised at the "General Meeting of Battleship Crews" on 1 March 1921, and included the re-election of the Soviet by secret ballot, freedom of expression, both written and spoken, for workers and peasants, and freedom for the trade unions and peasant associations.[3] But the Red Army, created by Trotsky, was ordered by the Communist Party to attack the Kronstadt mutineers on 7 March 1921. The Kronstadt Revolutionary Committee sent out the following radio message to the world.[4]

The first shot has thundered. But the entire world knows of it. The bloody Field Marshal Trotsky, who stands up to the waist in the fraternal blood of the workers, was the first to open fire against revolutionary Kronstadt, which rebelled

[1]Cf. Ruth Fischer, *Stalin and German Communism*, pp. 181–182.
[2]See p. 185 below.
[3]A. Rosenberg, *op. cit.*, p. 155, R. Fischer, *op. cit.*, pp. 166 and 611, and S. Leonhard, *op. cit.*, pp. 763 ff. Cf. also *Die Kommunistische Internationale*, No. 17 (1921), p. 392, and William H. Chamberlin, *The Russian Revolution 1917-1921*, London, 1935, p. 441.
[4]D. Shub, *Lenin, op. cit.*, p. 360.

against the government of the Communists in order to re-establish the real power of the Soviets. We will rise or fall under the ruins of Kronstadt, fighting for the bloodstained cause of the labouring people. Long live the power of the Soviets! Long live the world Socialist revolution!

The Kronstadt revolt was quickly crushed. The decision to beat it down in this manner showed that the leaders of the Soviet Party were prepared to employ methods which were incompatible with the development of genuine socialism in Russia.

## THE ACTION OF MARCH 1921

In Germany, too, the Communist revolution suffered a no less crushing defeat. After the 2nd World Congress, the United Communist Party of Germany (the VKPD) had begun to set up illegal militant organizations as required by para. 12 of the Comintern Statutes. For this purpose the VKPD made use of the former members of a clandestine underground organization built up inside the USPD by Ernst Däumig; and the so-called M.P. (Military-Political) organization was created.[1] The carefully chosen members were trained in the use of weapons and in conspiratorial manoeuvres and carried out night marches and similar exercises. A separate organization was the N-Apparat, whose task was to collect information. Sub-sections of the N-Apparat were concerned with subversive activity within the armed forces and the police. These clandestine organizations were acting in accordance with the revolutionary slogan put out by the 2nd World Congress and

[1] The military organization of the KPD was built up in 1920 and 1921 on the advice and with the assistance of Leon Trotsky, who was at that time People's Commissar for Military Affairs. The necessity for such an organization arose from the desire to exploit the current revolutionary situation. The organization, originally called the MP (Military-political) organization, was subordinate to the German Party. The Russian personnel, who included a number of generals, acted as advisers (in consonance with the relationship existing at that time between the German and Russian parties). In the course of the following years the influence of these "advisers" increased, an important factor, in view of the growing inflation, being the number of dollars they had at their disposal. After the collapse of the attempt at revolt in 1923, the organization and control of the secret military organization underwent an important change, in that control passed from the Red Army to the OGPU. G. W. Krivitsky gives indications of this in *I Was Stalin's Agent*, London, 1939, p. 64.

rhetorically reshaped to suit German conditions by Zinoviev at the USPD Party Congress in Halle in October 1920. They were preparing the way for the offensive with the bayonet.[1]

In February 1921, the ECCI sent Bela Kun, Josef Pogany and the Lithuanian August Guralski to Germany.[2] The orthodox Marxist view that a revolution in "advanced" Germany could save the Russian revolution, still heavily beset with internal problems, still prevailed and the theory developed by Bukharin and Radek of the "revolutionary offensive" was adopted by the German Communists.[3] A suitable jumping-off point for the offensive seemed to be the mining and industrial area of Mansfeld. In order to whip up the workers, members of the Communist underground organization, which was at that time under the command of Hugo Eberlein,[4] carried out such provocative action as setting off bombs in Breslau and Halle and sabotaging railways. The Prussian government took a grip on the situation and sent squads of police to Mansfeld before serious unrest could break out. There was fighting between the police and the miners and this provided the VKPD with an excuse for calling for a general strike for the whole of Germany.

However, the strike call was only followed in parts of Saxony, in the Ruhr and in Berlin, and not more than 300,000 workers came out on strike. The revolt was confined to a part of central Germany and was mercilessly crushed by the Reichswehr and the police.[5] A German Communist of the

[1]Erich Wollenberg, *Der Apparat*, Bonn, 1921, pp. 9 ff. Wollenberg, who long since ceased to have anything to do with Bolshevism, was described as Head of the South-West District and one of the most dangerous Communists in a judgment promulgated on 22 April 1925 by the State Court for the Protection of the Republic. See also Ruth Fischer, *op. cit.*, p. 112, and Walter Rist, *Der Weg der KPD* in the periodical *Neue Blätter für den Sozialismus*, 3rd year (1932), p. 89.

[2]In a letter to Clara Zetkin and Paul Levi of 16 April 1921, Lenin spoke of the "stupid tactics" of the Comintern representative (Bela Kun). See *Probleme des Friedens und des Sozialismus*, Berlin, 1958, No. 2, p. 12.

[3]O. K. Flechtheim, *op. cit.*, p. 74.

[4]Ruth Fischer, *op. cit.*, pp. 175 ff.; Paul Levi, *Unser Weg* (Wider dem Putschismus), Berlin, 1921, p. 33; Willy Brandt and R. Loewenthal, *Ernst Reuter*, Munich, 1957, p. 156.

[5]Walter Rist, *op. cit.*, p. 89; O. K. Flechtheim, *op. cit.*, p. 74; Ernst Meyer in *Volk und Reich der Deutschen*, Berlin, 1929, Vol. II, pp. 146 ff.

prominence of Paul Levi, who had left the Central Committee of the VKPD in February, together with Clara Zetkin, Ernst Däumig and others, sharply and publicly attacked the putschists in the VKPD and condemned the tactics of the Comintern.[1] He was thereupon expelled from the Party on 15 April 1921.[2]

Thus since the 2nd World Congress the Bolshevist revolution had suffered one defeat after another, not only internally (the consequences of war communism and the Kronstadt revolt), but also in the attempt to "advance" externally (in Poland, Italy and Germany).

THE THIRD WORLD CONGRESS
*(22 June—July 1921)*

The 3rd World Congress had to take account of these facts. In his report on the *World Situation and the New Tasks of the International*, Trotsky admitted that in 1919 the Bolshevists had expected world revolution to break out within a few months, but that now, in 1921, it had turned out that it might be some years before this happened. This view appeared in the theses of the 3rd World Congress, in which it was declared that the revolutionary advance of the proletariat had slowed down and that the revolutionary wave of 1917-1921 had not "swept away" capitalism, either in Europe or anywhere else in the world.[3] Nevertheless the 3rd World Congress still clung to world revolution as the ultimate aim. In a speech to members of a number of delegations, Lenin declared:

> But after we have won over the masses through our tactics of moderation, then comes the use of the tactics of offence, offence in the strict meaning of the word.[4]

The Congress remained faithful to the belief that the conditions of the proletariat could not show a lasting improvement under capitalism. At present, the theses said, there would have to be a

[1] See Levi's pamphlet, *Unser Weg*, p. 69 above, note 4, and Flechtheim, *op. cit.*, p. 75.

[2] The ECCI agreed to Levi's expulsion by a resolution of 29 April 1921 (see *Die Kommunistische Internationale*, No. 17, 1921, pp. 365 ff.).

[3] *Thesen zur Weltlage*, Library of the Communist International, Vol. 20, pp. 28 ff.

[4] This speech of Lenin's was not published until 1959 (see *Einheit*, the theoretical periodical of the SED, East Berlin, March 1959, p. 308).

struggle for the vital necessities of life of the proletariat and only
partial demands could be met until the proletariat were ready
for the fight for the ultimate aims. The 3rd Congress declared
in the resolution on the tactics of the Russian Communist
Party:

> This Congress unanimously approves the policies of the
> Communist Party of the Soviet Union . . . which is still
> concentrating all the forces of the proletariat they lead in
> order to maintain the dictatorship of the proletariat in
> Russia until the proletariat of Western Europe will be able
> to come to the help of their brothers.[1]

This made plain the situation of the international revolution.

The liveliest discussions during the 3rd World Congress
concerned the events of March in Germany. Mismanaged and
unsuccessful as the action was, its instigators, the leaders of the
VKPD, could plead that they had acted in accordance with
the revolutionary slogans of the 2nd World Congress. In fact,
as Clara Zetkin pointed out, the action in March had been
supported by the emissaries of the ECCI.[2] With the aim of
preventing any recurrence of interference by the International
in Section affairs, the French delegation demanded full details
regarding the ECCI's share in the events of March. Radek's
response was to attack the French so virulently that they
walked out of the meeting and stayed out for some time.[3] The
powerful German delegation, which included Ernst Reuter,
Fritz Heckert and August Thalheimer, were therefore surprised at the severity with which Lenin and Trotsky condemned
the March action and Bela Kun's part in it.[4] The Congress
also criticized the VKPD for having furnished the enemies of
the proletariat with grounds for stigmatizing the Communist
Party as "putschist". Furthermore, the Congress complained
that some Party comrades had described the offensive as the
most important militant method "in the present situation".
In this criticism of the revolutionary offensive no mention was
made of the fact that the 2nd World Congress had called not

---

[1]Library of the Communist International, Vol. 20, p. 104.
[2]Library of the Communist International, Vol. 23, p. 296.
[3]A. Rosmer, *op. cit.*, p. 179.
[4]Willy Brandt and Richard Loewenthal, *Ernst Reuter*, Munich, 1957, p. 167.

only on the German section but also on the Communist Parties of the world to take up the fight "with all available means, including weapons".[1] Although the decisions of the 3rd World Congress condemned the March action—in other words, although the Congress aligned itself with the criticisms that Paul Levi had made publicly—it still confirmed Levi's expulsion from the VKPD and forbade all members of the International to work with him. It has been said, "once you start purging, you don't know where you will end",[2] and in point of fact this was the start of a fateful process. From the cases of Levi, Reuter, Ruth Fischer, Maslow and Brandler there runs a thread that ends in the bloody purges of 1935 to 1938, in which Eberlein, Remmele, Hölz and a host of others were liquidated in the Soviet Union.[3]

THE THIRD CONGRESS AND THE WORLD REVOLUTION

From the point of view of the double-track Bolshevist tactics, there was probably nothing equivocal or contradictory in the resolutions of the 3rd Congress.[4] The resolutions embraced the tactics suggested by Lenin in *Left-Wing Communism*, in so far as they were relevant to the international situation in the summer of 1921. As Trotsky correctly put it,[5] "The slogan of the Third International did not simply read: 'To the masses!' but: 'To power through a previous conquest of the masses!' " The Dutch Communist Hermann Gorter thought that the 3rd World Congress had temporarily sealed the fate of the world revolution. Like Rosenberg, he was an adherent of the theory, originated by Marx and developed by Lenin, that world revolution was imminent.[6] This theory was based on Marx's concentration theory, which stated that the development of the capitalist economy in the highly industrial and "advanced" countries would lead to a concentration of capital

[1] Preface to the Comintern Statutes, Library of the Communist International, Vol. 22, p. 601.

[2] Lazich, *op. cit.*, p. 184.

[3] See p. 188 below.

[4] Rosenberg, *op. cit.*, p. 168; Hermann Gorter, *Die Moskauer Internationale*, Berlin, 1931, quoted by Rosenberg, *loc. cit.*

[5] Leon Trotsky, *The Third International After Lenin*, New York, 1936, pp. 90–91.

[6] See p. 48 above.

in the hands of the entrepreneurs and a concentration of poverty on the side of the workers, so that in the end a small number of capitalists would be faced with an enormous mass of poverty-stricken workers. When this centralization of the means of production and the corresponding degree of poverty are reached, then—said Marx in the twenty-fourth chapter of the first volume of *Das Kapital*—"the knell of capitalist private property will sound", "the expropriators will be expropriated".[1]

In the century which has gone by since *Das Kapital* was published, it has been shown that Marx's concentration theory, the most important theoretical lesson of Marxist economics, is false. Economic development in the highly industrialized countries, which ought to have led to a concentration of capital in the Marxist sense and was bound to lead to revolutionary situations with the "inevitability of a natural law", has produced a situation in which there has, it is true, been a certain concentration of capital, in that some large-scale businesses and industrial complexes have come into being. But there has been no evidence of a general development of this kind. There are some branches of industry which do not lend themselves to concentration, for example repair shops or the distribution of fuel. Thus there came into existence intermediate and artisan undertakings to stock, distribute or repair the products of industry. In the actual field of production itself—for example in the precision tool industry—small and medium-scale industries have developed and maintained themselves, contrary to Marx's expectations.

Nor has the "concentration of poverty" prophesied in Marx's theory of progressive pauperization come to pass—at least in the industrialized countries. The position of the workers under the capitalist economic system has assumed a form quite different from what Marx supposed it would take. The trade unions have developed into organizations of enormous power. The standard of living of the individual worker in the industrialized countries has risen remarkably. As the last forty years have shown, the view that proletarian revolution is bound to break out in the "advanced" countries is false. The picture of the development of world revolution envisaged by the

[1] Marx/Engels, *Ausgewählte Schriften*, Berlin, 1951, p. 434.

classical Marxists, including Lenin, and to which Rosenberg
and Gorter also clung, is a false one.[1] Gorter, however, correctly
pointed out[2] certain indications that the Communist parties of
Western Europe would for some time to come only be made
use of in order to keep the Russian revolution alive.[3] Russia's
internal problems occupied the foreground, which explains
why, at the 3rd Congress, when Lenin—unquestionably the
leading personality in the International—spoke, it was on the
situation in Soviet Russia, whereas his subject at the 2nd
Congress had been the *world* situation. It was Trotsky who
dealt with the world situation at the 3rd Congress.[4] The extent
to which the policies of the International were conditioned by
developments inside Russia was made plain by the international
effects of the tactics employed in creating the New Economic
Policy. In the theses on the world situation it was acknowledged
that capitalism had not been swept away and that the "self-
confidence of the bourgeoisie as a class and the exterior solidity
of their organs of State" had been strengthened, despite the
great revolutionary efforts of the Communists.[5]

For internal reasons the Russian party was incapable of any
further revolutionary effort. This is why the Communist parties
of the West were diverted from revolutionary aims to the
"indispensable necessities of life of the proletariat"; that is to
say, to economic questions. This new course was soon to lead
to a completely changed attitude—and one which had been
firmly rejected as recently as at the 2nd Congress—towards
the Social Democratic parties of the West, namely the policy
of the "United Front".

From the point of view of proletarian internationalism,
however, the 3rd World Congress meant this; that world

[1]To this very day, in spite of the developments of the last hundred years,
Marxist "political economists" still cling to this erroneous theory, as was
shown at the "international Economic Conference" which met in East
Berlin from 1 to 4 October 1958 (see Prof. I. I. Kusminov, "Factors of
Absolute Impoverishment" in *Neues Deutschland*, East Berlin, 21 October
1958).

[2]H. Gorter, quoted by Rosenberg, *loc. cit.*

[3]Cf. quotation on p. 96 below.

[4]Library of the Communist International, Vol. 23, pp. 48 ff.

[5]*Thesen und Resolutionen des III. Weltkongresses der Kommunistischen Internationale*, Library of the Communist International, Vol. 20, pp. 28 ff.

Communism—the world revolution—was subordinated to the requirements of the Russian party. Thus was laid the foundation-stone of the policy which Stalin was later to use to harness the Communist parties to the service of the Soviet party bureaucracy.

## THE UNITED FRONT, THE WORKERS' GOVERNMENT AND NEW SETBACKS (THE FOURTH WORLD CONGRESS)

The 3rd World Congress had dealt chiefly with the lessons to be drawn from the reverses of the years 1920 and 1921, and their resolutions were based on the realization that the Communist parties of the West would not be able to achieve power by revolutionary means within the foreseeable future, and that accordingly they ought to desist from revolutionary action and devote themselves to the fight for the "indispensable necessities of life of the proletariat". Their resolutions urged the Communist parties to get into the field of economic reform, the area in which the Socialist parties were most active—which was precisely the reason why the Socialists had been criticized by the Communists as "opportunists". The Sections of the Comintern were now told to concern themselves with "the masses", whose needs were to be satisfied by means of this new policy. Karl Radek, who had become the Comintern agent in Germany in place of Bela Kun after the failure of the March action, had been urging the adoption of this policy ever since 1921.[1] He became the main supporter of the idea of using the United Front policy in an attempt to win over the masses.

The United Front policy was not inaugurated at the 3rd World Congress, which came to no decisions regarding this new political line.[2] It was not until December 1921 that the United Front thesis was accepted and promulgated by the ECCI, who then called on the Communist parties to col-

[1] K. Radek, *Die nächsten Aufgaben der Kommunistischen Internationale*, in the weekly *Die Internationale*, No. 1/2 of 1 January 1922. Also Radek, *Genua, die Einheitsfront des Proletariats und die Kommunistische Internationale*, Hamburg, 1922, pp. 58 ff.

[2] In *Die KPD in der Weimarer Republik*, Offenbach, 1948, p. 47; O. K. Flechtheim is of a different opinion. R. N. Carew-Hunt, in *The Theory and Practice of Communism*, London, 1957, p. 173, also dates the beginning of the United Front policy from the 3rd World Congress.

laborate with the Socialists.[1] This collaboration was to be made to suit the conditions prevailing in the country concerned (for example, in Germany, the Communists were to co-operate with the Socialists in the formation of workers' governments; the British Communists were recommended to penetrate the Labour Party). The United Front policy broke away from the "Left" policies of the 2nd Congress, which had sharply opposed the "opportunists", and was one of those radical changes of the Party Line with which the Soviet Communists were so often to surprise the members and supporters in the future.

It is symbolic of the position of the World Congress that the ECCI was able to take such fundamental decisions. According to paragraph 4 of the statutes, it was the World Congress, the "supreme organ" of the International, which was supposed to deliberate and decide on the most important policy questions, yet in this case it had to be content merely to ratify the United Front policy a year later.[2] The change of line served the interests of the Soviet Party, which obviously put the decision into the hands of the ECCI because the Russians had more influence over the Comintern functionaries permanently resident in Moscow than they had over the delegates to the World Congress.

In order to implement the United Front policy, the Communists negotiated with the Second International they had rejected for years and with the "International Two-and-a-Half" they had so long derided. The negotiations took place from 2 to 25 April 1922 at a conference called by the Austrian Socialist, Friedrich Adler, on the suggestion of Radek, in the Reichstag building in Berlin. The conference was attended by such prominent politicians as Emile van der Velde, Camille Huysmans, Thorwald A. Stauning, Ramsay MacDonald, Friedrich Adler, Otto Bauer and Julius Martow, with the Comintern being represented by Karl Radek, Nikolai Bukharin and Clara Zetkin (and not, therefore, by the top-ranking Lenin and Trotsky).[3]

[1] Cf. *Die Kommunistische Internationale*, No. 20, p. 59.
[2] Library of the Communist International, Vol. 35, Hamburg, 1923, pp. 167 ff.
[3] See *Protokoll der Internationalen Konferenz der drei Internationalen Exekutiv-Komitees*, Vienna, 1922, p. 3; Ruth Fischer, *op. cit.*, p. 216.

The conference failed because the Western Socialists saw that what the Comintern wanted was to split the Socialist workers from their elected leaders, to win them over to the Bolshevist cause and thus destroy the Socialist parties. Emile van der Velde, the Belgian Socialist, said at the conference:

> There is an appeal to everybody for unity; there is a suggestion to us to make the United Front a reality; but there is no attempt to hide the *arrière-pensée*, first to embrace us and then to smother or poison us.[1]

This in fact was the hidden thought behind the United Front policy of 1922 and the Popular Front policy of 1935, and it is the motive that actuates the Bolshevists today when they continually call, as they have since 1946 and as they did at the 20th Party Congress of the CPSU,[2] for the unity of the working classes. Although Marx wrote in the Communist Manifesto,[3] "The Communists scorn to conceal their views and intentions", it is not often that the real purpose of the striving after the unity of the working classes and the unity of action has been so openly expressed as it was by Hermann Matern, a member of the Politbureau of the SED, when he said in February 1957:[4]

> Our striving for unity of action serves the main problem—the struggle for power. Unity of action merely for the sake of unity is not particularly important.

The United Front policy, based on tactical considerations, was to be fostered in the whole Comintern sphere.[5] However, it was rejected not only by the Socialists but also, in the beginning, by some senior Communist functionaries. The new line

[1] *Ibid.*, *Protokoll*, p. 13.
[2] Cf. M. S. Suslov's contribution to the proceedings at the 20th Party Congress of the CPSU, in L. Gruliow, ed. *Current Soviet Policies II*, New York, 1957, p. 76. Resolution of the 20th Party Congress in *ibid.*, p. 190.
[3] Marx and Engels, *Manifesto of the Communist Party*.
[4] *Neues Deutschland*, 16 February 1957. In a similar case, Karl Radek's opinion on this point, completely in agreement with the teaching of Lenin's *Left-Wing Communism*, was: "What the wise think to themselves, the stupid say out loud" (see K. Radek, *Der Kampf der Komintern gegen Versailles*, Hamburg, 1923, p. 92).
[5] Regarding Bulgaria, cf. the article in *Die Taktik der Einheitsfront* and *Arbeiter- und Bauernregierung in Bulgarien* in *Die Kommunistische Internationale*, 4th year, No. 28, p. 75, and for the USA see the article by John Pepper in the same publication, 4th year, No. 27, p. 82.

was opposed by the "Left" Communists, not only in the Communist parties but also at the 4th Congress. The French party had already said in January 1922 that the United Front could not be achieved in France.[1] In the Italian party a strong "Left" opposition was formed under Amadeo Bordiga. It was the struggle between the "Left" and the party-line Communists that facilitated Mussolini's assumption of power.[2]

In Germany, too, there arose a "Left" opposition led by Arkadi Maslow and Ruth Fischer, and their differences with the party-line Central Committee weakened the VKPD. If there ever was a revolutionary situation in Germany in the years 1922 and 1923, the United Front policy prevented the "Leftists" from exploiting it.

The 4th World Congress met on 5 November 1922 in Petrograd, and was continued in Moscow from 9 November until 5 December. At this Congress opposition to the United Front policy was expressed in speeches by Duret (France), Henryk Dombsky (Poland), Amadeo Bordiga (Italy) and Ruth Fischer (Germany),[3] but the Congress still approved the policies of the ECCI, and in particular the United Front policy, with 16 abstentions and one dissentient vote.[4] The opposition to the United Front policy caused the ECCI to have the following extract inserted into the resolution of the 4th Congress on the policies of the Communist International:

### International Discipline

In order that the United Front policy can be implemented both internally and in each individual country, the strictest international discipline is now more than ever essential, both in the Communist International and in the individual Sections.

The 4th Congress demands from all Sections and from all members the strictest discipline in carrying out the policy,

[1]Lazich, *op. cit.*, p. 200: Gérard Walter, *Histoire du Parti Communiste Français*, Paris, 1948, pp. 77 ff. and 89.

[2]Rosenberg, *op. cit.*, p. 189. Amadeo Bordiga left the Italian Communist Party and later founded the so-called "Italian Left".

[3]Library of the Communist International Vol. 37, pp. 27, 33, 34, 44 ff. Duret is probably identical with François Koral, the editor of the Paris paper *L'Humanité*.

[4]Library of the Communist International, Vol. 37, p. 55.

which will only bear fruit if it is implemented unanimously and according to plan, not only in word but also in deed.

At the 4th Congress Soviet interests played a still greater part than before. Lenin and Trotsky, the most respected Soviet delegates, spoke on Russian problems and particularly on the NEP, leaving Radek to expound on the international situation.[1] Whereas the 2nd World Congress had taken an optimistic view of the international stiuation, the discussions of the 4th World Congress no longer prophesied that world revolution was at hand. Nikolai Bukharin demanded that the Soviet State must be defended by the proletariat of the other countries,[2] giving the first intimation of something that was increasingly to characterize the Comintern—the fact that it was to be an auxiliary of the Russian party and of Russian foreign policy. Russian foreign policy, laid down by the Russian party, was at that time following a course—as illustrated by the Treaty of Rapallo of April 1922 and the co-operation between the Reichswehr and the Red Army—that had its parallel in the Stalin-Hitler Pact of 1939, even if on a different scale. Karl Radek had been in contact with German officers since 1919, and had had talks, for example, with von Seeckt and von Schleicher.[3] As the emissary of the Comintern, Radek was acting in the interests of Russian foreign policy when he advocated National-Bolshevist ideas and fostered National-Bolshevist activities in Germany. Radek's political-tactical considerations were reinforced on the theoretical level by Bukharin.[4]

National-Bolshevist ideas found support in Germany.[5] Shortly after Radek's return from the 4th Congress in January 1923, the Franco-Belgian occupation of the Ruhr created a

[1] *Ibid.*, pp. 56, 69, 76.

[2] Lazich, *op. cit.*, p. 213.

[3] On Radek's role see Ruth Fischer, *op. cit.*, p. 206. See also von Rabenau, *Seeckt*, Leipzig, 1940, pp. 309, 319. Further references in Alexander Dallin, *German Rule in Russia 1941–1945*, London, 1957, p. 5, note 2.

[4] Library of the Communist International, Vol. 37, p. 104.

[5] Cf. Radek's speech on Schlageter, delivered on 20 June 1923 at a meeting of the Expanded Executive of the Comintern and reproduced in the pamphlet *Schlageter*, which also contains contributions by Count Ernst Reventlow, Moeller van den Bruck and Paul Frölich. Also Ruth Fischer, *op. cit.*, pp. 268 ff.

new situation. The Cuno government and even nationalist circles now tended to seek an understanding with the Soviet Union. Radek, who was in close collaboration with Brandler, urged that the German Communist Party should participate in Workers' Governments in accordance with the United Front policy.[1] But in fact the only Workers' Government in which Social Democrats and Communists were represented was not formed until October 1923, when Heinrich Brandler, Paul Böttcher and Fritz Heckert entered Zeigner's Social Democratic government in Saxony. Prior to this, in the summer of 1923, the situation in Germany had taken a threatening turn. Inflation weighed heavily on the country's economic life. In return for their normal goods and services, craftsmen and farmers were receiving worthless paper currency. Many farmers refused to send their produce to market and thus aggravated the food shortage in the industrial areas. No sooner were wages and salaries paid out than they lost a large part of their purchasing power. In Berlin, Dresden, Frankfurt, Mannheim, Hamburg and Cologne there were riots outside food shops. In East Prussia, 120,000 agricultural workers went on strike. Inflation became so vicious that the State printing works could no longer produce sufficient paper money and some of the larger towns began to produce their own "emergency currency". The paper money crisis reached its culminating point when the employees of the printing works making bank-notes themselves went on strike and wages and salaries could not be paid. The printers' strike was followed by a mass strike in Berlin, which brought traffic to a stand-still. There were also wild strikes, accompanied by bloody street-fighting, in Saxony, the Ruhr, the Rhineland and Upper Silesia. Separatist movements in the Rhineland, the Ruhr and Bavaria won more and more supporters. On 11 August Cuno's government resigned and Stresemann formed a coalition cabinet.

In the summer of 1923 there were serious differences inside the German Communist Party. Ruth Fischer, who was a member of the Central Committee of the Party and is thus well informed on the Party's internal affairs, has given a con-

[1] Cf. Radek's speeches at the Leipzig Party Conference: Flechtheim, *op. cit.*, p. 87.

vincing description of what happened.[1] The "Right" group of
the Central Committee, led by Heinrich Brandler, stood by their
view that governments of workers and peasants should be
formed. Their attempt to enter into collaboration with the
Social Democratic government in Saxony by means of House-
wives and Consumers' Committees meant that they were
following a policy of "Communist Reformism", hoping by
this means to obtain mass support for a parliamentary workers'
government in Saxony and Thuringia. The "Leftists"—Ruth
Fischer and Arkadi Maslow—had no time for this kind of
reformism. They knew that the Party organization in Hamburg, Berlin and the Ruhr was in the hands of the radical
Communists who, in the summer of 1923, saw their task as the
organizing of military formations, the "Red Squads". They
were expecting fighting similar to civil war to break out and
were incensed by the passivity of Brandler and his supporters.
Brandler, however, had the support of Stalin and Zinoviev.
How the German situation was regarded at this period by
Stalin, the strongest of the three-man team at the head of the
Soviet Party, is indicated by a letter of his dated 7 August
1923, which was preserved for posterity by Trotsky:[2]

> Should the Communists at the present stage try to seize
> power without the Social-Democrats? Are they sufficiently
> ripe for that? That, in my opinion, is the question. When we
> seized power, we had in Russia such resources in reserve as
> (a) the promise of peace; (b) the slogan: the land to the
> peasants; (c) the support of the great majority of the working
> class; and (d) the sympathy of the peasantry. At the moment
> the German Communists have nothing of the kind. They
> have of course a Soviet country as neighbour, which we did
> not have; but what can we offer them? . . . Should the govern-
> ment in Germany topple over now, in a manner of speaking,
> and the Communists were to seize hold of it, they would
> end up in a crash. That, in the "best" case; while at worst,
> they will be smashed to smithereens and thrown away back.
> The whole point is not that Brandler wants to "educate the
> masses" but that the bourgeoisie plus the Right Wing Social-
> Democrats is bound to turn such lessons—the demonstration
> —into a general battle (at present all the odds are on their

[1]*Op. cit.*, pp. 292 ff. and 302.    [2]Trotsky, *Stalin*, pp. 368–369.

D

side) and exterminate them. Of course, the Fascists are not asleep; but it is to our advantage to let them attack first; that will rally the entire working class around the Communists (Germany is not Bulgaria). Besides, all our information indicates that in Germany Fascism is weak. In my opinion the Germans should be restrained and not spurred on.

About this letter Trotsky said:

This wretched document, every line of which testifies to crass ignorance, represents the beginning of Stalin's participation in the work of the Communist International and it is easy to understand why the leaders of the Russian Communist Party had kept him away from it.

### OCTOBER 1923

What neither the occupation of the Ruhr nor devaluation of the currency, neither mass strikes nor mass distress, had been able to achieve was brought about by Stresemann's agreement with Baldwin and the impending understanding with France— the Russians were persuaded to take action, which the fight over the succession to Lenin, already begun, had hitherto prevented them from doing.[1] During the whole of September and the first week of October 1923 there was a secret extraordinary session of the ECCI in Moscow.[2] The actual decision to prepare for revolt was taken by the Politbureau of the CPSU on 11 September 1923, after information had been received of the beginning of Franco-German negotiations, and all that the Comintern functionaries had to do was discuss with the German Communists how the decision was to be implemented.[3] The decision to carry on with the revolt was adhered to in spite of the failure of an attempt led by Dimitroff to overthrow the

---

[1] R. Fischer, *Stalin and German Communism*, pp. 311 ff.; A. Thalheimer, *1923, Eine verpasste Revolution,* Berlin, 1931, pp. 20 ff., and A. Rosmer, *Moscou sous Lénine,* pp. 275 ff.

[2] Apart from the Russians, only five parties were represented; R. Fischer, *op. cit.,* p. 312. A. Rosmer, *op. cit.,* pp. 276 ff., speaks of a secret conference which was also attended by delegates from the countries bordering on Germany.

[3] See R. Fischer, *op. cit.,* p. 316.

government in Bulgaria, an action which was to have been the start of the new revolutionary wave.[1]

There was not much time left to prepare the uprising in Germany. The KPD created a "Permanent Military Council", headed by Ernst Schneller.[2] But the German illegal organizations still did not have sufficient trained military forces and as a result the Soviet Politbureau decided to send a considerable number of Red Army officers to Germany with instructions to assist in the training and command of the Communist military formations.[3] The activities of the Russians in this period—for example, of Alexander Skoblevski, hailed as the "Victor of Kronstadt"—and the Russian origin of considerable sums in dollars found by the police in the possession of Communist functionaries, were revealed, after the collapse of the revolt, in the course of the trials before the Reich High Court and the State Court for the Protection of the Republic.[4]

The failure of this insurrection was certainly not due to the non-existence of a revolutionary situation in the autumn of 1923, for there had never been a situation so favourable to the Communists since the Kapp putsch. Nevertheless, from the beginning there were several factors which made it seem unlikely that the operation would succeed. The forces available for revolutionary action were confused by the United Front policy propagated by the ECCI in the preceding months. Moreover, there were only a few weeks in which to train and arm these forces for fighting. The Reichswehr had been

---

[1]Stella D. Blagoyeva, *Dimitroff, Aus dem Leben eines Revolutionärs*, Moscow, 1934 (German edition Berlin 1954, p. 69 ff.), and A. Rosmer, *op. cit.*, p. 277.
[2]*Zur Geschichte der KPD*, Berlin, 1954, p. 130.
[3]Krivitsky, *I Was Stalin's Agent*, pp. 55 ff.; R. Fischer, *op. cit.*, p. 324; A. Barmine, *op. cit.*, p. 203; Trotsky, *The Third International After Lenin*, p. 95.
[4]Judgments of the State Supreme Court: on Podubecky and others of 28 January 1925; on Felix Neumann and others (including Alexander Skoblevski, who called himself Gorev in Russia) of 22 April 1925; on Lamp and others (including Kleine-Guralski and other Russians) of 11 July 1925: all reproduced in *Die Kommunistische Partei in der Rechtssprechung des Staatsgerichtshofs zum Schutz der Republic und des Reichsgerichts*, published by the Stuttgart Police Headquarters in September 1925. Dr Arthur Brandt, in *Der Tschekaprozess, eine Denkschrift der Verteidigung*, Berlin, 1925, sharply attacked the proceedings in the so-called Cheka Trial (of F. Neumann and others). On the financing of the terror organization, see also Langemann, *Das Attentat*, Hamburg, 1956, p. 66.

strengthened and stood firmly on the side of the government. The intention not to unleash the revolt from Berlin and the Ruhr was a mistake, since not only were the strongest revolutionary forces concentrated there, but it was there that both the "bourgeois" government and the capitalist economic system could have been most effectively hit. Instead of that, and clearly owing to Brandler's influence, action began in Saxony. On 10 October the Social Democrat Zeigner formed a "Workers' Government" in Dresden, including in it the Communists Brandler, Heckert and Böttcher. The KPD believed that this had given them a favourable starting point for their campaign.

The Reich Government countered this threatening development by sending in Reichswehr troops under General Müller. The KPD leaders were unable to cope with this new situation. On 21 October there was a conference of workers' representatives in Chemnitz, attended by top-ranking functionaries of the KPD. In accordance with instructions by both the Comintern and the KPD (both of which were represented), the conference decided to call off the revolt which, on instructions from KPD headquarters, had been planned to start on 23 October in a number of towns. Couriers were despatched from Chemnitz to the centres of the revolt to bring the news of the cancellation of the operation. The Hamburg rising only came about because the courier bound for Hamburg, Herman Remmele, missed his train and arrived too late to prevent the fighting breaking out.[1]

[1] A. Thalheimer, *op. cit.*, pp. 26 ff. The story as related by Thalheimer is confirmed in its essentials by Heinz A. Habedank in *Zur Geschichte des Hamburger Aufstandes 1923*, Berlin, 1958, pp. 96, 112, 202 ff. Habedank, however, is inhibited from telling the historical truth by the fact that it is part of the SED "line" that the credit for the revolt belongs to Ernst Thälmann. Thälmann was at the head of the KPD North West Area, and Urbahns, as the leader of the "Wasserkante" District, was subordinate to him. It was not Thälmann who decided to begin the revolt, as Habedank claims on p. 202, for at this time Thälmann was probably away, attending the Chemnitz conference (Flechtheim, *op. cit.*, p. 96, note 2), where Urbahns also was. (See Hamburg Court Judgement, 15 L 157/24, against Hugo Urbahns and others, dated 18 February 1925.) The order to begin the rising had long since been issued by the headquarters of the KPD (in agreement with the ECCI representative, Radek). In Hamburg, this order was put into effect by Hans Kippenberger. It is interesting that Stalin, in Vol. 8, p. 121 of his *Works*, expressed his admiration for Urbahns' bearing before the court. Urbahns did admit during the proceedings that

The revolt of the Hamburg Communists, fighting alone, was quickly put down.

Thus ended in miserable failure the third attempt even before Lenin's death to bring about a Communist revolution in Germany. The Comintern had suffered a serious defeat. Heinrich Brandler, whose responsibility for the defeat was no greater than the ECCI's, was made the scapegoat and even the disappointed Party members turned against him.[1] The "Leftists", Ruth Fischer, Arkadi Maslow and Ernst Thälmann, took over the leadership of the Party. This also caused a weaking of Zinoviev's position in the Comintern, since up to that time Zinoviev had been a supporter of Brandler.

A further result of the defeat was that it at last became clear to the Soviet Politbureau how important developments in Germany were for world Communism. The belief that the proletarian world revolution would spread westwards via the "progressive" countries had to be revised.[2]

The Russian Military Intelligence Service immediately turned "The October" to account. W. G. Krivitsky, later one of the "Residents" of the Russian Service in Western Europe, said:[3]

> When we saw the collapse of the Comintern's efforts, we said: "Let's save what we can of the German revolution". We took the best men developed by our Party Intelligence and the *Zersetzungsdienst* and incorporated them into the Soviet Military Intelligence. Out of the ruins of the Communist revolution we built in Germany for Soviet Russia a brilliant intelligence service, the envy of every other nation.

This was no idle boast. Krivitsky's words are confirmed by

he had been preparing for violent revolution since the beginning of October 1923, which tallies with the fact (see p. 82 above) that the decision to prepare for the rising had been taken in September 1923. Urbahns said he had formed, together with two comrades whose names he did not wish to give, a triumvirate, in which he was the political leader and the other two were responsible for the organizational and military direction (Hamburg Court Judgement, p. 28). Thälmann, being Urbahns' superior, could not have been a member of the triumvirate, whose military member was probably Kippenberger.

[1]Z. W. Zeutschel, *Im Dienst der Kommunistischen Terrororganisation*, p. 27.
[2]Borkenau, *European Communism*, p. 57; Ruth Fischer, *op. cit.*, p. 364.
[3]Krivitsky, *op. cit.*, p. 64.

what Hans Kippenberger, Wilhelm Zaisser, and Arthur Illner
(alias Richard Stahlmann), to name only a few of those who
studied at the International Military School in Moscow,
achieved for the benefit of the Red Army's Intelligence Service.[1]
This was not the last time the Soviet Intelligence Service proved
its ingenuity in extracting advantage from a policy even after
it had been abandoned.

When Lenin died on 21 January 1924 the struggle for power
among the Russian members of the Politbureau—Trotsky,
Zinoviev, Kamenev and Stalin—was already in full swing.
Zinoviev was making efforts to improve his position by trying
to win over the "Leftist" forces of the Comintern to his side.
Stalin also was anxious to avoid any break with the powerful
"Left", as was shown in the course of the Party "trial" of
Arkadi Maslow, one of the leaders of the German "Left". Since
Maslow enjoyed a great measure of support from the German
"Left" and the Soviet leaders wanted to avoid trouble with this
group at the time, they allowed the case against Maslow to
take a course favourable to him. The problems of the German
party and the Comintern were regarded by Zinoviev and
Stalin only from the point of view of the role they might play
in the struggle for power inside the Russian Politbureau.[2]

### THE FIFTH WORLD CONGRESS
### (*17 June to 8 July 1924*)

The 5th World Congress demonstrated afresh the extent to
which Russian Party matters held the centre of the stage in the
Comintern. One of the subjects discussed by the Congress was
the fight against "Trotskyism" which had broken out in the
CPSU. Zinoviev saw to it that the statements made by "his"
Comintern delegates were in undisguised opposition to Trotsky.[3]
The Congress became the arena of the disagreements between
the members of the Soviet Politbureau. Zinoviev's anxiety
about his own position caused him to describe Brandler's
"Saxony tactics" of the autumn of 1923, which had been

---

[1] Wollenberg, *Der Apparat*, Bonn, 1952, pp. 12 ff. Also p. 178 below.
[2] R. Fischer, *op. cit.*, pp. 365–376.
[3] Boris Souvarine, *Staline*, p. 342; S. Leonhardt, *op. cit.*, p. 766.

whole-heartedly approved by the Comintern, as a "banal comedy".

The 5th Congress did not entirely abandon the United Front policy, but they did refuse to regard it as implying a political alliance with the Social Democrats. What they wanted was a united front "from below", one which would be made up of the Communist, Social Democratic and non-Party workers in the factory under the leadership of the Communist Party,[1] and they decisively rejected the United Front "from above", i.e. arising from negotiations with Social Democratic leaders. "The United Front is merely a method to be used for agitation and for the revolutionary mobilization of the masses."[2] In this sense the "Workers' Governments" were described as "synonymous with the dictatorship of the proletariat". The United Front policy was shortly to be re-employed to bring into being "international Trade Union unity".[3]

One decision of the 5th Congress had far-reaching effects—the decision to impose on the Sections the experiences of the Russian party "in so far as they were of international significance".[4] This contributed to the bolshevization of the Communist parties. The principle of "democratic centralism" (originally intended to mean the democratic election of Party organs by the membership, but with strict disciplinary powers granted to the organs thus elected) and "iron Bolshevist Party discipline" were to be enforced in all the Sections of the Comintern. These demands were not new; it was simply that the Sections had not really fulfilled them hitherto.[5] The principle of "democratic centralism" evinces at first sight some quite democratic features. It has, however, been constantly used by Party Executives to exercise authority, to nominate Party workers (full-time functionaries), to expel members or to neutralize functionaries who fall into disfavour. In this way the

[1]Zinoviev was already supporting the "United Front from below" after the failure of the Hamburg revolt. (See *Die Kommunistische Internationale*, 4th year, p. 3.)
[2]*Thesen und Resolutionen des V. Weltkongresses*, Hamburg, 1924, pp. 23, 25, ff.
[3]See p. 97 below.
[4]Rosenberg, *op. cit.*, p. 210: Souvarine, *op. cit.*, p. 343.
[5]Cf. Condition No. 11 of the *21 Conditions* adopted by the 2nd World Congress.

Executives and the functionaries composing them have influenced the composition of the Party Congresses: in other words, they have gained command over the highest organs of the parties.

In the years after 1925, the Secretary-General, Stalin, made use of the principle of democratic centralism to rule not only the CPSU but also the Comintern and its Sections with a grip of iron. The Central Committee of the national Communist parties and their top-ranking functionaries have also learned to use democratic centralism with such skill that with its assistance they also command their parties.[1]

The bolshevization of the parties was similarly furthered by another organizational demand made by the 5th Congress, that the organization of the Sections should be changed from the territorial system to that of factory cells.[2] All Communist parties were also required to become active among the young people, among the women and in the "reactionary trade unions".[3]

The 5th Congress displayed yet another symptom of increasing bolshevization in the curtailment of freedom of discussion. Eberlein had still been able to oppose the plans of Lenin and Trotsky to found the Comintern. At the 2nd Congress Serrati and Wijnkoop had voiced their opinions even when they differed from those of the ECCI. During the debates at the 3rd Congress, Alexandra Kollantai had put forward the demands of the *Workers' Opposition*, even though they had been rejected by the 10th Party Congress. At the 4th Congress the French had contradicted the United Front theses. At the 5th Congress, however, the delegates condemned Trotskyism with one accord, in spite of the fact that Leon Trotsky had many friends in the Comintern. The "iron Party discipline" was

---

[1] A. Balabanova, *op. cit.*, p. 233; Rosenberg, *op. cit.*, p. 148; S. Leonhard, *Gestohlenes Leben*, Frankfurt-am-Main, 1956, pp. 803 ff.; Hermann Weber and Lothar Pertinax, *Schein und Wirklichkeit in der DDR*, Stuttgart, 1958, pp. 149 ff.; R. N. Carew-Hunt, *A Guide to Communist Jargon*, London, 1957, p. 56. Interesting testimony as to the practical effects of this principle is contained in the report by Aksel Larsen, the Chairman of the Danish Communist Party, to his Central Committee on 18 July 1958, before he was relieved of his position.

[2] Gérard Walter, *Histoire du Parti Communiste Français*, Paris, 1948, p. 166.
[3] Kabakchev, *op. cit.*, p. 118.

having its effect. Trotsky himself made no reply to these attacks.[1]

It was during the 5th Congress that most of the delegates had their first sight of Stalin. He made no attempt to create an impression by a rhetorical performance and spoke only once or twice, in the "Polish Commission", where the proceedings were in Russian.[2] Otherwise he busied himself making personal contact with numerous European delegates. His policies and his influence were soon to take effect in the Comintern.

## STALIN AND THE GERMAN "LEFT"

The struggle for power inside the Politbureau of the Russian party, which was not without its effect on the Comintern, continued even after the 5th Congress. Influential Russian Bolshevists looked down on the Communists of Central and Western Europe because of the failure of their attempts at revolution. Stalin called the Comintern a *"Lavotchka"*, "a grocer's shop".[3] More than one "liquidator" may, even then, have thought of dissolving the Comintern.[4] Nevertheless the Comintern formed a concentration point for all those Communist forces of the world which saw in the Soviet Union the "fatherland of the working classes". As the Comintern was for the time being still a position of eminence for the members of the Russian Politbureau, Stalin too occupied himself with it following the 5th Congress and put his trusted confidant Dimitri Manuilski into the ECCI, where he attained a keyposition, which he occupied until the ECCI was dissolved.[5]

---

[1]Ruth Fischer, *op. cit.*, p. 404.     [2]Souvarine, *op. cit.*, p. 343.
[3]Krivitsky, *op. cit.*, p. 92; also Borkenau, *European Communism*, p. 61.
[4]Rosenberg, *op. cit.*, p. 210; Borkenau, *op. cit.*, pp. 63–64.
[5]Dimitri Zacharovitch Manuilski was born in Tarnopol in 1883, the son of a Greek Orthodox priest. He was deported to Yakuta for participating in the Kronstadt insurrection of 1908, emigrated to Western Europe and lived principally in France, where, in 1922, he reappeared as the Comintern delegate to the 2nd Congress of the French Communist Party. From 1925 onwards, he was permanent Comintern representative with the German Communist Party, which he managed to bring into complete subjection by 1928. From then on, until the dissolution of the Comintern, he held a key position in the ECCI. In 1945 and 1948 he took part in several United Nations conferences as the delegate of the Ukraine. He died on 22 February 1959. (See Ruth Fischer, *op. cit.*, p. 393, and *Neues Deutschland*, East Berlin, dated 24 February 1959.)

As long as the struggle for power had not been concluded, it was possible that the attitude of the KPD, the strongest Section of the Comintern, with three delegates (Thälmann, Maslow and Fischer) in the Presidium of the ECCI, might be extremely important for Stalin,[1] so that the schismatic tendencies the KPD was revealing were bound to be a source of anxiety for him. Ever since the 5th Congress the KPD had been trying hard to become less dependent on the Comintern. Without the knowledge of the Comintern, they sent delegates to the Communist Parties of England, Norway, France and Poland to discuss problems of common interest.[2] This earned them the reproach that they were crossing lines with the Comintern policies *vis-à-vis* the Sections.[3]

Various other differences arose. In the Trades Union section of the Central Committee of the KPD there were several Russian "experts" permanently working. Manuilski, who was stationed in Berlin as the Comintern's delegate, got these "experts" to keep him supplied with information on KPD internal affairs. The Central Committee of the KPD tried to curtail the activities of these Russians and thus came into conflict with Manuilski. The German Central Committee was also showing a tendency to become independent of the financial contributions which Mirov-Abramov, the representative of the OMS (Department of International Relations) in the Russian Embassy in Berlin, had been paying for years.[4]

Stalin did not stand idly by in the face of these developments. On 25 February 1925, he sent Arkadi Maslow a letter in which he tried to win over to his side the "Left" group of the KPD, which supported Zinoviev.[5] Maslow refused to go along with Stalin in his plot and informed Zinoviev, whom Maslow believed to be willing to work against the complete russianization of the Comintern. He also laid Stalin's letter before the

[1]Ruth Fischer, *op. cit.*, pp. 405 and 432.
[2]*Ibid.*, p. 432.          [3]Flechtheim, *op. cit.*, p. 133.
[4]The OMS (Otdel Mezhdunarodnoi Zvyasi=Department of International Relations) played an important role in the ECCI's control of national Communist parties. It was, for example, responsible for the transmission of ECCI funds to these parties. See pp. 136 and 169 for further details.
[5]This letter is reprinted in Stalin, *Works*, Moscow, 1954, Vol. 7, pp. 42 ff. Regarding Maslow, see Fischer, *op. cit.*, p. 361.

German Central Committee, who unanimously refused to join forces with Stalin against Zinoviev.[1]

The resolutions proposed by the "Leftists" at the 10th KPD Party Congress in July 1925 were unobjectionable from the point of view of the Comintern,[2] but Manuilski (alias Samuely) behaved so arrogantly at the Congress that his attempts to interfere with the election of the members of the Central Committee met with strong opposition. Shouts such as, "Clear off back to Moscow!" were heard.[3] The Soviet Politbureau were afraid that the KPD would break away from the Comintern. In order to prevent this happening, Stalin began to prepare the overthrow of the Maslow-Fischer group. First of all he got a German Communist, Heinz Neumann, who was devoted to him, to write a pamphlet called "Ultra-Left Menshevism".[4] In this pamphlet Neumann bitterly attacked the "anti-Moscowites" and the "ultra Leftists" in Poland, Italy and Germany, that is to say, Dombsky, Bordiga, Fischer and Maslow. The pamphlet concluded with these words:

> The Comintern must and will carry on a merciless fight to the end against ultra-Left Menshevism. . . . The Comintern must not tolerate at its summit the pace-makers of the anti-Soviet block. It must go over from the defensive to the offensive. Down with ultra-left Menshevism.

Two years later Neumann himself was to be stigmatized as an "ultra Leftist" and to fall a victim to the merciless fight he himself had demanded.

In the conflict with the "ultra Leftists" of the KPD, the Soviet Politbureau made Zinoviev persuade the ECCI to send an open letter to the Central Committee of the KPD calling for the removal of Maslow and Fischer.[5] While on a visit to Moscow, Ruth Fischer, as a member of the Presidium of the Comintern, was compelled to sign this letter and to make a

[1] R. Fischer, *op. cit.*, p. 439.
[2] Flechtheim, *op. cit.*, p. 138.
[3] Borkenau, *op. cit.*, p. 60; Flechtheim, p. 112; "Samuely" was the party name Manuilski used in Germany: R. Fischer, *op. cit.*, p. 442.
[4] Heinz Neumann, *Der Ultralinke Menschewismus*, Berlin, 1926: R. Fischer, *op. cit.*, p. 445.
[5] *Zur Geschichte der KPD*, Berlin, 1954, p. 180 (contains a version of this letter suitably tailored for the 1954 "party line").

public self-criticism—an example of Party discipline.[1] The "Left" group of the Central Committee of the KPD was destroyed. The Central Committee expelled Ruth Fischer, Arkadi Maslow, Werner Scholem and Arthur Rosenberg. Loyal supporters of Stalin (Heinz Neumann, Walter Ulbricht, Hermann Remmele and Franz Dahlem) took over the positions of these "Leftists", who had tried to preserve at least a modicum of independence.[2] The Central Committee of the KPD was thus made to toe Stalin's line, to which Ernst Thälmann was so faithful that he was able to remain at the top until 1933.

SOCIALISM IN ONE COUNTRY

In a *Letter to the Party Congress* of 24 December 1922, Lenin had described Trotsky as "probably the most capable man in the present Central Committee", and had suggested in a postscript that Stalin should be removed from the position of Secretary-General.[3] Trotsky, who had evolved the theory of the "permanent revolution", enjoyed enormous prestige in the Soviet Union and in the Comintern.[4] Stalin had not only to maintain his position in the Party *vis-à-vis* Trotsky; he also felt impelled to attack Trotsky on ideological grounds. Stalin developed a counter-theory with his lesson of "Socialism in one country". This said that the Soviet Union possessed everything necessary to build up a Socialist society.[5] Therefore Socialism must be established with the resources available to Soviet Russia.[6] This justified the continued existence of "Socialism"

[1] R. Fischer, *op. cit.*, p. 452. Even under these circumstances, Stalin, using Bela Kun as his intermediary, tried to attract Ruth Fischer to his side: *op. cit.*, p. 493.

[2] Flechtheim, *op. cit.*, p. 134. Of these, Neumann and Remmele died in the purges of 1936–8. Walter Ulbricht is First Secretary of the SED, and Franz Dahlem, after being rehabilitated by a decision of the 30th Plenum, now belongs to the Central Committee of the SED (*Neues Deutschland*, 3 February 1957).

[3] *Unveröffentlichte Dokumente, verteilt an die Delegierten des XX Parteitages der KPdSU*, reproduced in *Ostprobleme* 1957, pp. 964 ff.

[4] Trotsky, *The History of the Russian Revolution*, London, 1933, Vol. III, pp. 408 ff.; also Trotsky, *The Permanent Revolution*, New York, 1931, p. xxxiii.

[5] Stalin's essay, *The October Revolution and the Tactics of the Russian Communists*, reproduced in Stalin's *Problems of Leninism*, Moscow, 1954, pp. 112 ff.

[6] Stalin, *Concerning Questions of Leninism*, in *Problems of Leninism*, Moscow, 1954, pp. 188 ff.

in the Soviet Union, despite all the reverses suffered by world revolutionary forces from 1919 to 1923. This theory broke with the ideas of Marx, Engels and Lenin. In their *Address to the League by the Central Authority*, Marx and Engels had said:[1]

> While the democratic petty bourgeois want to conclude the revolution as quickly as possible and to satisfy at most the aforesaid demands, it is in our interest and is our task to make the revolution *permanent* until all the more or less propertied classes have been stripped of their authority, the governing power is in the hands of the proletariat, and the association of the proletariat, *not only in one country* but in all the leading countries of the world, is so far advanced that competition between the proletariat of these countries has ceased and at least the vital means of production are concentrated in the hands of the proletariat.

Lenin also had repeatedly stated his opinion after the October 1917 Revolution that Socialism could not survive in Russia alone. At the 7th Party Congress of 7 March 1918, for example, he had said:[2]

> Of course, if we look at it from a world historical scale, there can be no doubt that from the standpoint of the ultimate victory of our revolution, if it were to remain alone, if there were no revolutionary movements in other countries, then our position would be hopeless. When the Bolshevik Party tackled the job alone, took it entirely into its own hands, we were convinced that the revolution was maturing in all countries and that in the end—but not at the very beginning —no matter what difficulties we experienced, no matter what defeats were in store for us, the international Socialist revolution would come—because it is coming; would ripen— because it is ripening and will grow ripe. I repeat, our salvation from all these difficulties is an all-European revolution.

[1]Marx/Engels, *Ausgewählte Schriften*, Berlin, 1951, Vol. I, p. 97 (author's remarks).
[2]Lenin, *Selected Works*, London, 1947, Vol. II, p. 297; further statements by Lenin on this question are contained in Trotsky's *The Third International After Lenin*, pp. 11 ff.

In his speech on the policy of the CPSU at the 3rd World Congress, Lenin had declared:[1]

When we started the international revolution, we did so not because we were convinced that we could forecast its development, but because a number of circumstances compelled us to start it. We thought: Either the international revolution comes to our assistance, and in that case our victory will be fully assured, or we shall do our modest revolutionary work in the conviction that even in the event of defeat, we shall have served the cause of the revolution and that our experience will benefit other revolutions. It was clear to us that without the support of the international world revolution the victory of the proletarian revolution was impossible. Before the revolution and even after it we thought: Either revolution breaks out in the other countries, in the capitalistically more developed countries, immediately, or at least very quickly, or we must perish.

Thus Stalin was dishonest when he claimed—or got others to claim—that the lesson of Socialism in one country originated with Lenin,[2] and he tried to bolster up this claim by quoting statements made by Lenin in other contexts.[3] Stalin himself never had a great opinion of the prospects of a revolution in the West. Thus, in January 1918, when the Soviet Central Committee were debating whether or not to accept the harsh Brest-Litovsk treaty terms, Stalin had said, "There is no revolutionary movement in the West. There are no facts; there is only a possibility, and with possibilities we cannot reckon".[4] Yet in April 1924, a few months after Lenin's death, Stalin himself had clearly supported the "true" lesson in lectures he gave, *The Foundations of Leninism*, using the following words:[5]

[1] Lenin, *Selected Works* (12 volumes), London, 1937, Vol. 9, pp. 226–227.
[2] Stalin, *Problems of Leninism*, pp. 120 ff.; also *Short Course*, p. 432. Even today some authorities of the East Zone of Germany are trying to prove that the Bolshevists were thinking about the possibility of "Socialism in one country" even before their October revolution. See Walter Bartel, *Die Linken in der deutschen Sozial Demokratie im Kampf gegen Militarismus und Krieg*, Berlin, 1958, p. 334.
[3] Lenin, *Selected Works* (2 volumes), London, 1947, Vol. I, pp. 617 ff. (*The United States of Europe Slogan*).
[4] William H. Chamberlin, *The Russian Revolution 1917–1921*, London, 1935, Vol. I, p. 398.
[5] Stalin, *Problems of Leninism*, pp. 45–46.

But the overthrow of the power of the bourgeoisie and establishment of the power of the proletariat in one country does
not yet mean that the complete victory of Socialism has been
ensured. After consolidating its power and leading the
peasantry in its wake the proletariat of the victorious country
can and must build a socialist society. But does this mean that
it will thereby achieve the complete and final victory of
socialism, i.e., does it mean that with the forces of only one
country it can finally consolidate Socialism and fully guarantee that country against intervention and consequently also
against restoration? No, it does not. For this, victory of the
revolution in at least several countries is needed. Therefore,
the development and support of revolution in other countries
is an essential task of the victorious revolution. Therefore,
the revolution which has been victorious in one country
must regard itself not as a self-sufficient entity, but as an aid,
as a means for hastening the victory of the proletariat in
other countries.

Soon afterwards Stalin completely retreated from this
clearly-expressed position in favour of the new teaching of
Socialism in one country. The importance of Stalin's *volte-face*
for the study of international proletarianism does not lie in the
furious oratory with which he attacked Trotsky's theory of the
"permanent revolution" on the basis of his own new theory.[1]
More important are the inferences Stalin drew as far as the
Comintern was concerned.

The 3rd World Congress had seen the tasks of the Communist
parties as that of keeping "Socialism" alive in Russia. At the
4th World Congress Bukharin had said that the Soviet State
must be defended by the proletariat of the other countries.
Stalin's theory supplied the ideological justification for these
claims. At the 14th Party Congress of the CPSU in December
1925, Stalin demanded that the relationships between the
Soviet Union and the proletariat of the Western countries
should be completely changed, declaring that the working
classes of Europe had a moral responsibility to defend "our
State against capitalism" and "our interests against imperial-

[1]In the *Short Course* he had the claim made that to call this theory a Marxist
theory would be to insult Marxist theory.

ism".[1] Stalin was already arguing in 1927 that an Internationalist was someone who was unreservedly, unconditionally and unhesitatingly prepared to protect the USSR because the CPSU was the basis of the world-wide revolutionary movement.[2] In so saying, Stalin was laying the foundation for the view that was later to prevail, that the touchstone for every Socialist was his attitude towards the Soviet Union.[3]

It is from this point of view that the revolutionary movements in other countries have been judged and dealt with by the Politbureau of the CPSU ever since 1925; namely, from the point of view of whether the Bolshevist régime has seen any advantage to itself in helping them. The Chinese revolution of 1927 gave a striking demonstration of this view of "proletarian internationalism".[4]

Stalin used his theory of Socialism in one country to consolidate his position in his clash with Trotsky. Stalin did not want to give up the idea of world revolution, only it did not seem to him to be practicable at that time. Nevertheless he unequivocally declared at the 14th Party Congress:[5]

But in the last analysis, we cannot overcome the contradictions outside our country between the capitalist world and the socialist world solely by our own efforts; for that we need the assistance of a victorious proletarian revolution in a number of countries.

Without revolutionary mass action against capitalism in the countries of the West, the proletarian revolution could not be brought nearer, and the Comintern was given the job of organizing it.[6] England seemed to offer the greatest promise of starting a mass movement, provided that appropriate use could be made of the trade unions.

[1]Stalin, *Works*, Moscow, 1954, Vol. 7, p. 292.
[2]Speech at the Joint Plenary Session of the Central Committee and the Central Control Committee of the CPSU on 1 August 1927. Cf. Stalin, *Works*, Vol. 10, p. 53.
[3]For example, the resolution of the KPD Party leaders on the Yugoslav question (see p. 239 below).
[4]See p. 103 below.
[5]Stalin, *Works*, Vol. 7, p. 358.
[6]*Ibid.*, p. 300.

## "INTERNATIONAL TRADE UNION UNITY"—THE 1926 GENERAL STRIKE IN ENGLAND

The 5th World Congress put out the slogan "International Trade Union Unity" and ordered the West European Communist parties to interest themselves in the "reactionary trade unions".[1] The Bolshevists were well aware that in Western Europe, unlike Russia, the trade unions had been founded before the Communist parties and that the workers "regard the trade unions as their principal strongholds . . . in their struggle against the capitalists". This led them to the conclusion "firstly, that in the West the vast working-class masses cannot be won over unless the trade unions are won over, and secondly, that the trade unions cannot be won over unless we work inside them and strengthen our influence there".[2]

This attempt to continue the United Front policy by means of "International Trade Union Unity" was greeted with extreme mistrust by the European trade union leaders, who remembered that the Social Democratic "Yellow Amsterdam Trade Union International" had for years been the subject of violent attacks by the "Red Trade Union International."[3] At the same time some Western Socialists had been opposing the "reformist" policies of the Amsterdam Trade Union International, and this led to violent disagreements between German and British trade unionists at a congress of the Amsterdam International held in Vienna in May 1924. The British trade unionists were in conflict with the British employers and were in favour of "International Trade Union Unity", in which they wanted to include the Red International. The Germans were opposed to this *rapprochement* and persuaded the congress to pass a resolution confirming their opposition to it. However, the British trade unions made contact with the Russians direct, British trade union leaders visited the Soviet Union, and in April 1925 an Anglo-Russian Joint Advisory Council (on trade union unity) was created.[4]

[1] See p. 87 above.        [2] Stalin, *op. cit.*, p. 47.
[3] Rosenberg, *op. cit.*, p. 210, also No. 10 of the *21 Conditions* of the 2nd World Congress (see p. 339 below).
[4] Borkenau, *The Communist International*, pp. 277 ff. The exact name of the Bureau was *Joint Advisory Committee of the Trade Union Movement of Great Britain and the USSR.*

As far as the Bolshevists were concerned, this Council was nothing but a means to an end, since they were hoping that the radicalization of the British trade unions could be boosted up to the point of revolution (which showed how faulty their judgment of the situation was). Zinoviev had already given a hint of this hopeful attitude at the 5th World Congress, when he said that the revolution in England could just as easily enter through the trade union gate as through the Communist Party gate.

On 3 May 1926 the TUC issued a call for a general strike. The Soviet trade unions remitted 250,000 roubles to the Trade Union Council on 2 May and another 2,000,000 on 7 May,[1] but the TUC, fearful of the effect on public opinion, declined both the money and all other help. The general strike lasted only until 12 May, when it collapsed.[2] The Anglo-Russian Council was finally dissolved on 8 September 1927.

With the failure of "International Trade Union Unity", the United Front policy had miscarried once more. The Comintern had a further heavy defeat to add to the German debacle of October 1923. Although the chief sponsors of the Trade Union Unity policy had been Tomski and Stalin, Stalin utilized this defeat of the Comintern, of which Zinoviev was still President, to undermine Zinoviev's position still further.[3] He used quotations from Lenin's *Left-Wing Communism* as a basis for accusing Zinoviev, who had opposed the creation of the Anglo-Russian Council, of "ultra-Left" deviationism.[4]

### THE CHINESE DISASTER

In Europe, therefore, the Comintern—or more correctly the CPSU supported by the Comintern—had suffered both military

[1]Stalin, *Works*, Vol. 8, pp. 399–400, note 57.

[2]*Der Kampf um die Komintern (Dokumente der russischen Opposition)*, Berlin, 1927, pp. 110 ff. Leon Trotsky's article, *Der Kampf um den Frieden und das anglorussische Komitee.*

[3]His speech of 1 August 1927 (cf. Stalin, *Works*, Vol. 10, pp. 39 ff.).

[4]Whether Zinoviev organized the attempt at revolution in Esthonia in December 1924 in a desperate effort to increase his authority, and whether the attempt on Sofia Cathedral in April 1925 was organized by the Comintern, the OGPU or some other agency, is not really important for the problems of proletarian internationalism. On this aspect, see Ruth Fischer, d W. G. Krivitsky, *op. cit.*, pp. 65 ff.

and political reverses. The revolution had run aground on
"the stabilization of capitalism". What could be more appropriate than to start revolutionary upheavals in areas where this
stabilization was endangered—where the capitalist powers were
face-to-face with emotional forces of tremendous power—in the
colonial territories?

As far back as 1920, in the draft of the Theses on the *National
and Colonial Question* prepared for the 2nd World Congress,
Lenin had written:[1]

> . . . it is necessary to pursue a policy that will achieve the
> closest alliance of all the national and colonial liberation
> movements with Soviet Russia, the form of this alliance to
> be determined by the degree of development of the Com-
> munist movement among the proletariat of each country,
> or of the bourgeois-democratic liberation movement of the
> workers and peasants in backward countries or among back-
> ward nationalities.

Stalin had recognized the value of such an alliance. He
declared that in the Western imperialist countries "the national
factor as a factor in the struggle for emancipation" was lacking.[2]
In the colonies and dependencies on the other hand "the
national bourgeoisie, at a certain stage and for a certain period,
may support the revolutionary movement of its country against
imperialism" and that was where "the national factor, as a
factor in the struggle for emancipation" was a "revolutionary
factor". Thoughts similar to these animated the 7th Plenary
Session of the ECCI when they declared in December 1926
that the Chinese Revolution was the most important and
powerful of the factors liable to disorganize the stabilization of
capitalism.[3]

The Chinese Communist Party was weak. In 1922 it had
some 200 members and in 1925 about 1,000,[4] so that a revo-

[1]Lenin, *Selected Works*, Vol. II, p. 655. See p. 59 above.
[2]Stalin, *Works*, Vol. 10, p. 11. In the sense that Stalin meant, Germany
was a "dependency" after 1918, so that Radek was logically correct in
making use of the assistance of bourgeois and nationalist elements in his
attempt to push forward the revolution.
[3]Quoted by David Dallin in *The Rise of Russia in Asia*, New Haven, 1949,
p. 205.
[4]*Ibid.*, p. 217.

lution directed mainly against a group of imperialist powers
headed by Great Britain did not stand much chance of succeeding if it rested on the support of these scanty forces. On the
other hand, an alliance with the strongest anti-imperialist
force in China, the Kuomintang, offered much better prospects. It was the recognition of this fact that caused the Chinese
Lin Yen Ching to declare at the 4th World Congress that the
Communists would remain isolated if they did not join forces
with the Kuomintang. The Kuomintang, founded in 1912 by
Sun Yat Sen, was a national revolutionary party which, at the
beginning of 1920, was strongest in South China, in Canton
and Kwantung Province. In order to strengthen his movement
by appealing to national and mainly anti-British feeling among
the workers, Sun Yat Sen engineered strikes which, from 1922
onwards, broke out in Shanghai, Hong Kong and Canton.[1]
He subsequently came closer to the Communists, and in 1923,
following negotiations with the Russian Ambassador, Adolf
Joffe, he agreed to collaboration between the Kuomintang,
Chinese Communists and Russian Communists. Chinese Communists were now admitted to the ranks of the Kuomintang.
In the autumn of 1923, Chiang Kai-shek, at that time one of Sun
Yat Sen's young associates, went to Moscow for some months.
In September of the same year Michael Borodin, a Comintern
man with extensive experience of foreign countries, was plenti-
fully supplied with money and despatched to Canton with a
large staff and a number of officers, to act as "adviser" to the
Kuomintang.[2] Russian officers were seconded to each of the
Kuomintang armies, General Vassili Konstantinovich Blücher,
the most outstanding of these officers, becoming the adviser

[1] On this, see Borkenau, *The Communist International*, pp. 296 ff., and
D. J. Dallin, *op. cit.*, pp. 209 ff. See also the article by the Dutchman
Sneevliet (alias "Maring") on the railway workers' strikes in China in
*Die Kommunistische Internationale*, 1923, No. 27, p. 120, and Allen S. Whiting,
*Soviet Policies in China 1917-24*, New York, 1954, p. 95.
[2] Cf. Chiang Kai-shek, *Soviet Russia in China*, New York, 1957, p. 27;
before he was sent to China, Borodin had been dealing with the British
Communist Party (cf. his essay *Eine historische Anomalie* in *Die Kommunistische
Internationale*, 1923, No. 26, p. 48). Biographical details on Borodin are
given by Ruth Fischer, *op. cit.*, p. 574, Dallin, *op. cit.*, p. 212, and Isaacs,
*op. cit.*, p. 276. Borodin was later executed by order of Stalin (see Louis
Fischer, *Russia Revisited*, London, 1957, p. 23).

to Chiang Kai-shek.[1] Borodin and his staff, which included such
well-known Communists as the Indian Manabendra Nath
Roy, the Vietnamese Ho Chi Minh, the trade union leader
Salomon A. Losevski, the American Earl Browder, the Frenchman Jacques Doriot, Pavel Miff of the Far East Bureau and,
in the final phase, Heinz Neumann and Besso Lominadse (the
Russian youth leader: see pp. 152 ff.) were probably the most
imposing "mission" of its kind ever sent by the Comintern into
the territory of one of its Sections.[2] Borodin more or less completed his first task, which was to reorganize the Kuomintang
Party and its military forces. The Kuomintang consolidated its
position in the South, and in the course of 1925 the area controlled by the Canton Government was extended. Shortly
before his death in March 1925, Sun Yat Sen described the
collaboration between the Kuomintang and the Communists as
the foundation of the liberation of China.[3] The Moscow Communists regarded this collaboration as the result of their United
Front policy, which was characterized by the fact that "bourgeois elements" belonged to the United Front.[4] The connecting
link between the partners was their common "anti-imperialist"
views.

In pursuing this line, the Moscow Communists were adhering
to the plan that had caused them to create united fronts in
Europe, and especially in Germany.[5] When the European
Communist parties proved to be too weak to ensure the success
of the Bolshevist revolution, the Social Democrats or the trade
unions were supposed to form a ladder for them to climb up by.
In China there was no Socialist party and no trade unions to
speak of, and it was the Russians' idea that the Kuomintang
should provide the rungs of the necessary ladder. However,
Chiang Kai-shek seems to have made good use of his time in
Moscow, for he realized that the Communists merely intended

---

[1] D. J. Dallin, *op. cit.*, p. 213.

[2] See Losovski's article, "Hands off China", in the *Daily Worker* of 30
October 1924.

[3] D. Dallin, *op. cit.*, p. 214.

[4] Stalin, *Works*, Vol. 10, p. 22. It will be recalled that in Germany similar
attempts had been made to exploit nationalist sentiments from 1920 to
1923. See Ruth Fischer, *op. cit.*, p. 278.

[5] See p. 76 above.

to make use of him to gain power for themselves. In March 1926 he imprisoned not only Chinese Communists occupying influential positions in his army but also several Russian advisers, and even disarmed the bodyguard of Bubnov, a Central Committee member who had just arrived in Canton.[1] In order to avoid a break with Chiang Kai-shek, Borodin and Bubnov hastened to proclaim that the Communists arrested by Chiang Kai-shek were guilty (of "left deviationism"). Even the Politbureau of the CPSU seemed not to understand the import of Chiang Kai-shek's action.[2] How was it possible for the CPSU to ignore this warning? It was because the primarily anti-British strikes which had broken out from May 1925 onwards in Shanghai, Hankow and Peking, extending over a period of several months, aroused the hopes of influential Moscow Communists that 1926 would see a revolution in China. In February 1926 Manuilski wrote in the *Communist International*: "The events in Shanghai are ushering in a new era in human history".[3] The thought that in China they might at last achieve successes in the foreign policy field by employing the Kuomintang seemed to the Politbureau in this, as in other cases, more important than the loss of a few Communists.

The united front with the Kuomintang and Chiang Kai-shek continued. In the spring of 1926 the Comintern admitted the Kuomintang as a "sympathizing member". A "Chinese Commission", completely under the control of the Central Committee of the CPSU—and thus of Stalin—was created inside the ECCI. It was headed by Josef S. Unschlicht, a senior GPU official who enjoyed Stalin's confidence.[4] Thereafter it was this commission, and not the People's Commissariat of Foreign Affairs, which directed Soviet policy towards China.[5]

[1]D. Dallin, *op. cit.*, p. 216; Borkenau, *The Communist International*, pp. 307–8.

[2]The attacks which the opposition, led by Trotsky, made on this United Front policy need not be discussed here. (See Trotsky, *The Third International After Lenin*, pp. 180 ff.; D. Dallin, *op. cit.*, pp. 215 ff.; A. Barmine, *op. cit.*, p. 224, and also Zinoviev's *Thesen über die chinesische Revolution* in *Der Kampf um die Komintern* (*Dokumente der russischen Opposition*), Berlin, 1927, p. 14.)

[3]Quoted in D. Dallin, *op. cit.*, p. 222.

[4]Stalin, *Works*, Vol. 10, p. 19.

[5]D. Dallin, *op. cit.*, p. 227.

In June 1926 Chiang Kai-shek advanced northwards from Canton, achieving some astonishing military successes. By the end of 1926 he had reached the Yangtse-kiang, and in February 1927 his forces were approaching Nanking and Shanghai. Borodin and the left wing of the Kuomintang left Canton for Wuchang (Hankow), where they formed the Wuchang Government. Chiang Kai-shek, on the contrary, declared the capital of Kuomintang China to be Nanchang, where his headquarters lay. The first cracks were appearing in the united front. Chiang kept a distrustful watch on the activities of the Communists in the areas they controlled and kept a special eye on their expropriations.

As soon as Chiang had Shanghai firmly within his grasp, he had the town's leading Communists arrested and broke up the Communist trade unions. On 18 April 1927 he formed a National Government in Nanking, but included no Communists.[1] Similar measures followed in Canton. This meant the final break with the Communists and with the Wuchang Government. The Moscow Bolshevists, taken completely by surprise, were in a situation comparable to that of the biter bit, and they reacted accordingly. The Comintern branded Chiang Kai-shek as a traitor and an enemy of the working class and the International. Only just in time, Chiang Kai-shek had done to the Bolshevists what they had intended to do to him, for when Stalin was under attack from the Opposition for the China policy in May 1927, he admitted that he had never intended to support the Chinese national bourgeois but only to make use of them.[2] This had misfired, and the military and financial help provided by the Russians had been used by Chiang for his own purposes. Trotsky, who had vainly issued warnings against this China policy, sarcastically remarked that the only treason Chiang Kai-shek had committed had been against a Russian illusion, namely, the belief that they would be able to seize power in China with the help of the national bourgeoisie.[3]

Still Stalin and his supporters insisted that a Bolshevist

[1] Chiang Kai-shek, *Soviet Russia in China*, loc. cit., pp. 47–48.
[2] Stalin, *Works*, Vol. 9, p. 290.
[3] Trotsky, *The Third International After Lenin*, p. 181.

revolution could be brought about in China. Fresh Comintern emissaries, the Russian Besso Lominadse and the Germans Heinz Neumann and Gerhard Eisler, were sent off to China.[1] They now tried to carry through a revolution not only without the help of the strongest political force in China, the Kuomintang, but even in the teeth of opposition from the Kuomintang, which had now been considerably strengthened, thanks to Soviet help. In September 1927 Stalin declared that now that the Kuomintang had "disgraced and discredited themselves by their connection with the counter-revolution", the Chinese peasants and workers would flock to the banner of the Communists, thus giving notice of a new attempt at revolution.[2] Stalin had every reason not to admit that his China policy had failed, since the China question was one of the most important issues in his quarrel with the Zinoviev-Trotsky opposition. The 15th Party Congress, at which Stalin would have to maintain his position in the face of this opposition, was imminent. Stalin therefore suggested that it would be a promising proposition to utilize a revolutionary peasant movement in South China and an already existing revolutionary situation in Canton. Heinz Neumann and Gerhard Eisler went to Canton. There, in December, they organized a revolt, but it collapsed after a few days.[3] The Comintern emissaries managed to escape, but the Chinese Communists paid the reckoning in heavy and bloody losses. Not only that, but the Chinese Communists were also made to say that it was they who had been responsible for the catastrophe. On 17 July 1928 the Chinese delegate told the entire International at the 6th World Congress:[4]

The great Chinese revolution has suffered a heavy defeat.

[1]Borodin had left Hankow in July 1927 (see D. Dallin, *op. cit.*, p. 231, and Louis Fischer, *The Soviets in World Affairs*, Princeton, 1951, p. 291).

[2]Stalin, *Works*, Vol. 10, p. 162.

[3]Cf. Harold D. Isaacs, *The Tragedy of the Chinese Revolution*, Stanford, Cal., 1951, p. 291, and Chiang Kai-shek, *op. cit.*, p. 54. Pavel Mif, *Heroic China*, New York, 1937, pp. 55 ff., defends Stalin's policy when he represents the abortive revolt as "the Commune of Canton". A description of the Canton revolt as it was portrayed by H. Neumann is given by M. Buber-Neumann, *Potsdam-Moskau*, pp. 79 ff. It is likely that Heinz Neumann exaggerated the degree of support the masses gave to the rising (see Isaacs, *op. cit.*, p. 283).

[4]*Protokoll des VI Weltkongresses*, Berlin, 1928, Vol. 1, p. 10.

The reasons were the unfavourable international situation, the military intervention by world imperialism, the contemptible betrayal by the national bourgeoisie and the petty-bourgeois upper stratum and, above all, serious opportunistic mistakes by the leaders of the Chinese Communist Party.

Besso Lominadse, who was later to take his own life, also joined in this criticism.[1]

The Chinese were thus made to shoulder the blame which really attached to the Comintern, to the Comintern's agents and, above all, to Stalin, under whose direction the Chinese disaster had occurred. Stalin must be regarded as the author of the unsound China policy, not only because he continued to be attacked by the Opposition on that account,[2] but also because Stalin himself—in marked contrast to his usual habit—repeatedly and wordily pleaded in favour of the Soviet Union's China policy, not only before the failure of the attempted revolution, but even afterwards.[3]

### DEFEATS RESULT IN NEW MOVEMENT TO THE LEFT

At the end of 1927 the Comintern and Stalin could look back on a series of defeats. These reverses put an end to the "right" United Front policy which had been followed since 1925.[4] During this period Stalin had eliminated his "left" opponents, Trotsky, Zinoviev and Kameniev. Now he himself could apply their "left-wing" policies: and he employed them to combat the "right-wing" group of Bukharin and his followers. His turn to the left began in 1927, when he felt himself compelled by Chiang Kai-shek's "betrayal" to incite the Chinese Communists to their unsupported revolt in Canton. In his domestic

---

[1] B. Lominadse, *The Anniversary of the Canton Rising*, in *The Communist International*, London, dated 1 February 1929, pp. 135 ff.

[2] Trotsky, *The Third International After Lenin*, p. 180; Zinoviev, *Thesen über die chinesische Revolution*, loc. cit., pp. 14 ff.

[3] Stalin, *Works*, Vol. 9, pp. 225, 235, 243, 290 ff., and Vol. 10, pp. 10 ff. and 158 ff.

[4] Severe and well-founded criticism of this policy was contained in the so-called *Declaration of the Five Hundred*, addressed by five hundred veteran Bolshevists to the Central Committee of the CPSU in 1927. (See *Der Kampf um die Komintern* (*Dokumente der russischen Opposition*), Berlin 1927, p. 149.)

policies, too, from the end of 1927, Stalin veered to the left in his fight against the "wealthy peasants".[1]

THE SIXTH WORLD CONGRESS
*(17 July to 1 September 1928)*

Not only the circumstances under which this Congress was called but also the course it took give a good impression of the condition to which the Comintern and its "supreme organ", the World Congress, had been reduced. The 4th World Congress had already had no more to do than to ratify the ECCI's decision to introduce the United Front policy. It was now four years since the Comintern's "supreme organ" had been summoned, not since the 5th Congress in March 1924 in fact, even though the statutes said it was to meet once a year.[2] The full council of the ECCI made a show of being the deciding authority, but in point of fact the important decisions were taken by the Politbureau of the CPSU, which was in turn dominated by Stalin. Stalin had prevented the World Congress from being summoned between 1925 and 1928, evidently because he still feared the opposition of the "Left", which had already had a strong following in the International. The results of the 6th World Congress also give an indication of the extent to which Comintern policies were conditioned by the state of play in the struggle for power among the leading personalities of the CPSU. Although the leftward tendency of Soviet policy had already begun, the 6th Congress could not set a definite course to the left, as the "right" course had not yet been officially abandoned. The programme finally adopted by the 6th World Congress, after the 4th and 5th Congresses had already dealt with programmes years before, did contain world-revolutionary demands clothed in forceful slogans,[3] but there was no real preparation as yet for serious action designed to kindle revo-

[1] Borkenau, *The Communist International*, p. 333; *Short Course*, p. 267.

[2] The interval until the next, the 7th and last, World Congress, was to be still longer, namely, seven years.

[3] Trotsky, *op. cit.*, p. 229; Borkenau, *op. cit.*, p. 336. It is evident from the style of the theoretical passages in the programme that Bukharin had a good deal to do with drawing it up. (*Protokoll des VI Weltkongresses*, Vol. IV, pp. 43 ff.: C. L. R. James, *World Revolution 1917-1936 (The Rise and Fall of the Communist International*, London, 1937, p. 306).

lutionary workers' movements and to provide support for struggles for national liberation. Stalin was able to agree with Bukharin to the extent of turning away from the United Front policy.[1] The Profintern once more agitated against the "yellow" trade unions, and "red" unions such as the German Revolutionary Trade Union Opposition were founded. It is doubtful whether Stalin himself shared the anxiety expressed by the 6th Congress, that the imperialist powers might declare war on the Soviet Union, even if the fear of an imminent imperialist war was widespread among the Russian people.[2] It is possible that this war-anxiety was in fact created in order to pave the way for the impending Russian swing to the left.

### THE COURSE MOVES FURTHER LEFT

As soon as the power situation inside the Politbureau made it possible for him to do so, Stalin gave orders for the course to be altered a great deal further to the left. In November 1929 Bukharin was expelled from the Politbureau by the Central Committee of the CPSU.[3]

In the months that followed, in accordance with the decisions of the 6th Congress, which had described the danger from the "right wing" as being the chief danger, the Sections of the Comintern began to expel the "conciliatory groups".[4] In Germany, Heinrich Brandler, August Thalheimer, Paul Frölich, Jakob Walcher, August Enderle and others were expelled.[5] The American Communist Party expelled the General Secretary, Jay Lovestone, and his followers.[6] In Spain the purge included Andrés Nin and his supporters.

In 1926 and 1927 it was the left-wing Communists who had

[1]See Bukharin's speech, *Protokoll des VI Weltkongresses*, Vol. I, p. 50.
[2]For example, *Protokoll des VI Weltkongresses*, Vol. I, pp. 559 ff. and Louis Fischer, *The Soviets in World Affairs*, Vol. II, pp. 739 ff.
[3]*Short Course*, p. 270; Souvarine, *op. cit.*, pp. 456 ff.
[4]Theses of the Agit-Prop of the ECCI on the 6th World Congress in *Die Kommunistische Internationale*, Vol. II, Berlin, 1956, p. 160.
[5]Walter Ulbricht, *Zur Geschichte der Deutschen Arbeiterbewegung*, Vol. I, 1953, p. 351; O. K. Flechtheim, *op. cit.*, pp. 153 ff.
[6]W. Z. Foster, *History of the Communist Party of the United States*, New York, 1952, p. 270. Further details in Borkenau, *The Communist International*, pp. 348 ff. Cf. also Stalin, *Works*, Vol. 12, p. 21, *The Right Deviation in the C.P.S.U. (b)*. Jan Valtin describes the particular case of Arthur Ewert in *Tagebuch der Hölle*, Cologne, 1957, p. 158.

been eliminated, and now, with the purge of the "right wing", Stalin was getting closer to the aim of his "bolshevization", which was to ensure that the Comintern contained only functionaries who were known to be completely faithful to the Party line and who would loyally follow every alteration of the Moscow dogma and every change in Stalin's course.

There was no election of a new President of the ECCI to follow Bukharin after he disappeared from the scene. Stalin did not want to give anyone the opportunity to use that office to build a position for himself. Dimitri Manuilski and George Dimitroff, together with the Finn Otto Kuusinen, became his assistants in looking after the Comintern.[1]

In the Soviet Union the first Five Year Plan was accepted, and the expansion of heavy industry and the collectivization of the land were to be forced ahead. In the international sphere the fight against the Social Democrats was intensified to a degree surpassing what was required by the retreat from the United Front policy. The Social Democrats, so ardently courted by the Communists from 1924 to 1926, were known as "Social Fascists" from 1929 onwards.[2] Despite later attempts to whitewash this aspect, the grotesque description was applied by the Communists to the whole of Social Democracy.[3] To take only one example, a resolution by the 12th Party Congress of the KPD had said:

> Men and women of the working class! Have done with the SPD, the party that betrays and murders the working class. Drive the agents of Social Fascism out of all functions in the factories and trade unions. Vote red, for men you can trust. Vote for your own fighting leaders in the struggle for bread and pay!

PREPARATIONS FOR A NEW REVOLT IN GERMANY

Although the swing to the left, with its intensification of Bolshevist policies, had set in before the start of the world

[1]Borkenau, *The Communist International*, p. 339.

[2]See the message of greeting sent from the Central Committee of the CPSU to the 12th Party Conference of the KPD on 14 June 1929, reprinted in *Zur Geschichte der KPD*, p. 252; Douglas Hyde, *I Believed*, London, 1950, p. 56; Henry Pelling, *The British Communist Party*, London, 1958, pp. 65, 71.

[3]Walter Ulbricht's article in *Zur Geschichte der KPD*, p. 262.

economic crisis of 1928–9,[1] the effects of the crisis when it came gave an enormous fillip to the Comintern's radical policies and created something which had not existed in Europe since the autumn of 1923—a revolutionary situation. There were millions of unemployed in the industrial countries of Europe. In Germany alone there were 6 million registered unemployed, and it has been calculated that another 2 million did not register. Taking the dependants of the unemployed into account, it is probable that altogether one third of the entire population of Germany were living on inadequate unemployment doles.[2] The Bolshevists thought they could see in the misery and want of these unfortunate people confirmation of Marx's Theory of Increasing Pauperization.[3] The election results seemed to portend imminent reaction on the part of the "masses". In the Presidential elections of 13 March 1932, Thälmann received 5 million votes, while in the Reichstag elections in the same year, the Communists gained 800,000 more than in 1930, and reached a total of 5,370,000. The last free elections, on 6 November 1932, brought the KPD 6 million votes and the SPD 7¼ million. On the other hand the Communists appeared to overlook the much greater gains made by the National Socialists, who managed to poll more than twice as many votes as in 1930, receiving 11¾ million votes.[4]

There were some signs that the KPD figure was due not only to the votes of revolutionary workers primed for action, but to a large extent to the votes of the despairing and unorganized unemployed. Since only a small percentage of the workers who still had jobs belonged to the KPD, calls for a general strike put out by the KPD on a number of occasions between 1929 and 1932 evoked hardly any reaction,[5] and even the *coup d'état* carried out by von Papen's Government against the Prussian Social Democrat Government in July 1932 brought no greater response to the KPD's call for a general strike.[6] But Stalin paid no heed to these omens, while the Comintern appeared to be dazzled by the idea that they were on the threshold of success

[1]See p. 105 ff. above.   [2]Flechtheim, *op. cit.*, p. 167.   [3]See p. 72 above.
[4]Flechtheim, *op. cit.*, p. 179.
[5]Borkenau, *The Communist International*, p. 345.
[6]*Zur Geschichte der KPD*, p. 325.

in Germany. The 12th Plenary Session of the ECCI believed that the convulsion of the world economic system would give rise to revolutionary situations, which they were expecting to exploit. As regards Germany, the meeting pronounced that "the triumph of the German Revolution, together with the victorious revolution of October 1917" would mean the "most significant step on the road to world revolution", and that "the German Revolution would decide the fate of the proletarian revolution in West and Central Europe".[1] It certainly did: only, in the result, the victory went not to the Communists but to Hitler.

As the Resolution of the 12th Plenary Session of the ECCI indicated, the revolutionary course of these years was not confined to Germany. The 11th Plenary Session had previously named five countries in which the revolution was marching forward: Germany, Poland, Spain, China and India.[2]

This left-wing policy was not consistently adhered to. Whenever it seemed promising to do so, the Communists appealed to the Social Democratic workers (the united front "from below"), or offered to create a united front with the Social Democrats, whom they had called "the arch-enemy". This is true of the various calls for a united front which the Communists made to the SPD between 30 January and 5 March 1933.[3]

A characteristic of the Berlin transport workers' strike of November 1932, described by the KPD as "the great example", was the co-operation between the Revolutionary Trade Union Opposition (RGO) and the National Socialist Factory Cell Organization (NSBO) in opposition to the Social Democratic Trade Union leadership (ADGB). Most trade unionists and large sections of the public refused to co-operate, and the strike had to be called off after five days.[4]

[1]*Die Internationale*, Vol. XV, p. 54.
[2]Cf. Theses of the ECCI Plenary Session of 11 April 1930 in *Die Kommunistische Internationale, Auswahl von Dokumenten und Reden*, Berlin 1956, pp. 206, 213 ff.
[3]Flechtheim, *op. cit.*, pp. 181 ff.; *Zur Geschichte der KPD*, Berlin 1954, pp. 356–359.
[4]Flechtheim, *op. cit.*, p. 182; Ulbricht, *Zur Geschichte der Deutschen Arbeiterbewegung*, Vol. I, p. 647.

Nevertheless the German Communists went on with their preparations for armed revolt,[1] taking their theoretical guidance from the works of A. Lange, *The Road to Victory*, and A. Neuberg, *Armed Revolt*, both of which were published between 1928 and 1931.[2] The preparations were under the direction of Hans Kippenberger, who was responsible for the AM (antimilitary) Apparat. The main part of the work of this organization lay on the one hand in procuring the necessary material for an armed revolt, such as weapons, ammunition and explosives. It was on the other hand particularly important, in view of the impending fighting, to subvert the armed forces and the police, besides taking steps to ensure that the Party would be able to carry on its work if it should be proscribed. The armaments were often obtained by theft from arms factories and gunsmiths' shops or from firms which used explosives in their work. In 1933, for example, some thieves were charged before the Reich court with the theft of one heavy and 36 light machine-guns and 217 rifles from the Reichswehr garrison in Leipzig.[3] In 1932 alone the police investigated 1,225 cases of attempted subversion in the armed forces and the police and in the same year 169 persons were sentenced by the Reich court for subversion.[4]

In spite of these preparations, when Hitler took over power on 30 January 1933 the Communists remained inactive. There were no riots and the workers did not come out on strike when, on 27 February 1933, the Reichstag fire provided the Government with the excuse for arresting thousands of Communist functionaries, which struck a heavy blow at both the legal and

[1]Flechtheim, pp. 176 ff.

[2]"A. Lange" was a pen-name used by Hans Kippenberger, the leader of the German AM-Apparat, while "A. Neuberg" was probably a pseudonym of Heinz Neumann, one of the organizers of the Canton rising (see Isaacs, *op. cit.*, pp. 283, 367). The contents page and preface of "Neuberg's" book are reproduced in *House Report* No. 2243 of the U.S. House of Representatives, 29 May 1956. The preface to the edition which appeared in Switzerland in 1931 was written by the publishers. In criticizing the author—for example, in respect of his assessment of the Canton rising—the preface makes use of arguments which were being used against Heinz Neumann at about the same time.

[3]A. Ehrt, *Bewaffneter Aufstand*, Berlin, 1933, p. 102.

[4]Ehrt, *op. cit.*, pp. 85 ff. Ehrt's work, which appeared after Hitler's seizure of power in 1933, is only reliable when giving factual accounts.

the illegal KPD organizations.[1] The KPD was not to become an effective political force in Germany again until 1945, although Communists did do useful political work among political prisoners and in non-Communist anti-Fascist circles. The main value of this work during the war lay in the fact that it prepared the ground for Russian intelligence activity.

From 1930 to 1934 the Communists treated the Social Democrats as the arch-enemy. Advocates of an uncompromising war against National Socialism, such as Heinz Neumann with his slogan "Smash the Fascists wherever you meet them!", were disciplined for sectarianism.[2] This has led to the frequently-asked question, why did the Bolshevists permit Hitler to take over power? Did the Soviet Politbureau, in order to avoid a war with the Western imperialist powers, decided to forgo the chance of a Socialist revolution in Germany, and thus force Germany to become an aggressor nation, in the first instance against the West?[3] On this point there is this to be said. When one considers the revolutionary efforts made by the Comintern from 1919 to 1933 there seems to be no sign of strategic far-sightedness on the part of the ECCI or of the Soviet Politbureau. The action of March 1921 was no less bungled than the October 1923 action in Germany. "International Trade Union Unity" in England failed just as dismally as the Chinese Revolution of 1927.

Is there any reason to believe that the men behind these "operations", and particularly Stalin, were anything more than cunning despots with a good grasp of the internal Russian situation, but otherwise of limited understanding?[4]

There is more reason for assuming that until 1933 Stalin,

[1] It is unnecessary here to go into the question of who actually did start the Reichstag fire. It certainly was not the Communists.

[2] Jan Valtin, *op. cit.*, pp. 287 ff.; M. Buber-Neumann, *Potsdam-Moskau*, pp. 278 ff. Stefan T. Possony, *A Century of Conflict*, Chicago, 1953, p. 196; M. Buber-Neumann, *op. cit.*, pp. 285 ff.

[3] Stefan T. Possony, *A Century of Conflict*, Chicago, 1953, p. 296; M. Buber-Neumann, *op. cit.*, p. 285 ff.

[4] There can, of course, be no doubt about Lenin's breadth of vision in matters other than Russian. This was demonstrated on various occasions, including his suggested *Thesis on the National and Colonial Questions* for the 2nd World Congress (cf. Lenin, *Selected Works*, London, 1947, Vol. II, pp. 654 ff.).

blinded by his historically-rooted hatred of the Social Demo-crats—"social fascists", to use his words—underestimated the strength of the National Socialist movement.[1] Led astray by the world economic crisis, which on the face of it seemed likely to create a revolutionary situation, and by election results such as had never been obtained before, he worked to bring about a Bolshevist revolution, which he intended to be the climax of the "left" course he had been following since 1928.[2] However hopeless such a policy may have been in view of the situation in Germany, Stalin is not the only example of how dazzled a dictator can be when he has been fed for years on "rose-coloured" reports. Stalin wanted to exploit the revolutionary situation to establish a Bolshevik régime in Germany, thus giving himself security. When that failed, he tried to assure his predominance by co-operating with Hitler. In 1934 Hitler gave orders that the connection between the Reichswehr and the Red Army was to be broken off. Thereupon Stalin, in the guise of an "anti-fascist", made efforts to reach firm agreements with the French bourgeoisie.[3] This had no success, either, but the feelers that Stalin put out in the spring of 1939 to test the possibility of agreement with Hitler were favourably received. The 1939 pact seemed to offer both the dictators both security and plunder.[4]

[1]This was admitted by Wilhelm Pieck at the 7th World Congress (see summarized proceedings, Moscow, 1939, p. 38): it was confirmed by Dimitroff, as Jan Valtin (R. Krebs) has described, *op. cit.*, p. 167.

[2]Cf. Borkenau, *European Communism*, p. 71. The left-wing policy was not followed unswervingly, as can be seen from the number of "united front" offers the Communists made to the SPD in 1932–33 (see p. 110 above). The following is also worthy of note: Stalin told Heinz Neumann that if the National Socialists were to come to power in Germany, they would concern themselves so exclusively with the West that "we would be able to build up Socialism undisturbed" (M. Buber-Neumann, *op. cit.*, p. 284). Would it be correct to assume from this that Stalin hoped that the National Socialists would take over power?

[3]There are some signs that Stalin was trying to find a new solution in the West in the remarks made by Walter Ulrich (Urvich) to Richard Krebs in the spring of 1933. Ulrich said that the "decaying" Western democracies offered the Comintern opportunities for expansion, which, if exploited, would enable a "red ring" to be laid around Germany (Jan Valtin, *op. cit.*, p. 352). Ulrich (Urvich) was a Czech Communist who took Dimitroff's place in the WEB after 1933, appearing not only in Copenhagen but also in Paris.

[4]See p. 194 below.

E

### THE POPULAR FRONT POLICY IN FRANCE

It was traditional in the CPSU and the Comintern to alter the political course following a defeat. The left-wing policy had been abandoned in favour of the United Front policy after the failure of the March 1921 action, and in 1928 Stalin had moved away from the right-wing course following his "betrayal" by the Kuomintang. In the same way Stalin gave up the left course of the years 1929 to 1934 when the failure of that course became clear. This was also influenced by weighty factors of domestic policy. In January 1934 the 17th Party Congress, the "Congress of the Victors", took place, the victors being in fact the Party Bureaucracy, with Stalin at the head, and the defeated being the right and left deviationists and the kulaks; although the CPSU saw their victory as the accomplishment of the First Five Year Plan. The "dissolution" of the OGPU in the summer of 1934 could be regarded as signalizing the abandonment of the left-wing course.[1] In the foreign policy sphere, the most significant event of this period was Soviet Russia's entry into the League of Nations, which the 5th and 6th Congresses had still been anathematizing as "counter-revolutionary".

In the 'twenties, when the Comintern had to abandon the left-wing course, the method of revolutionary attack, it had turned to the United Front policy, seeking to win over the working masses and, with their help, to seize power. Thus the United Front policy led to co-operation with the Socialists and trade unionists in the hope of attracting them to the Communist side.[2]

[1] See Georg von Rauch, *A History of Soviet Russia*, London, 1957, p. 238. What actually happened was that the GPU was taken into the NKVD (People's Commissariat of the Interior) as a main department. It went on with its work (as the purges were to show when they reached their climax after 1935), was upgraded to the status of an independent People's Commissariat in 1943, and became the MGB (Ministry of State Security) in 1948. In 1947 the KI (Information Committee) was formed, but was dissolved again in 1951. The MGB was disbanded in 1953, and its work has been carried on ever since by the KGB (Committee of State Security). (Report of the Royal Commission on *Espionage*, Sydney 1955, pp. 230 ff. on the Petrov Case: see also David J. Dallin, *Soviet Espionage*, New Haven, 1955, pp. 2–3.)

[2] *Thesen und Resolutionen des V. Weltkongresses*, Hamburg, 1924, p. 27. In the 1920s, of course, the aim was the United Front "from below"; that is

In 1934 the difficulties in the way of political activity in Germany were so great that France seemed to offer the best possibility of going over to the United Front policy. In June 1933 French and Italian trade unionists and representatives of the German revolutionary trade union opposition (RGO) had banded together to form the *European Congress* with the idea of combining anti-fascism with the fight against war. In February 1934 demonstrations by right-wing supporters, developing into street fighting, had led to the fall of the Daladier government, a situation which the Communists were able to use to suggest to the Socialists that they should co-operate with them. France had, moreover, one anxiety in common with the Soviet Union—anxiety about Hitler's Fascism.[1] This combination of circumstances caused Stalin to make an energetic approach to the French problem and to initiate a policy which was successful for several years. In this way the French Communist Party became an important factor in European Communism.

The question of the tactics to be adopted for this led to differences of opinion within the Comintern. Anxiety about the increasing power of Fascism led the French author Henri Barbusse to suggest in Moscow in 1934 that "all lovers of peace"(!) should combine forces to form a Popular Front.

Dimitroff, Mao Tse-tung and Earl Browder supported Barbusse, as did the French Communists Thorez and Guyot, who were in Moscow at this time. Stalin had not yet made up his mind, so Manuilski, Gottwald, Kuusinen and the German Communists voiced objections.[2] The main counter-argument was that such a policy might give rise to "right-wing" devia-

---

to say, the Communists tried to separate the Social Democrats and the trade unionists from their leaders. The Popular Front policy, on the other hand, led to agreements between the Communists and the leaders of the West European Socialist parties, something which had hitherto been violently rejected. To give an example: In Stalin, *Works*, Vol. 6, pp. 431–432, note 56, Henrich Brandler was denounced for having "without regard to principles . . . entered into collaboration with the leaders of German Social-Democracy", in 1924.

[1]Borkenau, *European Communism*, p. 115; Krivitsky, *op. cit.*, p. 89.

[2]Manuilski, Stalin's closest adviser, was not unfamiliar with French problems. In the early 1930s he was often in France as a Comintern delegate (cf. *Ostprobleme* 1955, p. 616).

tionism and to the dilution of Communist parties.[1] Until Stalin gave his decision in favour of the Popular Front policy, the Communists' feelings of antagonism for the Social Democrats continued, even inside the concentration camps and in the Saar. While this lasted, the French Communists also continued to insist that the Socialists were "social fascists".[2] On 27 July 1927 the French Communists signed a pact of joint action with the Socialist Section Française Internationale Ouvrière (SFIO). This united front was then pushed out rightwards by means of an agreement between the Communists, Socialists, Radical Socialists, Confédération Générale du Travail, Confédération Générale du Travail Unitaire, the League of Human Rights, etc., leading to the creation of the Popular Front, 24 July 1935.[3] In the parliamentary elections in April and May 1936 the Popular Front obtained a majority[4] and the Communists proceeded a step further and tried to enter into close co-operation with the bourgeoisie—the army, the bureaucracy and the diplomats, the circles thought by Stalin to be the ruling circles in France. Maurice Thorez suggested the formation of a National Front, and even held out his hand to the Catholics, with the idea of making a common front of all Frenchmen from the Communists to the Catholics.[5]

The Communists used every kind of device to persuade their "partners" of the sincerity of their intention to co-operate. On 1 July 1934 Thorez gave an assurance that the Communist Party were not deceiving their partners. They were willing to renounce criticism of the Socialists and faithfully to abide by the agreement.[6] As a gesture the French party dissolved their trade union section, which entailed no sacrifice on the part of

[1]Eudocio Ravines, *The Yenan Way*, New York, 1951, pp. 113 ff.

[2]At the 7th World Congress, Wilhelm Pieck admitted that the Germans had thought "for a pretty long time" that the Social Democratic government had been fostering Fascism (*Protokoll des VII Weltkongresses*, Moscow, 1939, p. 38). Further evidence of this is in Borkenau, *European Communism*, pp. 120–121.

[3]The German Popular Front, composed of bourgeois, Socialist and Communist German émigrés in Paris, was not founded until the beginning of 1936.

[4]*Die Kommunistische Internationale*, Vol. 5, 1936, p. 446; *Ostprobleme* 1955, pp. 619 ff.

[5]Borkenau, *op. cit.*, p. 134; *Ostprobleme* 1955, pp. 619 ff.

[6]Quoted by Borkenau, *op. cit.*, p. 125.

the Comintern, since they had already bolshevized their party, extended the factory cells as the basic organization of the party and were now exercising their influence in the factories through these cells.[1]

Stalin made a personal contribution to deceiving the world when he gave an interview to an American journalist, Roy Howard, and, in reply to the question whether the USSR had renounced her revolutionary aims, declared that no such intention existed.[2] Nevertheless, it is definite that in spite of this statement by Stalin the world revolutionary aim remained alive. Thus Valentin Gonzales (El Campesino) has described how, when he attended the Frunze Academy in the autumn of 1939, the students, who were intended to fill the highest military posts, were instructed that they were to become "the leaders of the Red Army in the service of *world revolution*".[3] This indication ran exactly parallel with the decision of the 7th World Congress, which said in its *Resolution on the Activities of the ECCI*:

> The 7th World Congress of the Communist International draws attention to the fact that the transformation of the evolving political crisis into a victorious proletarian revolution is entirely dependent on the strength of the Communist parties and their influence on the broad mass of the proletariat and on the energy and self-denial of the Communists. Today, when the political crisis is coming to a head in a number of capitalist countries, the most important and decisive task of the Communists consists in not being content with the results so far achieved, but in striding forward to new successes, in extending the contact with the working class, winning the confidence of the millions of workers, converting the Sections of the Comintern into mass parties and bringing the majority of the working class under the influence of the Communist parties, thus creating the conditions necessary for the victory of the proletarian revolution.[4]

As Borkenau has said of Léon Blum, "no man on earth was

[1]Cf. p. 88 above.
[2]The interview appeared in *Kommunist* (April 1956) and in *Die Kommunistische Internationale*, No. 3, 1936, p. 185. It is reprinted in *House Report No. 2241* of the US House of Representatives, 29 May, 1956, pp. 320 ff.
[3]El Campesino, *Die grosse Illusion*, Cologne, 1951, p. 42.
[4]Abridged stenographic record of *Der VII Kongress der Komintern*, Moscow, 1939, p. 560.

less fit to resist the lure of the new Communist tactics than this suave, inhibited, deeply serious and honest but essentially guileless man"[1]—yet even Blum made public complaints that the "Pact of Joint Action" of July 1934 was being systematically abused.[2]

Thus the Popular Front policy contained the seeds of its own destruction from the very beginning. After the electoral victory of 1936, the Communists refused to take part in a Popular Front government, thereby showing that they were not interested in a genuine coalition with their partners. For the senior Comintern functionaries the anti-Fascist idea, the connecting link of the Popular Front, was merely an instrument of Russian foreign policy. Up to 1938 this policy was directed towards transforming the 1935 Franco-Soviet Pact into a military alliance, in furtherance of which Dimitroff called on the French masses to "exert the greatest possible pressure on the government's foreign policy".[3] Did Stalin and his confederates want to achieve genuine agreement with France, or was it all a manoeuvre designed to persuade Hitler to negotiate?[4] One thing is certain—when the Franco-Soviet military alliance did not come into being and Stalin drew closer to Hitler,[5] the Comintern lost interest in the Popular Front.

The Popular Front policy in France extended the alliance between Socialists and Communists to bring in anti-Fascist circles of the bourgeois Centre.[6] Something similar to this had been tried in China in the collaboration with the Kuomintang in 1927, when the unifying element had been "anti-imperialist" interests. The basis of the French Popular Front was the anti-Fascist feelings that animated the partners.[7] Borkenau sees in the French Communists' assurances to their partners of honest co-operation "a decisive step from Leninism to Stalinism".[8] In

---

[1]Borkenau, *op. cit.*, p. 135.    [2]*Ibid.*, p. 138.
[3]Quoted from *Ostprobleme* 1935, p. 620.
[4]See p. 195 below.    [5]See p. 196 below.
[6]Cf. Pieck's more general definition on p. 39 of the abridged stenographic record of the 7th World Congress, Moscow, 1939.
[7]Walter Gérard, *Histoire du PCF*, Paris, 1948, p. 260. Nazi works such as *Der Weltbolschewismus*, published by the "Anti-Comintern" and prepared by Adolf Ehrt, Leipzig, 1936, called anti-fascism "a demagogic invention of Willi Münzenberg's" (p. 19).
[8]Borkenau, *European Communism*, pp. 124–125.

*Left-Wing Communism*, however, Lenin had recommended the employment of ruses and practices of every kind in furtherance of Communist activity.[1] This was the strategy employed in the "Popular Front" era, since although the Communists did in fact enter into the Pact of Joint Action, they at no time observed it. The policy of the Popular Front was Leninist. Its success was due to the fact that it was more subtly handled than the clumsy United Front policies of the years before. In this success a not inconsiderable part was played by the so-called Front Publications of the publishing houses established in Paris by Willi Münzenberg.

### MÜNZENBERG IN PARIS

Münzenberg's publications were intended to make the fight against Fascism and the Popular Front idea internationally popular, especially among the intellectuals. They were not themselves a product of the Popular Front policy, but were the result of a long and carefully planned propaganda campaign skilfully created by Willi Münzenberg.[2] Münzenberg and his "concern", which had had its birth in the International Workers' Relief, were not subject to any of the Comintern Sections,[3] but worked directly for the OMS.[4] This meant that untrammelled by the Party bureaucrats—and much to their annoyance, of course—he could bring out attractively presented newspapers, periodicals, films and plays.[5] He reached the pinnacle of his

[1]See p. 50 above.
[2]See p. 150 below (The Youth International).
[3]On the extent of this concern, see p. 183 below (Agit-Prop activity).
[4]Krivitsky, *op. cit.*, p. 79. See p. 136 below. It is not clear from the material at present available whether Münzenberg had a functionary position in the Comintern organization (responsible, say, for Agit-Prop in the West European area?). Koestler, *op. cit.*, p. 314, calls him "head of the Comintern's West-European Agit-Prop Department". M. Buber-Neumann (*op. cit.*, p. 451) says that Manuilski suggested that Münzenberg should come to Moscow and become "the leader of the Comintern's Agit-Prop". Manuilski could not have made this suggestion unless Münzenberg was already a Comintern functionary, as people from outside the organization were not even considered for an ECCI post such as this.
[5]Arthur Koestler, *The Invisible Writing*, London, 1954, p. 207. During his émigré period, Münzenberg called his largest business undertaking *Editions du Carrefour*. Was this intended to be a pointer to the fact that he had reached the "crossroads" in his career?

activities as an émigré in Paris,[1] where he directed the Committee for Aid for the Victims of German Fascism, which became an important tool in the hands of the Comintern propagandists. Especially effective from a political point of view were his *Committee of Enquiry into the Background of the Reichstag Fire Trial* and his *Brown Book on the Reichstag Fire and Hitler's Reign of Terror*.[2] He had the Committee stage a counter-trial before the Reichstag Fire trial had even begun and was able to persuade well-known lawyers, such as Sir Stafford Cripps (later British Chancellor of the Exchequer) and the British King's Counsel, D. N. Pritt, to take part.[3]

The judgment in the counter-trial was given on 20 September 1933. It found that the Communists in the case were not guilty, a finding which was confirmed by the judgment of the Reich High Court on 23 December 1933. The *Brown Book* described how the real fire-raisers had got into the Reichstag building by an underground passage. It also contained powerful descriptions of Jewish persecution and of concentration camps.[4] The *Brown Book* was translated into seventeen languages and sold millions of copies. The result of this great campaign was that the demonstration that the Communists were innocent *in this case* led many people to the erroneous conclusion that they had had no part in insurrectionary activities anywhere else. Arthur Koestler, who was close to Münzenberg at this time, has this to say about this feeling:

> From now on Communist terrorism was regarded as a Nazi invention, with which the Nazis were trying to smear their chief opponents. In reality, so people thought, the Communists were honest defenders of freedom and democracy, braver and more determined than all the others. If anyone referred to Dimitroff as a "Comintern agent", he was just

[1]Valuable material on Münzenberg's work in Paris and the manner of his end are provided by Kurt Kersten in *Deutsche Rundschau*, Baden-Baden, 1957, No. 5, p. 464.

[2]Gustav Regler, in *Das Ohr des Malchus*, Cologne, 1958, pp. 211 ff., describes the birth—in which he played a part—of these books, and Münzenberg's work in Paris.

[3]Pritt is still active in the World Federation of Democratic Lawyers.

[4]Koestler, *op. cit.*, p. 199; M. Buber-Neumann, *Potsdam-Moskau*, p. 452; also *Braunbuch über Reichstagsbrand und Hitler-terror*, Basel, 1933, pp. 222, 270 ff.; *Braunbuch II, Dimitroff contra Goering*, Paris, 1934, pp. 14 ff.

speaking Nazi language. Dimitroff came to symbolize the courageous and upright type of modern liberal—the typical anti-Fascist.

Even more remarkable was that the Communists succeeded in erasing from the public memory the fact that they had preached violence and armed insurrection in Germany and elsewhere for years. The proof was there—on the front page of every Communist newspaper. Nevertheless, since the trial proved that they had not been planning armed revolt on the day of the Reichstag fire, the public regarded it as equally proven that they had never done anything of the kind and never would.

The anti-Fascist propaganda carried out by Münzenberg's organization after 1933 was enthusiastically received by hundreds of thousands of Western liberal intellectuals, actors, singers, lawyers and doctors. A mass basis had been won for all kinds of organizations and especially for the *League against War and Fascism*, also called the *Amsterdam Peace Committee against War and Fascism*.[1]

These Committees can be considered as the forerunners of the organizations established by the CPSU on a world-wide scale after 1945. Arthur Koestler has pointed out several parallels between the propaganda methods of that time and those of today:[2]

> The part of Pablo Picasso was then played by the equally innocent Henri Barbusse. Barbusse's pacifist novel *Le Feu* was the forerunner of Picasso's "Dove", and Barbusse's book on terror, *Fait Divers*, the forerunner of Picasso's "Guernica". The main task of the "Peace Rally" was to advocate rearmament against Nazi Germany and to fight the pacifism of the British Labour Party—which was being exploited by the rival "Peace Offensive" of the Nazis.

The results of this work were still making themselves felt up until the war years, but the men who were responsible for it, Willi Münzenberg and his chief associate Otto Katz, were

---

[1]Krivitsky, *op. cit.*, p. 79; Ruth Fischer, *op. cit.*, pp. 610 ff. Similar ideas were at the root of the World Peace Movement created in 1948 at the instance of the CPSU (see M. and M. Ferrara, *Palmiro Togliatti*, Berlin, 1946, p. 179).

[2]*The Invisible Writing*, p. 313.

brought down and finally done to death by the Bolshevist functionary clique. In 1937 Münzenberg had to hand over all his enterprises and functions to the Czech Comintern delegate, Bohumil Smeral. In letters which he wrote to Stalin (14 July 1937), Smeral (23 July) and Dimitroff (14 June and 30 August 1938), Münzenberg ascribed his deviationist attitude to differences between himself and the Ulbricht group, the ruling faction in the German party.[1] He had, he said, been in agreement with the Comintern leaders on all important questions ever since 1914. His actions in the conflict with the Ulbricht group were in consonance with Communist ideology and with the Communist movement and its traditions. There is no reason to suppose that Münzenberg was not expressing his true feelings in these letters.

Münzenberg died in France in 1940 under circumstances which point to the work of members of some Communist organization.[2] Otto Katz, who later called himself André Simon, was sentenced to death and executed in 1950 in connection with the trial of Slansky in Prague.[3]

### THE SEVENTH WORLD CONGRESS

The 7th World Congress met from 25 July to 20 August 1935, after an interval of seven years. It did nothing to alter the policies of the Comintern or of the CPSU, but merely ratified what the ECCI, on instructions from the Moscow Politbureau, had started in 1934—the "new style" United Front policy and the policy of the Popular Front "of all workers against Fascism". Marcel Cachin triumphantly reported to the Congress on the success of these movements.[4] The ECCI had begun to employ

[1] See Appendix VI to this book.

[2] Koestler, *op. cit.*, p. 407; Ruth Fischer, *op. cit.*, p. 614; M. Buber-Neumann, *op. cit.*, p. 456.

[3] The 25 November 1952 edition of *Neues Deutschland* referred to Katz as "a close collaborator of Münzenberg's Trotskyist group". Katz passed a last message to his former colleague and friend, Arthur Koestler, by quoting words from Rubashov's *Solar Eclipse*—an intellectual code—in his final speech before the tribunal in Prague (Koestler, *The Invisible Writing*, p. 405).

[4] See the abridged stenographic record of the 7th Comintern World Congress, pp. 557, 559, 565, also pp. 90 ff., and David T. Cattel, *Communism and the Spanish Civil War*, Berkeley and Los Angeles, 1956, pp. 24 ff.

the "new style" United Front policy when it instructed the Sections in the Spring of 1934 to negotiate with the Socialist parties. The ECCI itself offered the long-despised Second International the creation of "joint action in the fight against Fascism and the capitalist offensive and against war".[1] This "new style United Front" was nothing more than the "United Front from above", which the 5th Congress had so decisively rejected in 1924.[2]

The 7th Congress formulated an *Address of Greeting* to "Comrade Stalin, the Leader, Teacher and Friend of the proletariat and of the oppressed of the whole world"—the start of the cult of personality on the international level. Togliatti's proposal that Stalin should be honoured in this way corresponded to the real power situation. Since the 17th Party Congress of the CPSU in January 1934, Stalin was the acknowledged victor over the "right-wing" and the "left-wing" and was now the undisputed master of the CPSU and the Comintern. At the 7th World Congress there was no opposition whatever to the proposals made by the leadership.

The resolutions *On the Tasks of the Communist International in connection with Imperialist Preparations for a new War* confirmed what Stalin had been insisting since 1925—that "working-class policies and the fight for peace" should be regarded "from the point of view of the defence of the Soviet Union". In the event of war the Communists must call on workers everywhere "to help the Red Army to victory over the imperialist armies with all available means and at whatever cost".[3]

The aim of the International Communist movement— world revolution—was thus pushed into second place behind Stalin's requirement that the Soviet Union must be protected by the workers of the world. This did not mean, however, that world revolution was abandoned, as many people assumed following the 7th Congress.[4] It was only for tactical reasons that world revolution was no longer so openly mentioned as it had

[1]Abridged stenographic record, p. 557.
[2]See p. 86 above.
[3]See p. 96 above; abridged stenographic record of 7th World Congress, p. 585.
[4]Kermit E. McKenzie, *Einheitsfront 1935*, in *Ostprobleme* 1950, pp. 1310 ff.

been at previous congresses. In the *Resolutions on the Activities of the ECCI*, it was stated in terms perfectly comprehensible to every Communist:[1]

> Today, when the political crisis is coming to a head in a number of capitalist countries, the most important and decisive task of the Communists consists in not being content with the results so far achieved but in striding forward to new successes, in extending the contact with the working class, winning the confidence of the millions of workers, converting the Sections of the Comintern into mass parties and bringing the majority of the working class under the influence of the Communist parties, thus creating the necessary conditions for the victory of the proletarian revolution.

Dimitroff said in his closing speech:[2]

> The world—this world built by the hands of the toilers—belongs to us workers and not to the social parasites and idlers. The present lords of the capitalist world are only temporary. The proletariat are the real rulers of the world, the lords of tomorrow (loud applause), and they must claim their historic rights and seize the reins of power in every country in the whole world.

A manifest sign of the continued existence of the revolutionary aims was the attempted Communist revolt in Brazil in November 1935, a few months after the end of the 7th Congress. This attempt was led by the Brazilian Communist, Luis Carlo Prestes, whose adviser was the German Comintern agent, Arthur Ewert.[3]

[1]Abridged stenographic record, p. 560.
[2]Abridged stenographic record, p. 553.
[3]Jan Valtin, *Tagebuch der Hölle*, p. 194. Ewert, after spending a long time in a Brazilian prison, returned to the Soviet Zone of Germany in 1947 and died there on 3 July 1959 (Ravines, *The Yenan Way*, p. 162).

# Chapter IV

## THE ORGANIZATION AND METHODS OF THE COMMUNIST INTERNATIONAL

THE 1st and 2nd World Congresses decided that the Comintern was to be a world party made up of separate Sections, i.e. the national Communist parties. Its purpose was "to fight for the overthrow of the international bourgeoisie and for the creation of an international soviet republic", using all possible means, including armed force.[1] In consonance with this task the Comintern was organized on a strictly centralized basis and its methods corresponded to the requirements of the revolutionary struggle.

### THE ORGANIZATION

On the one hand the organization of the Comintern displayed all the elements of a Communist Party but on the other, unlike the national parties, it also had organizational features which enabled it to fulfil its role as a world party.

### THE WORLD CONGRESS AND THE ECCI

The supreme organ of the Comintern, according to para. 4 of the statutes, was the World Congress, to which the Sections were to send their delegates; so that the World Congress was to correspond to the Party Conference of a national Communist Party, at which the delegates of lower formations assembled. The World Congress was also to elect the Executive Committee, the ECCI, as its governing body. The ECCI can be compared with the Central Committee of a national Communist party, while the Politbureau of a national Communist party corresponded to the Presidium elected by the ECCI and presided

[1] *Leitsätze und Statuten der Komintern*, Verlag der Kommunistischen Internationale, 1920, p. 687 (Appendix IV to this book).

over from 1919 to 1926 by Zinoviev and from 1926 to 1929 by Bukharin.[1] At the time of the 4th Congress the Presidium consisted of Zinoviev, Bukharin, Radek, Fritz Heckert, Boris Souvarine, Egidio Gennari, Bela Kun and Jules Humbert-Droz. Like every Communist party, the ECCI boasted a Secretariat, also known as the Political Secretariat, as its implementing organ.[2] The 4th World Congress re-named it the "General Secretariat".

The principle of "democratic centralism" applied also to the Comintern, as can be seen from the 12th of the *21 Conditions* accepted by the 2nd World Congress. The application of this principle made the Presidium of the ECCI the commanding body of the Comintern, just as the Politbureau of the Central Committees of the national parties, thanks to "democratic centralism", have become their commanding bodies.[3] It may be taken as a visible sign of this development that after 1922 the World Congresses ceased to meet once a year, as laid down in the statutes, but were summoned increasingly seldom; the 4th Congress met in 1922, the 5th in 1925, the 6th in 1928 and the 7th and last in 1935.[4] A noteworthy parallel to this development may be seen in the fact that CPSU Party Congresses also only met at great intervals (17th Party Congress in

[1] On the election and duties of the Presidium, see the resolution of the 5th World Congress, *Statuten der Kommunistischen Internationale*, para. 18, reprinted in *Thesen und Resolutionen des V. Weltkongresses der Kommunistischen Internationale*, Hamburg, 1924, p. 85. Stalin did not appoint another Chairman. Following his "successes" in the Reichstag Fire trial and at the 7th World Congress, Dimitroff became "General Secretary" of the Comintern.
[2] Para. 25 of the 1928 statutes. The Secretariat grew out of the "little Bureau" elected by the 2nd World Congress. The Russian members at that time were Zinoviev, Bukharin and Radek, and the German representative was Ernest Meyer (see Brandt and Löwenthal, *Ernst Reuter*, pp. 141, 153). At the beginning of 1921, after the founding of the French Communist Party, Rosmer was taken into the Little Bureau. The Secretaries were Angelica Balabanova at the time of the 1st Congress, Radek between the 1st and 2nd Congresses and M. Kobiecky after the 2nd Congress (see A. Rosmer, *Moscou sous Lénine*, pp. 118, 149, regarding the working methods of the Little Bureau). At the time of the 4th Congress, the Secretariat consisted of Otto Kuusinen, Ossip Piatnitski, Walter Stoecker and Matthias Rakosi (cf. Degras, *The Communist International 1919-1943*, Documents, Vol. I, London-New York, 1956, p. 455).
[3] See p. 88 above.
[4] Thus the provisions of Article 8 of the 1928 statutes, according to which World Congresses were to be held every two years, were also ignored.

1934, 18th in 1939, 19th in 1952 and the 20th in 1956).

Instead of the World Congress, the ECCI began to be the deciding body. The 4th World Congress (November/December 1922) passed a resolution "On the Comintern Executive and its further Activities" and created an expanded Presidium consisting of the President, 24 members and 10 substitutes.[1] This "expanded Executive" often announced decisions on questions of the programme or on policy matters for which, according to para. 4 of the statutes, only the World Congress was competent. In fact, however, the deciding role was assumed by the Politbureau of the CPSU very early on.

Shortly after the formation of the "expanded Executive", on 11 September 1923, the Politbureau of the CPSU decided that a start must be made on preparations for an insurrection in Germany. The ECCI had no more to do than to discuss how this decision was to be implemented.[2] In May 1927 Ignazio Silone was present when the Soviet delegation, led by Stalin, demanded that a full meeting of the expanded ECCI should censure a letter by Trotsky to the CPSU Politbureau, although the delegates were not given an opportunity to see the letter. The Comintern élite were already so "bolshevized" that when Silone refused, some of the delegates, such as Ernst Thälmann, failed to understand him, while others, such as Otto Kuusinen, severely criticized him.[3] After Stalin had achieved his victory inside the Russian party, that is to say from about 1930, he alone was the "body" which *de facto* controlled the Comintern.

On the chain of command in the ECCI, at the beginning of the '40s, Castro Delgado has written:

Right at the top is Stalin, who gives orders to everybody. Those in the middle [of the ladder] obey those above them and give orders to those below them; and the underdog always obeys. There are two ways of giving orders. The top men give orders in a fatherly but firm tone while the

[1]See p. 75 above. Cf. *Thesen und Resolutionen des IV. Weltkongresses der Komintern*, Hamburg, 1923, pp. 72 ff. On the original size of the Presidium, see para. 8 of the statutes.

[2]Ruth Fischer, *op. cit.*, pp. 312 and 316. See p. 82 above.

[3]The contentious letter in question was Trotsky's *Probleme der chinesischen Revolution*, which revealed the weaknesses of Stalin's China Policy (Ignazio Silone in *The God that Failed*, London, 1950, pp. 112 ff.). See pp. 98ff. above.

small-time functionaries issue orders gruffly, like NCOs. But there is only one way of obeying. Disobedience is not tolerated, and it is disobedience to disagree with any point of the official dogma.

From about 1939 until the dissolution of the Comintern, Stalin filled the positions in the General Secretariat as follows.[1] The General Secretary was Dimitroff, with Alfred Kurella as his associate.[2] The Second Secretary, Manuilski, had as his assistant the Hungarian Gerö and the Bulgarian Stepanoff.[3] The members of the Secretariat, all "elected" by the World Congress, were Palmiro Togliatti (Italian), Otto Kuusinen (Finnish), André Marty (French), Wilhelm Pieck (German), Wilhelm Florin (German), Clement Gottwald (Czech), and José Diaz and Dolores Ibarruri (Spanish).[4]

Stalin had made Dimitroff General Secretary because he thought that the CPSU's dominant position in the Comintern would be less obvious if the General Secretary was a Bulgarian. After his "success" in the Reichstag Fire trial, moreover, Dimitroff was popular in the International—and he continued to be tractable. For several years Castro Delgado and Jesus Hernandez saw at close range how Dimitroff never gave an order that had not first been approved by Manuilski. In turn, Manuilski was completely dependent on Zhdanov, who was in charge of international affairs in the CC of the CPSU at that time. Manuilski's assistants, Gerö and Stepanoff, had much more influence than the "elected" members of the Secretariat.[5]

The Comintern's Sections sent their representatives to the ECCI. Thus after the 7th World Congress there were in Moscow Kopecki as representative of the Czech Party, Ulbricht for the KPD, Castro Delgado for the Spanish Party and Veljko

---

[1] Castro Delgado, *J'ai perdu la foi à Moscou*, p. 70.

[2] Details of the officials of the sub-departments of the ECCI will be given —as far as they are known—in the section on them, later in this book.

[3] Regler, *Das Ohr des Malchus*, p. 511. Since the 5th Party Conference of the SED, Kurella has been a candidate for election to the SED Politbureau.

[4] Castro Delgado, *op. cit.*, p. 18. The Abridged Proceedings of the 7th World Congress do not show the names.

[5] Delgado, *op. cit.*, pp. 60 and 207; Hernandez, *op. cit.*, p. 202.

Vlakovic for the Yugoslav Party.[1] The influence the Sections could bring to bear through their representatives declined in direct proportion to the increase in the authority of the CPSU in the Comintern.[2] In the years following the great purges, the representatives of the Sections played nothing more than walking-on parts; for example, the first that most of them learned of the dissolution of the Comintern was from the newspapers.[3] In addition to these top-ranking functionaries, there was a gigantic clerical staff of all kinds of translators, stenographers and other general personnel, to the number of 2,000–2,500.

## THE SECTIONS OF THE ECCI

Below the Presidium were the Sections of the ECCI, which were organized rather like the Central Committee of a national Communist party. In the decisions of the 4th Congress on the re-organization of the Executive there were mentioned an Organization Section (Org-Bureau), to which was subordinated the Statistics and Information Section, and a Section for Agitation and Propaganda.[4] There was also an Administrative and Correspondence Section. The 4th Congress gave the ECCI authority to create further additional Sections, an authority which the ECCI made use of when circumstances required.

As a world Communist Party, the Comintern could not manage without a cadre section, that is, a section concerned with the selection and employment of functionaries. In the first years the Comintern Cadre Section was headed by the Polish Communist Krajewski, a friend of Felix Dzershinski,[5] the

[1]Delgado says of Ulbricht (p. 71) that he was despotic and ignorant. He was the man who did the most speaking at meetings, says Delgado, but no one paid any attention to him, since he merely repeated what Dimitroff and Manuilski had previously said. See also Lazich, *Tito et la Révolution Yougoslave*, p. 117.

[2]Zinoviev had previously attached great importance to their presence; see p. 90 above.

[3]Delgado, *op. cit.*, p. 219.

[4]Hamburg, 1923, p. 72. The difference between the Org-Bureau and all the other Departments did not consist solely in its intrinsic importance. Following the passing of a *Resolution on the Statutes of the Communist International* of the 5th World Congress, the Org-Bureau was elected by the ECCI. Appeals against its decisions could be made to the Presidium.

[5]His real name was probably Vladislav Stein.

first Head of the Cheka. When the purges began, the Head of this Section was Alikhanov, but he, like his deputy Chernomordik, fell a victim to the purge in May 1937.[1] Later, and until the Comintern was dissolved, the Cadre Section was headed by Vilkov, who had previously been working in the CPSU Party Group in the ECCI.[2]

The Cadre Section was organized on a territorial basis and the most important sub-sections had their own heads. A Bulgarian woman, Stella Blagoyeva, worked in the "Latin Sector", for example,[3] while the German Sector was under the supervision of a certain Müller, whose associate was Grete Wilde.[4] To begin with, the Cadre Section was only responsible for the selection and employment of Comintern functionaries, but the more the CPSU penetrated into the Comintern, the more the services of the Cadre Section were demanded to assist the OGPU. The Cadre Section kept complete dossiers of every functionary and these dossiers contained full details of all the qualities and defects of the comrades concerned. These personal dossiers were a mine of information for the OGPU, not only making it possible to select Communists who might be considered for employment as secret agents, but also, in many cases, containing details of hostile remarks made by the members, which could be used as incriminating evidence in purges.[5] The training of the Cadres was the job of the Training Section, which, after the purges, was under the command of Vulko Chervenkoff.[6] The Resolution of the 5th Congress on "The Statutes of the Communist International" also mentioned an "Eastern Department".[7]

Krivitsky, Wollenberg and Borkenau have all testified to the

[1] Margaret Buber, *Under Two Dictators*, London, 1949, p. 6; Alfred Burmeister, *Dissolution and Aftermath of the Comintern*, New York, 1955, p. 2.

[2] Krivitsky, *op. cit.*, p. 81; W. Leonhard, *op. cit.*, p. 165; Delgado, *op. cit.*, p. 54.

[3] Delgado, *op. cit.*, p. 23; Hernandez, *op. cit.*, p. 200.

[4] Alfred Burmeister, *Dissolution and Aftermath of the Comintern*, New York, 1955, p. 2.

[5] Krivitsky, *op. cit.*, p. 82.

[6] Delgado, *op. cit.*, pp. 206, 228. In 1949 Chervenkoff became General Secretary of the Bulgarian party in succession to Dimitroff.

[7] Cf. the relevant resolution in *Thesen und Resolutionen des V. Weltkongresses der Kommunistischen Internationale*, Hamburg, 1924, p. 86. Regarding the composition of this Eastern Department, see p. 135 below.

existence of a Military Section, which had its heyday when the larger sections of the Comintern possessed secret military organizations, that is, in the '20s.[1] Its work in those years was the co-ordination of planning and execution, for example, in Germany in 1923. In all such enterprises, beginning with the Polish Campaign of 1920, the Red Army also played a leading part, of course.

The Comintern propaganda activity was ideologically directed by the "Agit-Prop" Section,[2] to which the entire Comintern Press was subordinated.[3] It may have been Münzenberg's successful press activity that prompted Manuilski to suggest to Münzenberg that he should stay in Moscow as Head of the Comintern's "Agit-Prop", a suggestion that Münzenberg turned down.[4]

The Comintern Press Bureau was responsible for providing Comintern functionaries with the publications they required. At the time of the 3rd World Congress it was under Tobia L. Axelrod.[5]

### THE ORG-BUREAU AND FINANCE SECTION

The most important Section was the Organization Section, also referred to as the Org-Bureau. Under this Org-Bureau were the International Relations Section or OMS (Otdjel Meshdunarodnoi Svyasi), "the heart of the Comintern", as Krivitsky calls it: the Finance Section and the Administration and Correspondence Section.[6] For many years the Org-Bureau was headed by Ossip Piatnitski, a Bolshevist with extensive experience of clandestine activity in the international field. Before the 1905 Russian Revolution, Piatnitski had been one of those engaged in smuggling the paper *Iskra* from Switzerland into Russia. He made himself notable on a number of occasions

[1]Krivitsky, *op. cit.*, p. 116; Wollenberg, *Der Apparat*, p. 139, and Borkenau, *The Communist International*, p. 139.

[2]Krivitsky, *op. cit.*, p. 78.

[3]See p. 183 below.

[4]See note 4, p. 119.

[5]Cf. *Probleme des Friedens und des Sozialismus*, Berlin, 1948, No. 2, p. 14.

[6]The financial duties of the Org-Bureau are mentioned in para. 19 of the 5th Congress's resolution *Die Statuten der Kommunistischen Internationale* (*Thesen und Resolutionen*, Hamburg, 1924, p. 85). (See also Krivitsky, *op. cit.*, p. 69, and p. 167 below.)

by his criticism of the poor results achieved by the Sections.[1] After 1933 he clashed with Manuilski.[2] It was also Piatnitski who made an abortive attempt to save Heinz Neumann, when Neumann fell into disfavour, by providing him with a Canadian passport to enable him to get away to Brazil. His independent and antagonistic attitude were probably sufficient reason for his liquidation during the purges.

### THE INTERNATIONAL CONTROL COMMISSION (ICC)

The 3rd World Congress had created a "provisional control commission",[3] which was confirmed by the 4th Congress as an "International Control Commission" and given the task of dealing with deviations from the "Party line", disciplinary offences or "anti-Party" behaviour on the part of Comintern members.[4] At the 6th World Congress Peter I. Stuchka said that the ICC was only supposed to deal with politically important cases.[5]

An example of the way the ICC worked is the well-known case of Maslow, in which the ICC was to be used to weaken the German "Left Wing".[6] The ICC also took action when Hans Jaeger, a German Communist, in a conversation with Willi Münzenberg and Leo Flieg in 1932, criticized KPD policy in attacking the SPD as the arch-enemy while according the NSDAP *de facto* toleration. While Flieg was temporarily absent, Münzenberg revealed to Jaeger that Flieg was in the confidence of the OMS and a member of the ICC. He was in fact one of the most influential Communists in Germany, even if he did operate from behind the scenes.[7] Jaeger did not have long to

[1] Borkenau, *The Communist International*, pp. 359–60; Jan Valtin, *op. cit.*, p. 114. There is no evidence that Piatnitski was ever "General Secretary" of the Comintern, in spite of M. Buber-Neumann's statement on p. 145 of *Potsdam-Moskau*. Before Dimitroff became General Secretary, Manuilski was the top man in the Comintern.

[2] Ravines, on p. 132 of *The Yenan Way*, describes Manuilski's severe criticism of Piatnitski prior to Piatnitski's being "purged".

[3] Library of the Communist International, Vol. 23, p. 1044.

[4] *Resolutions of the 4th World Congress on the Reorganization of the Executive*, Library of the Communist International, Vol. 36, p. 73.

[5] Cf. *Protokoll des VI Weltkongresses*, Vol. 1, p. 96.

[6] Ruth Fischer, *op. cit.*, p. 361.

[7] See p. 137 below and *Protokoll des VI Weltkongresses der Kommunistischen Internationale*, Vol. IV, Hamburg, 1928, p. 209.

wait before he was summoned to Moscow, where he had to defend himself before an "international commission", which included Radek, Kuusinen, Bela Kun and Knorin.[1] This commission was doing ICC work, for the ICC was responsible for investigating deviations from the Comintern line. Jaeger's critical remarks were of course a deviation from this line, which at that time prescribed "world-wide" antagonism to the "Social Fascists".

As will be shown later, the International Control Commission and the Cadre Section were utilized by the OGPU to extend the spread of OGPU influence on the Comintern. As early as 1923, when the investigations into the Maslow case began, the OGPU had two of its agents in the ICC—Joseph S. Unschlicht and Peter I. Stuchka.[2] This marked the beginning of the growing influence of the OGPU in internal Party affairs, which led eventually to the situation that interrogation by the ICC was a preliminary to arrest by the OGPU (NKVD). The fate of Heinz Neumann followed this course, as Margaret Buber-Neumann has related in detail, having had an opportunity to see how close the connection was between the NKVD and the ICC.[3] While he was still at liberty, Heinz Neumann had told her the content of his protracted interrogation by the ICC. After she herself had been arrested, the NKVD interrogator accused her of precisely the same offences as had been laid at her husband's door by the ICC.[4]

The ICC was also entitled to check Section accounts and financial reports if there were reason to suspect that Party funds had been dishonestly or incorrectly used. In 1924, for example, when Arthur König, the treasurer of the German party, was accused of speculating with OMS funds, it was the ICC which investigated his financial activities.[5] Again, the ICC was called in when Thälmann was accused of having tolerated the misuse

[1] This information was given to me by H. Jaeger himself. He now lives in London.
[2] Ruth Fischer, *op. cit.*, p. 361.
[3] M. Buber-Neumann, *Potsdam-Moskau*, pp. 290, 458. It is also she who relates (pp. 753 ff. of the same book) that Münzenberg was interrogated by the ICC.
[4] M. Buber, *Under Two Dictators*, p. 51.
[5] Ruth Fischer, *op. cit.*, p. 445.

of Party funds in connection with the case of his brother-in-law Wittorf in 1927. As the CPSU assumed a dominant influence in the International, the ICC lost its influence to the Soviet Central Party Control Commission (CPCC), in which the OGPU came to be the dominant power. During this period of the declining importance of the ICC (1935–1943), it was headed by the German Communist Wilhelm Florin.[1]

Inside the ECCI there were secretariats for groups of Sections (regional secretariats),[2] headed by Political Secretaries and containing functionaries delegated to the ECCI by the national Communist parties. In addition, *ad hoc* "Commissions" were set up to deal with special matters (e.g. the "Chinese Commission", which dealt with the attempted revolution in China in 1926–7). Outside the Soviet Union the ECCI established branch offices with limited territorial competence, the best-known being the West European Bureau, located until 1933 in Berlin and thereafter in Copenhagen. These bureaux were strictly supervised by Piatnitski's Org-Bureau and the OMS.

THE ECCI TERRITORIAL SECRETARIATS (REGIONAL SECRETARIATS)

The secretariats about which most is known were the Latin-American, the Anglo-American, the Central European, the West European, the East European, the Far Eastern, the Scandinavian and the Balkan Secretariats.[3] Of these the most important were for years the Central European and the West European, as until 1933 the nucleus of Comintern policy was the attempt to bring about successful revolution in Central Europe. After 1934 the main effort shifted to Western Europe, and was devoted to the Popular Front policy and the Spanish Civil War. The staff of the secretariats underwent frequent changes, especially as a result of the purges.

The Head of the Balkan Secretariat was Dimitroff, before he was sent to the West European Bureau in 1929.[4] After the

[1]*Neues Deutschland*, E. Berlin, dated 16 March 1959.

[2]Para. 27 of the 1928 Statutes.

[3]Cf. Lenin's reference in *Leitsätze über die Grundaufgaben des II. Kongress der Kommunistischen Internationale* in *Die Kommunistische Internationale*, No. 12, 1920, p. 52; Ravines, *The Yenan Way*, p. 135.

[4]Ruth Fischer, *op. cit.*, p. 308, note 2; Borkenau, *European Communism*, p. 228.

Reichstag Fire trial he returned to Moscow and became General Secretary of the Comintern. He was followed as Head of the Balkan Secretariat by Bela Kun, who later fell a victim to the purge. Kun's successor in 1936 was Wilhelm Pieck.[1] In the Balkan Secretariat the "reporter" on Yugoslav questions after 1936 was Tito (alias Walter),[2] while the man responsible for Cadre matters was Traitchko Kostoff.[3] The Balkan Secretariat covered Yugoslavia, Bulgaria, Greece and Rumania.

The Central European Secretariat, which covered Germany, Austria and Czechoslovakia, was headed until 1936 by Waldemar G. Knorin and his assistant, Grigori Smoliansky. When Knorin disappeared in the purge, his place was taken by Palmiro Togliatti, until then Head of the Latin-American Secretariat.[4] Togliatti was shortly afterwards sent to Spain and was replaced by Clement Gottwald. The Germans Sepp Schwab, Hermann Nuding and Fritz Heilmann were all employed at one time or another in the Central European Secretariat, in which the KPD representatives were Fritz Heckert, Hermann Schubert and, in the final years, Walter Ulbricht. Before the purges the Latin-American Secretariat, responsible for Spain, Italy and South America, was run by the Lithuanian August Guralski and the Russian Senani, and after the purges by the Bulgarian Stepanoff.[5] In charge of the Anglo-American secretariat was put T. Gusev, who before the revolution had lived for a time in the United States.[6] At the head of the Scandinavian Secretariat was Otto Kuusinen, who was succeeded by Wilhelm Florin. The "Eastern Department" mentioned on page 130 had the standing of a territorial

[1] Vladimir Dedijer, *Tito Speaks*, London, 1953, p. 97.

[2] *Ibid.*, p. 97.

[3] *Traitchko Kostoff und Seine Gruppe*, Berlin, 1951, p. 8 (no author's name given).

[4] That Togliatti was responsible for the KPD after the 7th Comintern World Congress is shown by his appearance as ECCI representative at the so-called Brussels Party Congress in October 1935. Cf. Ercoli Togliatti, *Die antifaschistische Einheitsfront und die nächsten Aufgaben der KPD*, Strassburg, 1935 or 1936. Further references in Buber-Neumann, *Potsdam-Moskau*, pp. 299, 414.

[5] Delgado, *op. cit.*, p. 65; Hernandez, *La Grande Trahison*, Paris, 1953, p. 12; Ravines, *The Yenan Way*, p. 135.

[6] Cf. the quarterly *Soviet Survey*, London, April-June 1960, No. 32, p. 113; No. 33, pp. 100 ff.

Secretariat. Until 1927 this Department was headed by Georgi Safarov, who was expelled from the CPSU at the 15th Party Congress for his membership of the opposition group within the Party. He was succeeded by Otto Kuusinen, who to a large extent left the affairs of Asian Communist parties in the hands of his assistants, Pavel Mif (alias Michael Firman) and L. Magyar.[1]

Discussion in the Secretariats of the problems of national Communist parties, and resultant suggestions made to the ECCI, had a certain influence on Comintern policies in the first decade of the Comintern's existence, although this influence became steadily less as time went on. After Stalin's victory over the "left wing" and "right wing", however, all important decisions on the policies to be followed by national Communist parties were taken by Stalin, who was already saying: "The Communist International means nothing, it is only thanks to our support that it exists".[2] Stalin began to build up the International Relations Sections in the CPSU Central Committee for the purpose of having in his hand a purely Russian instrument for the control of world Bolshevism.

### THE INTERNATIONAL RELATIONS SECTION (OMS)

The OMS sent special agents to the most important Sections of the Comintern to function as connecting links, and provided for communications between the ECCI and its agents in the various countries by means of a secret Apparat, which was used to convey money and instructions.[3] The OMS was also responsible for providing escorts to ensure that prominent Communist travellers reached their destinations safely. With the assistance of the OMS the ECCI directed the activities of Communist parties all over the world.

The OMS was subordinate to the ECCI's Org-Bureau, whose Head, Ossip Piatnitski, thus had the OMS organization and

---

[1]Walter Z. Laqueur, *The Soviet Union and the Middle East*, London, 1959, pp. 92 ff.; R. Jensen, *En omtumlet Tilvaerelse*, p. 81. The existence of a Far Eastern Secretariat is mentioned by Harold Isaacs, *The Tragedy of the Chinese Revolution*, p. 59, and Pavel Mif, *Heroic China*, pp. 21 ff.

[2]Boris Souvarine, *Staline*, Paris, 1935, p. 536.

[3]The word "Apparat" is used here to mean a specially selected group of functionaries operating under conditions of secrecy.

resources under his control and accordingly possessed considerable influence in the International. Three OMS agents of special interest were Jacob Mirov-Abramov, who served in Berlin from 1921 to 1930 and then became Head of the OMS; D. Petrovsky, who worked in England under the name of "Bennet"; and Henry Robinson, who was active in Paris.[1] The OMS and its representatives were never openly spoken of by the Comintern, as the OMS function, the financing of the Communist Party, was not one that could be openly admitted. Krivitsky has described how instructions and funds for Communist parties abroad were despatched by privileged diplomatic bag to the Comintern representative, who usually occupied a nominal post in the Soviet Embassy of the country concerned.[2] Mirov-Abramov, for example, belonged to the Press Department of the Soviet Embassy in Berlin and had, in 1923, when attempts to bring about a revolution in Germany were being intensified, a staff of more than 25 assistants and couriers.

The Communist parties received their allocations of funds covertly. The usual practice was for one trusted Communist to be selected to take over and look after large amounts. In Germany Wilhelm Pieck had this job for years and was followed by Leo Flieg. In South America it was the Argentinian, Vittorio Codovila, and of the Danish Communists, Richard Jensen was regarded by Moscow as particularly trustworthy.[3]

The Passport Section of the OMS was intimately concerned with the communications function of the OMS. Most of the couriers and others who had to travel on Comintern business needed passports, which were provided by the Passport Section. According to Krivitsky, this section did not manufacture passports itself, as the Soviet Secret Service did, but merely altered genuine passports by "touching them up".[4] When the OMS needed "first-class" faked passports, it could call on the

---

[1]Krivitsky, *op. cit.*, pp. 72 ff.; Ruth Fischer, *op. cit.*, p. 400. See also p. 152 below.

[2]Krivitsky, p. 71. On the OMS part in the transmission of funds, see p. 169 below.

[3]Krivitsky, p. 72; Ravines, *The Yenan Way*, p. 82; Jensen, *En omtumlet Tilvaerelse*, p. 75.

[4]Krivitsky, *op. cit.*, p. 73.

services of the passport organization of the KPD, which produced outstanding results during the heyday of the German
Apparats, from 1929 to 1933. This passport section of the
German Communist party manufactured identity documents
for a number of Comintern functionaries, such as the Swiss
Communist Paul Ruegg, who was operating for the Comintern
in the Far East under the name of Hilaire Noulens. Richard
Jensen, the Dane, also provided fake passports for Comintern
functionaries. Many clandestine Communists lived in Copenhagen after 1933, and a "passport factory" was started there as
well.[1]

For its communications with its own agencies abroad or with
national parties, the OMS relied on its courier system. In the
'thirties the International's seamen's and longshoremen's
maritime communications and shore bases were also used for
OMS purposes. From 1934–6 the OMS also made a start on
the establishment of radio links with its agencies abroad and a
few of the European national parties.[2] The most prominent
worker in this field in Western Europe was Johann Wenzel
(alias Hermann), who was trained in Moscow. Johannes Firl,
working from Paris, created a radio link for the émigré leaders
of the German Communist party from 1934 onwards. Daniel
Goulooze, also Moscow-trained, kept up radio connection with
the Comintern on behalf of the Dutch Communist party.[3]
During World War II the Comintern was in at least inter-
mittent touch with some of the Sections by radio.[4]

## THE COMMISSIONS

The ECCI created temporary or permanent Commissions for
special purposes. Originally there was no sanction for these in
the Comintern statutes, but the 6th World Congress gave
approval to the procedure the ECCI had been practising since

[1]David J. Dallin, *Soviet Espionage*, New Haven, 1955, p. 99; R. Jensen,
*Den Hellige Ko*, p. 98, and *En omtumlet Tilvaerelse*, p. 74.
[2]On the Wilson School which trained these radio operators, see p.175
below.
[3]During World War II Johann Wenzel and Daniel Goulooze worked as
radio operators for the RIS in Holland and Belgium (the so-called R.K.).
[4]*Cf. The Soviet-Yugoslav Dispute*, London and New York, 1948, p. 28, and
Dedijer, *Tito Speaks*, p. 100.

1924.[1] These Commissions were not elected but were appointed by the ECCI, and Stalin was able, thanks to his steadily increasing influence in the ECCI, to see to it that it was his adherents who were deputed to be members of them. So it came about that the Commissions became a further instrument for the weakening of the ECCI and the strengthening of the power of Stalin.

One of the *ad hoc* Commissions was the Chinese Commission, which was set up for the purpose of directing the attempted revolution in China of 1926-7.[2] As has been mentioned, Joseph S. Unschlicht, a senior GPU official and a confidant of Stalin's, was appointed as its Head. The Polish Commission of the ECCI and of the Central Committee of the CPSU had been in existence since the 5th World Congress. In 1926 it was engaged in trying to prevent Pilsudski from seizing power in Poland. Its members included Stalin, Zinoviev, Unschlicht and Dzershinski.[3] During the Spanish Civil War there was a Spanish Commission, to which Dolores Ibarruri, André Marty, Palmiro Togliatti, and Bielov and Blagoyeva, both ECCI cadre functionaries, were appointed.[4] The ECCI also established French, German, Czechoslovak and Yugoslav Commissions.[5]

### THE "PERMANENT BUREAUX" OF THE ECCI

Within a short time of its foundation the Comintern was setting up outposts in Western Europe, in those days the area of the main Comintern effort. Authority for this was contained in para. 9 of the statutes:

Where necessary, the Executive Committee shall organize technical and other auxiliary agencies in the various countries, these agencies to be completely subordinate to the Executive Committee. In fulfilling their political tasks the representa-

[1] Cf. para. 27 of the statutes adopted by the 6th Congress.
[2] See p. 102 above.
[3] Stalin, *Works*, Vol. 10, p. 4; Souvarine, *op. cit.*, p. 343.
[4] Togliatti had been in Spain, under the name of "Alfredo", as the Comintern's Chief Political Emissary. Cf. El Campesino, *op. cit.*, pp. 16 and 38; M. and M. Ferrara, *op. cit.*, p. 195. Blagoyeva has been quoted as "Blagoyev", but was probably Stella Blagoyeva, the daughter of Dimitur Blagoyev, one of the co-founders of the Bulgarian Communist Party, who died in 1924 (cf. *Handbuch des Weltbolschewismus*, p. 239).
[5] Stalin, *Works*, Vol. 7, pp. 58 and 69; Vol. 8, pp. 106 and 115.

tives of the Executive Committee shall maintain the closest contact with the Party Headquarters of the country concerned.

The Sections were obliged to carry out the instructions of the "Permanent Bureaux".[1] The statute of 1928 names the West European, the South American and the Eastern Bureaux. The South American Bureau was located in Buenos Aires in 1928 but was shortly afterwards transferred to Montevideo; and still later to Rio de Janeiro. In 1934 August Guralski held the leading position in this office, and he was followed by the Czech Frederick Glaubauf.[2] The Bureau was dissolved in 1935 after the failure of the attempted Communist revolution in Brazil.

A South-East Bureau was set up in Vienna, where it published the weekly paper, *Kommunismus*.[3] This South-East Bureau was the forerunner of the Balkan Bureau, which was located in Sofia and later in Vienna. After the 1st World Congress, acting on Lenin's instructions, the Dutch Communist Sebald J. Rutgers set up the "Provisional Amsterdam Bureau of the Communist International". In 1920 this Bureau organized a conference in Amsterdam, attended by Communists from Germany, England, Switzerland, Belgium, Holland and the USA (Louis C. Fraina). Michael Borodin attended on behalf of the Soviet party. In his *Left-Wing Communism* Lenin criticized the Bureau for its "miserable" sentiments on parliamentarism, which had been the subject of discussion at the conference.[4] The Amsterdam Bureau was dissolved after being in existence only three months.[5] At about the same time, in 1919, J. Thomas and Mieczislaw Warszawski organized a West European Bureau for the Comintern in Berlin, although in its early stages

[1] Cf. paras 20 and 21 of the 1928 statutes.

[2] Robert J. Alexander, *Communism in Latin America*, New Brunswick, 1957, pp. 35 ff.; Ravines, *op. cit.*, p. 79. Guralski worked for the Comintern in Germany from 1921 to 1923 (see p. 69 above).

[3] *Die Kommunistische Internationale*, No. 12 (1920), p. 364.

[4] Lenin, *Selected Works*, Vol. II, p. 599; also Lazich, *op. cit.*, p. 138, and *Die Kommunistische Internationale*, No. 12, p. 52; D. Shub, *Lenin*, New York, 1948, p. 349. Also Theodore Draper, *The Roots of American Communism*, New York, 1957, p. 235.

[5] Lazich, *op. cit.*, p. 138; *Die Kommunistische Internationale*, No. 12, p. 52.

the Bureau only produced propaganda material.[1] The work of the bureaux set up in the early days of the Comintern suffered from the lack of regular and speedy communication with the Soviet Union, due to the blockade by the "interventionist" Powers. Equally short-lived was the "Central Asian Bureau", which was set up in Tashkent at about the time of the 1st Congress of Eastern Peoples (see p. 61). The staff included M. N. Roy, Georgi Safarov and M. Sokolnikov. It was in Tashkent in those heady days that Roy tried to set up an "army" for the liberation of India. In 1921, however, when the Soviets lost interest in Central Asia, this Bureau was also closed down.[2]

The Comintern had also set up an outpost in Irkutsk, the so-called Irkutsk Bureau, which was intended to foster Soviet interests by co-operating with the Chinese Generals in control of North China—the policy known as the "Irkutsk line".[3] The Irkutsk Bureau ceased to be important when the Dutch Communist Henryk Sneevliet (alias Maring) and Ambassador Adolf Joffe took up contact with Sun Yat Sen on behalf of the Comintern and when this led to Michael Borodin's being despatched to China.[4] The Far East Bureau, at first located in Khabarovsk and later in Vladivostok, had a branch in Shanghai. This branch played an important part in the direction of Comintern activities in East and South-East Asia in the late 1920s. The Far East Bureau received instructions and funds through, *inter alia*, the West European Bureau in Berlin. The Comintern's operations in the trade unions in East and South-East Asia were under the control of the Pan-Pacific Trade Union Secretariat (PPTUS), which was founded in Hankow at a conference which included Salomon A. Losovski, the Profintern functionary, and the American Communist Earl Browder.[5]

[1]Ruth Fischer, *op. cit.*, p. 134, note 18. One of Warszawski's pseudonyms was "Bronski", the name under which he published the *"Kommunistische Rätekorrespondenz"* (Susanne Leonhard *op. cit.*, p. 205).

[2]Gene D. Overstreet and Marshal Windmiller, *Communism in India*, Berkeley and Los Angeles, 1959, pp. 34 ff.

[3]Isaacs, *The Tragedy of the Chinese Revolution*, pp. 61 ff. and 377.

[4]See p. 100 above.

[5]Charles A. Willoughby, *Shanghai Conspiracy*, New York, 1952, pp. 302 ff.

It was decided that the headquarters of the PPTUS should be in Shanghai.

Browder was also the Political Secretary of the Far East Bureau until he left Shanghai in 1929 or 1930, when his place was taken by Gerhard Eisler, the German Communist. Working alongside Eisler as Organization Secretary was Paul Ruegg, the Swiss, who operated in Shanghai from 1930 until June 1931, when he was arrested, a mishap which came about because his address was found among the papers of Joseph Ducroux when Ducroux was arrested in Singapore.

There was also, for a few months in 1930, an Asiatic Bureau in Hong Kong, responsible for Malaya, Indo-China, Thailand, Burma, the Netherlands East Indies and Australia.[1]

The bureaux located in Shanghai were forced to put a stop to their activities in 1931, when the Japanese occupied Shanghai. The Vietnamese Ho Chi-Minh played an outstanding part in the ECCI's control of these East Asiatic Comintern bureaux.

### THE WEST EUROPEAN BUREAU (WEB)

In the course of time, the modest propaganda agency set up by Warszawski and Thomas, which was re-established in 1928 and was located in Berlin until 1933, became the largest of all the branch agencies and the most important Comintern communications centre outside Moscow.[2] Disguised as the *"Führer-Verlag"*, it had its headquarters in Wilhelmstrasse and employed a number of "instructors", translators and office staff.[3] From 1930 onwards the agency was controlled by Georgi Dimitroff, who had at his disposal a large number of covert addresses and meeting places. Richard Gyptner, at one time an associate of Dimitroff in the WEB, wrote about the Berlin years, on the occasion of the seventy-fifth birthday of this "soldier of the proletarian revolution":[4]

[1]Harry Miller, *The Communist Menace in Malaya*, New York, 1942, pp. 23, 26.
[2]*Internationale Presse-Korrespondenz*, Berlin, 1928, p. 547; also Brandt and Löwenthal, *Ernst Reuter*, Brunswick, 1957, p. 130.
[3]Jan Valtin, *op. cit.*, p. 166.
[4]Cf. *Neues Deutschland*, East Berlin, 18 June 1957, p. 4. Prior to 1930 Gyptner was employed in the Communist Youth International and in the ECCI and is now Deputy Foreign Minister of the "DDR" (East Zone of Germany). The Foreign Service of the DDR employs a number of former Comintern functionaries, such as Sepp Schwab and Jonny Löhr.

During this period, Dimitroff, who lived for some years in Berlin, supported the work of the West European Communist parties with valuable advice. He developed particularly close friendships with Comrades Thälmann and Pieck.

It is not known for certain how many departments the West European Bureau had, but there were almost certainly more than the four which remained in the subsequent Copenhagen days, when there were departments for policy (Head: Otto Kuusinen, Finland), Organization (Head: Ernst Wollweber, Germany), Finance (Head: Richard Jensen, Denmark), and Counter Espionage (the 'S' Apparat, headed by Michael Avatin, Latvia). It was a truly international crew and they worked in Copenhagen under the guise of being an architectural and engineering agency, A. Salvo & Co., in the office block of Vesterport.[1]

Richard Krebs did not exaggerate when he wrote that the WEB's writ ran "from Iceland to Capetown". There is no doubt that all revolutionary activity in Western Europe and Scandinavia was directed from this Berlin agency. Sufficient proof of this is given by the "instructor" commissions Richard Krebs fulfilled in England, France, Denmark, Norway and Sweden on behalf of the Seamen's and Port Workers' International, which was subordinate to the WEB. In its role as a liaison point, the WEB's lines were even more widely spread. For example, as already mentioned, money intended for the Far East Bureau in Shanghai was sent by way of the OMS Liaison Department in the WEB in Berlin.

The Comintern's German policy ran aground in 1933 and the WEB had to be moved. It was split up, with one part being transferred to Paris and the remainder going to Copenhagen, where the records and files were also sent.[2] This action provided an example of how well the activities of the Bureau had been disguised all these years. While the Communist Party's Karl Liebknecht House was thought to be the headquarters of the revolutionary movement and was accordingly occupied by the police, Comintern agents were able to remove the WEB's

---

[1]Jan Valtin, *op. cit.*, pp. 166, 534 and 555, speaks of the Berlin Bureau having a dozen departments.
[2]On the Paris office, see p. 164 below.

confidential papers from the secret addresses where they had been stored, and had taken them to Copenhagen.[1] How little the Berlin police knew about the activities of the WEB is illustrated by the fact that during the trial of Dimitroff in connection with the Reichstag Fire, no mention was made of his function as Head of the WEB.[2] In fact the police only discovered that Dimitroff was in Berlin as the result of a tip-off given by a waiter, although he had been "working" in Berlin for three whole years.[3] Dimitroff told the Court that it was only to avoid threatened assassination by his Bulgarian political adversaries that he had lived in Germany under the names of Dr Schaafsma and Dr Hediger and had not registered with the police. In his evidence he said:[4]

> Regarding my activities in Germany. I repeat my statement of 20 March that while in Germany I have been engaged on the study of Bulgarian questions and on my Bulgarian literary work, chiefly concerning the position of political émigrés, a campaign for a political amnesty in Bulgaria and so forth.
>
> The texts of the appeal by the Communist International

[1] Jan Valtin, *op. cit.*, p. 319.

[2] The opinion held by many German émigrés, though unsupported by hard facts, that there was an agreement between the Gestapo and the OGPU to release Dimitroff (see Ruth Fischer, *op. cit.*, pp. 308–309, note 2) seems to have been disproved by the statements of the then Head of the Prussian Gestapo. Cf. Rudolf Diels, in his book *Lucifer Ante Portas* (Stuttgart, 1950, pp. 370 ff.). Diels' version gains support from Dimitroff's letter of 7 February 1934 to the then Reich Minister of Interior, Dr Frick, reprinted in Dimitroff's *Reichstagbrandprozess* (Berlin, 1946), p. 164. If Krivitsky (*op. cit.*, p. 67) says Dimitroff's bold and skilful tactics before the Nazi Court in Leipzig, "where he succeeded in fixing the guilt on the Nazis themselves, made him the Communist hero of the day", this at least does not contradict Diels' version. See also the report in *Braunbuch* II (Paris, 1934), p. 292, according to which the Soviet Government granted Dimitroff, Popoff and Taneff Soviet citizenship on 15 February 1934, whereupon the Soviet Ambassador in Berlin demanded the release of the acquitted.

[3] Details of Dimitroff's life at this time are given by M. Buber-Neumann, *Von Potsdam nach Moskau*, pp. 136 ff.

[4] Cf. Dimitroff's letter of 30 May 1933 to the judicial investigating authority, in Dimitroff's book, *Reichstagsbrandprozess*, p. 23. Diels (*op. cit.*, p. 185) believes that his Department IA was well informed on Communist illegal operations, but this is contradicted by the fact that, at least during the Reichstag Fire trial, no evidence was produced as to Dimitroff's activities as leader of the WEB which would support Diels' claim. (Cf. also Dallin, *Soviet Espionage*, p. 120.)

and the appeal for an international anti-Fascist Workers' Congress which were published in the *International Press Correspondence* and in the Communist Press all over the world, were sent to me by the Imprecorr editorial office for my information.

The first time I saw the KPD Press notice about the Reichstag fire-raisers was when the examining Magistrate showed it to me. I had never had and never read anything of this kind before.

Regarding my political associations in Germany. I was in touch with the editorial office of the *International Press Correspondence*, which published my articles on Bulgaria regarding the political amnesty and other things. I have also been in touch with the *International Workers' Relief* from time to time in connection with various matters to do with Bulgarian sections of that organization. In matters concerning Bulgarian political émigrés, I have had occasional contact when necessary with the International Secretariat of the Red Relief. For my work in Germany I did not need any other connections at all.

I am personally acquainted with leading German Communists who took part in the various Congresses of the Communist International and made public appearances in Moscow while I was there, such as Thälmann, Heckert and Pieck.

If it had been stated and proved to the Reich High Court that Dimitroff, as the Head of the West European Bureau, had been making preparations for armed insurrection on behalf of the Comintern ever since 1930, the High Court would certainly have found him guilty and sentenced him,[1] and it would not have been necessary to fabricate the patently unfounded charge that he had been one of those responsible for the Reichstag Fire.

The Comintern had had a subsidiary office in Paris since 1930 to assist in its work in Western Europe. This Paris office served as a post-office for international instructors and as a rendezvous for couriers, and was probably the most important

[1]During the trial Dimitroff claimed that the immediate task of the KPD at the time of the Reichstag Fire was in no way an armed revolt as part of the struggle for power (Dimitroff, *Briefe u. Aufzeichnungen aus der Zeit der Haft und des Leipziger Prozesses*, Paris, 1935, p. 107).

F

OMS agency in Europe, apart from the WEB.[1] This office, situated in the Rue de Seine, was skilfully directed by Roger Walter Ginsburger. After 1933 Paris became increasingly important for the Comintern, not only because it gave shelter to the so-called "Auslandsleitung" (the émigré leaders) of the KPD, hitherto the most important non-Russian party, but also because of the prominence of the successes of the French party, e.g. in the Popular Front. In those days Communists actively engaged on Comintern work in Paris included the Italian Luigi Longo, alias Gallo, the Hungarian Magyar, the German Adolf Deter, alias Maurice, and the Belgian Henry Robinson. Paris developed into an important meeting place for international Communists.[2] At the time of the Reichstag Fire trial and the World Anti-Fascist Congress, there were meetings in Ginsburger's home between leading German Communists— including Wilhelm Pieck, Bernard Koenen and Hermann Remmele—which left some of the participants with the impression that Wilhelm Pieck was so keen to become the leader of the Party that he would not have objected to seeing Ernst Thälmann remain in gaol and Ernest Wollweber continue with the Party work in Germany. The prospects of Thälmann's release were meagre and Wollweber's clandestine activities were almost certain to lead to his being caught.[3]

It was not only the German Communists who used to meet in Paris. The city was also of considerable importance for the South American parties and remained so until after the World War II.[4]

## INTERNATIONAL MASS ORGANIZATIONS

A number of international Communist mass organizations were closely connected with the Comintern. Among them were

[1]See p. 164 below.

[2]Jan Valtin, *op. cit.*, p. 575. On the end of Magyar, see Ravines, *op. cit.*, p. 314; Ruth Fischer, *op. cit.*, p. 308, note 2. The so-called Berne Conference of the KPD of 1939 also took place in Paris.

[3]Valtin, p. 380; M. Buber-Neumann, *Potsdam-Moskau*, pp. 256 ff. Some of these participants will have remembered how Wilhelm Pieck was treated by the members of the Guards Mounted Rifle Division, in contrast to the treatment of Rosa Luxemburg and Karl Leibknecht, who were arrested at the same time (see p. 37 above, note 3).

[4]Valtin, p. 155; Robert J. Alexander, *op. cit.*, p. 21: Ravines, *op. cit.*, pp. 25 ff.

the Red Trade Union International (Profintern), the Communist Youth International, the Women's Section and the International Red Relief (MOPR).[1]

## THE RED TRADE UNION INTERNATIONAL (PROFINTERN)

In July–August 1919 the International Federation of Trade Unions was re-established in Amsterdam. The Soviet Communists were always in bitter opposition to this "yellow" Amsterdam Trade Union International from the beginning. In the summer of 1920, Communist representatives of English, Italian, Bulgarian, French and Serbian trade unions, while on a visit to Russia, agreed with Soviet trade unionists on the formation of a new international organization of revolutionary trade unions.[2] The 2nd World Congress of the Comintern (July–August 1920) resolved in para. 14 of the statutes that the "Communist-based Trade Union International, combined under the leadership of the Communist International, should form a Trade Union Section of the Comintern". The first Congress of the Red Trade Union International (Profintern) finally took place from 3 to 19 July 1921.[3] The Profintern membership consisted of delegates sent by revolutionary trade unions of the various countries. In the 1920s, for example, the Spanish trade unionist Andrés Nin belonged to the Secretariat of the Profintern, which included in the '30s the German Communists Max Maddalena and Fritz Emmerich. The Trade Union Section was also represented in the ECCI, in which the role of its representative, S. A. Losovski, was of little importance.

The Profintern had no noticeable influence on the policies of the Comintern. Indeed, its history from its inception until

---

[1] This list is by no means exhaustive, for there also appeared: The Red Sport International, the Red Farmers' International, the International Workers' Relief, the Red Children's International, the Society of Friends of the Soviet Union, the Red Teachers' International, the International of Proletarian Freethinkers and the International League against War and Fascism.

[2] A. Losovski, *Amsterdam-Moskau-London*, Hamburg, 1921, pp. 14 ff., and A. Rosmer, *op. cit.*, pp. 188 ff. See also Borkenau, *The Communist International*, p. 196. The Profintern also founded a Central European Bureau in Berlin (see Brandt and Löwenthal, *Ernst Reuter*, p. 186).

[3] *The Communist International 1919-1943, Documents*, edited by Jane Degras, Vol. I, 1958, pp. 185, 274.

its dissolution shows how closely the Profintern was influenced by alterations in Comintern policies. When the Comintern was following a "left-wing" course, the Profintern had to try to divide the "yellow" trade unions. If the course was changed in a "right-wing" direction, as in the "United Front" policy, the Profintern was itself faced with dissolution, since the basis of the "right-wing" trade union policy was the attainment of ascendancy over the "yellow" trade unions from within them, which was hardly compatible with the existence of separate "red" trade unions.

After the Second World Congress, when the Comintern's "left-wing" policy reached its first climax, the Profintern did what they could to split the "yellow" trade unions. This attempt failed just as badly as the concurrent "left-wing" revolutionary efforts by the Comintern.[1] The swing to the right subsequently undertaken in the trade union sphere, e.g. in "International Trade Union Unity" and the Anglo-Russian Trade Union Commission, put the Profintern in danger of dissolution.[2] When the "left-wing" course was resumed after 1929, the Profintern revived again and in token of the change of direction the Seamen's and Port Workers' International (ISH) was founded. This "maritime" section was soon to become the most important in the Profintern. The important Far East Branch Office of the Profintern, the Pan Pacific Trade Union Secretariat (PPTUS), has already been mentioned.[3] Finally, at the subsequent high point of the "right-wing" policy during the "Popular Front" period, the Profintern was dissolved.[4]

The "traditions" of the *Red Trade Union International* were taken over by the World Federation of Trade Unions, founded in Paris on 3 October 1945.[5]

[1]See p. 64 above.
[2]Rosenberg, *op. cit.*, pp. 213 ff.; Borkenau, *op. cit.*, p. 279. See also p. 97 above.
[3]p. 141 above.
[4]Borkenau, *European Communism*, p. 223; Stalin, *Works*, Vol. 6, p. 434, note 63.
[5]Whose programme was reproduced in *Internationale Arbeiterbewegung und allgemeine Geschichte*, required reading in the Karl Marx Party High School of the Central Committee of the SED, Berlin, 1955, Vol. II, p. 321.

THE SEAMEN'S AND PORT WORKERS' INTERNATIONAL (ISH)

This "maritime" section of the Profintern was founded in 1931 at a conference held in Hamburg, its first president being an Englishman, George Hardy. Seamen and port workers were in a position to cause considerable damage to the enemies of the Comintern, the "imperialist powers", if they brought maritime and harbour traffic to a stand-still, and the ECCI was keen, by providing money and capable staff, to foster the development of the ISH, which was joined by seamen and port workers in the most important seaports.

The Profintern sent a leading and capable instructor, the Pole "Adolf", to Hamburg, where the General Secretariat was located and where he worked in close collaboration with Albert Walter, the General Secretary of the ISH. When Albert Walter was arrested by the Gestapo in 1933 and the ISH was transferred to Copenhagen (and later to Paris), Ernst Wollweber took over the command.[1]

Apart from the General Secretariat, there were in Hamburg a Japanese Section, a Chinese Section, a Scandinavian Bureau and a Latvian Section.[2] The Indonesian Section was in Marseilles (Rue Fauchier 10). This was headed for a time by Le Minter, whom Richard Krebs met in Antwerp.[3]

The importance of the ISH lay not only in the many strikes it engineered with the assistance of its skilled agents in many countries,[4] but also—and perhaps more important—in the fact that the ISH communications system, the ISH's many sections in ports and on board ships and among crews, provided a ready-made courier system. This network was possibly the most important overseas means of communication the Comintern possessed in the 1930s, and was used for the smuggling of propaganda material and human cargo from country to country. This led during this period to close co-operation be-

[1] Jan Valtin, *op. cit.*, p. 351; Richard Jensen, *Den Hellige Ko*, p. 42, and *En omtumlet Tilvaerelse*, p. 104 (Wollweber in Copenhagen), p. 105 (Transfer to Paris). Jensen gives "Adolf" the surname of "Schelley". One of "Adolf's" cover names was Adolf or Alfred Bem. He was a Pole. Regarding his end, see p. 189, note 3. Albert Walter was a Deutsche Partei (German Party) member of the Federal Bundestag in Bonn until 1957.

[2] Valtin, *op. cit.*, p. 249.     [3] *Ibid.*, p. 572.

[4] Jan Valtin, for example—*op. cit.*, pp. 233 ff. and 352.

tween the ISH and the OMS, which was responsible for Comintern communications.

After the 7th Comintern World Congress, the method of trying to take over the "yellow" trade unions through the "red" unions was abandoned and the ISH was accordingly dissolved. However, its communications system in the German and Scandinavian ports retained its extreme importance, for example in the building up of the Wollweber organization.[1]

## THE RED YOUTH INTERNATIONAL

During World War I some Socialist youth organizations had already been tending towards the radical anti-war policies of the Bolsheviks, as was evidenced at the Berne International Socialist Youth Congress and at the Zimmerwald Conference. The Berne Congress decided to publish a periodical, to be called *Jugendinternationale*. The editor of this paper was also the secretary of the *International Association of Socialist Youth Organizations*, Willi Münzenberg.[2]

This international youth work was continued after the First World War. On 20 November 1919, delegates from 14 countries, representing some 250,000 members, took part in an international youth congress in Berlin.[3] These delegates, described by Münzenberg as the active nucleus of the Berne Youth International, decided to transform the *International Association of Socialist Youth Organizations* into the *Communist Youth International*, which was to belong to the Comintern.[4] Youth organizations of Switzerland, Sweden, Norway, Spain, Austria, Rumania and the Soviet Union joined the Comintern after the 1st World

[1] Jensen, *En omtumlet Tilvaerelse*, p. 75, and *Den Hellige Ko*, pp. 12 ff.; D. J. Dallin, *Soviet Espionage*, pp. 127 ff. One of Wollweber's most valuable assistants was the Dutchman Schaap (Joseph Rimbertus), who had run the "Interklub" for the ISH in Rotterdam in 1932. Michael Avatin (Ernst Lambert) was called as a witness in the trial before the German People's Court which followed Schaap's arrest.

[2] See p. 34 above and Hermann Weber in the periodical *SBZ-Archiv*, 1958, No. 18, p. 289. Also *Deutschlands Junge Garde*, published by the Central Council of the FDJ (Freie Deutsche Jugend, Free German Youth), Berlin, 1954, p. 12—a "work" that completely suppresses any mention of Willi Münzenberg.

[3] *Die Kommunistische Internationale*, No. 12 (1920), pp. 332 ff., and W. Münzenberg, *Die Dritte Front*, Berlin, 1930, p. 293.

[4] Münzenberg, *op. cit.*, pp. 299 ff., 294 and 303.

Congress. Article 15 of the Comintern statutes laid down that the Youth International should have a voting representative in the ECCI. The 4th World Congress decided to include in the Presidium of the expanded Executive Committee a voting youth representative.

The Communist Youth International had its headquarters in Berlin, where it maintained secret offices. It attempted to build up its own organization for the purpose of ensuring reliable communications with the organizations affiliated to it.[1] Sub-secretariats were set up in various countries. From the very beginning the Communists tried hard to build up the Youth International into a mass movement, for which purpose they started the Sport International in 1921.[2]

The Communist Youth International never achieved the degree of influence that might have been expected in view of the attitude of large sections of the young people of those days. Able Communists who were active in the Youth International soon moved to other spheres. Its gifted founder, Willi Münzenberg, gave up youth work in the summer of 1921.[3] Leo Flieg, who started off by collaborating with Münzenberg in the Youth International, ended by occupying an important position in the organization in Germany and was one of Kippenberg's representatives among the leaders of the A.M.-Apparat. In this capacity, Flieg lived in Paris from 1935 to 1937, when he was called to Moscow, where he disappeared without trace.[4] At the 2nd World Congress of the Comintern, Münzenberg and Lazar A. Shatskin, who was Secretary of the Central Committee of the Komsomol, attended as delegates of the Youth International. At the 15th and 16th Party Congresses of the CPSU in 1927 and 1930, Shatskin was elected a member of the Central

---

[1] *Die Kommunistische Internationale*, No. 12 (1920), p. 332.

[2] W. Z. Foster, *History of the Three Internationals*, p. 294. The same purpose is served today, with tactical changes to conform with present-day conditions, by the World Youth Festivals.

[3] See p. 185 below (Agit-Prop activities) and Ruth Fischer, *op. cit.*, pp. 221 and 611; M. Buber-Neumann, *Potsdam-Moskau*, pp. 179 ff; Münzenberg, *Die Dritte Front*, pp. 346 and 348. In his book *History of the Three Internationals*, the American Communist W. Z. Foster calls Münzenberg an opportunist who insinuated himself into the Communist movement.

[4] Münzenberg, *Die Dritte Front*, p. 346; M. Buber-Neumann, *op. cit.*, p. 203.

Revision Commission. He aligned himself with the oppositional attitude of Lominadse and in 1936, when he was arrested in connection with the case against Zinoviev, he committed suicide.[1] Another leading functionary of the Youth International, the German Richard Schüller, was never heard of again after the purges.[2] Stanislav Hubermann, a brother of the violinist Bronislav Hubermann, was also active in the Youth International. In about 1926 he joined in the underground activity of the Polish party. In 1933 the ECCI sent him to Germany to advise the KPD in its underground work. He fell into disfavour in 1935 and finally lost his life in an aircraft accident.[3]

Besso Lominadse and Heinz Neumann, who probably met in Moscow while on Youth International business there, also gave up youth work within a short time. In 1923 Neumann began to operate in the KPD subversive organization, although frequent journeys to Moscow kept him in close touch with the Comintern and with Lominadse. In 1927 both of them, being regarded as loyal adherents of Stalin, were sent to Canton, and were in due course held to be responsible for the failure of the revolt there.[4] Lominadse joined the Opposition forces. He was removed from political work in 1930 and committed suicide after the murder of Kirov, while Neumann fell a victim to the purges.[5]

Henry Robinson was also concerned with the Youth International in the early 1920s. From 1930 to 1936 he was an OMS representative based in Paris and responsible for France, Switzerland and Great Britain. Later on, Robinson was closely connected with the Russian Intelligence Service, a connection which, in 1942, led to his falling into the hands of the Gestapo as a result of Leon Trapper's revealing his connection with Robinson after his arrest.[6]

---

[1] Cf. Ignazio Silone's contribution to *The God that Failed*, London, 1950, p. 108.
[2] Jane Degras, *The Communist International 1919-1943*, Documents, Vol. I, pp. 454 and 455.
[3] Krivitsky, pp. 84 ff.
[4] M. Buber-Neumann, *Potsdam-Moskau*, pp. 193 ff. Isaacs, *op. cit.*, p. 283, quotes a "self-criticism" by Lominadse.
[5] Buber-Neumann, *Potsdam-Moskau*, p. 234; *Ostprobleme*, 1951, p. 353.
[6] D. J. Dallin, *Soviet Espionage*, pp. 157 and 165.

In the final years of its existence, the Youth International ceased to be active and only a few secretaries, such as Michael Wolf and Raymond Guyot, remained. When the Germans were drawing near to Moscow in the autumn of 1941, it was transferred to Ufa, along with the Comintern, and was there dissolved. Unlike the Comintern, the Youth International did not retain offices in Moscow for the winding-up of its affairs.[1]

After 1945 the task of the Communist Youth International —that is, to attract young people all over the world to the Communist cause[2]—was taken over by the World Federation of Democratic Youth, which was founded in London on 7 November 1945.

### THE WOMEN'S SECTION OF THE COMINTERN
### (INTERNATIONAL OF COMMUNIST WOMEN)

As early as the nineteenth century the Socialists had realized how important it was to win over the women to their cause. Social Democratic policies were in step with contemporary popular opinion in demanding female suffrage and equality of the sexes. August Bebel's book *Women and Socialism*, published in the 1880s, had an enormous sale.[3] As early as 1889, at the foundation of the Second International, Clara Zetkin had championed the view that there could be "no final victory of the revolution without the women". The 1st World Congress had laid it down as "the imperative task of all parties affiliated to the Communist International to do their utmost to win over proletarian women".[4] In article 16 of the statutes, the 2nd World Congress put upon the ECCI the job of organizing a Women's Section. Clara Zetkin became the first Secretary General of the International of Communist Women and headed the "International Women's Secretariat", with headquarters in

---

[1]Delgado, *op. cit.*, p. 230; see also p. 205 below.

[2]On the programme, see *Die Kommunistische Jugendinternationale*, Vol. 13, p. 230.

[3]August Bebel, *Die Frau und der Sozialismus*, 147–151st thousand, Stuttgart, 1919.

[4]Resolution of the 1st World Congress "on the need to recruit women helpers for the fight for Socialism". Library of the Communist International, Vol. 7, pp. 68 ff.

Moscow.[1] When Clara Zetkin attended congresses of the French Party in Tours (1920) and of the Italian Party in Leghorn (1921) on behalf of the Comintern, she suggested that Communist women's organizations should be formed in these countries.[2] She was also Chairman of the Red League of Women and Girls, which was founded in Germany at the end of 1925.[3] Every year there was an International Women's Day, which was celebrated, on the suggestion of Clara Zetkin, to keep alive the tradition of Socialist women.[4]

Nevertheless these beginnings never led to the growth of any large-scale women's movement. The few other women who played a part in Comintern affairs, such as Alexandra Kollontai, Angelica Balabanova and Ruth Fischer, were concerned more with basic questions of policy and organization than with women's affairs.

After World War II, the International Federation of Democratic Women, founded in Paris on 2 December 1945, adopted the idea of an international "democratic" women's movement.

### THE INTERNATIONAL RED RELIEF (IRR OR MOPR)[5]

The International Red Relief, a Comintern creation, had its birth in the Soviet Union in about 1923, and formed numerous international sections under the guise of an "independent

[1] *Die Kommunistische Internationale*, No. 19, 2nd year, p 203, and Clara Zetkin, *Zur Geschichte der proletarischen Frauenbewegung Deutschlands*, Berlin, 1958, p 230.

[2] Hanna Ilberg, *Clara Zetkin*, Berlin, 1956, pp. 17 ff., and G. Walter, *Histoire du PCF*, p. 42.

[3] Ruth Fischer, *op. cit.*, p. 608.

[4] The proposal to celebrate 10 March as International Women's Day was first adopted at the 2nd International Conference of Socialist Women (Copenhagen 1910). Clara Zetkin, *op. cit.*, p. 219, and Elli Schmidt, *40 Jahre Internationaler Frauentag*, Berlin, 1950, p. 30.

[5] MOPR is the abbreviation of the Russian name of this organization (Mezhdunarodnaya organisaziya pomoshchi bortsam revolyutsii). It differed from the International Workers' Relief (IWR), founded in 1921, by reason of its purpose. The original purpose of the International Workers' Relief was to collect funds for the relief of the needy Russian people. This purpose was soon extended and the IWR was shortly afterwards claiming to be a non-party organization of the proletariat everywhere, ready to go into action and assist in cases of large-scale economic mass struggles and natural disasters. (Willi Münzenberg, *Für Brot und Freiheit, Die Aufgaben und das Ziel der Internationalen Arbeiterhilfe*, Berlin, 1931, p. 19.) See also p. 185 below (Agit-Prop).

relief organization not connected with the parties".[1] As early as 1927, as an "independent" organization, it had its own offices outside the Soviet Union, e.g. the "Central European Bureau of the IRR", under the chairmanship of the German Communist Eugen Schönhaar.[2] Clara Zetkin was the President of the IRR for many years and was followed by a Russian woman, Yelena Stassova.[3] The IRR proclaimed its aim to be "to accord assistance to all victims of the revolutionary struggle".[4] As it also recruited non-Communists, the Comintern regarded it as a suitable instrument of the United Front policy.[5] It was in connection with relief for the victims of Fascism and international Socialism that the IRR's public activities achieved the greatest importance. After 1933, when thousands of emigrants from Germany stood in need of help, the IRR maintained a network of relief agencies all over the world and also in the Soviet Union.[6] At the 7th World Congress, Dimitroff criticized the work of the IRR as inadequate and Stassova was replaced as President by Bogdanov.[7]

The activities of the IRR were not confined to charitable work. The Communists also made use of this widespread network of bases for their clandestine purposes, e.g. helping members of Communist Apparats who had got into difficulties. M. Buber-Neumann, for example, has described how the leader of the Swiss Red Relief arranged for her to be smuggled across the frontier into France in 1934.[8] The IRR was also concerned with the selection and transporting of volunteers for the Spanish Civil War.[9] In its Paris office it had dealing with this aspect the German Communists Hans Beimler (who was later killed in the Spanish war) and Siegfried Rädel. Nor, after 1924, did the German Red Relief confine itself to charitable activities in respect of arrested Communists or their

[1]*Protokoll des VI. Weltkongresses*, Vol. IV, Hamburg 1928, p. 208.
[2]Johannes Zelt, *Proletarischer Internationalismus in Kampf um Sacco und Vanzetti*, E. Berlin, 1958, p. 33.
[3]Hanna Ilberg, *Clara Zetkin*, p. 201.
[4]*Protokoll des VI. Weltkongresses*, Vol. IV, p. 205.        [5]*Ibid.*, p. 205.
[6]Buber-Neumann, *Potsdam-Moskau*, pp. 389, 397, 398; S. Leonhard, *op. cit.*, p. 25; and Wolfgang Leonhard, *Child of the Revolution*, London, 1957, pp. 164 ff.
[7]Delgado, *op. cit.*, p. 59.        [8]Buber-Neumann, *op. cit.*, p. 389.
[9]Krivitsky, *op. cit.*, p. 113.

relatives. For years it was engaged in arranging for Communists who had committed illegal acts to escape the clutches of the law.[1] In the Cheka trial, the examining magistrate, Landes-gerichtsdirektor Vogt, gave evidence that on 4 July 1924 he had initiated searches in the Reichstag and in the Prussian Landtag. The material that the Communist deputies had kept there demonstrated that the Red Relief for years regarded it as its job to help persons wanted by the police for crimes and offences by providing them with forged papers and to get them out of the reach of the law.[2] In this the Red Relief worked in close contact with the illegal sections of the KPD and especially with the forged passports section.

Communists played a part in the framing of the present-day International Association of Democratic Lawyers, which may be described as carrying on a part of the tasks of the IRR. National organizations still correspond to the national sections of the IRR today. In Germany, for example, the Central Council for the Protection of Democratic Rights has the job of looking after political prisoners and their relatives. In this work the functionaries of this organization have not scrupled to use illicit methods, as was stated by the Federal Supreme Court in its judgment of 20 May 1958 in the case of Dr Mertens and others (I. St-7/57).

### THE COMINTERN'S METHODS

In *Left-Wing Communism* Lenin had recommended Communist parties to combine legal methods with the illegal.[3] Regarding this, No. 3 of the *21 Conditions* said:

In almost every country in Europe and in America, the class struggle is entering on a phase of civil war. In such conditions the Communists can have no confidence in bourgeois legality. It is their duty to create a parallel illegal organiza-tion everywhere, which, at the decisive moment, will help

[1] *Die Kommunistische Partei in der Rechtsprechung des Staatsgerichts zum Schutz der Republik und des Reichsgerichts*, Stuttgart, 1925, p. 76.
[2] Dr Arthur Brandt, *Der Tschekaprozess*, Berlin, 1925, pp. 56 ff.
[3] For example in Lenin, *Selected Works*, Vol. II, p. 629. See also the Section "Über die Verbindung der legalen und illegalen Arbeit" in "*Leitsätze über den organisationischen Aufbau der Kommunistischen Parteien, über die Methoden und den Inhalt ihrer Arbeit*", adopted by the 3rd World Congress on *12 July 1921* (Library of the Communist International, Hamburg, 1921, Vol. 23, p. 138).

the Party to fulfil its obligations towards the revolution. In every country in which the state of siege and emergency laws make it impossible for the Communists to carry on their work legally, it is absolutely essential for them to combine legal and illegal activity.

To regard the words "legal" and "illegal" as equivalent to "lawful" and "unlawful" would be to misunderstand both Bolshevist semantics and Bolshevist practice. It would be more correct to substitute "overt" for "legal" and "clandestine" or "conspiratorial" for "illegal", although it must be remembered that not all of the Comintern's overt work was lawful. Thus their statutes, published to the whole world, and proclaiming that Communists were to fight "with weapons in their hands for the creation of an international soviet republic", definitely contained an unlawful intention. *Per contra*, not all clandestine Bolshevist activity was unlawful (for example, the financing of the "Sections", which was almost universally done by conspiratorial means; or the transmission of ECCI instructions to a Communist party by means of the OMS organization even when the Communist party was perfectly legal).

The essential features of the overt working methods of the ECCI and the World Congresses have already been touched on. Summarizing, one sees the following picture. The World Congress was only able to function as the "supreme organ" of the International until about 1922. Thereafter the ECCI began to take the decisions on "the most important questions of the programme and of policy". This development began, even while Lenin was still alive, with the ECCI's United Front theses of December 1921 and ended in 1935 at the 7th World Congress, which simply ratified what had already been put into effect—the Popular Front policy. Due to the steadily increasing influence of the CPSU in the ECCI, this international organ's powers of decision were also diminished. When Stalin had brought the CPSU under his control, he also controlled the International. A visible sign of the completion of this process was the extravagant ovation the 7th World Congress accorded Stalin. There are a number of parallels to these developments. Discussion at the 1st and 2nd Congresses was completely unhindered. At the 4th Congress, some "left-wing" speakers were still able to criticize the United Front policy, although this later led to their expulsion. For the delegates to the 7th World Congress there was no sign of unfettered discussion. The practice, begun in 1934, of summoning World Congresses at great intervals (1924–1928–1935) was contrary to the Comintern statutes but was a reflection of the real power situation. When Stalin summoned no congresses at all after 1935, he completely ignored the statutes. He exercised his dominion over the Comintern by infiltrating his "own" people (CPSU functionaries and OGPU officials) into its organization.[1]

### THE DIVISION OF RESPONSIBILITIES AMONG THE MEMBERS OF THE PRESIDIUM OF THE ECCI

The decisions of the 4th World Congress on the reorganization of the Executive uncovered a practice which had already become standard in the ECCI: the Presidium of the ECCI distributed the work among the members of the Presidium (later called Secretariat members) in such a way that each member of the Presidium was responsible for one of the most important countries or for a group of countries. The members of the Presidium supervised the work of the officials nominated to deal with each of the most important countries and employed in the territorial secretariats. This system of distributing the work was in operation from the Comintern's beginnings until it was dissolved.[2] In the early days Zinoviev dealt principally with German affairs, as is shown by his appearing at the Party Conference of the CPSU in Halle (12–17 October 1920). After Lenin's death, Stalin gradually drove his rival Zinoviev out of his position of responsibility for German affairs. After the defeat of October 1923, August Kleine-Guralski, who was closely connected with Zinoviev, was replaced as Comintern representative in Germany by Dimitri S. Manuilski, a former member of the Org-Bureau of the CPSU, who had been nominated for this post by Stalin's secretariat.[3]

Responsibility for France and Italy, on the other hand, lay

[1] See pp. 127 f. above.
[2] See Zinoviev in *Die Kommunistische Internationale*, Vol. 22, p. 595, and Castro Delgado, *op. cit.*, p. 43.
[3] Ruth Fischer, *op. cit.*, pp. 392 ff.

with Leon Trotsky during the time he was a member of the ECCI Presidium. During World War I Trotsky had been an émigré in France, spoke fluent French and was well acquainted with French problems.[1] Otto Kuusinen was in charge of Finland and the Scandinavian countries. Jules Humbert-Droz, as a member of the ECCI, dealt with Latin-American affairs at the time of the 4th World Congress, while after 1939 the Spaniard José Diaz handled Spanish, Italian and Latin-American affairs as a member of the Secretariat.[2]

### THE ECCI PLENIPOTENTIARIES

The ECCI made extensive use of its right to send to the individual countries representatives armed with plenipotentiary powers.[3] The Sections to which they were sent were obliged to admit these representatives to all their meetings and sessions and they were authorized to intervene, even against the central committee of the party concerned, if the central committee's line did not conform to the directives of the ECCI.[4]

There was a distinction between the permanent representatives who stayed in a country for a considerable time, and those who were deputed to attend specific assemblies, e.g. Party Congresses, of the Sections. Finally there were the international instructors dealing with particular matters.[5] Among the permanent Comintern plenipotentiary representatives in the early 1920s were Mieczyslav Warszawski (alias Bronski), Bela Kun, Yelena Stassova and Karl Radek in Germany, Matthias Rakosi in Italy and John Pepper (Pogany) in the USA. From 1924 Manuilski represented the Comintern *vis-à-vis* the KPD and D. Petrovski-Bennet was attached to the British party.

The activities of the permanent Comintern representatives often led to friction between them and the leaders of the national parties. The General Secretary of the German Communist Party, Ernst Reuter (alias Friesland), clashed with the Comintern representative, Radek, when he demanded that the

[1] *Ibid.*, p. 211.
[2] Robert J. Alexander, *Communism in Latin America*, New Brunswick, 1957, p. 33.
[3] Para. 9 of the Statutes and Resolutions of the 4th Congress on the Reorganization of the Executive, *op. cit.*, p. 73.
[4] Para. 22 of the 1928 Statutes. [5] See p. 165 below.

reports sent by Felix "Wolf" (Rackow) to the Comintern should be shown to the KPD Central Committee. The methods used by Yelena Stassova, who was the Comintern representative in Berlin somewhat later and who tried to control all international connections, also caused resentment in the KPD.[1] Manuilski also came into conflict with the KPD leaders when he was the Comintern representative. In 1924 he rented several flats for himself and his staff, sent observers to all local organizations and despatched reports to Moscow without the KPD's knowledge. He received visitors from widely varied Party circles, got journalistic commissions for intellectuals, collected information, arranged for journeys to Moscow, etc.[2] Mention has already been made of the violent reaction of the German Communists to Manuilski's attempts to interfere with the election of members of the Central Committee at the 10th Party Congress.[3] As the KPD became increasingly bolshevized, demonstrations of this kind of resistance died away.

The more the national parties accepted subjection to the Moscow centre the stronger the position of the Comintern plenipotentiaries became, and by the 1930s the leaders of the national parties to which they were delegated were practically under their control. Their influence extended even into the daily affairs of the party. Louis F. Budenz, for example, has told how in the 1930s the Comintern representative attached to the American Communist Party violently criticized an article by the editor-in-chief of the *Daily Worker*, Clarence Hathaway, during an editorial conference.[4]

Such friction was much less liable to occur in the case of temporary missions. When Clara Zetkin attended the congresses of the French and Italian parties at Tours and Leghorn in 1920 and 1921 as Comintern delegate, she was very popular

[1]Brandt and Löwenthal, *op. cit.*, p. 187.

[2]Ruth Fischer, *op. cit.*, p. 394.

[3]See p. 91 above. A remarkable parallel to these events occurred in Poland in October 1956, when Khrushchev and his delegation attempted to influence the elections to the Central Committee of the Polish Party. The attitude of Gomulka and his supporters, who had the backing of the mass of the people of Warsaw, corresponds to the antagonism of the German delegates at the 10th Party Congress. (Cf. 8th Plenary Meeting of the PVAP in *Ostprobleme* 1957, p. 188.)

[4]Louis F. Budenz, *This Is My Story*, New York, 1957, p. 135.

with the French and Italian Communists.[1] As a rule the instructors or plenipotentiary representatives of the Comintern were not nationals of the countries to which they were accredited. To mention only a few examples, the Russians Manuilski and Mirov-Abramov, the Lithuanian Guralski and the Bulgarian Dimitroff worked in Germany; Henry Robinson, born in Belgium, worked in France; Matthias Rakosi in Italy; Jonny Löhr, a German, in Rumania; D. Petrovski (alias Bennet) in England; Heinz Neumann in China and Spain; the Pole Professor H. Walecki, the Hungarian Josef Pogany (alias Pepper) and the German Gerhard Eisler (Hans Berger) in the USA.[2] At the beginning of the 1920s, the Indian M. N. Roy and the Japanese Sen Katayama were working in South America. In Mexico, from 1927 to 1932, the Italian Vittorio Vidali operated under the name of Sormenti.[3] The intention was obviously to avoid the possibility that Comintern representatives might identify themselves with the interests of the parties to which they were sent.

All this makes it only too easy to understand why there were continual differences between the Sections and the ECCI on account of the activities of the "instructors". Balabanova complained about their appearance in Italy; Zinoviev reported that Giacinto Serrati called the ECCI delegates "grey cardinals", although it is not clear whom Serrati meant by that.[4] Paul Levi described Kleine-Guralski and his Russian assistants, in view of their attitude before and during the "March action" of 1921, as "Turkestanis", thus jibing at Bela Kun's part as a guest delegate at the "Congress of Eastern Peoples" (in Baku in September 1920), and giving biting expression to his opinion of their lack of understanding of conditions in Germany.[5]

[1] A. Rosmer, *op. cit.*, p.148; Hanna Ilberg, *Clara Zetkin*, Berlin, 1956, pp.712 ff.

[2] Josef Pogany was a Hungarian and had acted as "President of the Military Council" during the short-lived Communist "soviet rule" in Hungary. Further biographical details are contained in House Report No. 2244 of the U.S. House of Representatives dated 29 May 1956, p. 43, and in *Die Kommunistische Internationale*, Vol. 3 (1925), p. 284. Details of Eisler's Comintern activities are contained in the report *The Shameful Years* by the Committee on Un-American Activities, U.S. House of Representatives 1952, pp. 42 ff. See also Louis Budenz, *op. cit.*, pp. 137, 241.

[3] Alexander, *Communism in Latin America*, pp. 32 ff. and 37.

[4] A. Balabanova, *op. cit.*, p. 235.      [5] Paul Levi, *op. cit.*, p. 54.

## ILLEGAL METHODS

Article 12 of the Comintern Statutes said:

The general situation everywhere in Europe and America forces the Communists of the whole world to create illegal Communist organizations alongside the legal organizations. The Executive Committee is charged with ensuring that this is brought about everywhere.

Not only the ECCI but also the Sections carried out this obligation. While official Communist publications occasionally admitted that the ECCI was engaged in "illegal" work (e.g. in the *21 Conditions*, in the statutes or by the Expanded ECCI as late as 1930), it was seldom that it was allowed to become known which parts of the organization were engaged on it.[1] At the 3rd World Congress Radek mentioned the "little Bureau" (sometimes called the "select Bureau") which had the job of looking after illegal work.[2] Radek stressed that this bureau would have to take on staff even if they had not been elected by the World Congress. On the other hand, the department of the ECCI which was of most importance for the illegal work was one which was never publicly mentioned by the Comintern —the Department of International Relations, the OMS.[3] The OMS transported and distributed the Comintern's financial contributions to the Sections and was responsible for the international communications system (e.g., the setting up of bases and the maintenance of courier routes) and for providing couriers and agents with the necessary travel papers.

Decades of experience of clandestine work by ECCI functionaries such as Radek, Zinoviev, Piatnitski and Dimitroff explains why they achieved such remarkable results in the building up of illegal (that is, covert) organizations and in the employment of conspiratorial methods. These methods, too, developed in step with the whole of the Comintern procedures. In the early 1920s Radek was living semi-covertly in Berlin. He conferred with officers of the Reichswehr on behalf of the Russians and was still able to exercise influence on the KPD

---

[1] *The Communist Conspiracy—Strategy and Tactics of World Communism* (House Report No. 2241), Part I, Washington, 1956, p. 216.

[2] Library of the Communist International, Vol. 23, p. 1045.

[3] See p. 136 above.

when he was sitting in the Moabit Prison. Ten years later Dimitroff adopted a better cover. Unknown to the police, he acted for three years as the Head of the extensive West European Bureau.

What methods did these people use? The covert worker conducted himself as self-effacingly as possible and gave himself the appearance of being totally harmless. He never carried compromising written matter or any other material on his person. He avoided contact with known Communists. He would only use covert premises if the tenants had been carefully checked beforehand. A man who worked in various districts of a town would use a different cover-name in each district. Cover-addresses and meeting-places were changed frequently. Any party comrade who asked questions not directly concerned with his party job was suspect. Strict punctuality was demanded of every "illegal worker".[1] These and similar methods enabled Dimitroff to maintain his cover through months of imprisonment on remand and in spite of the length of the Reichstag Fire trial.[2]

Following another basic rule, the "illegal" work was always kept strictly separate from overt Party activity. The illegal organization, i.e. the functionaries charged with illegal work, had nothing to do with Party activity and made use of covert offices which had no connection with premises used for overt Party work. Similarly the illegal organization kept its papers, files, etc., separate from those of the normal Party organizations.

### THE COMINTERN'S AUXILIARY OFFICES AND BASES

At the beginning of the 1930s, when the Comintern network was at its most widespread, the Comintern had at its disposal in great areas of the world—and certainly in Western Europe and America—permanent bases from which to conduct its operations. The most important of these was the West European Bureau in Berlin.[3] This Bureau had branch offices in Copenhagen and Paris and could depend for support on seamen's

[1] Jan Valtin, *op. cit.*, pp. 326 ff.

[2] Breaches of the rules of clandestine activity such as M. Buber-Neumann saw Dimitroff commit (*Potsdam-Moskau*, pp. 142 ff.) are of no consequence when set against Dimitroff's remarkable success.

[3] See p. 142 above.

clubs controlled by the Seamen's and Port Workers' International in every port in the Western hemisphere. These bases served as reporting centres for Comintern agents. For example, an instructor who had lost contact with his organization could report to one of them and would be supplied with shelter and money, as well as further instructions. Richard Krebs, having served a prison sentence for some years, had no contact with the Comintern organization. In Le Havre a distributor of Communist leaflets put him into touch with the leader of the local Comintern base, who finally got him to Berlin.

Regarding the job of the leader of such a base, Krebs said:[1]

> This kind of agent was to be found in every harbour and in every inland town. Their official work consisted of arranging contacts and providing passports for international functionaries delegated to or passing through their districts. They arranged for cover-addresses for covert correspondence and for the despatch of propaganda literature. They received and distributed Comintern funds intended for local organizations. . . . All official reports by the leading functionaries were checked for accuracy in Berlin and Moscow by being compared with corresponding secret reports by local agents. These agents were always natives of the country they worked in, and they were always in the pay of the OGPU.

Before Krebs made use of it, the base run by "Monsieur Cance" in Le Havre had served such illustrious guests as Romain Rolland, Bela Kun, Otto Kuusinen, Albert Walter, Tom Mann and Harry Pollitt—although it is doubtful whether Cance was faithfully observing the rules of secrecy in telling Krebs this. Still, René Cance's security precautions seem to have been adequate for the degree of clandestine work needed in Le Havre in 1930. Soon afterwards, Krebs made the acquaintance of another base which was really well disguised, Roger Walter Ginsburger's quarters in Paris, Rue de Seine 63.[2] Ginsburger was originally the representative of the Red Trade Union International (Profintern) and dealt with trade union matters and especially with the affairs of the Seamen's and Port Workers' International (ISH). The ISH premises and organization were very often utilized by the secret Apparats of the Inter-

[1] Jan Valtin, *op. cit.*, p. 152.     [2] *Ibid.*, pp. 154 ff. See also p. 145 above.

national and by the Russian Intelligence Service, so that the agency run by Ginsburger, who was completely loyal to the Communist cause, soon assumed much greater importance.[1]

Apart from these bases for disguised travellers and international instructors, there was also another group, the resident Comintern agents, whose job it was to maintain connection on behalf of the OMS with the Central Committee of the party of the country in which they were living. They had their headquarters in the same town as the Central Committee of the party they dealt with, which was normally in the capital of the country. Comintern financial assistance for national parties always went through their hands. From 1921 to 1930 the Berlin representatives for this work was Mirov-Abramov,[2] while in Paris Henry Robinson had this job from 1930 to 1936.

### THE "INTERNATIONAL INSTRUCTORS"

There was a close connection between the Comintern bases and the work of the "international instructors", i.e. the Comintern plenipotentiaries delegated to the Sections to provide guidance in certain sectors of Communist activity. They included specialists in agitation, strike specialists, specialists in women's affairs and experts in the various branches of industry and in military problems. These instructors were either asked for by the Sections or, more frequently, sent to the Sections in which the ECCI thought there was a need for them. They operated covertly, living under cover names in secret quarters,

---

[1]Jan Valtin (R. Krebs) first came into contact with Ginsburger in December 1929, when he had an opportunity to see the way in which Ginsburger was collecting material to use against an opponent, the German Communist Arthur Ewert. On Ginsburger's activities in the *Conseil National de Résistance* (CNR) during and after World War II see Borkenau's *European Communion*, pp. 331, ff., 441, and Jacques Soustelle's *Envers et contre tout*, Paris, 1950, Vol. 2, p. 171. Ginsburger and René Cance were still politically active in France in 1958, Ginsburger being a leading functionary of the French party and a member of the Chamber of Deputies under the name of Pierre Villon, and Cance being a Deputy for Le Havre.

[2]It is possible that while in Berlin Mirov-Abramov was not only responsible for the KPD but also headed the OMS section of the West European Bureau. This would mean that he was responsible for the entire area covered by this OMS section. The fact that he was entrusted with the leadership of the whole of the OMS on his return to Moscow in 1930 gives an indication of the value Piatnitski and Stalin attached to his services.

working in clandestine offices, using false identity documents, etc.[1]

The covert underground activities of such "Comintern agents" have occasionally been made known through cases in public courts. Probably the best-known case of this kind was the so-called Cheka Trial, which took place in Germany in 1925. In the course of this trial it was revealed that in 1922–4 Comintern agents had set up a "Cheka organization" for individual acts of terrorism and a so-called "partisan organization" to prepare for armed revolution.[2] The Supreme Court for the Protection of the Republic found it proven that the Russian Gorev-Skoblevski, a Comintern agent who was also arraigned and brought before the court, had established terrorist groups in Germany and had charged one of these with the task of murdering the Chief of the Army Command, von Seeckt, as well as two industrialists, Stinnes and Borsig.[3] As a result of this case Gorev-Skoblevski was sentenced to death. In another trial, held at about the same time, it was established that the Soviet nationals Kleine-Guralski, Golovin and Selenin had set up a "partisan organization" in preparation for armed revolt in Germany, and that this had been financed with dollar currency provided from the Soviet Union.[4] The chief defendant in this trial, Johannes Botzenhard, leader of the "Pomeranian partisan organization", became famous as a result of his escape and flight to the Soviet Trade Mission in Berlin.[5]

Revolutionary activity *of this type* was given up in Europe in 1925, and the weight of effort was transferred to political and trade union activity. Correspondingly the work of the Comintern

[1] Jan Valtin, *op. cit.*, pp. 165 ff.

[2] Judgment dated 22 April 1925, reproduced in *Die Kommunistische Partei in der Rechtsprechung des Staatsgerichtshofs zum Schutz der Republik*, pp. 59 ff.

[3] Ruth Fischer (*op. cit.*, p. 325, note 12) confirms that Heinz Neumann, who was mentioned in the court judgment along with Felix Neumann, was involved in the plan to murder von Seeckt, and says that it was Neumann himself who told her, "with youthful pride", about his part in it. When, therefore, M. Buber-Neumann (*Potsdam-Moskau*, p. 258) says that Heinz Neumann rejected individual acts of terrorism, the claim is only true of certain periods.

[4] Judgment of the Supreme Court against Lampe and others, 11 July 1925, *op. cit.*, pp. 297 ff.

[5] D. J. Dallin, *Soviet Espionage*, pp. 79 ff.

instructors also shifted into this field, with the object of achieving mass support for Communist aims among the workers. The activities of one of these "international instructors", working under the direction of the West European Bureau in Berlin and the Seamen's and Port Workers' International (ISH) in Hamburg, has been described by Richard Krebs.[1] He got to know the reporting centres of the ISH and the WEB in many of the important towns and harbours of Western Europe and in Scandinavia and was given the task of organizing mass demonstrations and strikes, with the help of local Communist functionaries. His experiences show up the disagreements between the international Communist organizations and the national Apparats. Georgi Dimitroff and Albert Walter wanted to use Krebs for international work among seamen, while Ernst Wollweber was thinking of employing him on work inside Germany. At first it was Dimitroff who had his way, and Krebs worked for the ISH. After 1933, however, when Dimitroff and Walter were in prison, Wollweber took control of the international organization and sent Krebs to Germany, where he fell into the hands of the Gestapo (although it will never be known whether Wollweber himself did not arrange this).[2]

### THE FINANCING OF THE COMMUNIST PARTIES

The ECCI used its financial resources not only for the accomplishment of its world revolutionary ambitions, but also to control the Sections of the Comintern and to keep them in a state of permanent thraldom. Boris Souvarine, who was elected to the Presidium of the ECCI at the 3rd and 4th World Congresses, and who knows Comintern practice in detail, writes:[3]

> With rare exceptions, the Communist parties of Europe, America and Asia needed financial help from the ECCI, that is, from the Bolshevist party. To lay down conditions for this form of solidarity is to exercise irresistible pressure.

The relationship of the Soviet State to the Comintern and its Sections is described by Karl Kautsky as follows:[4]

---

[1]Jan Valtin, *op. cit.*, pp. 165 ff.
[2]D. J. Dallin, *op. cit.*, p. 127; Valtin, *op. cit.*, pp. 398 ff.
[3]Souvarine, *Staline*, p. 342.
[4]Karl Kautsky, *Die Internationale und Sowjetrussland*, Berlin, 1925, p. 10.

Sitting in Moscow, the controllers of the Third International —which is only an instrument of the Soviet Government and is entirely dependent on Soviet financial support—consider themselves, by reason of the money they distribute, the absolute lords and masters of the Communist parties they sustain.

The distribution of Comintern resources was conditioned by the political aims of the moment. From 1919 to 1933 large sums flowed into Central Europe, and particularly Germany, for the reason that during this period the Comintern was concentrating its effort on bringing about revolution in Germany. At the time of the Comintern's collaboration with the Kuomintang in 1925–7 considerable sums of money passed through Borodin's hands. It is known that when Lominadse and Heinz Neumann were on the way to Canton, their luggage included a suitcase full of dollars.[1] Even before this, dollars had already played a prominent part in Germany, when Gorev-Skoblevski was building up his terrorist groups and Kleine-Guralski was gathering together his partisan organizations. Botzenhard, for example, as leader of the Pomeranian partisan organization, received his pay and expenses in dollars.[2] It was not until the beginnings of the Popular Front era that the Comintern began to devote a large part of its financial resources to Western Europe. During the Spanish Civil War, the Dane Richard Jensen was travelling about with millions on behalf of Moscow, buying up arms and equipment for Spain.[3]

Large amounts in dollars were also expended on fostering the activities of the Far East Bureau and the "Pan-Pacific Trade Union Secretariat".[4]

In the Comintern's early days funds were usually sent abroad in the form of money and jewellery confiscated by the OGPU. It was this practice which provided the basis for the accusation that Kamenev smuggled diamonds into Britain in 1921 to provide assistance for the Labour paper, the *Daily*

[1]Buber-Neumann, *Potsdam-Moskau*, p. 178.
[2]Judgment against Lamp and others, *op. cit.*, p. 302, in *Die Kommunistische Partei in der Rechtsprechung der Staatsgerichts zum Schutz der Republik und des Reichsgerichts*.
[3]Jensen, *Den Hellige Ko*, p. 83.
[4]Harry Miller, *The Communist Menace in Malaya*, p. 169.

*Herald.*[1] In the early 1920s Michael Borodin was sent to America with jewels alleged to have been worth a million roubles.[2] When the Soviet Union took up trade relations with the Western world from 1922 onwards, however, the necessary foreign currency could be got in less ponderous fashion.[3] The requisite amounts were often transmitted to their destinations by OMS special couriers, but wherever diplomatic relations existed between the Soviet Union and the "host country" in whose territory political activities were to be afforded financial assistance, the diplomatic bag was used as the means of transmission. This method of sending money was even simpler when the OMS representative in the country concerned was also a member of the Soviet diplomatic staff, as, for example, Mirov-Abramov, who handled large sums intended for the German party from 1921 to 1930. He belonged *pro forma* to the Press Department of the Soviet Embassy in Berlin.[4] On occasion, the Russian trade missions were also made use of for this purpose, and, in one well-known case, the Soviet Ambassador in Copenhagen, M. Kobetski.[5] The money itself would be handed over to a trusted representative of the party concerned.[6] In spite of clandestine handover procedures and notwithstanding security precautions, things did occasionally go wrong and the Soviet origin of the money came to light. As an example, it sometimes happened that British and American banknotes sent abroad through the OMS carried the stamp of the Soviet State Bank. There was also trouble when a Party treasurer (such as Arthur König in Germany in 1934) began to speculate with currency received from the Comintern.[7]

At the end of the 1920s, when the revolutionary preparations

[1] Louis Fischer, *The Soviets in World Affairs*, Vol. 1, p. 291.
[2] Draper, *The Roots of American Communism*, p. 218.
[3] Krivitsky, *op. cit.*, pp. 71 ff.
[4] *Ibid.*, p. 72. Diplomatic bags are still used for this purpose even today. According to the testimony of the MGB official Petrov, in January 1953 the General Secretary of the Australian Communist Party, Sharkey, was handed $25,000, forwarded from Moscow by diplomatic bag. It is noteworthy that in 1953 the OMS representative was an MGB official. (Report of the *Royal Commission on Espionage*, Sydney, 1955, p. 104.)
[5] Richard Jensen, *En omtumlet Tilvaerelse*, Copenhagen 1957, p. 95.
[6] Regarding the parts played in Germany by W. Pieck and Leo Flieg, see p. 137 above.
[7] Ruth Fischer, *op. cit.*, p. 444.

were on foot, the Comintern began to take steps to protect the funds belonging to its Sections from possible seizure by national Governments. This was done by taking advantage of the economic possibilities of the capitalist system, as in December 1929, when the firm of Diligentia A.G. was founded in Brisfelden in Switzerland and some part of the funds of the German Communist Party were transferred to it. The ECCI put this kind of economic manipulation into the hands of Hugo Eberlein, whose German confidant was Willi Langrock.

Since the Sections of the Comintern were mainly dependent on financial support from Moscow, they were required to inform the ECCI, through the OMS representative, of all projects entailing large-scale expenditure. The ECCI had the deciding voice on the financing of such projects, which meant that they also decided on all important political plans by the Sections. Apart from this, however, the Sections could hardly keep even their routine business alive without OMS help.[1] In the 1920s, the KPD, for example, employed several thousand full-time functionaries in order to fulfil the tasks laid upon it by the Comintern. It put out expensive propaganda and in doing so incurred expenses which it could not cover from its own resources.[2] However, accepting help from the ECCI entailed accepting the ECCI's instructions into the bargain. In 1921 the General Secretary of the German Communist Party, Ernst Reuter ("Friesland") was struggling to free the party from its financial dependence on the Comintern.[3] The German "left-wing" were also anxious to abolish the "sideways look at Moscow" when drawing up the budget (1925–6). Their efforts to achieve financial independence of the Comintern met with resistance from Manuilski.

As leader of the Yugoslav party (1938), Tito seems to have learned the value of financial independence. He declared:[4]

> . . . it was necessary to make the party independent of foreign financial assistance. That is one of the basic conditions for success. If assistance is expected only from abroad,

[1]Krivitsky, pp. 70 ff.; Jan Valtin, *op. cit.*, p. 199.
[2]R. Fischer, *op. cit.*, pp. 442, 503 ff.
[3]Brandt and Löwenthal, *op. cit.*, pp. 190 ff.
[4]Dedijer, *Tito Speaks*, p. 112.

a man gets into the habit of never trying to find support in the surroundings in which he lives and works. During the whole period of the Communist Party's work from 1919 to 1937 the receipt of money from Moscow had had only a harmful effect. From the moment I headed the party we discontinued the receipt of subsidies from abroad. We then had to rely on our own resources, because the financial problem had become a political one. The support we received depended upon the influence we had among the people. Furthermore, when our own money was money the workers had contributed from their salaries and the peasants from their small earnings, then the attention given to that money was much greater. Each dinar was spent with the utmost circumspection, the more so when the money was being spent not only for the purchase of printing presses, paper and printing ink, but in order to maintain our members who were being persecuted by the police or were unable to earn a living because of the undivided devotion with which they served the party.

## SCHOOLS AND UNIVERSITIES

It did not take the Bolsheviks long to realize the value of schools and universities. The "University of the Workers of the East" was founded in Moscow in 1921. The students fell into two groups: the first containing nationals of Eastern States already incorporated into the Soviet system (such as Turkmenis and Buryat), and the second consisting of Communists from colonies or dependencies such as Persia or India. The purpose of the University was to "forge these students into revolutionaries". It had branches in Irkutsk, Tashkent and Baku.[1]

The failure of the attempted revolution in Germany in October 1923 was the final item in a series of failures. The Soviet Communists thought that since their revolution had met with success, the Sections of the Comintern needed only to adopt Bolshevik principles in order to ensure success in their operations. This belief was partly responsible for the decision taken by the 5th World Congress (1924) to bolshevize the Sections. An effective means of bolshevizing was to educate the function-

[1]Stalin, *Marxism and the National and Colonial Question*, New York, n.d., pp. 206 ff. Also George Lenczkowski, *Russia, Iran and the West*, Ithaca (New York), 1948, pp. 126 ff.

aries in the Soviet way of thinking, and from 1924 onwards
selected Communists from all over the world were given training in political tactics, in guerilla warfare or in intelligence
methods.[1] It was the job of the OMS to co-ordinate the training
programme within the Comintern domain,[2] and the OMS
ran the so-called Lenin School, located not far from Moscow.
Here functionaries who had proven themselves within their
national parties were given their training. The school was
headed by a Director (Kirsanova, until the purges, and thereafter the Bulgarian Communist Vulko Chervenkoff),[3] together
with the Party Committee (as the deciding authority in Party
matters) and the Cadre Section. The school had German,
French, English and Russian sections, although the students
were not distributed among these sections according to nationality but according to their ability to receive instruction in the
language used in the section concerned. For example, French-
speaking Belgian students received their instructions in the
French Section, while their Flemish-speaking compatriots,
like the Dutch, attended the German Section. Norwegians who
spoke English belonged to the English Section, while those who
knew more German than English went to the German Section.
The students of the Russian Section were not Russian, but Poles,
Czechs and Serbs who understood Russian. Each section was
headed by a leader appointed by the Directorate of the school
and assisted by a secretary and one or more delegates elected
by the students. If their size warranted it, the sections were
sub-divided into circles. Thus after 1933, when there were a
large number of German Communists in Moscow, the German
Section consisted of two Party Circles and one Youth Circle.
In 1935 the school gave instruction to some 500 students, who
were completely isolated from the population and used cover-
names while they were at the school. The Cadre Section had the
job of ensuring that the rules of conspiratorial work were
strictly observed.

The courses at the school lasted one, two or three years, and

[1] The intelligence aspect of this training will not be dealt with in this
book.
[2] Krivitsky, *op. cit.*, p. 75.
[3] Eugenio Reale, *Nascita del Cominform*, Verona, 1958, p. 165.

there were also nine-month courses. Lectures were given by prominent Bolsheviks, such as Stalin and Bukharin, and Tito also lectured during his time as a member of the Balkan Secretariat of the ECCI.[1] The best-known German instructor was Fred Oelssner. The subjects taught included Communist ideology, mass agitation, the directing of strikes and guerilla tactics.[2] The students attended summer camps, where they had shooting practice and did practical training in field exercises and map-reading. However, by far the greatest part of the instruction was devoted to political subjects.

Hundreds of Communists from Western countries attended the Lenin School, and many of the students played prominent parts in the political life of their parties, men like Walter Ulbricht, Anton Ackermann and Karl Schirdewan in Germany, and Axel Larsen in Denmark. Many of the German students were later caught while engaged in illegal activity and executed (e.g. Wilhelm Knöchel). Others who later became very well known were Edvard Kardelj, the present Foreign Minister of Yugoslavia, and Sam Carr, who was involved in the Canadian Spy Case.[3] Like the other members of the Comintern staff, the strength of the instructors at the Lenin School was ravaged by the purges. The school was finally closed in 1938.

During the war there was a similar school in the neighbourhood of Ufa, where the Comintern had its headquarters. In this case, however, the students were not veteran Communists but were mostly the children of such Communists, who had been brought up in the Soviet Union and who were evidently

[1]Dedijer, *Tito Speaks*, p. 98.

[2]This Lenin School is not the same as the M-School mentioned by Wollenberg in *Der Apparat* (Bonn 1952, pp. 12 ff.). The first M-School was started after the failure of the revolution in Germany in 1923, and was intended to train officers for the future German Red Army. The German Communists who attended it, such as Hans Kippenberger, Wilhelm Zaisser, Arthur Illner (alias Stahlmann) and Albert Schreiner, went to work for the Red Army's Intelligence service after political developments prevented the formation of a German Red Army (Krivitsky, *op. cit.*, pp 56, 64; Dallin, *Soviet Espionage*, pp. 88 ff.). Later on M-Schools were started for the training of *Apparat* members. At one such school in Bakovka, near Moscow, German Communists were given six-month courses in guerilla tactics.

[3]*Report of the Royal Commission*, Ottawa, 1946, p. 104.

envisaged as the new blood of the future. This school catered only for students from countries which were at war with the Soviet Union. It was divided into national sections, to which all students from one particular country belonged. Both the students and the teachers used cover-names, and the students were subjected to strict "proletarian discipline". The instructors included such prominent Communists as the Pole, Jakob Berman, and the Germans, Bernhard Koenen and Paul Wandel. Some of the students have since achieved influential positions, e.g. Heinz Hoffmann, now a Lieutenant-General in the East German "National People's Army"; Lene Berg, Director of the Institute of Social Studies in the Central Committee of the SED, and Mischa Wolf, who came up from the Youth International, later worked alongside Manuilski and is today in a senior post in the East German Ministry of State Security.[1]

In addition to these schools, further establishments were set up, designed to meet the needs of particular races or groups of races. In 1925, at the height of the Comintern's collaboration with the Kuomintang, the Sun Yat Sen University was opened in Moscow. Of this university Karl Radek was the first Rector and Moses J. Lurje one of its best-known professors.[2]

Moscow was also the site of the Communist University for Western National Minorities (KUNMZ).[3] Originally of minor importance, it had been started in 1921 by Julian Marchlevski (Karski) for White Russians and Ukrainians living outside the Soviet Union, for example in Poland and the Carpathians.[4] There was also an Armenian sector. When large numbers of German Communists emigrated to the Soviet Union after 1933, a German sector was created for them and also took in Baltic Germans and Austrians. In 1934–5 the students totalled some 250, of whom half were German or Austrian. The Director of the school at this period was Maria Frumkina, who had originally come from the Jewish Social Democratic Party, known as

[1]W. Leonhard, *Child of the Revolution*, pp. 174 ff.; Castro Delgado, p. 230.
[2]R. Fischer, *Stalin and German Communism*, p. 574; R. Fischer, *von Stalin zu Mao*, Düsseldorf, 1956, p. 223; Krivitsky, *op. cit.*, p. 76.
[3]KUNMZ is the abbreviation for the Russian Kommunisticheski Universitet Natsionalnich Menshinstv Zapada.
[4]Dedijer, *Tito Speaks*, p. 99.

"der Bund", and who was later to die in the purges. The usual length of the courses at the KUNMZ was three years and they included not only political subjects but also cultural subjects, such as mathematics and literature. In 1933 special 14-month courses were introduced for German Communists, the principal subjects being Marxism-Leninism, Party History and Dialectical Materialism.[1] The KUNMZ was closed in 1936.

Also in the Comintern domain were courses in Leningrad, called by Richard Krebs "the international Department of the Communist University".[2] These courses dealt with Communist theory and practice, with the future Communist revolution and the dictatorship of the proletariat. That these courses were not without importance is indicated by the fact that such high-ranking Communists as Otto Kuusinen, Ossip Piatnitski, Heinz Neumann and Arthur Ewert acted as instructors. Another school which served Comintern interests was the so-called Wilson School, which trained wireless operators for the "Radio-Apparat" built up by the OMS in the 1930s.[3] A certain number—not, of course, very many—of North American and European Communists attended this school.

These schools and universities imbued their students with the way of thought prevailing in the Soviet Party and gave them the kind of knowledge which would enable them to work in the secret organization of the Comintern and its Sections. It was drilled into the students that the Soviet Party (and the Soviet Union) were to be regarded as the most precious possessions of every Communist, and it was with this attitude that they returned to their national parties. The students of the Comintern schools and universities became links in a chain, a chain used by the Soviet Party to bind to itself Communist parties all over the world. They also formed a reserve of manpower, and one which was also available to the Russian Intelligence Service, which is not the least of the reasons why the CPSU still runs "central schools" for foreign students in the Soviet Union today.

[1]Alfred Burmeister, *Dissolution and Aftermath of the Comintern*, New York, 1955.
[2]Jan Valtin, *op. cit.*, pp. 112 ff.        [3]See p. 138 above (OMS).

OTHER COMINTERN INFLUENCES ON THE INDIVIDUAL COMMUNIST

The Comintern also had other means of exercising influence on individual Communists as a means of improving its control over its Sections. The Comintern agents would, for example, try to win the confidence of members of the parties to which they were attached, the aim being to ascertain the real state of opinion within the parties, or to work up opposition groups in them, if this seemed desirable. Thus Manuilski made a number of friends among Party intellectuals, getting them journalistic commissions, for which they were paid. Hundreds of German Communists were given employment by the Soviet Trade Mission, their salaries, which were good, being paid in gold marks. These employees were naturally dependent on the good will of agencies in Moscow.[1] When there were disputes, the generous conditions of employment were an important factor in persuading them to side with the Soviet point of view. One of the employees of the Soviet Trade Mission in the 1920s, Willi Rumpf, managed to achieve the position of Minister of Finance in the "DDR", thanks to his devotion to his masters (1959).

Invitations to individual Communists to visit Moscow also served the purpose of creating closer links to the Comintern or to Stalin, as when Heinz Neumann was repeatedly summoned to Moscow during the days when he was still *persona grata*. It was during one of these visits that Stalin commissioned him to write a pamphlet against Maslow (see p. 91 above).[2]

Visits to the Soviet Union by workers' delegations also came into this category. Stalin had already spoken at the 14th CPSU Party Conference of the importance of these delegations for Soviet collaboration with foreign Communist parties.[3] Although he did not say so, it was obvious that the presence in the Soviet Union of Communists from abroad continually gave new opportunities for strengthening connections with them.

However, visits to the Soviet Union served purposes other than that of enabling guests to improve their contacts and friendships. A sojourn in Moscow could also be utilized for

[1]Ruth Fischer, *op. cit.*, p. 503.      [2]*Ibid.*, pp. 445–446, 503–504.
[3]Stalin, *Works*, Vol. 7, p. 290.

the bringing of heavy pressure to bear, as Ruth Fischer discovered when she arrived in Moscow in 1925—when the ECCI's battle with the German left wing was in full sway—and had her passport taken from her by Ossip Piatnitski. For ten months, although she was living in the Lux, the hotel of the Comintern stars, she was virtually a prisoner of state.[1] Again, in 1938, the Head of the secret service of the Spanish Republican Government, "Garcia", was detained in Moscow because Alexander Orlov, the NKVD emissary in Spain, wanted to carry out certain "operations" without interference from "Garcia".[2] In the 1930s it became the general practice to take away the passports of foreign Communists visiting the Soviet Union and to replace them with residence permits which did not entitle the holders to leave the Soviet Union.[3]

During the purge period the possession of a passport and an exit permit was often of vital importance. Münzenberg made desperate efforts to obtain an exit permit after he had been incautious enough to go to Moscow in 1936.[4] Hundreds of other foreign Communists would have escaped the purges if they had been as astute as Münzenberg, who managed to talk Togliatti into getting him an exit permit—though Münzenberg was still not to escape the fate that seemed to be destined for all but the utterly compliant Communists.[5]

### THE COMINTERN AND THE SOVIET INTELLIGENCE SERVICES[6]

The connection between the Comintern and the Soviet Intelligence Services reflected the relation in which the International stood to the Soviet Party and State.[7] When the Comin-

[1]Ruth Fischer, *op. cit.*, p. 454.
[2]Krivitsky, *op. cit.*, p. 128. "Garcia" is probably identical with Fernández Garcés, who was head of the Spanish intelligence service, S.I.M., in 1938.
[3]M. Buber, *Under Two Dictators*, p. 12.
[4]M. Buber-Neumann, *Potsdam-Moskau*, p. 455.        [5]See p. 122 above.
[6]In the initial years of its existence the Comintern, and the ECCI itself, ran its own intelligence service and had its own agents abroad for the collection of intelligence. However, the author does not possess sufficient material to be able to give a picture of this aspect of the Comintern's activities.
[7]For details of the various changes in the Soviet Intelligence Service, see p. 114 above, n. 1. Dallin's *Soviet Espionage* (pp. 4 ff.) gives more detailed information on the military intelligence service (RU or GRU).

G

tern was founded, the Soviet Party was merely one of a number of large Sections and Soviet security agencies exercised no noticeable influence on it. After 1920, however, the influence of the Soviet Party in the Comintern began to increase.[1] Once the civil war was a thing of the past, the Soviet State grew stronger. In 1921 the Foreign Section (INO) of the Soviet State Security Service was started,[2] and the Red Army's espionage section began to operate outside the Soviet frontiers. A case in point was that of the editor of *L'Humanité*, Robert Pelletier, who was recruited by the Soviet Intelligence Service. Trotsky, who at that time possessed considerable authority in the ECCI, wanted to avoid a situation in which the Sections of the Comintern might find themselves compromised through carrying out espionage on behalf of Russia. In this case, using his authority as Commissar for Military Affairs, he put a ban on any entanglement of the Red Army's espionage service with Communist Party activities, and Pelletier had to leave *L'Humanité*.[3]

In Germany, the Russian Military Intelligence Service had no such difficulties to cope with. After the failure of the attempted rising in October 1923, the Service was able to recruit a sizeable number of capable German Communists to work for it.[4] Conditions changed in France, too, before long, as Trotsky's influence waned and pride of place was taken by Soviet national interests. When the members of Jean Cremet's spy network were arrested in 1927, it was revealed that a large number of French Communists were involved and as a result the French Party was put in a very difficult position.[5] Nevertheless, this did not prevent the Soviet Military Intelligence Service from demanding its continued assistance. In 1929 the leader of the Party's Politbureau was Henri Barbé. He was in contact with a GRU agent named Honoré Muraille, who asked him to recommend likely members of Communist youth groups, with the idea of sending them to the Soviet Union for training. Muraille was arrested in April 1931 and charged with espionage, and the French Communist Party saw itself faced with another embarrassing situation. But when Barbé made

[1]See p. 58 above.      [2]D. J. Dallin, *op. cit.*, p. 3.      [3]*Ibid.*, p. 28.
[4]See p. 85 above.      [5]D. J. Dallin, *op. cit.*, pp. 36 ff.

representations to Piatnitski and Manuilski, they were un-impressed. "Regrettable as it may be that the Communist Parties get caught up in these affairs", said the head of the Org-Bureau, "the work must go on." Jan Berzin, the com-mander of the Military Intelligence Service, also refused to agree to Barbé's request that he should stop the recruiting of members of the French Party as agents. Since Barbé refused to give way, the Comintern dropped him, and he left the Polit-bureau at the end of 1931, his place being taken by the pliant Maurice Thorez.[1] Piatnitski, who was also in charge of the Department of International Communications, as has been said above, not only collaborated with the Military Intelligence Service, but was also in close contact with Michael Trilisser, the head of the Foreign Section of the OGPU. In 1926, for example, George Agabekoff was present at a discussion between Piatnitski and Trilisser on the best way of smuggling the Indian Communist M. N. Roy through Afghanistan into India with the assistance of the OGPU. The OGPU benefited by this collaboration even in those days. The "passport department" of the Comintern furnished the OGPU's agents with masterpieces of forged passports.[2]

In Germany, too, active Communists were continually being involved in espionage cases between 1929 and 1933. In a large number of industrial espionage cases German Com-munists such as Albert Knöpfle, Erich Steffen, Eugen Herbst and Karl Dienstbach were serving the interests of the Soviet State.[3] Needless to say, the KPD felt no qualms about the possibility of being compromised. The revolutionary course steered by the ECCI since 1929 and the subversive preparatory work on which the KPD was engaged on the ECCI's instructions made such considerations seem quite superfluous.[4]

While the Soviet Military Intelligence Service were utilizing the Sections and sub-sections of the Comintern for its operations against foreign powers, the OGPU were penetrating into the Comintern's internal organization. Within the Soviet Party,

[1] *Ibid.*, pp. 45 ff.
[2] George Agabekoff, *OGPU, The Russian Secret Terror*, New York, 1931, pp. 78, 274.
[3] D. J. Dallin, *op. cit.*, pp. 107 ff.
[4] See pp. 92 f. above.

Stalin not only dominated the Org-Bureau and the Central Party Control Commission (CPCC) but could also rely on the support of the OGPU. He therefore made every effort to see that senior Comintern posts were filled by people who had demonstrated their loyalty in these agencies.

Although Zinoviev was still President of the ECCI Presidium, he had not been able to depend on the Comintern organization since April 1925, and found it difficult, for instance, to pass information to his supporters outside Russia.[1] Stalin began his infiltration of the Comintern in the International Control Commission (ICC) and by the date of the Maslow affair, in 1923–4, he already had two influential OGPU men, Josef S. Unschlicht and Peter I. Stuchka, in the ICC. He also preferred to send OGPU men as delegates to the various Commissions formed inside the ECCI.[2] Unschlicht was not only Chairman of the Chinese Committee, but also belonged, together with Felix Dzershinski, the head of the OGPU, to the "Polish Commission", which also included Stalin and Zinoviev. The "Spanish Commission" included, in addition to Dolores Ibarruri, André Marty and Palmiro Togliatti, the two cadre functionaries Bielov and Blagoyeva, who were closely connected with the NKVD.

Dimitri Manuilski, who had worked his way up through the Org-Bureau of the CPSU, was one of the first of Stalin's adherents to appear outside the Soviet Union as a Comintern emissary.[3] OGPU staff were also sent abroad on behalf of the Comintern. There is reason to believe that the organizer of the partisan groups built up in Germany in 1923, "Willi" (Selenin), belonged to the OGPU.[4] The more Stalin's power over the Comintern grew, the greater the extent to which OGPU staff were involved in Comintern work; and by the time Stalin's "victory" was complete, the Comintern representatives abroad were working hand in glove with the OGPU men. Since Comintern affairs were increasingly conducted in an atmosphere of secrecy, the OGPU agents could not be distinguished by the mere fact that they worked clandestinely. Couriers carrying

---

[1] R. Fischer, *op. cit.*, p. 439.     [2] See p. 139 above.     [3] See p. 89 above.
[4] Walter Zeutschel, *Im Dienst der Kommunistischen Terror-Organisation*, Berlin, 1931, pp. 74 ff.

money and distributors of leaflets were just as cautious in their movements. It was a characteristic of the Soviet secret police that even outside Soviet territory the affairs they dealt with were always of a semi-police nature. If a "traitor" had to be disposed of, the OGPU attended to it, as in the murders of Ignaz Reiss, Walter Krivitsky and Leon Trotsky. Whenever "enemies of the Soviet Union" disappeared, as Generals Kutyepov and Miller did from France, the trail always led to officials of the OGPU.[1] The OGPU also took an increasing part in "looking into" anti-Party utterances, which meant that they were in fact usurping the functions of the ICC.[2]

Richard Krebs has provided a number of examples of OGPU operations in the Comintern area.[3] He saw much of the work of Michael Avatin, who was the OGPU representative in Hamburg, where the members of the ISH knew him as the head of the Latvian-Baltic Section.[4] When the West Bureau was transferred to Copenhagen in 1933, Avatin was in charge of the counter-espionage Apparat there.[5]

That OGPU officials in such influential positions in the Comintern were not only to be found outside Russia was seen at the 7th World Congress, when Michael Trilisser was elected one of the Secretaries of the ECCI. One of the jobs he was given was the dissolution of the Kippenberg organization of the KPD.[6] After the 7th World Congress the NKVD penetrated into Piatnitski's domain, the OMS. Mirov-Abramov's successor in the OMS, for example, was Shorkin, an NKVD official.[7]

The high-point of the OGPU's activity outside the Soviet Union came during the Spanish Civil War, when they kept a check on the movement of all "volunteers" to Spain, in order to remove "agents" from their ranks.[8] There was also a certain Orlov, who had belonged to the Foreign Section of the Moscow OGPU headquarters before being sent to Spain.[9]

---

[1]D. J. Dallin, *op. cit.*, pp. ix, 69.        [2]Krivitsky, *op. cit.*, p. 69.
[3]Jan Valtin, *op. cit.*, pp. 152, 241, 247, 499.        [4]See p. 149 above.
[5]Valtin, *op. cit.*, p. 554.        [6]D. J. Dallin, *op. cit.*, p. 123.
[7]Castro Delgado, *op. cit.*, p. 207.
[8]Krivitsky, *op. cit.*, p. 101.
[9]*Ibid.*, and Gonzales (El Campesino), *op. cit.*, p. 16. Regarding the identity of this Orlov with the author Alexander Orlov, who now lives in America, see p. 192 below, n. 1.

In Spain the OGPU initiated a reign of terror only equalled
by the purges in Russia. In December 1936 *Pravda* admitted
that the purge in Spain had been carried out with the same
energy as the one in Russia. On this, Krivitsky wrote:[1]

> Already in December 1936 the terror was sweeping Madrid,
> Barcelona and Valencia. The OGPU had its own special
> prisons. Its units carried out assassinations and kidnappings.
> It filled hidden dungeons and made flying raids. It functioned,
> of course, independently of the Loyalist government. The
> Ministry of Justice had no authority over the OGPU, which
> was an emgire within an empire. It was a power before
> which even some of the highest officers of the Caballero
> government trembled.

The domination of the State Security Services over the
Comintern was already so taken for granted at this period that
Leo Haikiss, a senior OGPU official, saw nothing out of the
way in discussing with Richard Krebs in Copenhagen the possi-
bility that Wollweber, then the most powerful man in the West
European Bureau, might be secretly in league with the Gestapo.[2]

The Cadre Section of the Comintern and the national parties
also played some part in the OGPU's infiltration into the
Comintern. They were in a position to provide the OGPU
with information on the personal characteristics, defects and
weaknesses of Party members; and did so without reserve.[3] The
NKVD succeeded in getting its people into these departments.
The last Head of the ECCI Cadre Section, Vilkov, has been
described as a member of the NKVD.[4] Through his co-operation, the Soviet Intelligence Service had at their disposal
a reservoir of loyal assistants after the Popular Front period.
The things these assistants were given to do were not so much
concerned with starting political movements, strikes, etc.;
they were more of an intelligence nature, that is to say, they
were to the direct benefit of the Soviet State.

OGPU influence was also responsible for the strict security
measures employed within the Comintern. Entry to Comintern
offices, and even to the Hotel Lux, which was used purely for

---

[1] *Op. cit.*, pp. 120–121.     [2] Jan Valtin, *op. cit.*, p. 513.
[3] Krivitsky, *op. cit.*, p. 81. Simon Weil and Robert M. Slusser, *The Soviet
Secret Police*, New York, 1957, p. 13 and p. 41, note 54, give further references.
[4] Castro Delgado, p. 207. But see p. 130 above.

accommodation, was denied to anyone who did not possess a special pass (*propusk*). As in the OGPU itself, the orders were that all papers were to be locked away after working hours and, even then, that windows, cupboards and office doors were to be sealed.[1]

### THE COMINTERN'S PRESS AND AGIT-PROP WORK

Lenin had always been aware of the importance of the press for the organizing of a political movement. In 1901, in an essay entitled "Where Shall We Begin?", written for *Iskra*, he wrote: "The newspaper is not only a collective propagandist and a collective agitator, it is also a collective organizer"—a view which he never ceased to hold.[2] Following this thesis, the Comintern had its own press organ from the start and also took steps to see that it ruled the press of the parties that joined it.

### THE PUBLICATIONS OF THE ECCI AND THE SECTIONS

Para. 9 of the statutes said:

The Executive Committee shall direct the entire work of the Communist International from one meeting to the next, shall publish the central organ of the Communist International (the periodical *Die Kommunistische Internationale*), shall issue the requisite announcements in the name of the Communist International and shall issue directions which shall be binding on all organizations and parties belonging to the Communist International.

Consequently the review *Die Kommunistische Internationale* appeared regularly in many languages up until the Comintern was dissolved. It is a valuable source of documentation on the international Communist movement and its subordinate organizations.

The Comintern also put out an International Press Correspondence in German, English and French. The title of the German edition, published in Berlin by the Hungarian, Julius Alpari,[3] was abbreviated to *Inprekorr*.[4] After 1933

---

[1] *Ibid.*, pp. 11, 12, 22, 24.     [2] Lenin, *Collected Works*, Vol. 4, part 1, p. 114.
[3] R. Fischer, *op. cit.*, p. 57; M. Buber-Neumann, *Potsdam-Moskau*, p. 159.
[4] The title of the English edition was *Inprecor*, and the French edition was called *La correspondance internationale*.

*Inprekorr* was published in Basle under the name *Rundschau* (Review)—of politics, economics and the workers' movement.[1]

It was a matter of particular concern to the Comintern that the press controlled by its Sections should follow the Comintern "line". On this point the *21 Conditions* laid down the following:

> The *entire* propaganda and agitation must be of a genuinely Communist character and must correspond to the programme and the decisions of the Communist International. All press organs of the Party must be directed by trustworthy Communists, who must have proved their devotion to the proletarian cause. . . . The periodical and non-periodical press and all Party publishing houses must be completely subservient to the Party Central Committee, irrespective of whether the Party as a whole is legal or illegal at the particular moment. It is not permissible for the publishing houses to abuse their independence and to follow policies which are not completely in accord with the policies of the Party.

Para. 11 of the statutes was equally unequivocal:

> The publications of all parties and organizations belonging to the Communist International and which are counted as sympathizing with the Communist International are obliged to publish all official decisions taken by the Comintern and its Executive Committee.

The entire Communist press and the publications of the Comintern Sections were fashioned to conform with these directions.[2]

The Communist press found itself in difficulty when the Comintern changed the "line", without issuing any guidance to its press regarding the change, so that it was impossible for Party publications to know how to treat the change. Douglas Hyde has given an illuminating picture of the situation in which the *Daily Worker* found itself when the Stalin-Hitler pact was followed by the outbreak of war in 1939 and the division of the spoils—Poland—between Germany and Russia.[3]

Press and publications were not the only means of carrying on agitation and Party propaganda, for which every possible means

[1] M. Buber-Neumann, *op. cit.*, p. 379.

[2] *Die Kommunistische Internationale*, Vol. 12, pp. 361 ff., contains a review of Comintern publications and literature for the year 1920.

[3] Douglas Hyde, *I Believed*, London, 1950; Borkenau, *European Communism*, pp. 243 ff.

was used. The pre-eminent expert in this field was Willi Münzenberg, who had been removed by Zinoviev from his position in the Youth International in 1921, after considerable difference of opinion with him.[1] Lenin commissioned him to start up a large-scale relief programme in the West for the benefit of the Russian people, who were still suffering from the consequences of war-Communism. This gave Münzenberg the opportunity to demonstrate his ability to master organizational tasks on a huge scale. He created the International Workers' Relief (IWR, 12 September 1921), founded publishing houses and started newspapers and periodicals. In 1926 his *Workers' Illustrated* had reached a circulation of something like a million.[2] His film-distributing agency popularized Soviet films of the 1920s, such as Eisenstein's *Potemkin* and Pudovkin's *Storm over Asia*, all over the world. In its heyday, Münzenberg's "concern" owned a number of businesses, producing newspapers, magazines, books and films, and even included a tobacco firm. The IWR appeals also met with success from both a material and a propaganda point of view. In 1921 twenty-one shiploads of gift contributions arrived in the Soviet Union, followed by seventy-eight more in 1922.[3] The actual collecting had a further effect, in that every donor, even if he himself was not a Communist, felt himself somehow linked with the people for whose benefit he was making his contribution.

Münzenberg was not only a capable organizer; he also developed an extraordinary talent for handling people, which he used to recruit many prominent personalities in support of his activities.[4] The "Anti-Imperialist League" he founded in 1927 attracted such supporters as Jawaharlal Nehru, U Nu (later Prime Minister of Burma), the leader of the American Negroes, James W. Ford, and Tremoko Garan Kouyaté (French Sudan), the General Secretary of the League for the

[1]See p. 151 above (Youth International).
[2]Münzenberg gave a report to the 4th World Congress on the International Workers' Relief (Library of the Communist International, Vol. 37, Hamburg, 1923, p. 125); and Münzenberg, *Für Brot und Arbeit, Die Aufgaben und das Ziel der internationalen Arbeiterhilfe*, Berlin, 1931. See also p. 154 above (Red Relief).
[3]R. Fischer, *op. cit.*, p. 611.
[4]Kurt Kersten in *Deutsche Rundschau* 1957, pp. 486 ff., and G. Regler, *Das Ohr des Malchus*, Cologne, 1958, p. 224.

GX

Defence of Negro Rights.[1] Albert Einstein took part in solidarity demonstrations. Henri Barbusse spoke at the opening of the Congress against Imperialist War in Amsterdam (1932), and a member of the English House of Lords, Lord Marley, wrote the preface to the *Brown Book*. Edu Fimmen, the Secretary of the International Federation of Transport Workers, and Ellen Wilkinson, a leading member of the British Labour Party, actively supported the League Against War and, Fascism. In keeping with its motto, "We must organize the intellectuals", Münzenberg was behind the brilliantly successful International Writers' Congress held in Paris in 1935.[2] André Gide's speech of welcome was addressed to such well-known personalities as André Malraux, Henri Barbusse, Louis Aragon, Jean R. Bloch, J. R. Lenormand, Bertolt Brecht, Heinrich Mann, Klaus Mann, Leon Feuchtwanger, Anna Seghers, Gustav Regler, Alfred Kerr, Alfred Kantorowicz, Johannes R. Becher, Erich Weinert, Robert Musil, Aldous Huxley, John Strachey, Martin Andersen-Nexø, Ilya Ehrenburg, Aleksei Tolstoy and Michael Kolzov.[3]

The Comintern propagandists also made great attempts to exploit the universal podularity of the European, and especially the German, theatre in the 1920s. In 1928 the Communists gained a decisive influence in the German Workers' Theatre Federation, the organization covering the combined Workers' Theatre Associations in Germany. Arthur Pieck, the son of Wilhelm Pieck and the Manager of the *Rote Blusen*,[4] became Chairman of the Federation.[5] In 1929 the Federation summoned a "Reich Conference" in Berlin, at which Friedrich Wolf spoke on "Art as a Weapon". In the summer of 1930 the first Conference of the International Theatre Federation met in

---

[1]See Overstreet and Windmiller, *Communism in India*, pp. 95 ff., 406, and the reproduction of portions of the *Arbeiterillustrierte* for 1931 in *Der Weltbolschewismus*, Leipzig, 1936, p. 220.

[2]Arthur Koestler, in *The God that Failed*, London, 1950, p. 72. Regarding Münzenberg's other activities while he was an émigré, especially during the Popular Front period, see p. 119 above.

[3]G. Regler, *op. cit.*, p. 314, has given details of the failure of the attempt to represent this congress as a non-party congress.

[4]One of the many Communist-inspired theatre groups that sprang up in Germany between 1924 and 1930.

[5]Jürgen Rühle, *Das gefesselte Theater*, Cologne, 1957, pp. 185 ff.

Moscow. This conference proclaimed that the objective of the working-class amateur theatre was to serve the Comintern and laid it down as the duty of workers' theatre groups everywhere "to transform the various amateur theatrical groups of the working-class, the popular stage and other organizations of the same kind into Agit-Prop groups". These Agit-Prop groups were to drum up new members for the Communist mass organizations. For this purpose they employed every kind of theatrical performance, including political revues, group recitations, sketches and popular songs.[1] Hermann Duncker, one of the founders of the KPD, formulated four principles of Communist cultural activity:[2]

(i) Art is not an end in itself, nor a matter of individual enjoyment.

(ii) For us art is agitation, an experience that revolutionizes and points out to us our goal.

(iii) For us art is collective striving, spiritual co-operation, a sensing of the feeling of the mass and an embodiment of the mass will.

(iv) For us art is a means of proclaiming our class-hatred of capitalism and of expressing our will towards Communism and the classless society. We do not waste time thinking about the future or searching through the tomes of the past. We are living today—it is in the present that we have to fight in order to bring about its revolutionary reshaping.

This was the frame of mind in which the artistic triumphs of the Comintern's propaganda were pressed into service.

[1] *Ibid.*, pp. 185 ff.    [2] *Ibid.*, p. 186.

# Chapter V

## THE END OF THE COMINTERN

### THE PURGES

*"Die Internationale erkämpft das Menschenrecht."*[1]

COMMUNIST parties and the Comintern had been expelling "opportunists" and otherwise undesirable members ever since the 8th Party Congress of the Russian Communist Party in 1919. The expulsion of Paul Levi, who publicly criticized the bungling of the March 1921 operations, was one of the first noteworthy examples.[2] In these cases, however, neither the life nor the liberty of the victim was in any way affected by the expulsions.

Hardly was Stalin the undisputed master of the CPSU, however, than he initiated the "purges", aimed at the physical destruction not only of his opponents but also of anyone who might one day become his opponent. These purges, which began after the 7th World Congress, followed the murder of Sergei Kirov, perhaps arranged and in any event made use of by Stalin, on 1 December 1934.[3] The Comintern and its staff, both inside the Soviet Union and outside the "fatherland of the working class", were hit by the purges, the greatest losses being in Spain and Germany.

Stalin had every one of the leading Bolshevists who had delivered the representative speeches at the World Congresses during the Comintern's first ten years—Zinoviev, Radek,

---

[1]Refrain of the song *Die Internationale*, composed by Eugene Pottier in 1871 (*Internationale Arbeiterlieder*, 24th edition, Berlin, 1953, p. 54).

[2]See p. 70 above.

[3]Sergei M. Kirov, the popular and influential secretary of the Leningrad Party organization, had been shot dead by a student in Smolny. Willi Schlamm, in *Die Diktatur der Lüge*, Zurich, 1937, p. 53, gives details of the trial of twelve Leningrad OGPU officials charged with "carelessness" in not having taken the ncessary security precautions.

Bukharin and Trotsky—branded as murderers, Gestapo agents and terrorists. The only exception was Lenin, who was dead.

In the Soviet Union, Stalin's fury, directed against any one who might be a potential opponent or who showed any signs of independent thought, was brought to bear even more viciously against the émigrés than against the hapless Russians.[1] The purges were carried out especially severely among those émigrés who could not hope for protection from their own governments, while as a rule American, English and French subjects remained untouched.[2] The East Europeans, the Germans and the Austrians, on the other hand, were defenceless in the face of the horrors that fell upon them.

Speaking of the fate of many of the leaders of the Polish "Agents' Party" (dissolved in 1938), Jerzy Morawski said after the 20th Party Conference, "Almost all the leaders and activists of the Polish Communist Party then living in the Soviet Union were arrested and sent off to camps".

Even the 70-year-old Comintern veteran Adolf Warszawski (Warski) disappeared, together with his wife.[3] The only one of the Polish Comintern functionaries who remained unharmed was the widow of Felix Dzershinski. Gomulka escaped being murdered because he stayed in Poland. Eugenio Reale accuses Togliatti of having taken part in the liquidation of Polish Communists while he was a Comintern functionary.[4]

The victims among the illegal Yugoslav Communist Party included no less than four former General Secretaries (Sima Markovic, Milan Gorkic, Anton Mavrak and Yovan Malisic-Martinovic) and the last two representatives of the Yugoslav

[1]Susanne Leonhard, *op. cit.*, pp. 23 ff., gives a graphic description of the situation of the German émigrés.

[2]Borkenau, *European Communism*, p. 226. The Dane Arne Munch-Petersen, who represented the Danish Party in the ECCI and who disappeared without trace in the Soviet Union in 1937, was just as much a victim of the purges as was Rose Cohen, D. Petrovsky's English wife. Nor has there been any reliable news of the Norwegian Communist Arthur Samsing since his sojourn in Moscow in 1936. (Richard Jensen, *Den Hellige Ko*, p. 49, and Jan Valtin, *op. cit.*, p. 556.)

[3]*Trybuna Ludu* of 27 March 1956 (quoted in *National Communism and Popular Revolt in Eastern Europe*, New York, 1956, p. 67); M. Buber, *Under Two Dictators*, p. 9. Richard Jensen tells of the fate of "Adolf Schelley" (Alfred Bems) in *Den Hellige Ko*, p. 17.

[4]Eugenio Reale, *Nascita del Cominform*, Verona, 1958, p. 21.

party in the ECCI, Ivo Grjetic and Vlada Copic. More than a hundred Yugoslav functionaries perished in the purges. When, at this time, Tito suggested that the leaders of the illegal Yugoslav party should be transferred from Paris (where they were in 1936–7) to Yugoslavia, the General Secretary, Dimitroff, said, "But *what* leaders? You are the only one left."[1] The toll was taken of the KPD, too. Hugo Eberlein, one of the founders of the Comintern; Max Hölz, once feted as a hero in Moscow; Hermann Remmele, who had still been a member of the Presidium at the 6th World Congress; Heinz Neumann, once Stalin's most fervent admirer; Leo Flieg, for years the liaison man between the OMS and the KPD; and the actress Carola Neher, who had been a great success in Berlin as Polly in Brecht's *Threepenny Opera*: all disappeared.[2] Fritz David, the editor of the *Rote Fahne* (*Red Flag*) until 1933, and thereafter in the Secretariat of the ECCI, admitted at the trial of The Sixteen in 1936 to having been concerned, on the instructions of Trotsky, in a plot to murder Stalin.[3] Hans Kippenberger, the head of the German AM-Apparat, and his deputy, Leo Roth ("Victor"), also perished. And with these there died thousands of other Communists, the prominent as well as the unknown.

The whole of the full-time Comintern functionary staff was cruelly decimated. Bela Kun, leader of the Balkan Secretariat of the ECCI until his arrest, died after enduring terrible torture.[4] Of the Cadre Section, the leader Alikhanov and his deputy Chernomordik, and of the German Sector the Head, Müller and his colleague Grete Wilde, were all arrested. The Head of the Central European Secretariat, Knorin, and his assistant Smoliansky both vanished. Ossip Piatnitski, the Head of the Org-Bureau, Jakob Mirov-Abramov, who had returned to

[1] Cf. Tito's remarks in the speech he made on 19 April 1959 on the 40th anniversary of the foundation of his party. (Yugoslav Information Service Rn.159/1–59 N S 7 and in *Kommunist* (Belgrade) of 16 April 1959 quoted in *Est et Ouest* (Paris), No. 216/59, p. 6.) See also Lazich, *Tito et la Révolution Yugoslave*, Paris, 1957, pp. 19 ff.

[2] M. Buber-Neumann, *Potsdam-Moskau*, p. 447. J. Rühle, *op. cit.*, p. 194.

[3] A. J. Vishinski, *Gerichtsreden*, Berlin, 1952, p. 505; Leo Trotsky, *Stalins Verbrechen*, p. 117.

[4] Krivitsky, *op. cit.*, pp. 217 ff. Bela Kun was rehabilitated after the 20th Party Conference of the CPSU. See an article by E. Varga in *Pravda* of 21 February 1956. See also p. 260 below.

Moscow after many years in Berlin and had taken over the OMS, and Josef Pogany (John Pepper), all perished.[1] Whole departments of the ECCI dwindled down to a few members.[2]

The ravages of the NKVD—or rather the OGPU still operating within the NKVD—were not restricted to the Soviet Union. The Spanish Civil War gave the Soviet State Security Service fresh opportunity to slaughter their own defenceless comrades. It was obviously from Abraham Slutsky, the then Head of the Foreign Section of the OGPU, that Krivitsky heard that Stalin had ordered Yagoda to set up a OGPU Section in Spain, and that the "Comintern operations in Spain" had been transferred to the OGPU.[3] This does not seem immediately compatible with the fact that Togliatti, alias "Alfredo", was, as a member of the ECCI, the Comintern representative and "the real boss" of Communism in Spain.[4] These contradictory views seem to show that it was not clear in whose hands the directing power lay. In any event the OGPU had no great desire to let their influence become patent.

The undisputed fact that Togliatti was in Spain in his capacity as a Comintern functionary helps to give the lie to his recent assertion that the political decisions and practical measures taken by the national parties between 1934 and 1939 —for example in Spain—were entirely the product of their own initiative and on their own responsibility.[5]

One OGPU official who was sent to Spain by the NKVD was

[1]Krivitsky, *op. cit.*, p. 72. Borkenau, *European Communism*, p. 227, says that the entire staff of the OMS were liquidated, as does M. Buber, *Under Two Dictators*, p. 34.

[2]Burmeister, *op. cit.*, pp. 1 ff.

[3]Krivitsky, *op. cit.*, p. 101. Krivitsky knew, of course, that the OGPU had been "dissolved" in 1934 (see p. 114 above). He obviously continued to use this name because the OGPU, too, was carrying on its work exactly as before.

[4]M. and M. Ferrara, *Palmiro Togliatti*, p. 196. Gonzales (El Campesino), *op. cit.*, p. 16; J. Hernandez, *op. cit.*, p. 122.

[5]Togliatti not long ago tried to gloss over his role in Spain in answers he gave to questions put by the publisher of *Nuovi Argomenti*, e.g. in No. 20 of 16 June 1956 (quoted in *The Anti-Stalin Campaign and International Communism*, New York, 1956, pp. 136 ff.). However, the real facts about his activities in Spain were confirmed by Alexander Orlov in the course of his questioning by the *Sub-Committee to investigate the administration of the Internal Security Act and other internal security laws*, on 14 and 15 February 1957.

Alexander Orlov,[1] at a time when Yezhov's henchmen were taking frequent advantage of the bitter fighting taking place against Franco's troops to settle accounts with their "comrades". A collaborator of Orlov's in Spain was "Carlos Contreras", who nowadays lives in Trieste under the name of Vittorio Vidali and is the leader of the Communists there.[2]

Another OGPU official, George Mink, had already carried out the murder of unreliable Communists (e.g. the German Hans Wissinger) on OGPU orders before he was sent to Spain.[3] In the Spanish War Mink had the job of keeping a watch on American volunteers serving with the Lincoln Brigade. According to the testimony of the former Communist Maurice L. Malkin, Mink was responsible for the death of a number of American volunteers who were shot from behind.[4]

The murder of the Spanish Communist Andrés Nin during the Spanish Civil War also caused a great sensation, Nin having been a friend of Lenin, Kamenev, Zinoviev and Trotsky. Jesus Hernandez, a Minister in the Republican Government, a member of the Central Committee of the Spanish Communist

[1]Krivitsky, *op. cit.*, p. 101; El Campesino, *op. cit.*, p. 16. This Orlov, alias "Nicolsky", alias "Shved", alias "Liyova", the author of *Kremlgeheimnisse* (Würzburg, 1956), admitted during his examination by the Sub-Committee (see previous note) that he had been in Spain as a member of the NKVD from September 1936 to July 1938 and had been intelligence adviser to the Spanish Republican Government. (*Hearings before the Sub-Committee to investigate the administration of the Internal Security Act and other internal security laws*, Washington 1957, p. 3422.) In view of the work Orlov did in Spain in succession to Krivitsky, Hernandez and Gonzales, it is easy to understand why he says so little in his book about his own part in the purges in Spain.

[2]Gonzales (El Campesino), *op. cit.*, pp. 16, 30; V. Serge, *The Case of Comrade Tulayev*, London 1951, pp. 128 ff. The "Carlos" spoken about by Gonzales is identical with Vidali (see M. and M. Ferrara, *op. cit.*, p. 196). In his evidence before the American Sub-Committee on 14 and 15 February 1957 (see note 1 above), Alexander Orlov said he had known the leader of the Triestino Communist Party, "Vidale", under the name of Contreras during the Spanish Civil War. This statement by Orlov confirms at least a part of Gonzales' story. According to Julian Gorkin (quoted in Leandro A. Sanchez Salazar, *Mord in Mexiko*, Frankfurt-am-Main, 1952, pp. 324 ff.; the English edition *Murder in Mexico*, London, 1950, does not include the relevant passages), Vidali was also involved in the preparations which preceded the murder of Leon Trotsky.

[3]Jan Valtin, *op. cit.*, p. 253.

[4]D. J. Dallin, *op. cit.*, p. 410. Mink survived the purges: Richard Jensen says in *Den Hellige Ko* that he reappeared in Copenhagen after 1945 on behalf of the Soviets, to look into conditions in the Danish Communist Party.

Party and later a member of the ECCI, has told how Alexander
Orlov started off by trying to obtain a warrant for Nin's
arrest, but failed. Thereupon Orlov's "demoniacal" colleague,
Carlos Contreras, simply kidnapped Nin and then, when even
frightful torture had failed to produce a confession from him,
murdered him and dumped his body in the sea.[1]

The NKVD's terrorism in Spain was not directed solely
against Spaniards, Germans and other "foreigners". Even
Soviet Russians who had been active for the Spanish Red
cause were recalled and liquidated. This fate overtook Marcel
Rosenberg, for example, the first Soviet Ambassador to the
Spanish Republican Government, and a similar fate awaited
Antonov Ovseyenko, who had been in the van in the storming
of the Winter Palace in St Petersburg in 1917.[2]

The picture of the purges in the Comintern would not be
complete without mention of the "collaboration" between the
illegal Communist underground organizations and the police
organizations of the countries in which the Communist parties
were banned. If a Communist marked down for "purging" was
out of the reach of the "Soviet State Security Services"—perhaps because he was in Germany—another effective method
was used, that of denouncing him to the Gestapo. KPD circular
letters sent out to large numbers of addresses contained exact
details of the illegal activities of such "comrades" as were
known to be anti-Stalin and who were therefore to be liquidated.
It was expected that circular letters distributed on such a large
scale were bound to fall into the hands of the Gestapo, who
would then take the necessary steps.[3]

Hans Kippenberger, the Head of the AM-Apparat, refused
to make use of such methods. Walter Ulbricht, nowadays First
Secretary of the SED, but in those days working in the Central
Committee of the KPD in Paris, sent Kippenberger to Moscow

[1]Jesus Hernandez, *La Grande Trahison*, Paris, 1953, pp. 74 ff. and 103 ff.
Also Hernandez's article in *Die Kommunistische Internationale*, No. 7, 193,
p. 35.
[2]Louis Fischer in *The God that Failed*, pp. 222–223.
[3]Wollenberg, *Der Apparat*, p. 17. There is a masterly description of this
side of the illegal Communist work in Germany in Manes Sperber's book,
*Der Verbrannte Dornbusch*, Mainz (no date), pp. 487 ff. See also G. Regler,
*Das Ohr des Malchus*, pp. 231, 234.

where, as has already been said, he vanished.[1] Adolf Deter, on the other hand, who in 1938 instructed Richard Krebs to write a postcard which would have delivered a German Communist into the hands of the Gestapo, is still a leading functionary in the Soviet Sector of Berlin.[2]

Ernst Wollweber, who was Minister of State Security in the Soviet Zone of Germany from 1953 to 1957, was also less scrupulous than Kippenberger. Richard Krebs (Jan Valtin), who worked in close collaboration with Wollweber in the Seamen's and Port Workers' International, has related that Wollweber deliberately played nineteen Communists into the hands of the Gestapo.[3] Under these circumstances one can understand only too well why all the "comrades" applauded loud and long when Wilhelm Pieck said at the opening session of the 7th World Congress:

> Our affectionate thoughts go out to all those imprisoned fighters who, by their fearlessness in the face of the fascist hangmen and by their outstanding devotion, have worked so outstandingly for the cause of the liberation of the proletariat.[4]

### THE STALIN-HITLER PACT—THE GRAVESTONE OF THE COMINTERN

*I cannot imagine a situation ever arising in which the interests of our Soviet Republic would require deviations to the Right on the part of our brother parties.*[5]

The purges had seen to it that all those, both in the Soviet Union and in the Comintern, who might be expected to have a high regard for the traditions of the Communist movement were either destroyed or silenced. The Society of Old Bolsheviks, to belong to which had been a rare honour up to the beginning of the 1930s, was banned in 1934.[6] This ban was

---

[1] See p. 190 above. It is likely that Kippenberger's death was not very much regretted by Wilhelm Pieck, who was aware that Kippenberger knew about the peculiar circumstances in which Pieck managed to avoid sharing the fate of Rosa Luxemburg and Karl Liebknecht, even though he was taken prisoner together with them. (Wollenberg, *op. cit.*, p. 17, note 3, and Appendix III to this book.)

[2] Jan Valtin, *op. cit.*, p. 575.      [3] Jan Valtin, *op. cit.*, pp. 499, 568.

[4] *Stenographic Proceedings of the 7th World Congress*, Moscow 1939, pp. 6 and 9.

[5] Stalin's words to the German Commission of the Expanded ECCI Plenum on 8 March 1926. (Stalin, *Works*, Vol. 8, p. 115.)

[6] See p. 188 above (Purges) and S. Leonhard, *Gestohlenes Leben*, p. 47.

followed by the dissolution of the Society of Former Political Prisoners and Exiles.[1]

This development cannot be laid exclusively at Stalin's door. Even while Lenin was alive, and indeed with Lenin's connivance, sincere but oppositional forces had already begun to suffer elimination, as, for example, when the CPSU, led by Lenin, took rigorous measures against the Workers' Opposition and the Kronstadt mutineers. After the failure of the revolutionary attempt in Germany in March 1921, Lenin approved Paul Levi's expulsion from the KPD and the Comintern, following his justified public criticism of the Comintern.[2] Zinoviev was involved in this development, which was later to prove so fatal for himself. After the 5th World Congress he pressed on with the bolshevization of the Communist parties. In this, of course, Stalin, with his campaign against the "left wing" (1926–7) and the "right wing" (1929–30), plus the physical destruction of his opponents in the purges, played the major part.

It would be wrong to regard the Stalin-Hitler Pact of August 1939 as a complete break with the policies hitherto followed by Stalin and the Comintern. The reader will recall the collaboration between the Red Army and the Reichswehr and the Russian attempts to reach agreement with the bourgeois Cuno Government at the time of the French occupation of the Ruhr.[3] A perfect example of close collaboration with nationalist elements (the Kuomintang) had been provided during the prologue to the abortive revolutionary attempt in China from 1925 to 1927. And in the late 1930s efforts were still being made to take up contact with the French "right wing", regarded by Stalin as the real wielders of power in France.

It was very probably the very failure of these efforts that led Stalin to lean towards the wielder of power in Germany, Adolf Hitler. It must be doubted whether Stalin had always hankered after this alliance ever since Hitler came to power, as Krivitsky thinks.[4] In view of the repeated swings in Stalinist tactical

---

[1] These bans have had a parallel in the Soviet Zone of Germany, where, in 1953, at the height of a party purge, the Association of Victims of Nazi Persecution was dissolved.
[2] See p. 70 above.     [3] See p. 79 above.     [4] *Op. cit.*, p. 18.

policies, it is probable that what happened was this. Stalin
tried to come to some arrangement with Hitler in 1933–4,[1] and
it was not until Hitler ordered the breaking-off of relations
between the Reichswehr and the Red Army that Stalin began
to look about for partners in the West and to initiate the Popular
Front policy in France.[2] The Popular Front was the starting
point of the attempt to conclude an agreement with the French
"right wing" and thus to gain security for the Soviet régime.[3]
When this attempt also failed, Stalin once more turned to
Hitler, despite the fact that the Anti-Comintern Pact signed in
Berlin in November 1936 did not seem to offer much encourage-
ment to Stalin's new attempt. Stalin's *volte-face* from his original
wooing of Hitler to the anti-fascism of the Popular Front was
equally reflected in his treatment of Trotsky. In 1933–4 Stalin
and the Comintern were accusing Trotsky of being an agent of
Anglo-Saxon imperialism and of France, whereas when Hitler
rejected further co-operation with the Soviet Union, Trotsky
was accused *in absentia* of conspiring with the Gestapo.[4]

Was there any foundation for the surmises regarding a
secret German-Soviet agreement that were bruited in the
West European countries following the Tukhachevsky trial in
Moscow? Ernst von Weizsäcker, at that time a senior official
in the German Foreign Office, wrote to the German Embassy in
Paris on 29 March 1938, probably in all good faith, that nobody
could believe any longer in the possibility of a *rapprochement*
between Germany and the Soviet Union.[5] Hitler's intention
was first of all to settle the problems of Danzig and the Polish
Corridor by means of an agreement with Poland. In October
1938 and again in January and March 1939 Hitler made an
offer to Poland of a common policy *vis-à-vis* the Soviet Union,

[1] *Ibid.*, pp. 22 ff.; E. H. Carr, *German-Soviet Relations Between the Two World Wars 1919-1939*, Baltimore, 1951, p. 109.

[2] Walter Görlitz, *Der Deutsche Generalstab*, p. 205. Krivitsky, *op. cit.*, p. 22. On p. 112 of his book, Carr points out the noteworthy parallel between the action of Wilhelm II in not renewing the treaty with Russia in 1890 and Hitler's stopping the collaboration between the Reichswehr and the Red Army.

[3] See p. 118 above.

[4] Leon Trotsky, *Stalins Verbrechen*, pp. 11, 16.

[5] *Documents on German Foreign Policy, 1918-45*, Baden-Baden, 1950, p. 744.

with special reference to the Ukraine.[1] When these intentions became known to Stalin, they caused him to make an attack on the Western countries at the 18th Party Congress in March 1939, declaring that they were trying "to incense the Soviet Union against Germany, to poison the atmosphere and to provoke a conflict with Germany without any visible grounds".[2] The following months made it plain that it was not only the Soviet Union that was interested in achieving an understanding. Since the Poles returned only evasive replies to Hitler's proposals, the Führer decided to settle the Polish question by force. In view of Britain's guarantee to Poland on 31 March 1939, Hitler hesitated to take military action as long as he had no ally. Stalin could provide the necessary security for his rearguard—and finally did so in the pact of 23 August 1939.[3] In taking this step, Stalin was undoubtedly thinking not only of the immediate advantages the pact would bring him—an alliance with the mighty Hitler and the acquisition of Polish territory. Moscow also expected that the impending European conflict would give rise to new Socialist states, as had happened in 1917–18.[4]

When Krivitsky says that on the day of the Stalin-Hitler pact the Popular Front came to an end with a resounding crash, he is identifying the Popular Front with the Comintern.[5] The Popular Front had already fallen into decay in 1938 in the course of the squabbles that broke out in France between the Popular Front partners.[6] Accordingly the Stalin-Hitler Pact

---

[1]A. Rossi, *The Russo-German Alliance*, London, 1950, p. 50; *Documents on German Foreign Policy*, Series D, Vol. V, p. 140.

[2]Stalin, *Problems of Leninism*, Moscow, 1954, p. 755.

[3]The course of the negotiations is described by Carr, *op. cit.*, pp. 166 ff. Hitler's intention to attack was in existence at least from 3 April 1939, as was revealed by Hitler's orders at this time in connection with Operation *Weiss* (*Dokumente der deutschen Politik und Geschichte*, Berlin, Vol. V, p. 39. The text of Stalin-Hitler Pact is reproduced in the same book, p. 89).

[4]Castro Delgado, *op. cit.*, pp. 51, 120.

[5]*Op. cit.*, p. 91. In *The God that Failed* (p. 223), Louis Fischer called the pact a gravestone of the Communist International.

[6]Borkenau, *European Communism*, p. 211. Admittedly the Popular Front period did not completely end in 1938. In January 1939 the German Communists received instructions to continue the Popular Front policy at the so-called Berne Conference in Paris. (*Zur Geschichte der Deutschen antifaschistischen Widerstandsbewegung 1933-1945*, East Berlin, 1957, p. 167.)

was less of a blow to the Popular Front politicians than to the adherents of the Comintern concept, the supporters of "proletarian internationalism". Within the higher levels of the Communist parties the pact had comparatively little effect, for the leading functionaries, having passed through the fiery furnace of the purges, had had devotion to the Party line burned into them. Not only that, but since most of them lived on funds provided by the Soviets, following the Party line was for them a matter of their livelihood. The chief problem for these functionaries was how to explain the new line to the rank-and-file, a difficulty which was to cause further embarrassment on the occasion of renewed changes in the Party line later on. A particularly vivid example occurred in the British party, which had been violently attacking Chamberlain's "Munich" policy until the Stalin-Hitler Pact. Immediately after 23 August 1939, the British Communists were maintaining that Stalin, by means of the pact, had stultified Chamberlain's attempts to divert Hitler's lust for conquest on to Russia. The pact, so it was argued, represented no betrayal of Poland and the other future victims of aggression.[1] A few days later, when Hitler's attack on Poland was followed by the outbreak of war between Great Britain and Germany, the British Communists proclaimed that the struggle must end with the destruction of fascism. At this time, John R. Campbell, a member of the Politbureau of the British party, was calling for the formation of a new government to ensure the effective prosecution of the war.[2] This position had to be completely disavowed when, on 17 September 1939, Soviet troops moved into Poland. Now the Comintern delegate to the British party succeeded in enforcing his version, which was that Britain's war against Germany was an imperialist war.[3] This explanation of the "true state of affairs" was soon

---

[1]Borkenau, *European Communism*, pp. 236 ff., with quotations. Douglas Hyde, *op. cit.*, p. 69; Victor Gollancz, *The Betrayal of the Left*, London, 1941, pp. 1 ff.
[2]Borkenau, *op. cit.*, p. 237.
[3]Douglas Hyde (*op. cit.*, p. 70) makes the astonishing claim that the Comintern representative produced an instruction to this effect, sent to him by Dimitroff on a post-card, before a meeting of the Central Committee. In contradistinction to this, it is probably true that David Springhall, the then representative of the British party in Moscow, arrived in London on 23 or 24 September 1939 with the appropriate Soviet instructions. (H. Pelling, *The British Communist Party*, p. 211.)

followed by an appeal to British workers to end this "unjust" war by Marxist methods.[1] This "revolutionary" slogan had as little practical effect in England as the speech in the House of Commons by the Communist M.P., Willie Gallacher, on 3 October 1939, when he demanded the immediate initiation of peace negotiations.

In France developments took a different course. The French party also began, it is true, by being uncertain of its attitude towards the war. In the Chamber, for example, the Communists voted in favour of war credits on 2 September. But in October, after the Soviet Union had occupied the eastern regions of Poland, the Comintern line was unequivocally laid down in an article by Dimitroff.[2]

The French party opposed the war "among the soldiers in the army, the workers in the factories, the peasants in the villages, the refugees in the evacuation centres, the wives of the men who had been called up, everywhere".[3] Since the French party had had some success among broad sections of the French people during the Popular Front era, their defeatist propaganda sapped the fighting spirit of some parts of the French forces and in this way contributed to their defeat in the summer of 1940.

When Ribbentrop returned from Moscow, he surprised those in his entourage by remarks favourable to the Bolsheviks.[4] Hitler, too, thought that Stalin seemed to be steering away from the "Jewish-international type of Bolshevism" and trying to work towards a kind of "Slav-Muscovite nationalism". After the Germans had occupied France, Trotsky's works were

[1]Hyde, *op. cit.*, p. 72. A similar attitude was adopted by the American Communist Party in a declaration of 19 September (Foster, *History of the Communist Party of the United States*, New York, 1952, p. 387).

[2]The article was entitled *War and the Working Class in the Capitalist Countries*. It was published in large numbers under the false cover-title of *The Truth about the War: How is it to be won?* (A. Rossi, *The Russo-German Alliance*, London, 1950, p. 104, note 2). Soviet instructions to the French party were probably brought to France by Raymond Guyot, who arrived in Paris from Moscow at the end of September 1939 (Pelling, *op. cit.*, p. 111).

[3]Maurice Thorez in an interview given to *L'Humanité*, banned at that time (Rossi, *op. cit.*, p. 107, note 3). The French party had been dissolved by a Government decree of 26 August 1939. (A. Rossi, *Physiologie du Parti Communist Français*, Paris 1948, p. 1.)

[4]*Ciano's Diary, 1939-1943*, London, 1947, p. 162.

included in the list of banned books, but Stalin's were not.[1]

One might imagine that it would have been difficult for the German Communists to cease their battle against Hitler, since the reign of terror being carried on by the National Socialists against the "comrades" on the scaffold and in the concentration camps never paused for a moment. However, the KPD leaders, living in exile in Moscow and completely dependent on Stalin, did not deviate one inch from "the line". Walter Ulbricht let himself be seen arm-in-arm with the Nazis. On 9 February 1940 he wrote in *Die Welt*, the Comintern paper run from Stockholm, that the German workers now had proof before their very eyes that the ruling class in England was carrying on the war against the working class. If Germany should be defeated, the German worker could expect the same treatment. Not only the Communists, Ulbricht went on, but also many Social-Democratic and National-Socialist workers regarded it as their duty not to allow a breach of the Hitler-Stalin Pact under any circumstances[2] . . . but when the time came, these supporters of the Nazi-Bolshevik "united front" were not asked whether they wanted to allow a breach of the Stalin-Hitler Pact or not!

The Soviet Union was most careful to fulfil all its obligations under the pact. As late as 13 April 1941 Stalin made public demonstration of his desire for friendship when he said to the German Ambassador, von der Schulenburg, on Moscow Station: "We must remain friends and you must do everything to that end".[3] So it was that when Hitler began his "Russian campaign" on 22 June 1941, Stalin stood there as the dupe who had left all warnings unheeded—duped, just as he had been by Chiang Kai-shek in 1926–7.[4]

The change of line that had to be undertaken following the outbreak of the Russo-German war was of course easier for the European Communists to accept than the one they had had to

[1]Rossi, *The Russo-German Alliance*, pp. 75 ff.

[2]Ulbricht's article is reprinted in Gollancz, *The Betrayal of the Left*, pp. 302 ff.

[3]Rossi, *The Russo-German Alliance*, p. 197.

[4]Regarding the warnings Stalin received of Hitler's aggressive intentions there is not only Khrushchev's "secret speech" of 25 February 1956 but also Winston S. Churchill, *The Second World War*, Vol. III (*The Grand Alliance*), pp. 320 ff., and David J. Dallin, *op. cit.*, p. 134 and Alexander Dallin, *German Rule in Russia*, p. 4, note 2.

make in August 1939. Now the call was for a revival of the old United Front Policy.[1] Once again an Anglo-Russian Committee of Trade Union Unity was formed. Yet in Asia many Asiatics saw the Germany of those days as battling against their traditional enemy, British imperialism, and this prevented the growth of an anti-fascist United Front feeling there. What came about after Hitler attacked Russia, in fact, was this. In November or December 1941, Harry Pollitt, the General Secretary of the British party, sent a letter to the leading Indian Communists, who, like Nehru and Gandhi, had been put in gaol for their boycott of the British war effort. Through Pollitt the Comintern now called on the Indian Communist Party to support the British and thus make possible the more effective prosecution of the war against Hitler Germany, the common enemy. The Indian Communists were at first doubtful, but in the end they obeyed. Since they now proclaimed the war to be a "people's war", they were released from Deoli Camp and the ban on their party was lifted. However, the part they played as war allies of British imperialism was to cost them their prestige among the mass of the Indian people for a long time to come.[2]

All efforts at a United Front during this period had to be made without the usual energetic support of the Soviet Union, for the Russians, fighting for their very lives in the first years of the war, could do nothing to help.

### THE DISSOLUTION OF THE COMINTERN

The outbreak of the Russo-German war brought about a severe restriction of the ECCI's work.[3] Some functionaries were infected with the panic that made Wilhelm Pieck scuttle through the corridors of the Lux Hotel in October 1941 shouting: "The Germans are coming".[4] When the staff of the Comintern were forced to leave Moscow, the General Secretary,

[1] Borkenau, *op. cit.*, p. 272.

[2] Minoo R. Masani, *The Communist Party of India*, New York, 1954, p. 80. Overstreet and Windmiller, *op. cit.*, p. 197, say that it was widely believed in India that such a letter was delivered to the Deoli Communists with the connivance of the British authorities.

[3] Castro Delgado, *op. cit.*, p. 41. Kurt Krupinsky gives details, admittedly one-sided, of the Comintern's propaganda activities preceding the outbreak of the Russo-German war in *Die Komintern seit Kriegsausbruch*, Berlin, 1941.

[4] Castro Delgado, *op. cit.*, p. 318.

Dimitroff, went with a small staff to Kuibishev, while the greater part of the Comintern staff were found accommodation in Ufa. Here the Information Section put together a daily communiqué. The ECCI did its best to support Russian military action by means of propaganda. The Italians broadcast from the "Milan Freedom Station", Ana Pauker on "Radio Free Rumania" and Dolores Ibarruri from "Radio Independent Spain". The "Deutscher Volkssender" and the "Freies Osterreich" transmitter were beamed to Germany and Austria. The ECCI did hardly any real Comintern work in the sense of the direction and control of the Communist parties. Even before its dissolution the Comintern was in its death-throes.

The ECCI's decision to dissolve the Comintern, taken on 15 and made known on 22 May 1943, was signed only by Zhdanov and Manuilski and those national party leaders who happened to be in the Soviet Union, and who were in the main nationals of the countries under the control of the Axis powers: Dimitroff and Kolaroff from Bulgaria, Pieck and Florin from Germany, Thorez and Marty from France, Ercoli (Togliatti) from Italy, Kuusinen from Finland, Koplenig from Austria and Gottwald from Czechoslovakia.[1] The proclamation said that the decision to dissolve had been taken by the ECCI, which, if it was true, meant that the Communist International had been dissolved by an executive organ that, according to Articles 4 and 5 of the statutes, was not even formally competent to take such a decision.[2] Manuilski admitted as much to Jesus Hernandez in a conversation on 22 May 1943. Shortly afterwards *Pravda* also wrote that it had not been possible to call a world congress.[3] Hernandez also learned from Manuilski that it had been thought preferable to take the necessary action first and talk about it afterwards. In this way it had been possible to achieve complete surprise.[4] Bearing in mind what has already

[1]Borkenau, *European Communism*, p. 283, is correct in suggesting that the emergence of Andrei Zhdanov, who signed the proclamation for the CPSU along with Manuilski, is evidence that Zhdanov had assumed responsibility for international affairs in the Politbureau of the CPSU. Zhdanov was repeatedly to reappear in this capacity in the future (e.g. in connection with the founding of the Cominform).

[2]Cf. also Art. 8, para. 2, second sentence of the 1928 statutes.

[3]Quoted in *Keesings Archiv der Gegenwart*, 1943, pp. 5949 ff.

[4]Hernandez, *La Grande Trahison*, Paris, 1953, p. 248.

been said, it need not be stressed that it was not the ECCI which decided to dissolve the Comintern. It only made the announcement of what Stalin had previously decided. There was, it is true, a meeting of the Comintern Presidium, at which the question of the dissolution was discussed, but the first that the majority of the ECCI functionaries heard of the decision to dissolve was what appeared in the newspapers.[1] It should be said, however, that some of the national Communist parties were consulted beforehand. The Yugoslav party, for example, received a radio message about it.[2] In the actual decision to dissolve, dated 15 May 1943, it was said that

> the course of events in the last quarter of a century and the experience gained by the Comintern have incontrovertibly demonstrated that the organizational form of the working-class association chosen by the First Congress of the Comintern was becoming increasingly out of step with the times, even though it answered the requirements of the initial period of the working-class movement. The movement outgrew its tasks, which themselves became more and more complicated in the various countries. In the end the Comintern became in fact an obstacle in the path of the further consolidation of the working-class parties.

This version was intended to give the imdression that the decision to dissolve the Comintern was the result of a thorough examination of the position of the Communist parties, and that while the Comintern had in the past controlled the national Communist parties, it had now proved to be a hindrance to the consolidation of those parties. Four years later, when the Cominform was founded, Zhdanov said that the dissolution of the Comintern had once and for all put an end to the slander, put about by the enemies of Communism and of the working-class movement, that Moscow interfered in the internal affairs of other countries and that the Communist parties acted not in accordance with the interests of their own people but on orders

[1]Veljko Vlakovitch, who took part in the meeting of the Presidium, in *Kommunist* (Belgrade), dated 20 April 1959, quoted in *Est et Ouest*, Paris, No. 216/59, p. 7; Castro Delgado, *op. cit.*, p. 190; Hernandez, *op. cit.*, p. 248.

[2]Dedijer, *op. cit.*, p. 197. Regarding the existence of a Comintern radio station in Zagreb, see *The Soviet-Yugoslav Dispute*, London and New York, 1948, p. 28.

from abroad.[1] All this was said in order to disguise the fact that in spite of the dissolution of the Comintern, the Central Committee of the CPSU still led world Communism and that the real reason for dissolving the Comintern was to be found in the international situation.

The dissolution of the Comintern was clearly intended to persuade Russia's allies that the old revolutionary plans had been abandoned and that Moscow was willing to give up its control over national Communist parties. It is also likely that Roosevelt's wish to see an end of Communist propaganda in America played a part.[2] Although the American Communist Party had already quit the Comintern in 1940, it still went on with its propaganda.[3] Roosevelt accordingly appealed to Stalin, whose loyalty he trusted. There is a possibility that this naïve belief of Roosevelt's was encouraged by some senior American government officials, such as Alger Hiss, subsequently Roosevelt's adviser at the Yalta Conference, and Harry Dexter White, with whom the Russian Intelligence Service, taking advantage of the Popular Front atmosphere, had been for years in fruitful contact.[4]

Dissolving the Comintern would also make it easier for the Western Communist parties to exploit the wave of sympathy that arose after Hitler's declaration of war, and which was strengthened by the Russians' stubborn defence of their homeland.[5] This particular purpose was achieved. The American Communist, William Z. Foster, believed in fact that the dissolu-

[1]See p. 219 below.

[2]Cf. Veljko Vlakovitch, *loc. cit.*, and Lucien Laurat, *Du Comintern au Cominform*, Paris, 1951, p. 7.

[3]See the *Sunday Worker*, New York, 17 November 1940. The American Communists found themselves compelled to take this step as a result of the Voorhis Act of October 1940 (William Z. Foster, *History of the Communist Party of the United States*, New York, 1952, Chapter 27). The Voorhis Act did not prevent the American Communists from declaring that they held unshakably to the principles of proletarian internationalism in the spirit of Marx, Engels, Lenin and Stalin. (Earl Browder, *The Way Out*, New York, 1941, p. 191.)

[4]D. J. Dallin, *Soviet Espionage*, pp. 442 and 475 ff.; Toledano/Lasky, *Seeds of Treason*, New York, 1950, pp. 59 ff.; Don Whitehead, *The F.B.I. Story*, New York, 1956, pp. 283 ff.

[5]Douglas Hyde, *op. cit.*, p. 170 and the Stalin interview reprinted in the German edition of W. Leonhard, *Child of the Revolution* (*Die Revolution Entlaesst Ihre Kinder*, Cologne-Berlin, 1955, pp. 259–260).

tion of the Comintern contributed appreciably to the Allied decision to open the "Second Front".[1] But it was not only the Communists who gave optimistic voice. On 22 May 1943, for example, Reuter's chief diplomatic correspondent wrote:

> The recommendation made by the leaders of the Communist International that the Moscow headquarters of the national Communist parties should be liquidated means that in future Communism will be a national, native product of each individual country. It will cease to be an international organization, and in each country the Communist Party will be a national party. In the Allied countries these national Communist parties will devote themselves to the furtherance of the Allied war effort. This step ought to have particularly beneficial effects on relations between the United States and the Soviet Union.
>
> In Great Britain it will introduce a new element into the differences between the Labour Party and the British Communist Party, differences which have arisen as a result of the Communist Party's demand for affiliation to the Labour Party.

German circles declared in 1943 that the dissolution of the Comintern represented the greatest propaganda action Stalin had ever set on foot.[2] Borkenau, too, thinks it "one of the biggest public stunts of Russian propaganda".[3] Certainly this step by the Soviets made a powerful impression on world opinion.

Borkenau, relying on Castro Delgado's statements, maintains, in common with some other commentators, that the Comintern carried on its work in Ufa, where its offices had been since they were evacuated in 1941, and shortly afterwards returned to Moscow (Textilshchikov St. 10); but the evidence does not seem to bear this out.[4] Borkenau said: "The Comintern exists to this day, and it would therefore be useful to reintroduce the word into ordinary political parlance instead of bowing to the hoax term 'Cominform',"[5] but when Borkenau made this

[1]William Z. Foster, *History of the Three Internationals*, New York, 1955, p. 439.

[2]*Keesings Archiv der Gegenwart*, 1943, pp. 5949 ff.

[3]*European Communism*, p. 283.

[4]Castro Delgado, *J'ai perdu ma foi à Moscou*, Paris, 1950, p. 227.

[5]Borkenau, *op. cit.*, p. 283. See also Ruth Fischer, *op. cit.*, p. 393, note 5 and *Report of the (Canadian) Royal Commission*, Ottawa, 1946, pp. 37 ff.

recommendation in 1952 the Comintern had been dead for years and the Cominform was nothing more than a shadow. The dissolution of the Comintern was genuine, as will shortly be shown in detail. Yet the international Bolshevist movement did not go out of existence on 15 May 1943. On the contrary, it stayed alive and is still alive to this very day. But the aspect of world Bolshevism that was called the Comintern ceased to exist soon after 1943.

A gigantic organization such as the Comintern, with its world-wide network, could not be liquidated within a few days. It would take months, if not years, to dissolve a comparable organization anywhere in the world. So it was quite in accordance with normal practice that certain Comintern agencies, such as the office building in the Textilshchikov Street in Moscow, should remain in use following the announcement of the dissolution, and that functionaries should go on working there.[1] Some part of the work the ECCI had been doing was also continued virtually unchanged, for example the editing and preparing of radio propaganda in the so-called *Institut 205*, which was located in the former Comintern offices in Rostokino.[2] Archive work and general winding-up operations were also carried on. The non-Russian functionaries had an interest in keeping their jobs going in order that they could retain their entitlement to rationed food. Igor Guzenko, the Russian intelligence service official, who later achieved fame in the Canadian spy trials, saw Comintern staff still working in Moscow in the summer of 1943. At the beginning of 1943 he also saw, written on an index card in the Soviet Embassy in Montreal regarding the Communist Sam Carr, a note which read: "Detailed biographical material is available in Comintern Headquarters".[3] Guzenko therefore assumed that the dissolution had meant only the disappearance of the Comintern's name, while the organization itself went on working.[4]

Guzenko may have observed the facts correctly, but he went too far in the conclusion he drew from them. He left Moscow

[1] Borkenau, *op. cit.*, p. 282; Castro Delgado, p. 227.
[2] W. Leonhard, *op. cit.*, p. 242.
[3] *Report of the Royal Commission*, Ottawa, 1946, p. 104.
[4] *Op. cit.*, p. 37. Borkenau relies on this point in *European Communism*, p. 282.

in the summer of 1943. At that date—and even later—there undoubtedly were Comintern staff still active in Moscow.[1] Yet the evidence that the Comintern archives were still being worked on and the fact that an index card referred to biographical information being available in the "Comintern Headquarters" do not prove that the Comintern continued to exist. To continue to use the archives and the information collected by the Cadre Section (such as was meant in the case of Sam Carr) was the common-sense thing to do. It does not justify the conclusion that the Comintern remained in existence.

There are by contrast a number of circumstances which point to the conclusion that the dissolution of the Comintern was genuine. The Yugoslav party, a Section of the Comintern, received a radio message on 2 May 1943, asking for their views on the suggested dissolution.[2] The Central Committee of the Yugoslav party agreed with the suggestion. Then again, the discussion which preceded the foundation of the Cominform proceeded on the basis that the Third International had long since ceased to exist.[3] Dedijer's book was written after the Yugoslavs broke away from the Soviet Union and Dedijer would have had every reason to expose the Russians if the truth was that they had only pretended to dissolve the Comintern. In fact, he does not even hint at the possibility. Milovan Djilas was told by Dimitroff—one of the few really wellinformed functionaries—that the idea of dissolving the Comintern had come up once before during the period when Stalin was collaborating with Hitler.[4] Djilas also is convinced that the Comintern really came to an end.

Following the announcement of the decision to dissolve, a start was made on liquidating the Comintern agencies. A Liquidation Commission, consisting of Manuilski, Dimitroff and Togliatti, was formed, with the task not only of supervising the dissolution but also of issuing guidance to the representatives of the Communist parties. The Liquidation Commission, significantly enough, had its headquarters in the Foreign Section (Department of International Relations) of the Central Com-

[1] Castro Delgado, *op. cit.*, p. 227; W. Leonhard, *op. cit.*, pp. 242, 249.
[2] Dedijer, *Tito Speaks*, p. 197.  [3] *Ibid.*, p. 300.
[4] Milovan Djilas, *The New Class*, New York, 1957, p. 179.

mittee of the CPSU.[1] This was made known only to the members of the Politbureau of the national parties, and even to them only verbally. Everyone else had to accept the official version.[2] Wolfgang Leonhard relates that the Comintern school in Kushnarenkovo, which he was attending in May 1943, was closed down immediately after the announcement of the dissolution.[3] What purpose would have been served in closing this school—unknown as it was either to the Russian or the international public, with both staff and teachers brought there in conditions of secrecy—if it had not genuinely been intended to do away with the Comintern? If any part of the Comintern organization could have remained in existence without prejudicing the propaganda effect intended to be produced by a pretended dissolution, then it was this school. Leonhard also quotes a remark by Mikhailov, the head of the school, that the school was being dissolved in common with all other Comintern agencies.[4] In July 1943 Leonhard could already see that Mikhailov's remark was not just a figure of speech. The former Comintern offices in Rostokino were being used by the *Institut 205*, which was now only engaged on editing work for the various "illegal" transmitters whose programmes were beamed to Germany or the countries occupied by German troops.[5]

Leonhard himself was working in Moscow at this time as an editor on the staff of the paper of the National Committee of Free Germany. This agency of the exiled KPD was controlled in the final instance by senior CPSU functionaries such as Alexander Shcherbakov, a candidate for the Politbureau since the 18th Party Congress.[6] This did not mean that there had been any change in the system that had been working for years, only now the decisions of the Central Committee of the CPSU went directly to the national Communist parties, without having to

[1]Lazich, in *Tito et la Révolution Yougoslave* (p. 117), confirms that Manuilski was in the Central Committee of the CPSU after the dissolution of the Comintern.

[2]Hernandez, *La Grande Trahison*, p. 249.

[3]Leonhard, *Child of the Revolution*, p. 223.

[4]*Op. cit.*, p. 220. Mikhailov is not identical with Michael Koltsov, mentioned by "El Campesino", *op. cit.*, p. 31, but is probably identical with "Miguel", whose description by Castro Delgado tallies with Leonhard's.

[5]Leonhard, *op. cit.*, p. 242.      [6]*Ibid.*, p. 254.

go through the intermediary of the ECCI.[1] The abolition of
the ECCI as a link in the direction of the national Communist
parties by the CPSU can be regarded as the principal result
of the decision to dissolve the Comintern.

If this is so, it follows that the dissolution of the Comintern
constituted no real concession by Stalin to his allies, but merely
a gesture—and a sham gesture at that. In an interview published
in *Pravda* on 30 May 1943, Stalin tried to create the impression
that it was not true that "the activities of the Communist
parties of the various countries were not governed by the
interests of the people of the countries but by orders from
abroad".[2]

Stalin did not need the assistance of the Comintern to ensure
that national Communist parties obeyed the "orders from
abroad". One of the means he used in order to achieve this
was to have prominent former Comintern functionaries sent
back to their homelands to carry on political work. Thus
Dimitroff went to Bulgaria, Togliatti to Italy, Pieck and
Ulbricht to Germany, Johann Koplenig to Austria, Rakosi to
Hungary and Maurice Thorez and André Marty to France.
Anyone who believes that the Comintern remained alive must
be prepared to answer the question: who took over the functions
of these people in the Comintern? And when did these "successors" ever show themselves? These are questions to which
there is not likely to be any satisfactory answer.

A review of the history of the Comintern and of the factors
which led to its dissolution must lead one to the conclusion that
the Third International, exactly like the First and Second
Internationals, foundered on the rock of nationalism. Both of
the first two Internationals fell apart as the result of conflicts
between the European national states. The Comintern was
offered up by Stalin as a sacrifice to Soviet power politics.[3] Its
existence clashed with the national interests of the Soviet

[1] Cf. Laurat, *op. cit.*, p. 8. William Z. Foster, in his *History of the Three
Internationals*, confirms that the Comintern, overshadowed by the importance
of the CPSU, was out of date.

[2] Leonhard, *op. cit.* (German edition), p. 259.

[3] As far back as 1930 Trotsky prophesied that Stalin's policies would lead
to the liquidation of the Comintern (in *The Permanent Revolution*, New York,
1931, p. xv).

H

Union, whose founders believed that if anyone should be the champion of proletarian internationalism, it ought to have been the Soviet Union.

# Chapter VI

## THE COMINFORM

BEFORE moving on to consider the forms taken by proletarian internationalism after 1945, it is necessary to glance at the general situation.

From 1944 onwards there arose in Eastern Europe a number of states whose governments, originally coalitions of bourgeois parties with Socialists and Communists, came increasingly under Communist domination. Without going into detail regarding this process, it can be said that by 1948 it was complete in all the East European states with the exception of Yugoslavia, where there had been a People's Republic from the beginning.[1] Soviet domination of the countries which had become Soviet satellites did not rest only on the fact that the CPSU controlled their national Communist parties, although party connections undoubtedly did form the mainstay of Soviet power and were evident in every aspect of life. Further factors strengthening the position of the Soviet Union were the presence of the Soviet armed forces, whose importance varied from country to country, the despatching of Soviet "advisers" into the most important branches of public affairs (e.g. the state security service) and close economic ties.[2] Of these, the presence of Soviet troops in the "People's Democracies" played a very considerable, and in some cases decisive, role. The popular risings in the Soviet Zone of Germany in June 1953 and in Hungary in October-November 1956 were only put down by Soviet troops stationed in those areas, and in some cases strengthened by reinforcements from elsewhere. Poland was always a particularly sensitive point for the Soviet despots,

[1] H. Ripka, *Czechoslovakia Enslaved*, London, 1950; Ferenc Nagy, *The Struggle behind the Iron Curtain*, New York, 1948; Ulam, *Titoism and the Cominform*, pp. 39 ff.

[2] Nagy, *op. cit.*, p. 137; Dedijer, *Tito Speaks*, pp. 262 ff.

who sent Marshal Konstantin Rokossovski there as Minister of Defence and member of the Polibureau.[1]

The building up of the Soviet position of power in the East European countries had a considerable influence on Soviet policies towards them. In the course of his visits to Moscow in June and September 1956, Tito, for example, observed that some of the Russians he dealt with had a conception of Soviet relations with Yugoslavia quite different from their conception of Soviet relations with countries such as Poland and Hungary, in which it was Soviet military victories which had brought the Communists to power.[2] It was only in respect of Yugoslavia, which had been liberated by her own military action, that the "Stalinists" seemed willing to admit the principles of equality of rights and non-intervention.

The relations of the Communist parties to one another after 1945 were roughly as follows. The Comintern had been dissolved.[3] Control over the national Communist parties was being exercised by the Central Committee of the CPSU, the actual control being in the hands of the Department of International Relations of the Central Committee.[4] The Secretary within the Central Committee responsible for this department from 1943 onwards was probably A. Zhdanov, who signed the decision dissolving the Comintern in May 1943 on behalf of the CPSU. He also delivered the principal speech on the occasion of the founding of the Cominform.

The dissolution of the Comintern did not do away with CPSU control over the national parties.[5] In Eastern Europe it was not only party connections which shackled the "liberated" countries so tightly to Moscow but also the presence of the Red Army, the influence of the MGB and economic ties.[6] The most impressive demonstration of the extent of this domi-

[1]Regarding Rokossovski's role in the events of October 1956 in Poland see p. 272 below.
[2]See p. 276 below.
[3]It is one of the weaknesses of Borkenau's case that in *European Communism*, pp. 517 ff., he proceeds on the basis that the Comintern was still in existence.
[4]This is not to say that the Department of International Relations of the Central Committee of the CPSU still maintains an *apparat* comparable to the OMS *apparat*.
[5]See p. 209 above.
[6]Seton-Watson, *The Pattern of Communist Revolution*, pp. 253 ff.

nation was provided when Czechoslovakia accepted the Franco-
British invitation to attend a conference in Paris in July 1947
to discuss the Marshall Aid plan. The Czechs were ordered to
send a delegation to Moscow with all speed. As a result of the
"conversations" in Moscow, Czechoslovakia withdrew her
agreement to take part in the Paris discussions.[1]

Dedijer has given a description of Moscow's procedures on
such occasions. Yugoslavia and Bulgaria had told the Soviet
Union about their plan to established a Balkan Federation.
When Dimitroff, in an interview, voiced his opinion that the
peoples concerned would settle this question on their own,
Yugoslav and Bulgarian delegations were summoned to Moscow
in February 1948 and peremptorily told by Molotov and Stalin
that this plan had caused serious differences between the Soviet
Union on the one hand and Yugoslavia and Bulgaria on the
other. Stalin maintained that the Yugoslavs were getting into
the habit of not asking the Soviet Government for its advice in
matters of foreign policy. On 10 February 1948 he told the
Yugoslav delegation that they were to sign an agreement in the
name of their government covering mutual discussions with the
Soviet Government in foreign policy matters. At midnight (!)
on 11 February Edvard Kardelj, the leader of the delegation,
was summoned to Molotov's presence. In Molotov's room all
preparations had been made for Kardelj to sign an agreement
he had never seen. Kardelj had no opportunity to consult his
government. "I was looking at two sheets of paper inserted in a
blue folder, I was listening to the harsh voice of Molotov,
ordering 'sign this', and I was boiling with rage."[2] He signed.

The intimate intermingling of the affairs of government and
party, both in respect of staff and of policies, makes it likely that
negotiations at the Party level must have been conducted in
much the same atmosphere. In view of this relationship and the
dependence of the national parties, it is reasonable to enquire
why the Cominform was ever established. There does not seem
to be much justification for the view that there was a kind of

---

[1]*Ibid.*, p. 255; Ripka, *op. cit.*, pp. 56 ff.; Robert Bruce Lockhart, *My
Europe*, London, 1952, pp. 124–125.
[2]Quoted in Dedijer, *Tito Speaks*, p. 333.

"interregnum" prior to the founding of the Cominform.[1] The events of the period 1946–8 show the results of Soviet control over the East European states and parties. In every country the Socialist and Communist parties were amalgamated.[2] The Russians began this process in April 1946 with the compulsory merger of the KPD and the SED in the Soviet Zone of Germany. The corresponding amalgamation in Czechoslovakia took place in the summer of 1948 and in Poland in December 1948. The modest role the bourgeois parties had been permitted to play in the governments of the East European countries after 1945 was gradually diminished and finally extinguished. The Hungarian Prime Minister, Ferenc Nagy, resigned in May 1947.[3] The leader of the Peasant Party, Stanislav Mikolajczyk, left Poland in December 1947.[4] In December 1947 King Michael of Rumania was forced to abdicate by the Soviet special emissary, A. J. Vishinski. In February 1948, with the assistance of the Soviet Deputy Foreign Minister Valerian A. Zorin, the Communist *coup d'état* took place, resulting in the death of Jan Masaryk, the Foreign Minister, and the resignation of President Benes.[5]

There were nonetheless unmistakable signs of a certain relaxation. The Czech attempt to share in the Marshall Aid Plan has already been mentioned. In Poland, Yugoslavia and Rumania there had also been some popular demand for participation in the Paris Conference, even if these countries did decline the invitation in the end. Even the French Communists had spoken in the Chamber in favour of accepting the

[1]As Borkenau thinks (*European Communism*, p. 520).

[2]In Germany, the Russians and the German Communists did not try to bring about this "unification" immediately after May 1945. In typical fashion they misjudged the situation in Germany, assuming that the KPD would attract a much greater following than the SPD. It was not until it became plain that the SPD was the stronger of the two that the cry was raised, "Brothers, forward hand in hand" ("Brüder, in eins nun die Hände": third verse of the song *Brüder, zur Sonne, zur Freiheit* in *Internationale Arbeiterlieder*, Berlin, 1953, p. 83).

[3]Nagy, *op. cit.*, pp. 417 ff.

[4]S. Mikolajczyk, *The Rape of Poland*, New York—Toronto, pp. 243 ff.

[5]Robert Bruce Lockhart, *My Europe*, London, 1952, pp. 130 ff.; Ripka, *op. cit.*, pp. 240, 244, 306. Ripka relates that Zorin had thought it necessary to travel to Prague to check the position on Soviet wheat consignments. This is a good example of the conjunction of power and deceit in the Stalin era.

American offer, but they, like their Czech comrades, were
forced to change their minds.

Events such as these led Stalin and his functionaries to the
conclusion that the co-ordination of the Communist movement
was not functioning as well as it had functioned under the
Comintern. Since 1945, moreover, one country—Yugoslavia—
had been making desperate efforts to free itself from Soviet
control and to take its place in the system of people's democracies as a partner with full and equal rights. This attitude on
the part of the Yugoslav party and state was not only due to the
energetic leadership of Tito, who knew and saw through
Stalin's tactics. It was strengthened by the fact that Yugoslavia, in the shape of Tito's partisan guerillas, had fought
against the German conquerors in open warfare and—in spite
of Stalin's opposition in the first years of the war—had battled
for the achievement of Communist rule in Yugoslavia; and was
the only East European country to have achieved this.[1] The
Yugoslavs could make the proud claim that they themselves
had liberated the greater part of their own country unaided.[2]
The Soviet representatives in Yugoslavia ignored these facts.
The behaviour of the Soviet troops was hardly any different
from their behaviour in the conquered territories.[3] In their
efforts to exercise unrestricted rule, the Soviet forces employed
the same methods in Yugoslavia as they employed in other East
European countries. The Soviet intelligence services began to
recruit members of the Yugoslav party and state officials and
military officers, "for the Soviet Union, the great power for
peace".[4] Yugoslavia was also exploited economically by means
of treaties loaded in favour of the Soviet Union.[5] In the field of
foreign policy, the Soviet Union took decisions affecting
Yugoslav interests (e.g. in Trieste) without consulting the

---

[1]Josip Broz Tito, *Workers Manage Factories in Yugoslavia*, Belgrade, 1950,
pp. 14 ff.; Ernst Halperin, *The Triumphant Heretic*, London, 1958, pp. 20 ff.;
Lazich, *Tito et la Révolution Yougoslave*, pp. 110, 160.

[2]Dedijer, *Tito Speaks*, pp. 264 ff. and 384; M. Pijade, *About the Legend that
the Yugoslav Uprising Owed its Existence to Soviet Assistance*, London, 1950,
pp. 3 ff.

[3]Regarding the raping of Yugoslav women, see Dedijer, *op. cit.*, p. 271.

[4]Dedijer, *op. cit.*, pp. 268, 270; Hamilton Fish Armstrong, *Tito and
Goliath*, New York, 1951, pp. 69 ff.

[5]Dedijer, *op. cit.*, p. 276.

Yugoslavs, while at the same time forcing the Yugoslavs to sign an agreement in February 1948 compelling the Yugoslavs to consult the Soviet Union on every aspect of foreign policy.[1]

It is in the light of these events that the foundation of the Cominform must be considered.

### THE FOUNDING OF THE COMINFORM

Tito had already suggested to Stalin in 1945 that a new international organization should be set up. In June 1946, when Tito was again in Moscow, Stalin asked him whether he still thought a new International should be established; this one, however, to serve only as a medium for the exchange of information between the members. When Tito assented, Stalin suggested that the Yugoslavs should take the initiative in the matter. That same evening, in the course of discussions with the Yugoslavs and the Bulgarians, Stalin criticized Dimitroff's erstwhile activities in the ECCI and declared that while the Comintern would not be revived, there was a need for a purely informational body whose decisions would not be binding on any party. At this stage there was no unanimity on who should take the first steps.[2] It seems that Stalin, characteristically enough, was already trying to sow the seeds of discord between Tito and Dimitroff. Still, both of them knew Stalin well enough not to swallow the bait.

A year later, at the instigation of the CPSU, the Polish party invited the Communist parties of Yugoslavia, Bulgaria, Rumania, Hungary, Czechoslovakia, Italy and France to attend the inaugural session of the new organization.[3] The meeting took place on 22 to 27 September 1947 in Schreiberhau

---

[1] See p. 213 above; Hamilton Fish Armstrong, *op. cit.*, pp. 64 ff.

[2] This description of these events is based on Dedijer, *op. cit.*, p. 301, who was given authentic information by Tito and his associates. Boris Meissner (*Shdanow in Osteuropa*, Zeitschrift für Gegenwartsfragen des Ostens, 1952, p. 98) says that the "re-establishment of the Communist International in the shape of a Cominform" was due to Zhdanov's initiative, but in view of the course of events described here, this cannot be correct, even if Zhdanov did have a great deal to do with the foundation of the Cominform and its direction in the first year. Djilas also confirms that the Cominform was founded on Stalin's initiative in *The New Class*, p. 179.

[3] Eugenio Reale, *Nascita del Cominform*, Verona, 1958, p. 16.

(Szklarska Poreba) in the Riesengebirge.[1] The delegates were Andrei Zhdanov and Georgi Malenkov for the CPSU; Edvard Kardelj and Milovan Djilas for the Yugoslav party; Vulko Chervenkoff and Vladimir Poptomoff for the Bulgarian Workers' Party; Ana Pauker and Gheorge Cheorghiu-Dej for the Rumanian party; Jacques Duclos and Etienne Fajon for the French party; Wladyslav Gomulka and Hilary Minc for the Polish party, Rudolf Slansky and Stefan Bastanovski for the Czech party and Luigi Longo and Eugenio Reale for the Italian party.[2] The hosts accommodated their guests in a large hotel, cut off from the outside world by a military cordon.[3]

Zhdanov spoke on the international situation, while Gomulka's speech concerned the exchange of information on the experience of Communist parties and the co-ordination of their activities. Regarding the international situation Zhdanov said, *inter alia*:[4]

> The anti-imperialist and anti-fascist policy of the USSR, with its growing international influence, stands as a bulwark in the path of America's attempts at world domination. These attempts are also thwarted by the countries of the new democracy, who have shaken off the control of Anglo-American imperialism, and by the workers everywhere, including the workers of America herself, who have no desire to go to war again on behalf of the domination of their oppressors. That is why the expansionary and reactionary policy of the USA is directed against the USSR, against the countries of the new democracy, against the working-class movement in every country and against the anti-imperialist forces of freedom everywhere. . . .
>
> Just as the Nazis cloaked the preparations for their predatory aggression under the cover of anti-Communism,

---

[1]Reale, *op. cit.*, pp. 16 ff., and Dedijer, p. 302. The belief that this meeting took place in Viliza Gora (*Ostprobleme* 1950, p. 287) or in "a secret meeting place near Warsaw" (von Rauch, *A History of Soviet Russia*, London, 1957, p. 392) is contradicted by Reale and Dedijer.

[2]Reale, the author of the book mentioned in note 3, p. 216 above, was a Neapolitan Communist and is not identical with Togliatti, as Borkenau mistakenly thinks (*European Communism*, p. 519). Reale was expelled from the Italian Communist Party in 1956.

[3]Reale, *op. cit.*, p. 19.

[4]*Informationskonferenz der Vertreter einiger kommunistischer Parteien in Polen*, Moscow, 1948, pp. 16, 22, 24, 42.

in order to make it possible to oppress and enslave all peoples, and especially their own, so the present ruling clique in the USA are covering up their expansionist policies and their offensive against even the vital interests of England, the weaker of the competing imperialist powers, with allegedly defensive anti-Communist tasks. . . .

There came about a new grouping of political forces. The further we recede from the end of the war, the more obvious it becomes that two main tendencies have formed in the post-war political scene, corresponding to the division of the political forces of the world arena into two main camps: the imperialist and the anti-democratic camp on the one side and the anti-imperialist democratic camp on the other.

The Soviet Union is tirelessly fighting for the principle that the political and economic relations between different states must be governed exclusively by the principle of the equality of the partners and mutual respect for their sovereign rights. Soviet foreign policy, and particularly Soviet economic relations with foreign countries, are based on the principle of equal rights and the guaranteeing of mutual advantage from the agreements concluded. . . .

The Comintern politicans, too, frequently used to raise the charge that the capitalists were preparing for war (as in 1928, at the 6th World Congress) in order to cover up their own offensive preparations (in 1928, the introduction of the "left-wing" policies of the years 1929–34). Similarly, in his speech at the inaugural Cominform meeting, Zhdanov accused the United States of warlike preparations in order to distract attention from the Soviet offensive policies he announced in the very same speech. This offensive manifested itself in the attempts by the French and Italian parties to come into power soon after the founding of the Cominform. The left-wing trend also displayed itself in the satellite countries, whose Communist parties achieved absolute power in the years following the foundation of the Cominform. In the sphere of foreign policy the Soviet offensive revealed itself in the menacing gesture of the Berlin Blockade (June 1948—May 1949). When, therefore, Reale, one of the participants in the conference, described the founding of the Cominform as a gigantic conspiracy against peace, he was not far wrong.[1]

[1]Reale, *op. cit.*, p. 11.

Regarding the relations between the Communist parties, Zhdanov said:[1]

The dissolution of the Comintern, which corresponded to the requirements of the development of the working-class movement in the new historical situation, had its positive side, in that it once and for all put an end to the slanderous allegations by the enemies of Communism and of the working-class movement that Moscow was interfering in the internal affairs of other countries and that the Communist parties of the various countries acted not in accordance with the interests of their peoples but on orders from abroad.[2]

The Comintern was created after the First World War, when the Communist parties were still weak, when there was hardly any contact between the working classes of the various countries, when the Communist parties still had no generally acknowledged leader for the working-class movement. The value of the Comintern lay in the fact that it re-created and stabilized the links between the workers of the different countries, that it worked out the theoretical questions of the working-class movement in the new post-war situation, that it provided universal standards for the propagation of Communist ideas and simplified the further training of the leaders of the working-class movement. This created the conditions for the transformation of the young Communist parties into mass parties of the working class. However, this transformation made the direction of these parties from one central point impossible and inappropriate. As a result, the Comintern, which had originally been a factor in the fostering of the development of the Communist parties, began to change into a factor hindering that development. The new stage in the development of the Communist parties demanded a new type of relationship between the parties. It was this circumstance which made it necessary to dissolve the Comintern and create new forms of contact between the parties. In the four years which have gone by since the dissolution of the Comintern, there has been a significant consolidation of the position of the Communist parties, and they have increased their influence in almost all the countries of Europe

[1] *Informationskonferenz der Vertreter einiger kommunistischer Parteien in Polen*, Moscow, 1948, p. 43.

[2] The resemblance between this wording and Stalin's remark on the dissolution of the Comintern (p. 209 above) will not have escaped the reader.

and Asia. This influence has grown not only in Eastern Europe but in nearly every one of the countries in Europe in which fascism used to rule, as well as in the countries occupied by the German fascists—France, Belgium, Holland, Norway, Denmark, Finland, etc. The influence of the Communists has particularly increased in the countries of the new democracy, in which the Communist parties have become the most influential parties in the State.

The present situation of the Communist parties has, however, its disadvantages. Many comrades have taken the dissolution of the Comintern to mean the breaking off of all connection and every contact between the Communist brother parties. But experience has shown that this kind of isolation of the Communist parties one from another is wrong, harmful and at bottom unnatural.

Zhdanov's description of the "value" of the Comintern is not in the slightest degree compatible with the real nature of the Third International.[1] His assertion that the transformation of the Communist parties made the centralized direction of these parties impossible contradicts the principle of "democratic centralism", insisted on by the Comintern until the very last, and is in striking contrast to the continual Soviet interference in the internal affairs of the "brother parties" both before and after the Comintern was dissolved.[2] Zhdanov gave an indication of another purpose behind the dissolution when he spoke of the comrades "who have taken the dissolution of the Comintern to mean the breaking off of all connection and every contact between the Communist brother parties". The intention was to tighten up the bonds between the CPSU and those who had already begun to slacken them during the war and had been trying ever since 1945 to attain the standing of equal partners. This applied principally to the Yugoslavs, but the Czechs (in the case of the Marshall Plan) and the Poles (Gomulka) had also been making gesture of independence.[3]

Zhdanov went on:

The greatest danger for the working class today lies in

[1] See pp. 87 and 123 above.
[2] See p. 87 (democratic centralism) and p. 90 above (interference).
[3] Djilas, *The New Class*, p. 179. On Tito's deviations from the Moscow line during the war, see Halperin, *The Triumphant Heretic*, London, 1958, pp. 19 ff.

underestimating its own strength and in overestimating the strength of its enemies. Just as in the past the Munich policy paved the way for Hitler's aggression, so a policy of appeasement towards the new course being steered by the USA and the imperialist camp will make its instigators still more impudent and aggressive. The Communist parties must therefore take the lead in every field—governmental, political, economic and ideological—in the campaign of resistance to these imperialist plans for expansion and aggression. They must close their ranks, unite their efforts on the basis of a common anti-imperialist and democratic platform and gather around them all the democratic and patriotic forces of the people.

The Communist brother parties of France, Italy and England have a special job. They must raise the banner of the defence of the national independence and sovereignty of their countries. If the Communist parties hold unshakably to their position, if they refuse to let themselves be intimidated or blackmailed, if they courageously watch over a lasting peace and the people's democracy, over the national sovereignty and the freedom and independence of their countries, and if, in their struggle against all attempts at the political and economic enslavement of their countries, they can succeed in gathering round them all the forces determined to defend the cause of honour and national independence, then every plan aimed at the enslavement of Europe will be thwarted.

Zhdanov's call to the Communist parties to align themselves against "imperialist aggression of a governmental, political or ideological nature" is explained by the Soviet assertion that the Marshall Plan represented aggression of this kind. The Marshall Plan had proved attractive to Czechoslovakia and Poland only a short while before.[1]

Zhdanov's declaration was uttered in a tone of authority. He had no intention of initiating a discussion among equal partners, but rather, in parallel to the position of his Party, of laying down the line the others were to follow. The contents of Malenkov's report *On The Activities of the Central Committee of the CPSU(B)* were in general the same as those of Zhdanov's speech, but they did reveal a difference in the attitude of these two functionaries. Zhdanov delineated the position from the

[1]See p. 214 above.

point of view of the Soviet state, the USSR, and based his thesis principally on power-political arguments, making only occasional reference to Stalin and the CPSU. Malenkov, on the other hand, continually referred to Stalin, to the brief given to him by the Central Committee of the CPSU, and to the decisions of the Central Committee. Zhdanov sharply attacked the "right-wing" Socialists, such as Schumacher and Bevin, and made it evident that his position among the Bolsheviks was a "left-wing" one. Malenkov gave no support to these attacks. He stressed quite firmly that co-existence between the capitalist and Soviet systems was inevitable—a thesis which would point to a "right-wing" position on his part.[1] It was on this level, with Malenkov being a "right-wing" Bolshevik and Zhdanov a supporter of the expansionist (and to this extent "left-wing") Soviet foreign policy, that the contrast between the two men was to be seen.[2] At the same time, Zhdanov was not a revolutionary internationalist of the old school.[3] He might be called a Russian nationalist who made use of a few left-wing revolutionary arguments.

In the course of the inaugural conference, the Communist representatives reported on developments in their individual countries, as had also been the practice at Comintern meetings. Zhdanov had not only referred in his speech to the special job devolving on the brother parties of France and Italy, but before this he had also instructed the Yugoslav delegates, Djilas and Kardelj, that during the discussions they should criticize the policies being used by these two parties.[4] In France the Communists had made unceasing if vain attempts ever since 1944 to gain a share in the government, either by "left-wing" methods (the Resistance forces) or by parliamentary means

[1] *Die Informationskonferenz, op. cit.,* p. 133.

[2] Similar differences have been observed between the Russians working in the Soviet Zone of Germany, e.g. between Col. Sergei Tulpanov and Ambassador Vladimir S. Semyonov, since 1946 (Boris Meissner, *Russland, die Westmächte und Deutschland,* Hamburg, 1953, p. 185). Tito gave a hint of similar groupings within the present Central Committee of the CPSU in his Pola speech. (See p. 279 below.)

[3] On this point, see Halperin, *op. cit.,* p. 76.

[4] Reale, *Nascita del Cominform,* pp. 38, 41. The way in which this criticism, engineered by Zhdanov, was later used as ammunition in the conflict between the Russians and the Yugoslav party is described on p. 234 below.

("United Front" with the Socialists). They had managed to get themselves into various coalition governments, it was true, but they had never been able to attain control of one of the ministries (Defence or Interior) whose possession had been used in the East European countries to create the "People's Democracies".[1]

The Italian party had had more success with their United Front policy, thanks to Palmiro Togliatti's adroit tactics and to the attitude of the Italian Socialists, particularly Pietro Nenni. In 1946 they still had four seats in the first de Gasperi government. Togliatti was Minister of Justice, Mauro Scoccimaro was Minister of Finance, Pietro Nenni had the Foreign Office and Giuseppe Romita the Ministry of Interior. But, powerful as this position was, the Communists could not manage to hold on to it. The United Front began to totter when the Socialists split on the question of co-operating with the Communists. In January 1947 Giuseppe Saragat formed his own group, attracting to it 50 of the 115 Socialist deputies. From May 1947 onwards Alcide de Gasperi ruled without the Communists or the Nenni Socialists.[2]

The results of the efforts of the Italian and French parties did not provide a sufficient answer to Moscow's demand that the leading positions achieved in France and Italy should be maintained. The Yugoslavs, hustled along by Zhdanov, expressed their criticism of the two parties, and finally Duclos and Longo gave way under the attacks engineered by Zhdanov.[3]

Gomulka's speech on the exchange of information and the co-ordination of the activities of the Communist parties was followed by a discussion which showed that Gomulka did not agree with Zhdanov on the road Poland should take on the way to Socialism. Moreover, it turned out that there was also considerable disagreement between Gomulka and Zhdanov and the majority on the question of whether a new international

[1]Borkenau, *European Communism*, pp. 466 ff.        [2]*Ibid.*, pp. 478 ff.
[3]Dedijer, *Tito Speaks*, p. 304. The published proceedings (*Informations-konferenz der Vertreter einiger kommunistischer Parteien in Polen*, Moscow, 1948) give, in the wording of the speeches by Kardelj (p. 47), Djilas (p. 78), Duclos (p. 137) and Longo (p. 241), some indication of the criticism and self-criticism, but it is in the highest degree improbable that they give the full text of all the discussions at Schreiberhau.

organization should be established and on whether the Schreiberhau meeting and the establishment of the Cominform should
be publicized. Gomulka expressed his complete disagreement
with the intention to form a new International. In the end,
however, all the declarations and resolutions embodying
Zhdanov's ideas were unanimously adopted and published.[1]

A common declaration on the international situation
reaffirmed the political line laid down by Zhdanov. The second
resolution dealt with the organization of the Information Bureau
of the Communist and Workers' Parties. It said:

> It is acknowledged that the lack of contact between the
> Communist parties taking part in this conference is a
> serious disadvantage in the present situation. Experience
> has shown that the non-existence of such connections between
> Communist parties is wrong and harmful. The necessity for
> an exchange of information between the parties and for a
> voluntary co-ordination of their actions has become particu-
> larly urgent today in view of the difficult international post-
> war situation, in which this lack of contact between the
> Communist parties of the working class can impair their
> interests.
>
> As a result of these considerations the participants in this
> conference have agreed upon the following:
>
> First: That an Information Bureau should be set up,
> consisting of representatives of the Yugoslav Communist
> Party, the Bulgarian Workers' Party (Communists), the
> Communist Party of Rumania, the Hungarian Communist
> Party, the Polish Workers' Party, the All-Union Com-
> munist Party (Bolsheviks), the Communist Party of
> France, the Communist Party of Italy.
>
> Second: The Information Bureau shall be charged with
> the task of organizing the exchange of information and,
> where necessary, with the co-ordination of the activities
> of the Communist parties on the basis of mutual consent.
> Third: The Information Bureau shall be composed of
> representatives of the Central Committees, two from each

[1]Dedijer, *Tito Speaks*, p. 306. Eugenio Reale, on page 35 of *Nascita del Cominform*, says only that Gomulka was surprisingly cool towards the sug-gested formation of a new organization. The text of the declaration and resolutions given here is taken from *Keesings Archiv der Gegenwart*, Vienna, 1950, Vol. 1946/7, pp. 1207 ff. (See also *Informationskonferenz der Vertreter einiger kommunistischer Parteien in Polen*, Moscow, 1948, pp. 7 ff.)

Central Committee, the delegations to be nominated and, if necessary, replaced by decision of the Central Committees.

Fourth: The Information Bureau shall establish a newspaper, to appear twice a month initially, and later weekly, and to be published in French and Russian and also, if possible, in other languages.

Fifth: The Information Bureau shall be located in Belgrade.

The final point of this resolution—the location in Belgrade—raises once again the question of why the Yugoslav party was brought into such close contact with the new organization. The Yugoslavs themselves see this as an indication of the Soviet intention to bind their party as closely as possible to the new organization, "in order to facilitate the blow that was to follow".[1] There are a number of other factors which seem to lend credence to this. The necessity for an exchange of information was a world-wide necessity, but the limitation of the Cominform to a few European parties seems to take no account of this. The real purpose in setting up the organization was not the one given in the resolution. Why did the resolution put Yugoslavia first in the list of names, and why was it the representatives of just that party who were called upon to criticize the French and Italian parties? It could not be that this symbolized the Russians' implicit trust in the Yugoslavs, since of all the East European countries it was Yugoslavia which had evinced the strongest urge towards independence ever since 1945. In Yugoslavia the Communists ruled unchallenged. Neither in their policies nor in their revolutionary propaganda did they need to pay as much respect to bourgeois and Social-Democratic coalition partners as other Communist parties still had to do at this time. This meant that Yugoslavia was well on the way ot achieving a position at the side of Moscow, respected and admired by many Communists.[2] Was it not therefore the mistrustful Stalin's real intention to send trustworthy watch-dogs into the country that was making suspiciously great efforts to be treated as an equal? Do not Stalin's efforts to create discord

[1]Dedijer, *op. cit.*, p. 304. Djilas, too, says (*op. cit.*, p. 179) that the Cominform was founded for the purpose of guaranteeing Soviet domination in the satellite countries.

[2]Halperin, *The Triumphant Heretic*, London, 1958, pp. 42 ff.

between Dimitroff and Tito fit into this picture?[1] When Zhdanov forced Djilas and Kardelj to criticize the French and Italian parties, is it not likely that the *arriére-pensée* was that, in the case of a subsequent Soviet-Yugoslav dispute, the resentment aroused by the criticism could be profitably exploited? In the light of these and other events which were soon to follow —the offensive policies of the Communists in France and Italy and the seizure of power in the East European countries (and even more, in view of the fact that membership of the Cominform was restricted to the very parties that took part in these events)—it can be shortly said the Cominform was to serve, both towards the satellite countries and towards the free world, as an instrument of the Soviet offensive policy which was announced at its foundation.[2] The function of the Cominform's news-sheet was not only a propaganda function, but was also that of making known the Moscow line to the Communist parties of the world. It was originally envisaged that the Cominform would have certain functions of supervision over some of the People's Democracies, and particularly over Yugoslavia.

Borkenau interprets these events differently. He is quite right, of course, in regarding as highly important the decision to make Belgrade the headquarters. But is it right to say, as he does, that the highest "command post" of the "Comintern" was transferred from Russia? Is it really possible to see in this decision an "act of rebellion" by Zhdanov against Stalin? Did Stalin really have "no majority in the Politbureau" at this time?[3]

Zhdanov asked Stalin to decide on the location of the Cominform's headquarters—and Stalin decided on Belgrade.[4] Borkenau's idea that a senior Soviet official could rebel against Stalin seems incompatible with the events of the period 1934–47. Stalin was powerful enough to "purge" any opponent, even a potential opponent, or in fact anyone who dared to give utterance to independent thought. Men who had had much more real power than Zhdanov—Tukhachevski, Yagoda,

---

[1]See p. 216 above.    [2]Eugenio Reale, *op. cit.*, p. 27.
[3]Borkenau, *European Communism*, pp. 521 and 524.
[4]Dedijer, *op. cit.*, p. 304.

Yezhov—had disappeared. Did Stalin in fact *need* a majority in the Politbureau?[1]

In his "secret speech", delivered at the 20th Party Congress on 25th February 1956, Khrushchev had this to say about the atmosphere in the Central Committee of the CPSU:[2]

It is obvious that such conditions put the members of the Politbureau in a difficult position. And when we also bear in mind that in the last two years there were no plenary sessions of the Central Committee and that the Politbureau only met occasionally, we can understand how difficult it was for the individual member of the Politbureau to protest against this or that unjust or improper action or against errors and defects in the actions of the leadership.

As we have already shown, many decisions were either taken by one individual or else in wholesale fashion without thorough discussion. Everyone knows about the tragic fate of the member of the Politbureau, Comrade Voznessenski, who fell a victim to Stalin's oppression. It was typical that the decision to expel him from the Politbureau was never brought up for discussion, but was the result of an unfair manoeuvre. It was the same in the case of the decision to remove Kuznyetzov and Rodionov from their positions.

The importance of the Politbureau of the Central Committee was reduced, and its work was broken into fragments, by the creation of various commissions within the Politbureau, to so-called "quintets", "sextets" and "septets". Here, as an example, is a resolution by the Politbureau dated 3 October 1946. Stalin's proposition:

1. The Politbureau's Commission for External Affairs ("sextet") shall in future deal not only with external affairs but also with domestic construction and questions of domestic policy.
2. The "sextet" shall co-opt the Chairman of the State Commission for Economic Planning, Comrade Voznessenski, and shall henceforth be called a "septet".

(signed) J. STALIN, *Secretary of the Central Committee*.

What card-player's language! (laughter). It is obvious

[1]A correct assessment of the relationship between Zhdanov and Stalin is given in Halperin, *op. cit.*, p. 76.

[2]Stalin had already created "commissions" within the Comintern to ensure that certain spheres of activity remained in the hands of people on whom he could absolutely rely (see p. 139 above).

that the creation of these Commissions in the Politbureau—
"quintets", "sextets" and "septets"—is a violation of the
principle of collective leadership. The result of this procedure
was that some of the members of the Politbureau were denied
contact with vital affairs of state.

In view of Stalin's powerful position indicated by Khrushchev's words, it is extremely unlikely that Zhdanov would have
tried to start and to carry through such a "rebellion". Zhdanov
died on 31 August, under circumstances which have admittedly
never been completely explained.[1] However, if his death was
not due to natural causes, the explanation may just as well
lie in the impending failure of his offensive policies, both against
Yugoslavia and against Western Europe. Borkenau's views are
based on the belief that the Comintern was not dissolved and
that "the command" was moved "out of Russia to Belgrade".[2]
What in fact happened was quite different. The Comintern
really was dissolved. After 1943 the Central Committee of the
CPSU controlled the national Communist parties without the
intermediary of the Comintern. This situation was not in any
way changed by the formation of the Cominform, which was
in no sense a "highest command-post".[3]

### THE ORGANIZATION AND ACTIVITIES OF THE COMINFORM

According to the resolution which founded it, the Cominform
was to organize the co-ordination of the work of the Communist parties and the exchange of information between them,
on the basis of mutual agreement. It was also to produce a
newspaper in various languages.[4] The long-winded name of this
paper, *For Lasting Peace, for People's Democracy*, was thought up
by Stalin himself.[5] The Cominform first of all turned to the
problem of producing the paper. The first issue appeared in
Belgrade on 1 November 1947.

Yudin, who had been in Belgrade since October 1947,

[1] See p. 244 below, note 2.
[2] See p. 245 below and Borkenau, *European Communism*, pp. 282, 521.
[3] See p. 245 below.
[4] The Cominform newspaper finally appeared in eighteen languages.
(*Ostprobleme* 1955, Vol. II, p. 1152.)
[5] Reale, *op. cit.*, p. 51. For purposes of clandestine distribution, the
German Communists used to call the paper by the name of a once-popular
German family magazine, *Die Gartenlaube*.

demanded and was given one of the largest buildings in the centre of the city for accommodating the Cominform head-quarters. Radiotelephone and teleprinter communication with Moscow was immediately established. Yudin brought with him several compositors from Moscow to work on the paper.

The paper was printed on presses belonging to *Borba*, which was also required to provide separate premises for the make-up and printing work. All stages of the work were treated as secret. During work-breaks and at night Yudin's assistant, J. Olenin, locked up the rooms and sealed the doors, a method used by the Russian secret service when security requires it. Dedijer says of Yudin that he was regarded in the Soviet Union as "the leading philosopher among the NKVD men and the best NKVD man among the philosophers".[1] Yudin, too, was in close contact with the Central Committee of the CPSU.

The paper was pre-censored in Moscow. When the first hundred copies had been printed, the printing was suspended and the sample copies were sent by air to the Central Com-mittee. If the contents were approved, the Central Committee would telephone through the order to resume printing. The articles were frequently amended, and it sometimes happened that the amendments were so extensive that whole pages had to be reset, printed and sent off to Moscow again. Sometimes it was Yudin himself who took the sample copies to Moscow. The Yugoslav envoy to Moscow, Vladimir Popovitch, had an opportunity to observe the servile respect Yudin paid to Zhdanov when Popovitch happened to be visiting Zhdanov at the end of 1947.[2] In view of the power of the Soviet censor-ship, the editorial conferences in Belgrade to discuss what should appear in each issue were of minor importance. This censorship was liable to be applied even in the case of articles by prominent authors. The Polish representative, Finkelsztajn, once protested—in vain—against amendments to an article by a Polish statesman. Finkelsztajn seems not to have understood that the Soviet position was just as dominant within the editorial

---

[1]Dedijer, *op. cit.*, p. 306. All these details of Yudin's editorial activity are taken from Dedijer, *op. cit.*, pp. 306 ff.

[2]Dedijer, *op. cit.*, p. 307.

sphere of the Cominform as it was in the political life of the East European states. It was in token of this that Yudin introduced a number of Soviet journalists into the editorial offices, even though he was not formally entitled to do so.

On 1 February 1948 it was announced that representatives of the nine member parties had met in Yugoslavia and had decided to form a permanent editorial staff for the paper about to be published.[1]

In the first years of its existence, the Cominform's "offices" were organized and staffed as follows. The editor-in-chief was the former director of the Soviet trade union paper *Trud*, Pavel F. Yudin.[2] Further editors were Giancarlo Pajetta (Italy), Julian Finkelsztajn (Poland), Pierre Hentges (France), Boris Ziherl (Yugoslavia), Zoltan Biro (Hungary) and B. Voda-Peska (Czechoslovakia). There was also, although he was not publicly named, an "English representative", that is, a Russian who was responsible for the English edition of the paper, and who had two English Communists as assistant editors.

The organization of the "office" was conditioned by the task of publishing the paper in different languages. There were a Russian, a French, a Yugoslav and an English department, the Russian department not only having the largest staff but also being responsible for administration. Yudin, as head of the Russian department, gave the heads of the other departments details of the instructions he received from Moscow, and told them what articles were to appear. Altogether, the staff consisted of between forty and fifty persons, of which some thirty were employed in the Russian department. The Yugoslav department, headed by Ziherl, was closely supervised by the Russian department, for which purpose Ziherl had as his

[1]*Keesings Archiv der Gegenwart*, Vol. 1948/49, p. 1354. Dedijer, *op. cit.*, p. 289, mentions a meeting which took place in Yugoslavia on 15 December 1947, at which technical questions to do with the publication of the paper were discussed. This is probably the same meeting as the one mentioned by the Cominform on 1 February 1948.

[2]Togliatti recently claimed that in 1951 Stalin suggested to him that he might like to give up his post as General Secretary of the Italian Communist Party to take over the post of General Secretary of the Cominform. Togliatti claims that he refused, on the grounds that such a nomination would have given the appearance of a return to the Comintern organization. (See *Unita*, 26 June 1956.)

assistant a Russian national, Vladimir Pavlovitch Milyutin.

In their efforts to introduce into the Information Bureau working conditions similar to those which obtained in their own country, the Soviet Russians made clear distinctions in the treatment of the staff. Heads of departments received preferential treatment of every kind. They were given better accommodation and bigger rations, irrespective of the size of their families, and in the canteen they had a room specially reserved for them.

There is no evidence that the Bureau—that is to say, the "organization" composed of the representatives of the nine parties—did anything other than produce the paper *For Lasting Peace, For People's Democracy* during the period preceding the conflict with Yugoslavia. After the transfer of the Cominform headquarters to Bucharest the paper went on appearing.

The Cominform did, however, occasionally hold meetings of a political nature, at which decisions taken in Moscow were "adopted". In this respect Togliatti was correct in saying in June 1956 that the Italian Communists had never found it necessary to discuss their policies at international meetings, apart from the inaugural (Cominform) meeting.[1] It was not necessary, simply because on such occasions the Moscow line was adopted *nemine contradicente*. In saying this, Togliatti did not reveal whether he ever discussed his views, which did not coincide at all points with the Moscow line with regard to the 1947 offensive policy, with the representatives of the Soviet state security service attached to the Soviet Embassy in Rome. From 1945 onwards the Soviet state security service had begun to take over the role of the OMS as the intermediate link between the Moscow headquarters and the national Communist parties in individual cases.[2]

The Cominform Bureau, staffed with journalists and not with high-level functionaries, consisted of nothing more than a group of editors. Yet its publications were of considerable importance, for thanks to the precensorship by the Central

[1] In his answer to the ninth question by the publisher of *Nuovi Argomenti* in issue No. 20 of 16 June 1956 (quoted in *The Anti-Stalin Campaign and International Communism*, New York, 1956, pp. 136 ff.).

[2] Regarding the intermediary role of the state security service in the financing of a Communist party, see p. 316 below, note 3 (Australia).

Committee of the CPSU nothing went into print that was not
in consonance with the Soviet party line or which ought not
to be published for any other reason. Thus the paper was
valuable to the Communist parties of the world as representing
a kind of Guide to Communist Usage. From the way in which
their articles were published, or the manner in which they were
"improved", the authors could see whether or not they were
following the Moscow "line".

Both the new left-wing Moscow line announced at the
founding of the Cominform and individual articles in the
Cominform paper had their effects, but these effects were not
confined to the parties belonging to the Cominform. The
Indian Communist Party for example had, in agreement with
the British party, been supporting Nehru's Government since
15 August 1947, when India gained her independence.
Zhdanov's thesis that the world was divided into two antagonistic camps, together with the demand made by Edvard
Kardelj when the Cominform was founded, that the Communists must attack the bourgeoisie as a whole, now changed
the picture for the radical elements among the Indian Communists. At a meeting of the Central Committee in December
1947, they rejected the policy of support for Nehru as opportunist and replaced the General Secretary, Puranchandra
Joshi, by the radically-minded Bhalchandra Trimbak Ranadive.[1] Led by Ranadive, his radical supporters tried to overthrow the government by force of arms in 1948-9, an attempt
which led to the arrest of numbers of leading Communists and
the banning of their Party (e.g. in West Bengal), and finally
brought the Indian Party to a state of crisis.[2] In the case of
Japan, an article in the Cominform paper of 6 January 1950,
during this period of left-wing policies, rejected the conciliatory tactic being pursued by Sanzo Nosaka, the then
General Secretary of the Japanese Communist Party, and this
finally led to Nosaka's fall.[3]

However, the Cominform paper was only one of the means

[1]Overstreet and Windmiller, *op. cit.*, pp. 266 ff.
[2]M. R. Masani, *op. cit.*, pp. 90 ff.
[3]John H. Kautsky, *op. cit.*, p. 202, and Ruth Fischer, *Von Lenin zu Mao*,
Düsseldorf/Cologne, 1956, p. 208.

used by the Central Committee of the CPSU to control and direct world Communism.

## THE CONFLICT WITH YUGOSLAVIA

The significance of the Cominform was made clear by the fact that the Soviet letter of 27 March 1948 (signed by Stalin and Molotov "on behalf of the Central Committee of the CPSU"), which began the conflict, was sent by the Central Committee of the CPSU not to the Yugoslav party alone but also to the member parties of the Cominform, with the request that they should send their comments on the Soviet letter to the Central Committee of the CPSU.[1] On 16 April 1948 Yudin went to see Tito and gave him a letter from Zhdanov enclosing the text of a resolution by the Central Committee of the Hungarian party. The Yugoslavs thereupon sent their reply to the Soviet letter of 27 March to all the parties belonging to the Cominform. The Yugoslav party received the comments of these parties one after the other *via* the Central Committee of the CPSU and the Soviet representative in Belgrade.[2]

The Yugoslavs suggested to the CPSU that a delegation should be sent to Yugoslavia to examine the question of whether the charges contained in the Soviet letter of 27 March were true.[3] The CPSU, on the other hand, in their letter of 4 May 1948, demanded that the matter should be brought before the Cominform.[4] Tito would not agree to this. It was clear from the comments he had already received from the other parties that his representatives would be in a hopeless minority in the event of such a discussion in the Cominform.[5] But this was precisely

---

[1]Dedijer, *op. cit.*, pp. 357–358 and 341, and the *Soviet-Yugoslav Dispute*, London and New York, p. 15. The letter condemned the fact that prominent personalities in Yugoslavia had uttered "malicious" criticism of the Soviet Union. Considering that Stalin had Trotsky first expelled and then murdered, it is worthy of note that the letter of 27 March said, *inter alia*, that Trotsky had also started by uttering this kind of criticism. "We regard Trotsky's political career as instructive enough." Similar clumsy threats were to be repeated when Yugoslavia left the Cominform. The Yugoslavs also published the correspondence (cf. "*Brief des ZK der KPJ und Brief des ZK der KPdSU (B)*", Beograd, 1958 (with comments).

[2]Dedijer, *op. cit.*, p. 359.

[3]Letter of 13 April in *The Soviet-Yugoslav Dispute*, p. 28.

[4]The letter is reproduced in *Keesings Archiv der Gegenwart, loc. cit.*, p. 1501.

[5]Dedijer, *op. cit.*, p. 364, and *Keesings Archiv der Gegenwart*.

the reason why the Soviet Communists began to prepare a Cominform meeting. On 20 May the Yugoslav Central Committee reaffirmed their already expressed refusal to attend such a meeting, whereupon a Soviet letter of 22 May reminded the Yugoslavs that they themselves had contributed to the criticism of the French and Italian parties at the inauguration of the Cominform.[1] If they now declined to submit to criticism themselves, then this had nothing to do with equality but meant that the Yugoslavs thought they were entitled to a preferential position in the Cominform.[2]

Unless they wanted to surrender completely, the Yugoslavs could do nothing else. Their standpoint was justified, considering the resolution on the organization of the Cominform.[3] If the exchange of information and the co-ordination of the activities of the Communist parties was to be organized "on the basis of mutual agreement", as the resolution put it, then this implied that there must be agreement in each single instance of future collaboration, irrespective of whether this concerned attendance at meetings or reporting at Cominform conferences. The attitude of the Soviet representatives in the Security Council of the United Nations and in the Allied Control Council in Germany demonstrates that the Russians understood and made the most of a comparable right, so far as their interests were concerned.

There was another thought in the minds of the Yugoslavs—that there was no guarantee that their representatives would be able to leave such a conference safe and sound: a fear which was not wholly unjustified. Dedijer remarks that when Stalin summoned the Ukrainian Politbureau to the Kremlin for conversations in 1937, every one of the members was arrested by the NKVD. The Yugoslavs were also aware that in March 1945 several Polish politicians, including General Leopold Okulicki, the Commander of the *Armiya Krayova* (Home Army), had been invited to Moscow to take part in discussions on the formation of a unified Polish government. Thereafter nothing more was heard of these Poles until the Soviet delegates at the

[1] See p. 222 above.
[2] *Keesings Archiv, loc. cit.*, p. 1506, and Dedijer, *op. cit.*, p. 367.
[3] See p. 224 above.

United Nations conference in San Francisco (April—June 1945) announced that they had been sentenced by a Soviet court for crimes against the Red Army.[1]

The Cominform meeting which finally set the seal upon the breach between Yugoslavia and the Soviet bloc took place in Bucharest at the end of June 1948. Taking part were Andrei Zhdanov, Georgi Malenkov, and Michael Suslov for the Soviet Union; Traitchko Kostoff and Vulko Chervenkoff for Bulgaria; Gheorge Gheorghiu-Dej, Ana Pauker and Vasile Luca for Rumania; Matthias Rakosi, Michael Farkas and Ernö Gerö for Hungary; Rudolph Slansky, Viliam Siroky, Bedrich Geminder and Gustav Bares for Czechoslovakia; Palmiro Togliatti and Pietro Secchia for the Italian party; Jacques Duclos and Etienne Fajon for the French Communist Party and Jakob Berman and Aleksander Zavadski for the Polish Workers' Party.[2]

The resolution unanimously adopted at this conference said:

> The Information Bureau has come to the unanimous conclusion that the leaders of the Communist Party of Yugoslavia, by their anti-Party and anti-Soviet views, which are incompatible with Marxism-Leninism, by their refusal to take part in the meetings of the Information Bureau, have taken up a position of opposition to the Communist parties belonging to the Information Bureau. They have set foot on the path of renunciation of the united Socialist front and trodden the road leading to the betrayal of the cause of the international solidarity of the working class and have adopted a nationalistic attitude. The Information Bureau condemns the anti-Party policies and attitude of the Central Com-

[1]Hugh Seton-Watson, *The East European Revolution*, London, 1956, p. 118. A similar case, equally contrary to the principles of good faith and to international law, occurred more recently, on 4 November 1956, when the Hungarian General, Pal Maleter, went to see Russian staff officers to conduct negotiations with them and was arrested.

[2]The reader will note the fates suffered by the various participants in this conference in the purges of the subsequent years and in the upheavals following the death of Stalin. Zhdanov died in 1948, Kostoff was hanged in 1949, Slansky and Geminder were executed in 1952, Ana Pauker and V. Luca fell in disgrace. The upheavals after Stalin's death drastically affected the careers of M. Farkas, E. Gerö, M. Rakosi, and even Chervenkoff. It is not without significance that neither Dimitroff nor Gomulka took part in the conference.

mittee of the Communist Party of Yugoslavia and is of the opinion that in view of all this it has put itself and the Yugoslav Party outside the family of fraternal Communist parties, outside the united Communist front and consequently outside the ranks of the Information Bureau.

The Information Bureau is of the opinion that the basic reason for all these defects in the leadership of the Yugoslav Communist Party is indisputably the fact in the last five or six months nationalist elements have managed to achieve a dominating position in the senior ranks, where they had always been, although well in the background; and that as a result the leaders of the Yugoslav Party have broken with the international traditions of the Yugoslav Communist Party and have taken the road of nationalism. The Yugoslav leaders grossly overestimate the nationalist forces of Yugoslavia and their influence and believe they can maintain the independence of Yugoslavia and build up Socialism in their country without the support of the Communist parties of other countries or of the People's Democracies or of the Soviet Union. They believe that the new Yugoslavia can manage without the assistance of these revolutionary forces.

Revealing their defective understanding of the international situation and the fact they have been intimidated by the blackmail and threats of the imperialist powers, the Yugoslav leaders think they can win the good opinion of the imperialist states by making concessions to them. The Yugoslav leaders obviously do not understand—or pretend not to understand—that this kind of nationalist line may well lead to the decline of Yugoslavia into an ordinary bourgeois republic, to the loss of her independence and to her transformation into a colony of the imperialist countries.

The Information Bureau has no doubt that inside the Yugoslav Communist Party there are sound elements which are still sufficiently loyal to the principles of Marxism-Leninism, the international tradition of the Yugoslav Communist Party and to the united Socialist front. It is their task to force the present leaders to admit their mistakes frankly and honestly, to break with nationalism, return to internationalism and to use every means to strengthen the united Socialist front against imperialism. If the present leaders of the Yugoslav Communist Party prove unequal to this task, then these sound forces must replace them by others and produce a new international leadership for the Party. The Information Bureau has no doubt that the Yugoslav Communist Party will be able to fulfil this honourable task.

The headquarters of the Cominform was transferred from Belgrade to Bucharest.

The Cominform resolution repeated the gist of the charges the Soviet Communist Party had previously raised against the Yugoslavs by letter. The new feature was that the resolution made an appeal to the "sound elements" in the Yugoslav party and called on them to force their "present leaders" to admit their mistakes and to return to internationalism. This was interference in Yugoslavia's internal affairs, but the hopes of the Soviet leaders contained in the wording of the resolution, that they could encourage an opposition group in the Yugoslav party, were not fulfilled. The only reaction among the Yugoslav people was a wave of antagonism towards the Russians when the Cominform resolution was made public in Yugoslavia.[1]

In July 1948 the 5th Congress of the Yugoslav Party took place and the resolution of the 28 June was put before the delegates. Tito made a report to the congress in a speech lasting several hours. Although he defended his policies in his speech, he made no attempt to attack the Soviet Union, and said it was his party's aim to improve relations with the CPSU. The overwhelming majority of the delegates voted for his re-election to the Central Committee, only five dissenting.[2]

Halperin is certainly correct when he says that what was at stake in the Yugoslav conflict was the security of the Soviet monopoly over world Communism, a monopoly that was threatened by Tito.[3] This factor, as has already been clearly shown, also played a part in the founding of the Cominform, which Halperin elsewhere described as the most important

---

[1] C. H. Dewhurst, *Close Contact*, London, 1954, p. 111.

[2] Josip Broz Tito, *Political report of the Central Committee of the Yugoslav Communist Party* (speech at the 5th Congress), Belgrade, 1948, pp. 175 ff. Also *Neues Jugoslavien*, Belgrade, No. 19, 25 June 1950, p. 6, and Charles P. McVicker, *Titoism—Pattern for International Communism*, New York— London, 1957, p. 17. See also Dedijer, *op. cit.*, p. 380.

[3] *The Triumphant Heretic*, p. 67.

success of the left-wing extremists.[1] The foundation of the Cominform is part of the pattern of the left-wing offensive of this period, but it was equally important as an attempt to recreate complete Soviet control over Yugoslavia (and over other countries of the Eastern bloc).

C. H. Dewhurst's surmise is that it was the advice of the Soviet secret service which led Stalin to commit this, the greatest Soviet mistake.[2] It is true that the intelligence services in totalitarian states have a habit of reporting to the dictators what the dictators want to hear. Stalin, however, tended to approach problems with such firmly preconceived ideas that he simply took notice of any reports to the contrary. A good example of this was his attitude in the period preceding the outbreak of the Russo-German war.[3] In the Yugoslav affair, his conversations wth Tito, Kardelj and Djilas gave Stalin an opportunity to form his own opinion. It is possible that he brought the conflict with the Yugoslavs to a head in the unshakable belief that Tito, who had had "proletarian discipline" hammered into him through his long years as a Communist, would give way.

In this work there is no room for more than a bare description of the Yugoslav conflict with the Soviet bloc which developed out of the Comintern controversy.[4] The Soviets employed a number of devices in the attempt force Yugoslavia to submit. They set economic sanctions on foot. Hungary cancelled her trade agreement with Yugoslavia in June 1949 and Czechoslovakia broke off trade negotiations with her in the same month. In the July Poland stopped deliveries of goods to Yugoslavia, and after August Hungary paid no further reparations to her.

Then there was the anti-Yugoslav propaganda campaign.

[1] *Op. cit.*, p. 57.

[2] *Op. cit.*, pp. 111–112. It is open to doubt whether Western eyes would see this mistake as a "lamentable step" (Dewhurst, *op. cit.*, p. 112).

[3] See p. 200 above, note 4; D. J. Dallin (*Soviet Espionage*, p. 134) also reports that when Hitler's war preparations were reported to him, Stalin ordered the punishment of the originator of this "British provocation".

[4] In his *History of the Three Internationals* (pp. 495 ff.), the American Communist William Z. Foster gives a completely distorted account of the conflict. This account has since been contradicted by the Soviet statements of May 1955.

Communist parties all over the world, even those which were not members of the Cominform, unanimously condemned the behaviour of Yugoslavia. The press and radio of the Soviet Union and the satellites directed a stream of propaganda against the Yugoslav party and its leaders, maintaining not only that the party had fallen into the hands of "enemies of the people, murderers and spies", but also that it was an espionage network engaged in carrying out missions on behalf of the Tito-Kardelj-Rankovic-Djilas clique and so forth. In September 1949 the Soviet Union abrogated the treaty of assistance it had concluded with Yugoslavia in April 1945 and this example was followed in the succeeding months by Hungary, Rumania and Bulgaria.

In the October and November Soviet and satellite troops were seen to be concentrating on the Yugoslav borders. In October the Soviet Union demanded the recall of the Yugoslav Ambassador, Mrazovic, and in November the Yugoslav *chargé d'affaires* was declared *persona non grata* and was requested to leave the Soviet Union.

The trials of alleged supporters of Tito were of considerable importance politically. Their main purpose was probably that of strangling any attempts at independence in East Europe. At this period there was an intensive campaign against national movements in all Communist parties, the intention being to enforce acknowledgement of the leading position of the Soviet Union.[1] This "leading position" of the Soviet Union had developed out of the policy of subordinating the interests of world Communism to the requirements of the Soviet party, the policy that had been followed ever since the 3rd World Congress in 1921.[2] In 1949 the KPD declared in one of its published documents:[3]

Ever since the Soviet Union came into existence the proof

[1]There has hitherto been no evidence that the trials of the Titoists had their origin in the so-called "Leningrad Affair" (the trials of Nikolai Voznessenski, Alexei Kuznyetsov and others).

[2]See p. 71 above.

[3]"Guidance on the consideration of the Resolution of the 14th Meeting of the KPD Party Executive, 28–30 December 1949, entitled *On the Ideological-political consolidation of the Party on the basis of Marxism-Leninism.*" Published by the Party Executive, Frankfurt-am-Main, 1949, pp. 86–7.

of international proletarianism has lain in the attitude and
demeanour towards her. Since the Second World War, since
the American imperialists took over the inheritance of
fascist German imperialism and have been preparing for
war against the Soviet Union with all the means at their
disposal, this has been more than ever true. Today, the term
proletarian internationalist can be applied only to him who
unconditionally supports the defence of and friendship with
the Soviet Union, who unconditionally recognizes the leading
position of the Soviet Union and the CPSU in the peace
camp, who devotes himself completely to the unity and
indivisibility of the camp of world peace and who gives his
support to the Chinese People's Republic, the struggle of the
nations oppressed by imperialism and the struggle of the
world's peace forces. . . . Today, the only internationalist is
the one who fights with all his might against the enemies of
the Soviet Union, of peoples' democracy and in particular
against the fascist Tito clique and other agents of imperialism.

In Albania, Kochi Dzodze was executed on 10 June 1949
for collaboration with Yugoslav Titoists. On 14 June the
prominent Bulgarian Communist and Deputy Prime Minister,
Traichko Kostoff, was arrested on charges of being a "close
collaborator of the spy and traitor, Tito," and was sentenced to
death on 15 December.[1] The trial of the former Foreign
Minister of Hungary, Laszlo Rajk, and seven others took place
in Budapest from 10 until 24 September 1949. It was not only
"proved" that the accused had been guilty of espionage on
behalf of Yugoslavia, but they were also charged with having
attempted to overthrow the Hungarian Government and
trying to "collect the Peoples' Democracies around Yugoslavia
with Belgrade as the focal point". Rajk and two others were
sentenced to death, the rest being given long prison sentences.[2]

These trials were followed by those of the General Secretary
of the Czech Party, Rudolf Slansky, and thirteen others. In
November 1952 Slansky and ten of the others were sentenced to
be hanged. The Communists proclaimed that this trial, too, was
an action in the battle against Tito's "band of conspirators":[3]

[1] *Traitschko Kostoff und seine Gruppe*, Berlin, 1951, pp. 7 ff.
[2] *L. Rajk und Komplizen vor dem Volksgericht*, Berlin, 1949, pp. 372 ff.
[3] *Neues Deutschland*, the SED newspaper, E. Berlin, 25 November 1952.

The trial of Slansky and his accomplices belongs to the same group as the conspiracy trials of Rajk, Kostoff and other bands of traitors working in the popular democratic countries with the same methods and the same aims. The Tito band had a direct connection with the Prague conspiracy. Slansky and his accomplices were in secret contact with it for years.

In fact the prime significance of the Slansky trial lies elsewhere. Eleven of the fourteen accused were Jews. Some of them were charged with "Zionist" connections, i.e. the connections between Czechoslovakia and Israel, but this was only a cover for the anti-semitic nature of the trial.

All the instructions concerning the purges carried out in the Peoples' Democracies emanated from Moscow.[1] The CPSU's anti-semitism had its roots in Russian history, but its appearance in 1950 and 1951 is explained by the international character of Jewry.[2] The most outstanding theoretician of revolutionary internationalism, Leon Trotsky, came of Jewish stock, just as Karl Marx did. Many Communists who had worked on the international level, who had emigrated to Western countries or who took part in the Spanish Civil War, were Jews. These Communists were devoted to an internationalism, which, true to the classic teaching, saw its aim as world revolution, but not as world domination by the Soviet state. Yet it was just this world domination that Stalin was striving for. Thus the Slansky trial served to destroy men who, in their own countries, might threaten the Soviet hegemony. And because the Soviet hegemony seemed threatened, Stalin had war declared on the "deviationism" represented by Zionism or cosmopolitanism.[3] It was also the desire to eliminate

[1]This is clear from the statements of Josef Sviatlo, a senior official of the Polish security service. (See *Die Affäre Gomulka/Spychalski* in the special supplement to the periodical *Hinter dem Eisernen Vorhang*, Munich, 1955, No. 4.)

[2]The culmination of the anti-semitic campaign in the Soviet Union came with the "unmasking" of the "terrorist" group of Jewish doctors in January 1953 (TASS report of 13 January 1953).

[3]"Cosmopolitanism", just like "internationalism", underwent a change in significance. In 1935, a "cosmopolite" was still being defined in a Soviet lexicon as "a citizen of the world". In 1952 the *Short Philosophical Lexicon* was calling "cosmopolitanism" a reactionary theory which preached indifference to the fatherland, to national traditions and to national culture. (See Carew Hunt, *A Guide to Communist Jargon*, pp. 36 ff.)

J

opponents of the Soviet hegemony which lay at the root of the
purges carried out in Poland and East Germany.

Gomulka was not a Moscow émigré. During the first years of
the war he had already joined up with a group of Polish Communists, who asked the Comintern to let them ally themselves
with the national resistance forces fighting against the Germans.
The Comintern sent a refusal, explaining that such resistance
was premature (Hitler had not yet started the war against the
Soviet Union) and was not in the interests of Moscow. Gomulka
had given further demonstrations of opposition to the Moscow
line, not only in the matter of the foundation of the Cominform
but also in connection with the break with Yugoslavia.[1] The
Polish party later admitted that although Gomulka was
allegedly arrested on suspicion of "diversionist activity", the
real reason was "merely" nationalist deviationism.[2] It was not
least because of his handling of the Gomulka affair that Jakob
Berman, a loyal adherent of Moscow and the man in the Politbureau responsible for controlling the security police, was
made to resign in May 1956, after senior officials of the Polish
state security service, such as the Deputy Minister, Roman
Romkovski, had already been called to account for it.[3]

The German Communists Kurt Müller, Paul Merker, Bruno
Goldhammer, Willi Kreikemeyer, Lex Ende, Leo Bauer and
Maria Weiterer, who were arrested in 1950–1, also belonged to
the category of former émigrés to the West, Spanish Civil War
veterans and Jews.[4] Walter Ulbricht himself gave the instructions on the course the investigations were to take. Leo Bauer
was told by Erich Mielke, the Deputy Minister of State Security

[1] Halperin, *op. cit.*, p. 77; H. F. Armstrong, *op. cit.*, pp. 144 ff. See also
pp. 223 f. above.

[2] E. Ochab in *Trybuna Ludu*, 7 April 1956, quoted in *National Communism
and Popular Revolt in Eastern Europe*, p. 81.

[3] Leon Wudski's statements at the 8th Plenary Session of the Polish party.
Wudski was a member of the Party Control Commission (*Nowe drogi* 1956,
No. 10, quoted in *Ostprobleme* 1957, p. 189. Also *Trybuna Ludu*, 27 January
1955, quoted in *Ostprobleme* 1955, p. 438).

[4] Cf. *Lehren aus dem Prozess gegen das Verschwörerzentrum Slansky* (Resolution
of the Central Committee of the SED, 20 December 1952), reproduced in
Hermann Matern, *Uber die Durchführung des Beschlusses des ZK der SED,
Lehren aus dem Prozess gegen das Verschwörerzentrum Slansky*, in which all the
fabrications accepted by the courts in the trials of Rajk and Slansky are
faithfully re-echoed.

in the Soviet Zone of Germany, after his arrest in August 1950 that the SED intended to sentence the accused in February 1951 after a public mass trial similar to the trials of Rajk and Kostoff. The charge that the accused had collaborated with the "spy" Noel Field also played a considerable role in the preparations for the German "Rajk trial". The investigations could not be completed by February 1951 because neither persuasion nor severe interrogation could induce the accused to make the requisite confessions. In April 1951 the accused were handed over to the Soviet state security service. There was no propaganda trial. The accused were sentenced to death by a Soviet court, but the death sentences were later commuted to life imprisonment. In 1955 two of them, Leo Bauer and Kurt Müller, returned to the Federal German Republic.[1]

At least one of the accused, Willi Kreikemeyer, died in prison. The persons responsible for the investigation in the Soviet Zone of Germany were never called to account, as comparable people were in Poland and Hungary. On the contrary, Erich Mielke, who was in charge of the investigations, was appointed Minister of State Security after the dismissal of Wollweber.

There is no doubt that Halperin is correct when he says that these purges hung together as part of one and the same plan.[2] At the same time it is doubtful whether this plan consisted in trying to join forces with some German movement of revenge, present-day national-socialists.[3] What evidence there is only points to Stalin's unremitting efforts to wage war on all national movements and genuinely international activities within his sphere of domination in order to maintain the pre-eminent position of the Soviet Union.

The Rajk trial was followed by such weighty measures against Yugoslavia as the abrogation of treaties of mutual assistance and the recalling of diplomatic staffs.[4] When Rajk

---

[1]Leo Bauer, *Die Partei hat immer Recht*, in *Aus Politik und Zeitgeschichte* (Supplement to the weekly *Das Parlament*), Bonn, 4 July 1956, p. 409.

[2]*Op. cit.*, p. 201.    [3]*Ibid.*, pp. 203, 209.

[4]See p. 238 above. Borkenau says (*op. cit.*, p. 543) that the Rajk trial had no political character at all. But is this political character not evident from the way the trial was used? If the trial was the result of Rakosi's enmity towards Rajk, why were Palffy, Dr Szöny and Szalai also hanged?

was rehabilitated in 1956, the posthumous ceremony on 6 October assumed the character of a moving demonstration of the true feelings of the Hungarian masses.[1]

None of the reprisals taken against Yugoslavia by the Soviet Union and the satellites were Cominform measures. The Cominform neither planned them nor carried them out, but merely expressed views at a meeting held in Hungary in the second half of November 1949. The Soviet Party was represented by Michael A. Suslov and Pavel Yudin.[2] The *Resolution by the Information Bureau of the Communist Parties of November 1949* repeated the well-worn charges against the "murders and spies, the hirelings of Belgrade", together with the appeal to the "forces loyal to Communism" in Yugoslavia to drive out the "Tito-Rankovic clique".[3]

Another resolution "on the defence of peace and the struggle against the warmongers" described the "Socialists of the Right", of whom Ernest Bevin, Clement Attlee, Leon Blum,

[1] *Nie wieder*, an article in *Szabad Nep*, Budapest, 6 October 1956, quoted in *Ostprobleme* 1956, p. 1524.

[2] Suslov was originally in the Central Party Control Commission and the Org-Bureau, i.e. the organizations in which Stalin had always put his adherents (*Ostprobleme* 1951, p. 360). He had become the Secretary of the Central Committee in general charge of relations with foreign Communist parties after the death of Zhdanov. Whether Zhdanov died a natural death is not certain. After his death his name was hardly ever mentioned. His supporter, N. A. Voznessenski, who was also a member of the Polit-bureau, was removed by Stalin, as Khrushchev admitted in his secret speech in February 1956. An indication that Zhdanov's death was not a natural one may lie in the charges against the Kremlin doctors in January 1953. Nine doctors (six of them of Jewish descent) were accused of the responsibility for the deaths of prominent Soviet personalities, including Zhdanov, as the result of faulty diagnosis and deliberately incorrect treatment. After Stalin's death the accusations against the doctors were revealed as "fabrications".

Was it not part of Stalin's underhand method to accuse others of murders that he himself had ordered? One has only to think of the murder of S. M. Kirov, which was "proven" in the purge trials of Zinoviev and Trotsky. (See *Short Course*, p. 318.) As early as in the great purges doctors (including Dr L. G. Levin and others) had confessed to murdering well-known Bolsheviks and had been sentenced for it. (Vishinski, *Gerichtsreden*, Berlin, 1952, pp. 706 ff.) The question therefore arises whether Stalin did not have the false charges made against the Kremlin doctors in 1953 because he needed to present some scapegoats for the misdeeds he himself had instigated. This possibility is not affected by the fact that Zhdanov really was a sick man. (Bedell Smith, *My Three Years in Moscow*, and Halperin, *op. cit.*, pp. 76–77.)

[3] *Für Dauerhaften Frieden, für Volksdemokratie*, 29 November 1949.

Guy Mollet, Henri Spaak, Kurt Schumacher, Giuseppe Saragat and Karl Renner were specifically named, as "the worst enemies of peace", the "prime enemies of the working class" and "executioners in the service of the warmongers and imperialists". The tenor of this abuse indicates the "left-wing" course being followed at this time by the Central Committee of the CPSU, and is reminiscent of the policy of the years 1930–4, when the Social Democrats were regarded as the arch-enemy—a policy which made a great contribution to the triumphs of the National Socialists in Germany.[1]

Fortunately, as a result of the policies of Stalin and his supporters, political conditions had changed for the worse as far as the Bolsheviks were concerned. In 1948 their attacks on the "arch-enemy" could not even produce the negative result they had brought about in 1933.

## WHAT THE COMINFORM WAS NOT

Some authors ascribe to the Cominform an importance comparable with that of the Comintern. This might not be completely wide of the mark if these authors meant that the Cominform, like the Comintern in its final years, had no *decisive* influence on the direction of world Communism. But anyone who believes that the "highest command post" was no longer in Russia because Belgrade was chosen as the headquarters of the Cominform does the servile Yudin, the head of this "command post", too much honour.[2] Similarly, the view that the Communist International was resuscitated in the shape of the Cominform fails to comprehend the true significance of the Information Bureau.[3] The Comintern was a world party composed of the Sections, the Communist parties of the entire world. Stalin had not the slightest desire to revive this kind of world party, in which the Russian Party would be merely one of the Sections. This was the reason why he always believed that the new "International" should be formed "for informa-

[1]See p. 112 above.
[2]Thus Borkenau in *European Communism*, p. 521. The experience of Vladimir Popovic described on p. 229 is indicative of the character of Yudin and of the Cominform.
[3]Dedijer, *Tito Speaks*, p. 300.

tional purposes".[1] Djilas confirmed this when he wrote in 1950:

> The Cominform is not the leading body of the international working-class movement. . . . This organization has only met twice in two years; in reality, in fact, only once. The first meeting was concomitantly the inaugural Cominform meeting, while the second (and only real) one was the meeting convened for the purpose of censuring the Yugoslav Communist Party. . . .
>
> The Cominform was in reality only a formality. . . .[2]

Another thing that speaks against the belief that the Cominform was a high-level "command post" is the fact that the staff did not include any of the most senior Communists. Until its dissolution, the ECCI had had among its members such top-flight functionaries as Dimitroff, Manuilski, Togliatti, Pieck and Kuusinen. The representatives the Communist parties sent to the Cominform could not compare with this Comintern élite. Even Pavel Fyodorovitch Yudin was no exception. Until he was given his Cominform post he had occupied himself only as a "philosopher" and "journalist" (*Trud, Sovietskaya Kniga*).[3] At the date of the 18th Party Congress, in 1939, he was not even a member of the Central Committee of the Communist Party. Indeed, it is probable that it was only his Cominform post that enabled him to be accepted as a candidate for the Central Committee and to be elected a full member at the 19th Party Congress in 1952.[4] The subordinate position of the Cominform became quite clear in the conflict with Yugoslavia. Stalin's letter of March 1948—six months after the formation of the Cominform—was sent to the member parties with the request that the replies should be sent to the Central Committee of the CPSU, not direct to the Yugoslav party and not to the Cominform, either. The replies from the member parties, beginning with the Hungarian comments, were sent on to Tito by Zhdanov, with Yudin

---

[1] *Ostprobleme* 1950, p. 829, note 4.
[2] M. Djilas, *Lenin über die Beziehungen zwischen Sozialististischen Staaten*, Belgrade, 1950, p. 4, note 2.
[3] *Ostprobleme* 1952, pp. 1675/6. *Ostprobleme* 1951, pp. 361 ff.
[4] Dedijer, *op. cit.*, pp. 357 ff.

merely functioning as a post-box.[1] Regarding this, Djilas wrote in 1950:[2]

> The real quarrel is between the Yugoslav Communist Party and the CPSU . . . while the quarrel between the Central Committee of the Yugoslav Communist Party and the Cominform only serves as camouflage for the real one.

*Kommunist*, the theoretical organ of the CPSU, put the position correctly when it said:[3]

> The Information Bureau merely linked a number of Communist parties without in any way forming an organizational structure. Nor were there any statutes. The tasks of the Information Bureau were limited. It was not created to control the parties from one central point.

The "left-wing" offensive policy initiated by Zhdanov in his speech at the inaugural meeting of the Cominform in September 1947 was not Cominform strategy.[4] It was rather the Central Committee of the CPSU which made use of the Cominform in order to announce its new line. The "left-wing" activity of the West European Communists, such as the strikes and unrest in France and Italy in the autumn of 1947, were not ordered by the Information Bureau: they arose from the offensive policy of the Soviets.[5] There is a fairly strong probability that Yudin and his colleagues first learned of the actions in France and Italy through the newspapers, since at this time they were only just beginning to assemble in Belgrade.[6]

Borkenau thinks that the Cominform pulled off its greatest coup—and its only successful one—in Czechoslovakia.[7] The Prague *coup d'état* of February 1948 was successful, it is true. But was it a Cominform coup? Valerian Zorin was sent to Prague by Moscow to pull the strings behind the scenes.

Zorin did not take part in any Cominform meetings. At this

[1]Dedijer, *op. cit.*, pp. 357 ff.

[2]Cf. M. Djilas, *Lenin über die Beziehungen zwischen Sozialistischen Staaten*, Belgrade, 1950, p. 3, note 1.

[3]Quoted in *Neue Zeit* (the newspaper of the Communist Party of the Saar), 16–17 March 1957.

[4]Boris Meissner, in the monthly *Osteuropa*, Stuttgart 1952, p. 99, thinks otherwise.

[5]Borkenau thinks otherwise (*op. cit.*, p. 529): ". . . The Cominform had given orders to do something violent".

[6]See p. 228 above.     [7]*European Communism*, p. 532.

time he was a Soviet Deputy Foreign Minister and was, as head of the *Komitet informatsii*, concerned with the coordination of the Soviet intelligence services. Nor did Zorin belong to Yudin's editorial board.[1] The Prague *coup d'état* was engineered by the Soviets, and the Cominform had no hand in its execution.

Dedijer mentions that while he was in Belgrade, Yudin was not only concerned with publishing the Cominform newspaper, but also took an active part in the preparations for the "final reckoning with Yugoslavia".[2] He made particularly strong efforts, says Dedijer, to poison relations between Bulgaria, Albania and Yugoslavia. This is undoubtedly true, but it does not alter the character of the Cominform Bureau as the editorial office of a newspaper, even if it was a great and important newspaper—and Moscow's mouthpiece.

Various commentators, for example F. O. Miksche and Otto Heilbrunn, believe that the Cominform did intelligence work.[3] Did the Cominform run an intelligence service? During the nine years of the Cominform's existence not a single "Cominform agent" was arrested in the free world. Not a single pass-

---

[1]Cf. the statements made by the MGB officer Nikolai Khokhlov at the press conference organized by HICOG (Bonn/Mehlem) on 22 April 1954 and the *Report of the Royal Commission on Espionage*, Sydney, 1955. Also Seton-Watson, *The Pattern of Communist Revolution*, p. 259.

[2]Dedijer, *op. cit.*, p. 308.

[3]In his book *Unconditional Surrender*, London, 1951, pp. 347 ff., F. O. Miksche expresses the view that the Third International never ceased to exist. He claims it was divided up into:

  (i) The Cominform, formerly the Comintern, a kind of central head-quarters, to which the Politbureaux of the individual Communist parties in the various countries were subordinated.
 (ii) The Communist parties, which, under the leadership of the Politbureaux, represented the rank-and-file soldiers of the movement.
(iii) A secret organization consisting of innumerable invisible threads in and between the different countries.

In a sketch on page 349 of his book, Miksche connects up all the European Communist parties with the Cominform, including the "Politbureau Germany" in Berlin, i.e. the SED, even though the SED was not a member of the Cominform. The Cominform, says Miksche, had a central committee made up of representatives of the various Communist parties. Under this central committee were ranged five departments, Propaganda, Economic Warfare, Political, Military, and Information. Each of these departments had territorial sub-sections for Germany, France, Italy, etc. The Cominform had a staff of 675 employees.

The most important of these departments was the Military Department

port was impounded that could be shown to have been "fixed up" by the Cominform. Is one to assume that the Cominform worked in such complete secrecy that its activities could remain undiscovered? If so, the Cominform must be the only intelligence service in recent years to have achieved this feat for so long. Between 1947 and 1956 hundreds of Soviet, Polish, Czech or Hungarian agents were caught in Western Europe, but never a "Cominform agent". Why was this? The answer is, because there were no Cominform agents. That is why, when Tito complained to the CPSU in March 1948, it was not the activities of Cominform agents in Yugoslavia that he complained of, but attempts by the Soviet service to recruit secret agents in his country.[1] Yudin paid Tito a visit at the same time, not to defend the activities of his agents, but to ask Tito for an article for the Cominform newspaper.[2]

Officials of all kinds of Eastern services have defected to the West since 1947, and have told all they knew. Neither Josef Sviatlo nor Vladimir and Evdokia Petrov, neither Yuri Rastvorov nor Nikolai Khokhlov ever said a word to indicate that the Cominform ran an intelligence service.[3]

(F. O. Miksche is a lieutenant-colonel). It was highly secret, so the author was not in a position to give details of its organization and equipment. In spite of this, however, F. O. Miksche can reveal that the Military Department had a staff of 249, that it directed intelligence services and conspiracies, arranged for the forging of identity documents, and was equally responsible for running civil wars and the training of agents.

Miksche obtained these details from a secret document whose origin he cannot reveal. Now the contents of even secret documents can be untrue, and this would seem to be the case with the document Miksche is referring to.

A central committee of the Cominform such as the one Miksche proceeds from is never mentioned in any place whatever, nor has its existence been observed in any other manner. After their conflict, the Yugoslavs would certainly not have kept the fact secret from the world if there had been such an organization. Nor have any other details come to light to confirm Miksche's claims regarding the composition of the "central committee".

[1]Dedijer, *op. cit.*, pp. 339, 355.    [2]*Ibid.*, p. 339.

[3]Discovering that the Cominform did not run an intelligence service should not blind anyone to the fact that all Communist parties give assistance to the intelligence services of the Soviet Union and the Peoples' Democracies in one way or another. Every convinced Communist sends up pieces of information which might be of interest to the "political movement", either through Party channels or through the organization he happens to belong to. In the case of the so-called "factory reporting", indeed, this passage of information is well organized. The reader is also reminded of the well-authenticated fact that suitable members and supporters of the Communist

Heilbrunn, too, gives details of intelligence activity by the Cominform.[1] He says that the Comintern, "now probably the Cominform", had the job of checking on agents whom the Soviet secret service intended to recruit. The Soviet intelligence service used to make use of the Comintern's archives, and still does, that is true.[2] This fact, however, is not a valid reason for believing in intelligence activity by the Cominform.

In the appendix to his book, Heilbrunn includes the well-known *Protocol M*, which first appeared in the West Berlin paper *Kurier* on 15 January 1948.[3] This document said, *inter alia*, that the "Communist Information Centre" coordinated the struggle of all socialist movements. Heilbrunn also thinks *Protocol M* may possibly be a fake, but refers to a statement by the British Minister Hector McNeil on 19 April 1948, according to which there were certain credible reasons for believing that even if the document was not genuine, it had been compiled from genuine Communist sources. Heilbrunn ought to have mentioned that Hector McNeil added that the investigations had thrown up a German employee who had admitted authorship of the document.[4] This disposes of the question of the document's authenticity. As the author admitted, *Protocol M* was a fake. It cannot be utilized as a source.

On the question of Cominform intelligence activity there is this to be said. It is known as a result of statements by former permanent officials of Eastern intelligence services, confirmed by others of the same kind, that the Soviet intelligence service, and particularly the Second Directorate of the Information Committee (the KI), were working in the satellite countries in the heyday of the Cominform.[5] These statements underline the decisive factor. By 1934 Stalin had brought all the Communist parties under Soviet control and between 1944 and 1948 had his grip firmly on the East European states. He would never

parties and their "front" organizations are available to the Eastern intelligence services for recruitment as secret agents. This does not, however, make the Communist parties into espionage organizations in the sense of organizations whose job is the systematic obtaining of state secrets.

[1] Otto Heilbrunn, *The Soviet Secret Service*, London, 1956, p. 131.

[2] See p. 207 above.          [3] Heilbrunn, *op. cit.*, pp. 192–195.

[4] Reuters, 19 April 1948.

[5] Appendix 3 to the *Report of the Royal Commission on Espionage*, Sydney, 1955, p. 431, and M. Khokhlov, *Ich sollte morden*, Frankfurt, 1956, pp. 16, 44.

have tolerated the formation outside the Soviet Union—for example, in the satellite countries—of political centres for the purpose of controlling the work of a large number of Communist parties. This is why the Balkan Federation planned by Dimitroff and Tito was shattered; and this is why it was never the intention to make the Cominform into an agency possessing any considerable political influence.

### THE DISSOLUTION OF THE COMINFORM

Ever since the death of Stalin, the Central Committee of the CPSU had been making efforts to improve Soviet relations with Yugoslavia, still strained and still weighted down by the Cominform resolutions of 1948 and their consequences.[1]

When the Soviet delegation arrived at the airport in Belgrade on 26 May 1955, Khrushchev declared:[2]

We sincerely regret what has happened, and are determined to clear away the things that have piled up during this period. Among the things that have piled up, we on our side unhesitatingly include the provocatory role which Beria, Abakumov and others, since unmasked as enemies of the people, played in relations between Yugoslavia and the USSR. We have carefully examined the material on which the grave charges and insults directed against the Yugoslav leaders were based at the time. The facts show that this material was fabricated by enemies of the people and by despicable imperialist agents, who had cunningly insinuated themselves into the ranks of our Party.

Tito listened to this in icy silence and said no word of greeting to his visitors. Was this silence intended to make it clear that he felt exactly the same about the amount of truth contained in Khrushchev's words as he had felt about Stalin's letters of 1948?[3]

In this speech of Khrushchev's, the words "Information

---

[1]Halperin, *op. cit.*, pp. 211 ff. and 246 ff.

[2]*Ostprobleme* 1955, p. 978. The Central Committee of the CPSU withdrew the allegation that the conflict with Yugoslavia had been provoked by "the Beria gang" in its resolution of 30 June 1956, saying that it had been "gross arbitrary action" by Stalin that had led to the conflict. (See *Ostprobleme* 1956, p. 960.)

[3]Halperin goes into detail regarding the significance of the events at the airport, *op. cit.*, pp. 263 ff.

Bureau of the Communist Workers' Party" were never mentioned. At the conclusion of the conversations a mutual declaration was issued. This was announced to be in the names of both governmental delegations, although Khrushchev's greetings to "the leaders of the Federation of Yugoslav Communists" had been uttered in the name of the Central Committee of the CPSU as well. Nor did the bilateral governmental declaration, the wording of which was undoubtedly thought out very carefully, make any mention of either of the parties or of the Cominform.

In the succeeding months Tito made efforts to ensure that the desired consequences followed from the admissions Khrushchev had made while in Belgrade. During the summer of 1955 he repeatedly demanded a re-examination of the proceedings against Kostoff, Rajk and Slansky. On 27 July, according to *Tanjug*, he said in a speech at Karlovac:

> We can only regret that there are still some people in neighbouring countries in the East who are not happy at the prospect of this normalization of relations. They are afraid to open their mouths. For years they stood in fear of Stalin, and therefore they think they are not allowed to speak even today. Instead, they are intriguing against us behind the scenes, are unwilling to stand by what the Soviet leaders have said and are trying to put a spoke in our wheel wherever they can.

These words, obviously intended for people like Rakosi and Ulbricht, are evidence of the fact that in the summer of 1955 the Stalin atmosphere was still present in the Eastern bloc.

The silence on the subject of the Cominform was broken by Khrushchev on 27 December 1955, when, on the occasion of his and Bulganin's report on their journey to Asia, he told the Supreme Soviet:

> Finally, I should like to deal with the question of the continued existence of the Information Bureau of the Communist and Workers' Parties, or, as it is called in the West, the Cominform.
>
> Actually there is no reason for the question, but foreign journalists often asked us while we were in India, "Why don't you dissolve the Cominform? Can't the activities of the Communist parties in other countries be stopped?" . . .

Following the example of the Communist Party of the Soviet Union, the activities of the Communist parties of all countries are indissolubly linked with the vital interests of the working classes—with the interests of the people. And that doesn't please those who would like to keep the people in permanent subjection. They don't like the international solidarity of the working class, and naturally they want the Cominform to be abolished. But that doesn't depend on them!

These words cannot be taken to mean that it was the intention to let the Cominform remain alive. Khrushchev carefully avoided answering the question, in fact—which may be regarded as an indication that it was by no means certain whether the Cominform would continue to exist. Another pointer was provided by the failure of the 20th Party Congress even to deal with the question of the Cominform at all.

On 17 April 1956 there appeared in the Cominform newspaper an *Informational Announcement regarding the Discontinuance of the Activities of the Information Bureau of the Communist and Workers' Parties*.[1] This said:

The creation of the Information Bureau of the Communist and Workers' Parties in 1947 played a positive role in abolishing the separation of the Communist parties from one another which had arisen after the dissolution of the Comintern; and was an important factor in strengthening proletarian internationalism in the ranks of the international Communist movement and in continuing to unite the working class and all toilers for the struggle for lasting peace, democracy and Socialism. The Cominform Bureau and its paper, *For Lasting Peace, for People's Democracy*, played a positive role in the development and strengthening of the fraternal relations and mutual exchange of information between the Communist and Workers' Parties, in the elucidation of questions of Marxist-Leninist theory in relation to the actual conditions in the individual countries, and in illustrating the experiences of the international Communist and Workers' movement. This contributed to the ideological, organizational and political strengthening of the brother parties and to the raising of the influence of the Communist parties among the masses.

[1] No. 16/1956.

In recent years, however, changes which have taken place in the international situation, such as the emergence of Socialism from the limits of one country and its transformation into a world system; the creation of an extensive zone of peace, embracing both Socialist and non-Socialist peace-loving countries in Europe and Asia; the growth and consolidation of many Communist parties in the capitalist countries and in the dependencies and colonies and the activation of their fight against the danger of war and against reactionary forces, the fight for peace and the vital interests of the workers and for the national independence of their countries; and finally the tasks, particularly urgent today, of repairing the split in the working-class movement and of strengthening the unity of the working class in the interests of the successful struggle for peace and Socialism; all this has created new conditions for the work of the Communist and Workers' Parties. Neither the composition of the Information Bureau nor the tenor of its activities corresponds any longer to these new conditions.

The Central Committees of the Communist and Workers' Parties belonging to the Information Bureau have had an exchange of views on the question of its activities and agree that the Information Bureau they established in 1947 has now fulfilled its task. In this connection they have reached general agreement to suspend the activities of the Information Bureau of the Communist and Workers' Parties and the publication of its newspaper *For Lasting Peace, For People's Democracy.*

The very first sentence of this announcement ("a positive role in abolishing the separation of the Communist parties from one another") is dishonest. Soviet control over the majority of the Cominform parties was never more complete than in 1947, when Stalin, the "Liberator" of Eastern Europe, stood at the peak of his might. It may be assumed that the author wanted to give the impression that the Cominform really was "an important factor in the strengthening of proletarian internationalism", a factor which was now to be abolished. The truth was that in this respect the Cominform had played a very modest role. The control of the Communist world movement had shown no weakness worth mentioning even after Stalin's death and up to the 20th Party Congress.[1] It was only the acceptance of individual roads to Socialism, the open admission of mistakes and even of certain crimes by Stalin, together with changes that took place in the Soviet Union and in international Communism as a result of Stalin's death, that led to indications of lessening of control which culminated in the events in Poland and Hungary in the autumn of 1956.

Nor are the reasons adduced for the dissolution very convincing. If the Cominform had really played the positive role that the announcement ascribed to it, what ought to have been the consequence of the "emergence of Socialism from the limits of one country and its transformation into a world system"? Surely it would have been desirable to extend the Bureau, instead of dissolving it? If this view is correct and if the version of the role of the Cominform contained in the announcement was untrue, then the question is, what was the real reason for dissolving the Cominform? When Stalin was considering the creation of the Cominform, he was very largely influenced by the need to be able to exercise better control over tendencies towards independence on the part of Yugoslavia and the other countries of the Eastern bloc. If this is so, there was no longer any point in keeping the Bureau in existence by the spring of 1956. The sovereignty of Yugoslavia and the principle of non-interference in her internal affairs had already had to be expressly acknowledged. It is probable that Yugoslavia demanded the dissolution of the Cominform as one of the conditions for healing the breach. This seems to be confirmed by the fact that after the visit of the Soviet delegation to Belgrade in May 1955, the Cominform was never again mentioned by the Soviet leaders in any unequivocally positive fashion and that on the other hand the announcement of the dissolution made no mention of Yugoslavia whatever.[2]

There seems to be no valid reason to doubt that the Cominform really was dissolved.[3] In the final years it had done nothing more than produce its newspaper, and that has never appeared

[1]See p. 202 above.

[2]Reale says (*op. cit.*, p. 15) that Khrushchev told the Yugoslav representative, Vukmanovic Tempo, that the Cominform was going to be dissolved as early as in March 1956, at the funeral of Bierut.

[3]Heilbrunn, *op. cit.*, p. 125, note 2.

since. Remarks by prominent Communists—for example, Karl Schirdewan, who said: "The dissolution of the Information Bureau is very important for the future development of the Communist and Workers' parties",[1] may be regarded as having some truth in them, to the extent that they can be said to have confirmed that the dissolution did take place.

[1]Report by Politbureau of the SED delivered at the 29th session of the Central Committee (*Neues Deutschland*, East Berlin, 28 November 1956). See also the article by I. P. Pomelov in No. 1/1957 of *Kommunist*, entitled *Die Entwicklung des Sozialismus und des Proletarischen Internationalismus*.

# Chapter VII

## PROLETARIAN INTERNATIONALISM
## AFTER THE DEATH OF STALIN

*"Beneath Stalin's rule of terror there reigned an iron logic."*[1]

THE history of the Comintern demonstrates that although in 1919 the Communist parties voluntarily came together and founded the new International as members possessing equal rights, the ascendancy of the Russian Party in the Comintern was making itself felt as early as 1920. Ever since the 5th Congress in February 1924, the Comintern became the arena for the contests which broke out between the Soviet members of the Politbureau. These contests were accompanied by the start of the bolshevization of the Sections of the Comintern. Stalin made his first appearance on the international scene. When Stalin's conquest of the Soviet Party was made manifest at the 17th Party Congress in 1934, he was also dictator of the Comintern.[2] During the purges, his NKVD ravaged the Comintern just as much as the Soviet Party. Stalin remained the dictator of world Communism until his death. The demand for the acknowledgement of the leading role of the Soviet Party was directed at making every Communist subject to Stalin's domination. Describing the situation during this period, Gomulka said at the 8th Plenary Session of the Central Committee of the Polish Party:[3]

> In the bloc comprising the Socialist states it was Stalin who stood at the summit of this hierarchy of adulation. All those who were below him bowed their heads before him. It was not only the other leading personalities in the CPSU and the

[1]Edda Werfel in *Przeglad Kulturalny*, No. 44, 1956.
[2]Nenni in *Avanti*, 24 June 1956 (quoted in *The Anti-Stalin Campaign and International Communism*).
[3]*National Communism and Popular Revolt in Eastern Europe*, New York, 1956, p. 228.

Soviet state who kow-towed to him, but also the leaders of the Communist and Workers' Parties in other countries of the Socialist camp. . . . The object of this cult was omniscient, knew how to handle everything, solved every problem and directed and decided everything that lay in his sphere of action.

The system Gomulka was describing was not so much the result of the cult of personality as a characteristic of the relations between the parties in the era of "Stalinism".

The death of the dictator was bound to have its effect on the Communist world movement. Even in July 1955 Tito was quite correct in saying at Karlovac that nobody in the Eastern bloc dared to open his mouth.[1] Everyone was still trying to find his bearings in the new situation.

The place of Stalin, who had enveloped himself in an aura of monumental glory and a still greater one of fear, and who had had the unrestricted use of the mightiest secret police force in the world, was taken by a collective leadership of Party functionaries. These men had come through difficult and anxious years, during which they had indeed gone in fear of their lives.[2] If any proof of this had been needed, it was provided by Khrushchev in his secret speech:

In those days I often used to have conversations with Nikolai Alexandrovitch Bulganin. One day when we were driving together in a car, he said: "It sometimes happens that a man goes to visit Stalin as his friend and at his invitation. And then, when he is sitting together with Stalin, he does not know where he will go when he leaves—home again or to gaol."[3]

It is understandable that in the first months of their collective leadership these men came out with a number of measures designed to prevent the concentration of power in the hands of

[1] Cf. p. 522 above.

[2] The background to the charges against the Kremlin doctors in January 1953 is only one example of this. These charges can only be understood as the prologue to a purge—under Stalin a bloody one, naturally. See Halperin, *op. cit.*, p. 248, and W. Leonhard, *Kreml ohne Stalin*, Cologne, 1959, pp. 75 ff.

[3] Mikoyan was also on the list for purging before Stalin died. (See L. Fischer, *Russia Revisited*, London, 1957, p. 65.)

one man. Malenkov's tenure of office as both First Secretary of the CPSU and Chairman of the Council of Ministers lasted only a few days and Beria had to pay with his life for his attempt to "put the Ministry of Interior above the Party". The collective leaders succeeded in cutting back the power of the secret police.[1] The ebbing of tension in the Soviet Union also manifested itself in the *New Course*. The *New Course*, with its great efforts to increase the production of consumer goods, is characteristic of the period when Malenkov was Prime Minister (March 1953 until February 1955).

In the international sphere the Soviet collective leaders themselves gave advance notice of impending changes by undertaking the journey to Yugoslavia, where their statements, publicly made, provided the prince of the erstwhile hateful "Titoism" with a triumph without parallel in the Communist world. This step could not help but have far-reaching effects. Every Communist now had proof that stubborn opposition to the Moscow line was not necessarily followed by liquidation. It became clear to many that the secret police would no longer be employed to the extent they had been used by Stalin to destroy opponents. In the result many a Communist now felt emboldened to utter criticism of the Soviet Union that would have been unthinkable hitherto. The proportions this criticism was to assume was to be demonstrated at the 20th Party Congress, when the Soviet collective leadership, headed by Khrushchev with his secret speech, handed one argument after another to the critics within their own ranks.

### THE DISCUSSION AT THE TWENTIETH PARTY CONGRESS

Proletarian internationalism as a concept played no part at the 20th Party Congress of the CPSU (14–25 February 1956), an indication of how small a problem the question of international relations between the Communist parties seemed to the organizers at this time. Various speakers referred to the importance of "fraternal relations between the countries of the Socialist camp", without, however, going into detail as to what

---

[1]The Soviet public also experienced a drop in the number of arrests by the secret police. (L. Fischer, *Russia Revisited*, p. 20.)

this "fraternity" consisted of. Khrushchev mentioned "proletarian internationalism" once at the conclusion of some remarks on the nationalities question within the Soviet Union; but he too failed to go any further into the elements of this internationalism.

By contrast, the factors which had been coming to the fore ever since Tito's rehabilitation in 1955, and which were to have their effects on relations between the Communist parties in the course of 1956, were all the more thoroughly discussed—the question of the various forms of the transition to socialism and the problem of the Stalin cult, with which Khrushchev in particular dealt, speaking with a frankness which had not been known for decades.[1] The Presidium of the Central Committee of the CPSU seems to have been slow to appreciate the effect these factors would have on the relations between the Communist parties if they became known. How different the results of the 20th Party Congress were expected to be in Soviet circles can be guessed from an article in *Pravda* of 16 July 1956, which included this passage:

> The decisions taken at the 20th Party Congress have opened up majestic prospects for the unifying of all the forces supporting peace and Socialism.

This would mean on the face of it that the "right" tendencies displayed at the 20th Party Congress, including the criticism of Stalin, were intended to consolidate the unity of the Socialist camp and to foster the Popular Front policy in the countries of the West. But this does not tell the full story of the tactical significance of the "right-wing" policy. From the point of view of domestic politics, Khrushchev's right-wing policies were undoubtedly used to open the battle against the proponents of a severe "left-wing" course and against the closest associates of Stalin, especially Molotov, Kaganovitch and Malenkov.[2]

---

[1] Khrushchev in his *Central Committee Report to the 20th Congress of the CPSU* in L. Gruliow, ed., *Current Soviet Policies II*, New York, 1957, pp. 37–38, and Suslow, *ibid.*, p. 76.

[2] It will be recalled that when Stalin was conducting his war against the "left-wing", Zinoviev and Trotsky, he went over to a right-wing policy and then changed to a "left-wing" policy when he wanted to eliminate the "right-wing" Bukharin.

The resolution on the dissolution of the Cominform, published in mid-April 1956, contained nothing that would contribute to the discussion of proletarian internationalism. The Politbureau of the CPSU seems to have assumed that its degree of control over the Communist parties was still great enough to keep them "toeing the line". The resolution followed the pattern set by the announcement of the end of the Comintern, in that it made no mention whatever of the activities of the body which really controlled the Communist parties—the Central Committee of the CPSU.[1]

### THE EFFECTS OF KHRUSHCHEV'S SECRET SPEECH

It is a commentary on the situation of international Communism and of the mentality of leading Communists that the discussion of Khrushchev's speech only began after the publication of the speech by the US State Department on 4 June 1956, even though many non-Soviet Communists, in Moscow as guest delegates, had heard about it. Not only that, but the Soviets had also sent to Central Committees of the Communist parties of the Iron Curtain countries a version of the secret speech intended for them. Articles in the Yugoslav paper *Borba* of 20 March 1956 and Walter Ulbricht's speech to the district delegates conference of the SED in Berlin (16–18 March 1956) make it evident that the secret speech was known about. It is also fairly certain that leading Communists living in the free world were aware of the content of the speech. This is evident from Togliatti's report to the Central Committee of his party, reprinted in *Unita*, of 15 March 1956.[2]

Nevertheless the American announcement of 4 June 1956 was followed by a wave of discussion unparalleled in the history of international Bolshevism during the previous thirty years. The essential feature of this discussion was not whether the secret speech actually had been delivered but whether the American version was authentic. Outside the Soviet Union

[1]See p. 203 above.
[2]The only criticism uttered by the French and British parties was that up to June 1956 they had not received an official version of the speech. (Statement by the Politbureau of the French Party of 18 June 1956 in *L'Humanité* of 19 June and the statement by the Political Committee of the CPGB of 21 June in the *Daily Worker* of 22 June 1956.)

only isolated individuals denied its authenticity and even they only in the first few days after the announcement.[1]

Neither Khrushchev nor the Central Committee of the CPSU offered any comment on this point at the time.[2] It was not until May 1957, fifteen months after the 20th Party Congress, when the international discussion sparked off by the secret speech was at its height, that Khrushchev touched on the question of whether the version published in the United States was genuine. Speaking to the publisher of the *New York Times*, he said:[3]

> I don't know what you mean by the text of my speech. There was one text which was apparently concocted by the American Intelligence Service. This publishing firm, led by Allan Dulles, enjoys no very high reputation with us. I am not interested in what it publishes.

The second sentence of this utterance contradicts the first, since it shows that Khrushchev knew very well what was meant. And the third sentence does not chime with the second, since one cannot come to the conclusion that something is a fake until one has interested oneself in it. What Khrushchev wanted to avoid at this point in time was an admission that the American version had given a fairly accurate account of his secret speech. More recent utterances by Khrushchev get rather nearer the truth. In May 1959, for example, at the Soviet Writers' Congress, he asked:

> Did anyone force us to make our statement at the 20th Party Congress on the cult of personality and its consequences?

Other credible witnesses had already mentioned the speech before this. Anastas Mikoyan, for instance, did not deny to Louis Fischer at the end of 1956 that the speech was genuine.[4]

[1] Cf. the Luxemburg *Zeitung Vom Letzeburger Vollek* of 6 January 1956 and *De Waarheid*, Amsterdam, of 7 June quoted in *The Anti-Stalin Campaign and International Communism*, p. 97.

[2] The fact that the speech was delivered by Khrushchev is clear from the footnote to Dennis's article in *Pravda* of 17 June 1956 and from the stenographic record of the proceedings of the 20th Party Congress (cf. *20th Congress of the CPSU*, stenographic record (in Russian), Moscow 1956, Vol. II, pp. 402, 498).

[3] *New York Times*, 11 May 1957, International Edition, p. 3.

[4] L. Fischer, *Russia Revisited*, p. 64; also *Pravda* of 24 May 1959 on the Writers' Congress.

Nor can it be overlooked that neither Khrushchev nor the Central Committee of the CPSU nor yet *Pravda* rejected any of the numerous commentaries on the Stalin problem, whether they emanated from Tito, Gomulka, Togliatti or from other prominent Communists, on the grounds that the commentary was based on a fabrication or that no secret speech had been delivered, that the contents of the speech had been quite different or for any other reason.

Discussion of the secret speech was linked with criticism of the Soviet leaders. In so far as this criticism was concerned with the way in which Khrushchev's speech had become public knowledge, the reproach was unusual enough, but it still did not touch the really tender points.[1] These were revealed by Togliatti when he allowed the publication of an interview he gave to Alberto Moravia, the publisher of the Italian periodical *Nuovi Argomenti*.[2] Togliatti did not confine himself to criticizing the present Soviet leaders for allowing Stalin's one-man régime a free hand for so long, until it was no longer possible to save the situation without serious harm to all concerned. He added that to put the abuses down to Stalin's mistakes was to remain in the arena of the personality cult. Togliatti demanded from the Soviet comrades a detailed answer to the question of how the course of the development of Soviet society could have given rise to general disorders and defects, against which the entire Socialist camp must be warned. In saying this, Togliatti had come out into the open and criticized the Soviet system, and he was not afraid to give frank expression to his critical views. Unless he was much mistaken, he went on, it was the Soviet party which had been the original source of all the harmful restrictions on democracy and the source of the gradual spread of all forms of bureaucracy. The criticism of Stalin, he maintained, had brought to the surface the "problem of the dangers of bureaucratic degeneration, the stifling of democratic life and the alienation of the leaders from initiative, from criticism and from the masses".

[1] As in the American *Daily Worker* of 6 June 1956 and the declarations by the French and British parties referred to on p. 261 above, note 2.

[2] *Nuovi Argomenti* No. 20 of 16 June 1956. *Ostprobleme* 1956, No. 28, p. 938, also reproduces a corresponding article from *Unita* of 17 June 1956 containing a part of Togliatti's statements.

Just as important as Togliatti's criticism of the system were his remarks on the relations of the national Communist parties to one another and their attitude to the CPSU. He hoped, he said, that nobody would any longer believe the stupid fable that Communist parties received instructions and orders for their every move.[1] As far as the post-war era was concerned, said Togliatti, the Italian party had never had to discuss their policies at international meetings except at the inaugural meeting of the Cominform.

This may be true, but Togliatti gave no hint of the number of times he or his party's representatives had had confidential discussions about their policies with Zhdanov, Suslov, or even with Stalin. At the time of the Yugoslav crisis, how did Togliatti react to Stalin's instruction that the comments of the Italian party on the Soviet letter of 27 March 1948 were to be sent to the Yugoslavs *via* the CPSU? Why did he agree to the Bucharest resolutions of June 1948 expelling the Yugoslav party from the Cominform?[2] Nowadays he calls the Cominform resolutions "the unfortunate intervention against the Yugoslav Communists". From 28–30 May 1956, that is, shortly before the publication of this interview, Togliatti paid a visit to Tito. Did he also explain his behaviour to him by saying that in Bucharest in 1948 he had arrived at his decisions without any pressure from outside?

In the relations between the CPSU and the national parties Togliatti distinguished between three groups. In countries which had Communist governments, "the movement" could and must exercise its influence in various ways. There were also countries in which the desire to build up Socialism was present, even though the Communists were not the leading party. In a third group the road to Socialism was the target on which the efforts of various political movements were concentrated, but these movements had not reached any understanding between themselves. In this way the whole system was becoming "polycentric".

Extracts from Togliatti's statements appeared in Polish,

---

[1] *Nuovi Argomenti*, No. 20, quoted in *The Anti-Stalin Campaign and International Communism*, p. 135.
[2] See p. 235 above.

Hungarian and East German newspapers.[1] The Norwegian party newspaper *Friheten* of 19 June 1956 praised him for his "important contribution to the discussion" just as heartily as did the Belgian *Drapeau Rouge* of the same date. The French Politbureau echoed the Italian criticism of the present Soviet leaders, saying that the explanation of the origin of Stalin's "errors" was unsatisfactory. A thorough Marxist analysis was essential in order to clarify the circumstances under which Stalin had been able to exercise such a degree of personal power.[2] Thus the French were also pointing out the discrepancy in blaming the cult of personality for Stalin's crimes.[3] The French party also put into words what almost all the Communist parties wanted—guidance, an official line, which they could use in discussion with Party members and others in order to explain the attitude of their party to the Stalin question. The long delay that ensued before the Soviets provided such elucidation caused considerable uncertainty and discontent within the Communist parties.

On 24 June 1956 Togliatti spoke once more, this time to a Plenary Session of the Central Committee of his party, and explained what he meant by a "polycentric" system:[4]

> The solution which probably most nearly corresponds to the new situation may be to grant the individual Communist parties complete autonomy and to set up bilateral connections between them, so that complete mutual understanding and mutual trust can be achieved, conditions which are essential for the unifying not only of the Communist movement but also of the whole of the progressive working-class movement. Also, such a system can probably make possible a better extension of the relations between the Communist movement and the non-Communist, Socialist-orientated movement. . . .
>
> It is clear that in the new situation, while we are working towards the creation of new contacts with the other sections

[1] *The Anti-Stalin Campaign and International Communism*, p. 167; *Neues Deutschland*, 20 June 1956.

[2] Declaration by the Politbureau of the PCF, 18 June 1956, published in *L'Humanité* of 19 June.

[3] Bertram D. Wolfe, *op. cit.*, p. 89.

[4] *L'Unità*, Rome, 26 June 1956, quoted in *The Anti-Stalin Campaign and International Communism*, pp. 215 ff.

of the international Communist movement, we must energetically reaffirm and fight for the spirit of proletarian internationalism, in order to reinforce it in our own ranks, in the working class and in the people.

In accordance with this line of thought we have been working towards a solution of the question of our own relations with the Federation of Yugoslav Communists. My visit to Belgrade had excellent results. We have set up bilateral contact with the Federation of Yugoslav Communists, based on solidarity and trust. . . .

In this new situation, relations with the CPSU and the great Soviet Communist movement appear in a new light. . . . The situation itself demanded that these relations should be re-examined and clarified on a new basis. . . . It is unnecessary to repeat that during the whole of the period following the October Revolution and up to the outbreak of the World War—and even afterwards—the position taken up by the CPSU provided the requisite fundamental guidance for the vanguard of the working class in Europe and the world. In this frightful decade in the history of Europe the Soviet Union was the strongest bulwark and the most consistent defender of the principles of democracy, freedom and peace.[1] That is why she . . . led the broad masses of the peoples of the whole of the Western world. . . . It is true that this happened at a time when, as they now tell us, a wave of illegality, violence and breaches of revolutionary legality led to the demoralization even of Party functionaries. We could neither know this nor even imagine it. . . .

It is a lie to say that the Communist International only contained one group of people who gave orders and groups of non-Russians who obeyed . . . serious disputes did arise in the Comintern through the years, and it cannot be denied that they were attended with severe disciplinary measures. . . . Later on, however, and after the war . . . the autonomy of the parties increased. . . . In this most recent period the Communist movement has developed a large degree of autonomy.

Togliatti's statements are a remarkable mixture of diffident admission of fact (e.g. the influence of Moscow on the Communist parties until World War II) and downright untruth, culminating in the claim that he had known nothing of the

[1]Togliatti meant the period 1930–1940.

breaches of revolutionary legality, indeed that he could not imagine such a thing. During the critical years Togliatti was employed in the West European Secretariat in Moscow. He knows very well what went on during the purges![1]

Togliatti's words in June 1956 were in direct contrast to his actions during the Yugoslav conflict of June 1948.[2] Nevertheless his remarks indicate that he regarded the relations between the Communist parties and the CPSU with a certain amount of realism. There do in fact exist groupings among the Communist parties, differing according to the closeness of their connection with the CPSU and with the Soviet Union. The inner circle is formed by the Communist parties of the countries which were "liberated" by the Soviet armed forces.[3] Next after them come the Communist parties of the countries which gained their freedom entirely or to a very large extent by their own resources (e.g. the Yugoslavs and the Chinese). The third group is composed of the Communist parties of the countries of the free world. These parties are indeed linked with the CPSU by ties of all kinds, but they have—at least in theory—the possibility of taking up independent attitudes.

The thorough Marxist analysis of the situation from Moscow took a long time to arrive.[4] On 27 June 1956, however, *Pravda* printed an article by the then General Secretary of the National Committee of the CPUSA, Eugene Dennis, which had appeared in the American *Daily Worker* on 18 June. Dennis's article was amended in Moscow, exactly as articles by foreign Communists

[1]See p. 189 above. In fact Togliatti himself had something to do with Münzenberg's escape from the Moscow purges (see p. 177 above).

[2]See p. 235 above.

[3]There are also considerable degrees of differentiation between these parties of the Peoples' Democracies, for example between the Polish party and the SED. Still, any possibility these parties may have of realizing their varying ideas are very much restricted, e.g. because of the presence or proximity of the Red Army.

[4]It was also called for by the British party in a declaration by the party's Political Committee on 21 June 1956, published in the *Daily Worker* of 22 June.

On 11 November 1956 Tito correctly described the situation when he said that the Soviet statesmen were wrong to regard Stalin's policies as a result of the personality cult and not of the system, and that the cult of personality was in fact a result of the system. Still, one can appreciate why the Soviet leaders could not bring themselves to criticize the system when they had all played a considerable part in keeping it going.

for the Cominform paper used to be amended. His statement that a great number of Jews of cultural prominence had also been liquidated during Stalin's régime did not appear in the reprinted version. Dennis's article was permitted to appear because it revealed an attitude of approval towards the Soviet Union and its present-day leaders and because it expressed a belief in the beneficial effects of the 20th Party Congress on collaboration with "progressive" groups—trade unionists, Liberals, Socialists and Communists. The publication of the article in *Pravda* confirmed that certain portions of the declarations by the Soviet leaders at the 20th Party Congress (e.g. the admissibility of individual roads to Socialism) were intended to foster the new Popular Front policy of the Western Communists.

They did not fulfil this purpose everywhere, as was shown in an article by Pietro Nenni in the Socialist newspaper *Avanti* on 26 June 1956. Nenni, an Italian Socialist, had for many years been a supporter of close collaboration between the Socialists and the Communists and had in fact allowed the Italian Socialist Party to split on this issue in 1947. He wrote that the dissolving of the Cominform seemed to be based on a tendency in Moscow to loosen the bonds with other Communist parties, something which would have been inconceivable in the days of the Third International. The Comintern had been a world party, whose national Sections had not only tolerated but had even demanded that the Soviet state should lead them. A Communism divorced from Moscow would no longer be the Communism of the last thirty-six years.[1] Certain as it is that this last phrase of Nenni's is true, the question arises whether the dissolution of the Cominform can be regarded as the expression of a Soviet tendency to loosen the ties between the CPSU and the other Communist parties.[2]

While these discussions were still in full swing, Tito made a return visit to Moscow, at the conclusion of which, for the first time since the resumption of friendly relations, a mutual declaration by the CPSU and the Federation of Yugoslav Communists was published. The communiqué started with the

[1]Quoted from *The Anti-Stalin Campaign and International Communism*, p. 189.
[2]See p. 255 above.

statement that the relations between the parties were bilateral and went on to say that they would be in a form which would be "based on equality of rights, sincere, democratic and comprehensible to world public opinion".[1] This meant that—at least officially—the Russians were disowning the kind of tricks and subterfuges Stalin had used, together with the conspiratorial methods of the Comintern. In his speech at Pola, Tito remarked that in his opinion the Moscow declaration of 20 June 1956 was directed at a wider audience than just Yugoslavia and the Soviet Union.[2]

## THE "MARXIST" ANALYSIS

The resolution by the Central Committee of the CPSU of 30 June 1956 was obviously put together and published in response to the many demands for a "thorough Marxist analysis".[3] In it the Central Committee of the CPSU declared that it could be regarded as a sign of the strength of the CPSU and of Socialist society that certain errors could be so frankly admitted. In this it knew it was supported by the French party.[4] The resolution also said that at the 20th Party Congress the CPSU "had told the whole truth, bitter as that might be". This "whole truth" did not include any mention of the murder of Polish officers at Katyn or the numerous crimes committed against the Soviet oppositional forces, such as the murder of Leon Trotsky, to mention only two examples.

The resolution emphatically rejected any suggestion that "Stalin's errors, particularly as regards the violation of Soviet law", might have had their origins in the nature of the Soviet social order. All the abuses, it said, were attributable to the cult of personality centering on Stalin. The cult of personality was brought about by conditions which were already a thing of the past—and not by the Soviet system itself. With regard to Togliatti's criticism, the resolution said there was no reason to pose the question of whether Soviet society had assumed some degenerate forms.[5] It did not go into Togliatti's ideas on

[1] *Neues Deutschland*, E. Berlin, 21 June 1956.
[2] *Ostprobleme* 1956, No. 49, p. 1703.
[3] *Pravda*, Moscow, 2 July 1956, quoted in *Ostprobleme* 1956, pp. 955 ff.
[4] Declaration by the PCF of 18 June 1956 (*L'Humanité* of 19 June 1956).
[5] See p. 263 above.

a "polycentric" system of international Communism. The Central Committee of the CPSU, it said, abided by the view that "the marxist parties of the working class" must strengthen their "ideological unity and international fraternal solidarity" and must naturally maintain their links to each other in fidelity to the principles of proletarian internationalism. Although the "leading role of the Soviet Union" was not expressly mentioned anywhere in the resolution, it did say that the Soviet people were justifiably proud that it was their homeland which had been the first to pave the way for Socialism.

With this resolution the Central Committee of the CPSU neither replied to the criticism of the system expressed in international Communist circles, nor did it discuss the question of the way in which the relationships between the Communist parties should be ordered in the future. Some of the severer strictures voiced at the 20th Party Congress were toned down (e.g. "Stalin's errors") and certain meritorious acts by Stalin were given their due. The Soviets had seen what harmful effects frankness—or even partial revelation—could have.

The subject of "individual roads to Socialism" was not gone into in detail in the resolution of 30 June, clearly because as yet no one wished to deal with the first effects of this decision taken at the 20th Party Congress—effects such as the discussion which had been raging in Poland ever since February 1956.

### POLAND AT THE CROSS-ROADS—OCTOBER 1956

The workers' rising in Poznan in June had been described in a resolution by the Central Committee of the CPSU of 30 June 1956 as the work of "provocateurs and deviationists".[1] The Soviet leaders held to this line. Thus Bulganin, in the course of a visit to Poland in company with Zhukov, declared on 21 July that the rising had been instigated by hostile agents.[2] In Polish circles, however, a different opinion had grown up in the course of the summer of 1956. The 7th Plenary Session of the Polish Central Committee (18–27 July) acknowledged that the events

[1] On 28 June 1956, workers had organized a demonstration in reinforcement of certain trade union demands. The demonstration turned into an uprising, which was quelled the following day.

[2] *Trybuna Ludu*, 22 July 1956 (quoted in *National Communism and Popular Revolt in Eastern Europe*, p. 143).

in Poznan had had their origin in the clumsy handling of justified complaints by the workers of Poznan. Looked at in the light of the atmosphere at the time, this divergence is very significant as an indication of a leaning to independence on the part of the Polish party. A few months later, on 19 October, there was to be a manifestation of very much more powerful claims to independence, and these claims were to have to maintain themselves in the face of clumsy Soviet efforts to interfere in the Polish party's internal affairs.

On 4 August Wladyslaw Gomulka was re-admitted to the Party.[1] On 15 October the Polish Politbureau had a meeting to prepare for the 8th Plenary Session of the Central Committee of the Polish party. On 16 October it was announced that Gomulka had attended the Politbureau meeting.[2] On the morning of 19 October he was co-opted into the Central Committee by the 8th Plenary Session.

The impending resumption of the leadership of the Polish party by Gomulka and his followers created alarm in the Central Committee of the CPSU. At about midday on 19 October a strong Soviet delegation, headed by Khrushchev, arrived at Warsaw airport. The delegation included not only Kaganovitch and Mikoyan but also Molotov, who had "proved his worth" as a militant opponent of Yugoslav national independence.

The aircraft had to wait for some time before it received permission to land. During the hour's respite this afforded, Gomulka, Marian Spychalski, Ignaz Loga-Sowinski and Zenon Kliszko were voted into the Central Committee.[3] In the discussion which followed the arrival of the Soviet functionaries, the Russians made grave—Ochab called them "monstrous"—charges such as: "Traitor—have you been bought over by the Americans and Zionists?"[4]

The "Soviet friends" left Warsaw in the early hours of 20 October, without having achieved anything, even though they had not only urged their anxiety about the situation in Poland

---

[1] *Trybuna Ludu*, 5 August 1956.    [2] *Ibid.*, 16 October 1956.
[3] *Ostprobleme* 1957, p. 184.
[4] Cf. the extracts from the discussion at the 8th Plenary Session in *Nowe drogi* 1956, No. 10, quoted in *Ostprobleme* 1957, p. 188.

but—which was a much more massive argument—had also given Konstantin Rokossovski, the Russian Marshal in the Polish Government (and a member of the Polish Politbureau), orders to undertake troop movements. On 21 October Gomulka was elected First Secretary of the Central Committee of the Polish party.

Regarding the visit, Alexander Zawadski said at the 8th Plenary Session:

> The Soviet comrades gave as the reason for their sudden arrival the profound disquiet felt in the Presidium of the Central Committee of the CPSU at the course of developments in Poland. They wanted, together with us, to settle the course of future developments and to find out what was in our minds—the particularly disquieting issues being the various forms of anti-Soviet propaganda and our lack of action, or at all events insufficient reaction, to this propaganda. The Soviet comrades painted a picture of these matters against the background of our internal situation and in particular against the background of the friendly relations between our countries. This last they described to us with unusual vividness. As proof of the propaganda against the Soviet Union they produced extracts and examples from various of our newspapers.
>
> The comrades were also interested in our intentions regarding the composition of our new leading body, to be elected by the 8th Plenum. They pointed out that the suggested membership was known about all over Poland but that we had not kept the Soviet comrades informed. Furthermore, they described it as a defect in our relations that there had not been sufficient contact between us recently and that we had not sent them any authorized and authentic information on the situation in Poland.
>
> As far as the membership of our leading bodies is concerned, I should like to make it clear that this matter was discussed from beginning to end on the basis that it was an internal affair of our Party and its Central Committee.
>
> For the most part the discussions were carried on in a Party spirit, and at times animatedly, on both sides. We did our best to calm down our Soviet comrades and to explain to them the essential features, the purpose and the irrevocability of our process of democratization.

Zawadski was followed by Edward Ochab, whose remarks also give a good indication of the atmosphere in which the negotiations were carried on:

In recent months we experienced—and I myself had to tolerate—so much malevolence that it seemed that we could only swallow the bitter pill with the greatest difficulty. People were saying that it couldn't have been bitterer. But in both of the last two days there was a new virulence, so bitter that one can only say we have never experienced such acerbity. I myself, for example, was forced to listen to completely unfounded and monstrous charges by our Soviet friends, while at the same time I was facing a phenomenon which was to some extent the cause of these discussions and yet is a problem on its own. I mean the declarations, resolutions and speeches by people at meetings all over Poland, declaring that the Central Committee would be defended against the troops alleged to be threatening the Central Committee, or in other words, the Soviet Army. Who could ever have dreamed that he would find himself in a situation in which Party members, people who fervently believe in the victory of the Communist cause, would be faced with this problem and would be driven to the despairing realization that they were threatened either by the troops or by their friends . . .?

This desperate talk about defending the Central Committee against the Red Army comes from people who unquestionably want to see the victory of Communism and the strengthening and consolidation of the friendship between Poland and the Soviet Union. The consciences of the people have been profoundly disquieted by what is happening in connection with real or imagined troop movements. Are we to condemn the students or the young workers for talking like this?

In saying this, Ochab had introduced a factor which had made a considerable if not decisive contribution to the outcome of the negotiations—the attitude of the people of Warsaw. Some members of the Natolin Group in the Polish Central Committee (Boleslav Ruminski and Franciszek Joswiak), faithful to Moscow, claimed at the 8th Plenary Session that the Warsaw party organizations had organized anti-Russian demonstrations

K

during the Soviet visit. To this Romana Granas, a member of the Warsaw Party Committee, replied:[1]

> The provocative slanders that have been put out against the Warsaw Party Committee during the whole of this meeting have got to be nailed for what they are, and with all possible force. As a member of the Warsaw Committee I say that the Warsaw party organization was mobilized with exceptional skill in support of the Central Committee. Particularly outstanding were the efforts of the Zeran party organization, the Kasprzak and other factories and the high-school party organization. In face of these facts, how can one describe the accusations of those who charge the Warsaw Committee and its members with having organized an anti-Soviet street demonstration by the factories? Can one describe these methods otherwise than by calling them the methods of the Beria gang?

Gomulka himself had intelligence enough to oppose the anti-Soviet elements, pointing out how too aggressive an attitude might seriously prejudice the vital interests of the Polish state. Developments in Hungary were to show how right he was.

Soviet interference in the affairs of a brother party has seldom taken place with so much publicity as this intervention in Poland. It will be remembered from the history of the KPD how Manuilski, in his capacity of Comintern plenipotentiary, tried to influence the election of the Central Committee at the 10th Party Congress on 12 July 1925.[2]

Khrushchev had described the task of Soviet foreign policy as "consolidating fraternal relations with Poland . . . in every possible way". The significance to be attached to this was demonstrated by the clumsy attempt to bring into being a Polish Central Committee consisting of personalities acceptable to the CPSU. Like Stalin, the collective leaders of the Central Committee of the CPSU paid only lip-service to the principles of mutual trust and equality of rights.[3]

[1] All these quotations are taken from the extracts printed in *Nowe drogi* 1956, No. 10, reproduced in *Ostprobleme* 1957, p. 188.

[2] See p. 91 above.

[3] Cf. the final communiqué issued at the conclusion of Tito's visit to Moscow in June 1956 (see p. 269 above), and Gomulka's speech at the 8th Plenary Session. (*National Communism and Popular Revolt in Eastern Europe*, p. 227.)

This was to be shown once again, only a few days after the failure of the attempted interference in Poland, by the Soviet intervention in Hungary.[1]

## "PROLETARIAN INTERNATIONALISM" IN HUNGARY

The relationship in which the CPSU stood to the Hungarian party (and the Soviet Union to the Hungarian People's Republic) was made clear by Tito in what he said about his conversations in Moscow:[2]

When we were in Moscow, our conversations naturally included Poland, Hungary and other countries. We said that Rakosi's régime and Rakosi himself lacked the requisite qualifications for governing the Hungarian state and for leading it to internal unity: if anything, they would only lead Hungary into serious trouble. Unfortunately, the Soviet comrades did not believe us. They said Rakosi was an old revolutionary, a decent chap and so forth. He is old, that's true—but that isn't enough. As to being a decent chap—I couldn't agree with that on my knowledge of him, especially after the Rajk trial and other matters. As far as I am concerned, these people are the least "decent" people in the world. The Soviet comrades said he was clever, and that he would be a success—and besides, they didn't know who else they could rely on in Hungary.

This confirms that the Soviet leaders, whether Stalin or Khrushchev and his associates, control the top functionaries in the Peoples' Democracies. This control is one of the means they use to keep the power over these countries in their hands ("they did not know who else they could rely on in Hungary").

---

[1]A description of the actual course of events in Hungary does not properly belong to this book. These events will only be touched on in so far as they illustrate the relations between the Soviet and Hungarian parties.

Imre Nagy, who led the Hungarian Government for a few days, was an old Communist who had been a prisoner-of-war in Russia during World War I, and had been a member of the Bolshevik Party there before he joined the Hungarian Communist Party, founded in 1918. He was also in the Soviet Union during World War II, returning to Hungary in the wake of the Red Army (*Imre Nagy on Communism*, New York, 1957, p. 241 and p. vii).

[2]Cf. the speech he delivered at Pola on 11 November 1956, reproduced in *Ostprobleme* 1956, pp. 1702 ff. The Moscow visit Tito is speaking about is obviously the one he made in June 1956.

At last, Tito went on, "the Soviet comrades realized that things could no longer go on as they were going on, and they agreed to the removal of Rakosi". Mikoyan took part in the meeting of the Central Committee of the Hungarian party on 18 July 1956, at which Rakosi was relieved "at his own request" of his membership of the Politbureau and his function as First Secretary.[1] The situation in Hungary was again discussed during Tito's second visit to the Soviet Union at the end of September 1956. It was during these discussions that Tito was told by some of the Russians with whom he had talks that they regarded their relations with Yugoslavia in a different light from their relations with East European countries such as Poland and Hungary, in which the Communists had been helped to power by the Soviets.[2] As Tito remarked, some of the Soviet leaders had "erroneous" views about relations with Poland, Hungary and other countries.[3] After the events in Poland and Hungary Tito said that in September 1956 he had not been clear as to the strength of the Stalinist group among the Soviet leaders. Enlightenment was provided by the discussions at the June 1957 Plenary Session of the Central Committee of the CPSU, together with the public self-criticism by Bulganin and Pervukhin and the charges made by Kusmin and others against the "enemies of the Party". The nucleus of the opposition was formed by Malenkov, Kaganovitch and Molotov. Bulganin, Pervukhin and Shepilov joined forces with this group, first on isolated questions and later altogether.[4] It was the existence of this strong Stalinist opposition that made it difficult for Khrushchev to persuade the Presidium of the Central Committee of the CPSU to accept the line given out at the 20th Party Congress, a line which at this time was still his own.

[1] *National Communism and Popular Revolt in Eastern Europe*, p. 338, with an extract from *Szabad Nep* of 19 July 1956.

[2] On p. 174 of his *The New Class*, Djilas also points out how important it is in these states whether the Communists came to power by their own efforts or not.

[3] Cf. the quotation of Tito's speech at Pola in *National Communism and Popular Revolt in Eastern Europe*, p. 521.

[4] Cf. Bulganin's self-criticism in *Pravda* of 19 December 1958, Pervukhin's speech at the 21st Party Congress and Kusmin's attacks on him in *Pravda* of 4 and 5 February 1959.

The Soviet Russians' attempt to interfere in Poland alone showed that the Soviet leaders were acting as Stalin would have done, and the Soviet actions in Hungary gave further proof of the extensive influence the Stalinists had in Moscow. To take the place of Rakosi the Russians chose Ernö Gerö, whose loyalty to Moscow was well known and who had been partly responsible for Rakosi's policies.[1]

They began their military intervention on 24 October 1956, thus adding fuel to the flames of the revolt: and it was again Stalinist to include in the Soviet Government's declaration of 30 October an assurance that the Soviet Union based its relations with the Socialist nations "only on the principles of complete equality, respect for territorial integrity, national sovereignty and mutual non-interference in each other's internal affairs".[2] At the time these high-sounding words were being uttered, Soviet military forces were withdrawing from Budapest and preparing, together with reinforcement troops, for a second attack.[3] On 1 November Mikoyan and Suslov, in the presence of the Prime Minister, Imre Nagy, negotiated with Ferenc Münnich (a Spanish Civil War veteran and Nagy's Minister of the Interior) and Janos Kadar, at that time First Secretary of the Party, regarding the "withdrawal" of the

[1]It was unquestionably a mistake on Tito's part to receive Gerö in Belgrade and thus to accord him a certain degree of recognition. (See Richard Löwenthal in *Der Monat*, No. 121, October 1958, pp. 6 ff.) On 30 October Nagy declared that it was not he who called for Russian troops. From 24 to 28 October he was virtually a prisoner in the Central Committee offices (United Nations Report on Hungary, parts of which were quoted in *Ostprobleme* 1957, p. 721). On 11 November, at Pola, Tito said it was Gerö who asked for the intervention. It is possible that the Russians began their first intervention without being asked, just as they prepared and carried out the second without the agreement, indeed against the will, of the Hungarian Government. Gerö fled secretly from Budapest on 26 October. (See *United Nations Report of the Special Committee on the Problem of Hungary*, New York, 1957, pp. 41 ff.)

[2]*Ostprobleme* 1956, p. 1630.

[3]Cf. Nagy's telegram to the Secretary General of the United Nations on 1st November 1956, reproduced in *National Communism and Popular Revolt in Eastern Europe*, p. 462. In *Der Monat* of October 1958 Richard Löwenthal reports that a Yugoslav confidant told him that Khrushchev visited Tito on the island of Brioni at the very beginning of November to try to gain Yugoslavia's political support for the projected action (although this has not been confirmed elsewhere).

Russian troops.[1] In view of Nagy's presence, there cannot have been any negotiations on the impending intervention and the formation of the "Hungarian Revolutionary Workers' and Peasants' Government".

On the evening of 1 November, Münnich and Kadar visited the Soviet Embassy.[2] It is probable that during the course of this visit there were discussions aimed at overthrowing Nagy and forming a government under Kadar. This assumption is strengthened by the open letter by Kadar and Münnich of 4 November, claiming that they had withdrawn from the Nagy Government on 1 November and had taken the initiative in forming a "Hungarian Revolutionary Government of Workers and Peasants". On 2 November Kadar was still in evidence in the parliament building, and until 4 November he said nothing to indicate his opposition to Nagy. The Government felt no doubts about the loyalty of the Minister of the Interior and the First Secretary of the Party.

Kadar and Münnich played their double game against Nagy at the instigation of their "Soviet friends", who wanted political cover for their second military intervention. This was the "respect for national sovereignty" and the "mutual non-interference" which the Soviet Government's declaration of 30 October had so hypocritically spoken of. The Commander-in-Chief of the Russian forces was acting quite in the Stalin tradition of coupling power and deceit when he tried to give the impression that his "operation" was the result of an appeal by the "Revolutionary Workers' and Peasants' Government".[3] In contrast to this, the Nagy Government declared in the early hours of 4 November:

> This is Imre Nagy, the Prime Minister. In the early hours of this morning Soviet troops began an attack against our capital with the obvious intention of overthrowing the rightful democratic Hungarian Government. Our troops are in

[1] United Nations Report on Hungary, German edition, Bonn, 1957, p. 83. Münnich's behaviour showed once again how right Dimitroff had been when he said after the defeat in Spain that the Spanish War veterans would still prove invaluable to the cause of Communism. (Cf. Jesus Hernandez, *op. cit.*, p. 202.)

[2] *United Nations Report of the Special Committee on the Problem of Hungary*, p. 44.
[3] *National Communism and Popular Revolt in Eastern Europe*, p. 48.

action. I hereby inform the Hungarian people and world public opinion of these facts.

On the same day *Pravda* wrote that the operations of the reactionary forces in Budapest were the product of long-standing agitation by the imperialist powers. "The peoples of the Socialist countries", *Pravda* went on, "united in the common aim of the building up of Socialism and the noble principles of proletarian internationalism, have rightly given expression to their disquiet over the situation which has arisen in Hungary."

On 2 December 1959, however, Khrushchev went much further towards admitting that these "noble principles of proletarian internationalism" had been used by the Soviet leaders as whitewash to cover the Red Army's intervention. Speaking in a Budapest factory, he said:

In 1848 Tsar Nicholas did not hesitate for a moment to help Austria in crushing the glorious Hungarian revolution. How could the Soviet Union have refused to give such help in 1956, at a time when we had troops available in the country . . .?

The comparison was a just one, although not perhaps in the way Khrushchev had intended. The reactionary Nicholas had crushed a revolutionary fight for freedom in Hungary. Khrushchev had done exactly the same.

### THE CRISIS OF INTERNATIONALISM

The events in Hungary unleashed a spate of discussion on proletarian internationalism, the bases for which had already been provided by the Soviet Government's declaration of 30 October. Apart from the problem of military intervention itself there were three main constituents of this discussion—the question of non-intervention in the internal affairs of Socialist states or parties, the problem of the leading role of the Soviet Union and, thirdly, how the Communist parties were to collaborate internationally in the future.

### THE PROBLEM OF THE MILITARY INTERVENTION

On 11 November 1956 Tito said at Pola:[1]

I am firmly convinced that the blood which has been shed

[1] *Ostprobleme* 1956, pp. 1706 ff.

in Hungary and the terrible sacrifices made by the Hungarian people will have a positive effect, and that the comrades in the Soviet Union, even the Stalinist elements, will see the light and will realize that things can't be done like this any more. Things *cannot* be done like this any more. It is our tragedy, the tragedy of all of us together, that Socialism has been dealt a fearful blow. Socialism is compromised.

Whether it was Socialism that had been compromised, as Tito felt, is open to doubt, for the bureaucratic domination by the functionaries of the Soviet Union was as little deserving of the name of Socialism as was the Rakosi régime, which Kadar now carried on in Hungary.[1] But the Soviet Union herself had been severely compromised in the eyes of the free world and of the Communist "world" by the contrast between the Soviet assurances regarding "the noble principles of proletarian internationalism" and the actions of the "Leninist Central Committee" which made a mockery of every principle of law and decency.

Even in the Soviet Union it had to be admitted that "a complicated situation for international Socialism" had arisen "as a result of the events in Hungary".[2]

On the occasion of his visit to Moscow, Gomulka said that his negotiations with his Soviet partners had shown that the Soviet Government's declaration of 30 October had contained not empty phrases but a living content.[3] These words by Gomulka give a good indication of the defensive attitude the Soviet comrades were forced to adopt in view of the world's indignation at the Hungarian bloodbath. Only a year or two before it would hardly have been conceivable that the leader of a party within the direct sphere of Soviet influence should even have mentioned the possibility that a declaration by the Soviet Government contained empty phrases.

Now, however, the Central Committee of the CPSU began a counter-offensive designed to regain the ground lost by proletarian internationalism. In a leading article on the

[1] Djilas, *The New Class*, pp. 33 ff.

[2] A. Rumyantsev in *Kommunist*, Moscow, No. 18/1956, quoted in *Ost-probleme* 1957, pp. 340 ff. In No. 1/57 of *Kommunist*, I. P. Pomelov later denied that internationalism was going through a crisis.

[3] *Pravda*, 19 November 1956, quoted in *Ostprobleme* 1956, p. 1726.

significance of the Soviet-Polish negotiations, *Pravda* said on 22 November 1956:

> The Soviet-Polish negotiations have proved that the defects in the relations between the Socialist countries can and must be completely eradicated. There can be no doubt that this fact will considerably strengthen the faith in internationalism of the peoples of the Socialist countries and of Socialists all over the world. . . .
>
> All Socialist countries, all Socialist parties and Socialists all over the world are, so to speak, in the same boat and must fight their way through the storm to the shore of victory. The enemy who opposes us is a mighty one. Only if we consolidate the unity of our Socialist ranks, the unity between the Socialist countries and parties and unity within each country and each party can we reach our great, common goal.

The same argument was used in respect of Tito's Pola speech, which contained such frank remarks about "Stalinists" and "non-Stalinists" in the Central Committee of the CPSU and about the terrible blow the Soviets had dealt to "Socialism".[1] The Soviet appeal for the consolidation of the Socialist ranks was intended to muffle the criticism which had been raised even in the Socialist camp by the military action in Hungary.

Behind the Iron Curtain it was only in Poland that such criticism retained any sort of intensity. *Po prostu* said in No. 45/56:[2]

> We need unity as much as we need air to breathe. But not unity with Stalinists. Not unity at any cost, at the cost of truth and the renunciation of revolutionary honour.

And:

> . . . this is why the attitude to the Hungarian tragedy is not simply *a* problem. It is the *key* of the whole international working-class movement.

A Polish woman writer boldly asked whether a strategic victory in Hungary made up for the tremendous moral defeat suffered by the Communists of the whole world.[3] In 1924 Stalin

---

[1] See page 280 above and *Pravda* of 19 November 1956, p. 1708.
[2] Quoted in *Ostprobleme* 1957, p. 52.
[3] *Po prostu*, No. 49/56 (Yadviga Siekierska). One is reminded here of similar thoughts by Rosa Luxemburg regarding the October Revolution in 1917 (in her book *Die Russische Revolution*, Hamelin, 1957, pp. 67 ff.).

KX

had been faced with a similar choice. The revolutionary attempts in Europe had failed. The Soviet revolution had not spread to the progressive countries as might have been expected according to classic Marxist teaching. At this time Stalin could choose between admitting the bankruptcy of the teachings of internationalism and adopting a policy which was no longer proletarian-revolutionary and no longer Socialist.[1] Stalin stayed in power and invented the "Leninist" teaching "Socialism in one country".[2] He followed a nationalistic policy which was incompatible with Socialism and internationalism alike. In October 1956, in a parallel situation, the Moscow collective leaders, in an access of genuine Stalinism, decided to hold the position in Hungary at all costs.

The attitude of the other Communist parties was conditioned by the fact that throughout the years the only functionaries to reach the most senior positions were those who had unconditionally acknowledged the leading role of the Soviet Union. This is the reason why it was only in the days immediately following the rising that some of the Communist parties in the countries of the free world (for example the American, Danish and Norwegian parties on 11 and 12 November) condemned the Soviets' military intervention.[3] The Chinese People's Republic did not expressly condemn the Russian action, but by laying stress on the independence of the Socialist countries tacitly showed her disapproval of the Soviet step.[4] Chou En-lai displayed a similar attitude when he visited Poland in the middle of January 1957.[5] Considering the feud which was in full swing at this time between the journalists of Soviet and Polish papers, Chou En-lai's statements—e.g., "I drink to the correctness of the work of the leaders of the Polish Party"— contained a measure of cautious support for the Polish standpoint. The Polish and Chinese Governments indirectly retreated from the Soviet intervention in Hungary by declaring, without even mentioning the Russians' military action, that they were

[1]S. Leonhard, *op. cit.*, p. 820.        [2]See p. 92 above.
[3]*Ostprobleme* 1956, p. 1683, and 1957, p. 27.
[4]Declaration by the Government of the Chinese People's Republic of 1 November 1956, quoted in *National Communism and Popular Revolt in Eastern Europe*, p. 492.
[5]*Trybuna Ludu*, 17 January 1957, quoted in *Ostprobleme* 1957, p. 249.

prepared to support the programme of the Kadar Government.[1]

In the British Communist Party the rank-and-file members were harder hit than the functionaries. The British Party tried hard to counter the considerable drop in membership at a specially convened Party Congress, at which an extremely critical minority opposed a report by the Party leaders.[2]

The American Party, at their Party Conference in February 1957, went so far as to declare its independence of outside influence and its loyalty to the American Constitution in an attempt to avoid the damaging effects of the Hungarian affair on its membership.[3] Jacques Duclos, in a letter of 21 January 1957 to the American Party, had previously tried to counteract these gestures of independence.[4] These events had an historical parallel in the CPUSA's action in leaving the Comintern in 1940, when the Stalin-Hitler Pact made the Comintern unpopular in the United States and diminished the American Party's prospects of making an appeal to the broad masses of the people. There had also been a previous instance of Duclos's interfering in the American Party's internal affairs, when in April 1945 his violent newspaper attack on Earl Browder, the leader of the American Communists, started the process which led to Browder's expulsion from the Party.[5]

The modest efforts by some Communist parties—excepting the Polish Party—to form an independent judgment of the events in Hungary was stifled by the dead weight of the larger European parties, which unanimously ranged themselves at the side of Moscow. While the French and Czech parties and

[1]Joint declaration of 16 January 1957 (*Ostprobleme* 1957, p. 250). Previous to this, some Chinese had admittedly approved the Soviet intervention. (See quotation from the Peking People's Newspaper in *Ostprobleme* 1956, p. 1714, and the article from *Yen Min Jih Pao*, Peking, 29 December 1956, quoted in *Ostprobleme* 1957, p. 130.)

[2]*The Observer*, London, 18 November 1956. The Party Congress was held at Easter 1957. At this Congress it was revealed that the British Party had lost 7,000 members, or 20 per cent of its membership. (*The Manchester Guardian*, 22 April 1957 and the *Daily Worker*, London, 20 April 1957. Also H. Pelling, *The British Communist Party*, p. 175.)

[3]*New York Herald-Tribune*, 15 March 1957.

[4]*New York Times*, 10 February 1957.

[5]It is noteworthy that the CPUSA did not sign the peace manifesto published on the occasion of the 40th anniversary of the October Revolution.

the SED of the Soviet Zone in Germany did this completely without reserve, the Italian Party, in a resolution adopted at their Party Congress of 14 December 1956, did what they could to represent the Soviet intervention as "a painful necessity brought about by circumstances".[1] The excuse which all these "Party liners" employed to justify their attitude was the allegation that the Soviet troops had been forced to take action in Hungary against "imperialist provocation" and against "counter-revolutionary machinations".

### THE PRINCIPLE OF NON-INTERVENTION

There seems to be no necessity to reproduce here the many Communist statements which were made following the Soviet declaration of 30 October 1956 approving the principle of non-intervention.

This declaration said quite plainly:

The unshakable basis of the USSR's foreign relations is, as it has always been, the policy of peaceful co-existence, friendship and co-operation with all states.

The profoundest and most consistent expression of this policy is seen in the mutual relations between the Socialist countries.

According to this, the Central Committee of the CPSU made no distinction between the policy of co-existence which was to be applied to Socialist states and relations with other states. I. P. Pomelov, however, did make such a distinction. Following the events in Poland and Hungary in the autumn of 1956, he wrote in the Moscow paper *Kommunist*:[3]

The principle of co-existence is the principle of the peaceful association of countries which have differing and opposing social and economic systems. It is not difficult to see that it

[1]*Unita*, Rome, 15 December 1956, quoted in *Ostprobleme* 1956, p. 6. Italian Communists who left the Italian Communist Party as a result of the Hungarian tragedy claimed that Togliatti only made use of the slogan about the Italian road to Socialism in order to mask his complete devotion to the Soviet Union. (*Ostprobleme* 1957, p. 547.)

[2]*Pravda*, Moscow, 31 October 1956.

[3]*Kommunist*, Moscow, the theoretical and political journal of the Central Committee of the CPSU, No. 1/1957, reproduced in *Aus der Internationalen Arbeiterbewegung*, Berlin, 1957, No. 4.

would be a great mistake to carry this principle of co-existence over to the reciprocal relations between similar Socialist
states or to the relationships between Communist parties,
which have a common aim and a common ideology.

Pomelov's theory contradicted the Soviet Government's
declaration of 30 October, but this declaration was itself in such
opposition to the Soviet Union's actions in Hungary that it was
obviously thought necessary to provide a theoretical under-
pinning for the Soviet intervention. Pomelov managed to find
the theoretical justification, to the extent that on the one hand
he called the intervention in Hungary an act of "international
working-class solidarity" against the "alliance between the
Horthy-Fascist gang and international imperialism", while on
the other hand maintaining that it was important to distinguish
between the relations existing between "Socialist" states and
those between capitalist and Socialist states.[1]

Pomelov would have got nearer the real truth of the matter
if he had said that the Soviet Union only accepted the principle
of co-existence with other states where Soviet intervention in a
state, no matter what its social system might be, would result
in a war which the Soviet Union did not feel able to cope with
or which she wanted to avoid for some other reason. It was this
attitude of mind which made Russia begin the war against
Finland in the winter of 1939 and also gave rise to the use of
military force to crush the uprising by the Hungarian people in
1956. *Per contra*, it was this same attitude which inhibited the
Russians from taking military action against the recalcitrant
Yugoslavs in 1948, lest this should cause a general conflagration,
as it probably would have done.[2]

In the light of Pomelov's theory, the principle of non-intervention *vis-à-vis* "Socialist" countries assumes the following
form. The Soviet Union claims the right to interfere in the

[1]In saying this, Pomelov was also rejecting the argument of the Yugoslavs, who had been demanding equality for all "socialist" states ever since
1949 (cf. Josip Broz Tito and Mosche Pijade, *Über Beziehungen zwischen
Sozialistischen Ländern*, Jugoslavenska Kniga, Beograd, 1949, pp. 25 and 42)
and had pointed out that according to Lenin's teachings, the principle of
equality also applied to Communist states (see Milovan Djilas, *Lenin über
die Beziehungen zwischen Sozialistischen Staaten*, Beograd, 1950, p. 40 ff.).
[2]Djilas, *The New Class*, p. 174.

internal affairs of a "Socialist" country at any time if that
country shows signs of deserting the popular—democratic—
system.

### THE LEADING ROLE OF THE CPSU AND THE SOVIET UNION

When Stalin was at the summit of power, the attitude to the
CPSU and to the Soviet Union was described as the test of
proletarian internationalism.[1] This implied that Stalin had
made the "leading role" of the CPSU into a dogma, giving the
CPSU authority to lead and control the national Communist
parties. Following the 20th Party Congress, Soviet agencies,
and in particular the Soviet Government in its declaration of
30 October, at first silently passed over the question of whether
the CPSU still claimed the "leading role", Suslov merely
asserting in his speech on the 39th anniversary of the October
Revolution that some of the basic features of the Soviet revolution were of international significance.

But then, at about the end of November, and obviously in
response to instructions, there began among the satellite parties
a campaign designed to restore the damaged standing of the
CPSU and to secure it the leading role it still claimed. In the
report of the Politbureau of the East German SED to the 29th
Plenary Session of the Central Committee of the SED (12–14
November 1956), not published until 28 November, during
this campaign, it was said: ". . . we acknowledge the leading
role of the CPSU among all Communist and Workers' Parties".[2]
The Deputy Prime Minister of Czechoslovakia, Vaclav
Kopecky, in the course of a funeral oration for Gottwald,
demonstratively quoted Gottwald's own slogan "With the Soviet
Union forever" several times.[3] At the same time the Bulgarian
Communists were stressing that they regarded the experience
of the Soviet Union as providing valuable guidance.[4] The

[1] See pp. 239 f. above.

[2] *Neues Deutschland*, E. Berlin, 28 November 1956. There are also variations
between the adherents of Moscow to the extent that the most loyal are in the
habit of stressing not only the leading position of the Soviet Union but also
that of the CPSU.

[3] *Rude Pravo*, Prague, 23 November 1956, quoted in *Ostprobleme* 1956,
p. 1764.

[4] *Rabotnichesko delo*, Sofia, 27 November 1956, quoted in *Ostprobleme* 1956,
p. 1766.

faithful Stalinist Enver Hodja was scrupulously following the
1949 line when he said at the plenary session of the Albanian
Workers' Party in February 1957:[1]

> Recent events confirm that the attitude of a person, party or
> state to the Soviet Union, the appreciation of the international
> role of the Soviet Union in the Socialist camp and in the
> Communist movement as a whole and the appreciation of
> the universal character of Soviet experience characterize
> better than any other criterion the political and ideological
> attitude to Marxism-Leninism of the person, party or state
> concerned.

In his report to the Central Committee of the French Communist Party, Raymond Guyot described the attitude to the
Soviet Union and to the CPSU as a question of principle.[2]
There is no doubt how the tried and true French Stalinists will
respond to that question.

At its Extraordinary Party Congress at Easter 1957 the
British party also adopted the standpoint that the Soviet Union
stood at the centre of proletarian internationalism. The Italian
party made at least a gesture of independence, as they had in
their evaluation of the events in Hungary ("a painful necessity"). They said that instead of talking about the leading role
of a state or party (i.e. the Soviet Union and the CPSU) there
ought to be more stress laid on the leadership provided by the
principles of Marxism and the interests of the Italian working
class, even if there was no denying the incontrovertible function
of the Soviet Union in the Socialist world.[3]

Only the Polish party, together with the Yugoslav Communist Federation, has so far publicly acknowledged neither the
leading role of the Soviet Union nor that of the CPSU.

The influence of these recalcitrant forces was attested by the
declaration published in November 1957 by "representatives
of the Communist and Workers' Parties of the Socialist countries" following the 40th anniversary celebrations of the
October Revolution.[4] The declaration included the assertion

---

[1] *Aus der Internationalen Arbeiterbewegung*, E. Berlin, No. 6/1957, p. 22.
[2] *L'Humanité*, Paris, 21 November 1956, quoted in *Ostprobleme* 1957, p. 10.
[3] Resolution by the 8th Party Congress of the Italian Communist Party,
*Unita*, Rome, 15 December 1956, quoted in *Ostprobleme* 1957, p. 5.
[4] See p. 295 below and *Neues Deutschland*, E. Berlin, 22 November 1975.

that peace was being defended by the unconquerable "camp of the Socialist states with the Soviet Union at their head".

Friedrich Ebert went even further, and declared at the 34th meeting of the East German SED that Mao Tse-tung had acknowledged the leading role of the CPSU in the comity of Communist and Workers' Parties, as well as the leading role of the Soviet Union at the head of the states composing the "Socialist camp", during the discussions in Moscow.[1] The communiqué issued after this meeting of the SED Central Committee accordingly said it was "particularly to be welcomed that all parties are of one mind in acknowledging that the glorious CPSU" stood "at the head of the Communist and Workers' Parties".[2]

The declaration issued by the twelve parties, however, included no such acknowledgment. Since "documents" of this type are usually formulated with great care, it must be assumed that not all the signatories of this one found themselves able to acknowledge "the leading role of the CPSU and of the Soviet Union". One of the signatories, Gomulka, said on his return from Moscow that in the mighty association of Socialist states first place belonged to the mightiest of them all, the Soviet Union.[3] This remark accords both with the facts—for the Soviet Union is undeniably the mightiest of the Socialist states —and with the declaration by the twelve states. Nevertheless, it does not contain any acknowledgment of the leading position of the CPSU, an acknowledgment which had been used in the past by functionaries devoted to Moscow for the purpose of

[1]*Neues Deutschland*, 30 November 1957, p. 4. In his report on the discussions in Moscow, Ebert named seven representatives of Communist countries in addition to Khrushchev, Mao Tse-tung and Ulbricht who had acknowledged that "only the CPSU can stand at the head of the Socialist camp". Gomulka and the Hungarian representative were not mentioned. Mao Tse-tung's action in this respect shows that the Chinese party had drawn closer to the Soviet position during 1957.

[2]*Neues Deutschland*, 29 November 1957, p. 1. This was an attempt by the Central Committee of the SED to shift the accent from the Soviet state to the CPSU. The SED resolution was a fiction, if only because the "partners" were so far from agreeing on this point that the Yugoslavs did not even sign the declaration by the party representatives. The most they would sign was the unimportant "Peace Declaration" (see *Neues Deutschland*, 22 and 23 November 1957).

[3]*Trybuna Ludu*, 29 November 1957, p. 4.

making their parties into imitations of the Soviet party, ideologically, politically and organizationally.[1]

## NATIONAL COMMUNISM

Djilas was one of the few people in the Communist-controlled countries who had the courage to say openly that Communism only existed in the shape of national Communism. According to him, the divergences between Communist countries are as a rule proportionate to the extent to which the Communists in them came to power by their own efforts; in other words, without the help of the Soviet Union.[2] The functionary caste ruling in the countries of the Eastern bloc have condemned other and less realistic remarks as "national Communism" or "national opportunism". I. P. Pomelov, for example, a functionary of the CPSU Central Committee, attacked "national opportunism", which, in the building up of Socialism, sets up national characteristics against what is typical of all countries completing the transition from capitalism to Socialism.[3] *Einheit*, the theoretical organ of the SED, called national Communism an ideological lever used by imperialism against the Socialist camp.[4] The only thing right about that is that the name "national Communism" is frequently used in the free world. Yet the conditions which have led to movements towards freedom (1948 in Yugoslavia and 1956 in Poland and Hungary) were created by the Soviet Union and her lackeys in the Peoples' Democracies.

Ever since 1945 the Soviet Union has been making every effort to shackle the East European states to herself by means of Party, military, intelligence and economic ties. After Yugo-

[1]Wolfgang Leonhard, in his *Kreml ohne Stalin* (Cologne, 1959, p. 379), agrees with this assessment of the 12-Party declaration.

[2]Djilas, *The New Class*, p. 174.

[3]In *Kommunist*, No. 1/1957, quoted in *Aus der internationalen Arbeiterbewegung*, No. 4, 23 February 1957, p. 6. There is no convincing evidence that the CPSU (or the Soviet Government) sent a letter to the Peoples' Democracies in August 1956 condemning Titoism, as the *Washington Post* claimed on 17 October 1956 (Louis Fischer, *Russia Revisited*, p. 118). It is probable, however, that in discussions held in the autumn of 1956 the Central Committee of the CPSU expressed its antagonism to national Communism.

[4]*Einheit*, March 1957, No. 3, p. 260.

slavia's revolt she gave instructions to the Peoples' Democracies
for a campaign to destroy all potential opponents of the Soviet
hegemony; and the instructions were obeyed (e.g. in the trials
of Kostoff, Rajk and Slansky.[1] The attitude to the Soviet Union
was declared to be the touchstone of proletarian internationalism. Notwithstanding that Soviet functionaries wordily
proclaim "the noble principles of proletarian internationalism",
Soviet national Communism has tyrannized the international
Communist movement ever since 1925, and the peoples of
East Europe since 1945, with a severity unequalled by any
imperialist power.

NEW FORMS OF COLLABORATION—A NEW INTERNATIONAL?

Acknowledging the supremacy of the Soviet Union after the
events of the autumn of 1956, the loyal devotees of Moscow
simultaneously showed that all was not well with the collaboration between the Communist parties. The Politbureau of the
SED, for example, in a report to the 29th plenary session of the
SED Central Committee, declared that the present international situation called for new forms of meeting and consulta-
tion.[2] In saying this the SED was not voicing its own ideas. The
November issue of *Mezhdunarodnaya Zhizn* had already asserted
that it was urgently necessary to set up new forms of connection
and contact between the Communist and Workers' Parties to
correspond with the changed international situation.[3]

The Austrian paper *Osterreichische Volksstimme* also published
a declaration on 28 November, saying that the Austrian party
had already taken steps to achieve "the creation of an international organ of the Communist parties" for the discussion of
international questions and the exchange of information.[4] The
Austrian party added that there were still differences of opinion

[1]See p. 240 above.
[2]*Neues Deutschland*, 28 November 1956.
[3]Quoted from *Ostprobleme* 1956, pp. 1752 ff. When the Japanese Communist paper *Akahata*, in an article in the issue of 23 October, complained
of the lack of information on the results of the 8th plenary session of the
Central Committee of the Polish party, the issue was not the founding of a
new organization of the Communist parties. *Akahata* was only suggesting
improving the informational side of the Communist press by the formation
of an international news network of proletarian newspapers.
[4]*Ostprobleme* 1956, p. 1752.

among the brother parties regarding the putting of these plans into effect.

An example of these differences of opinion was given shortly afterwards, when a resolution by the Italian Communist Party at the 8th Party Congress included the statement that while the idea of "a return to the centralized organization of relations between Communist parties" was rejected, it might be useful to organize meetings between the representatives of the working classes.[1] In 1947 Gomulka had shown great reluctance to agree to the creation of the Cominform.[2] His experiences since then had doubtless led him to feel no great enthusiasm for the idea of joining an international organization. The silence from the direction of the Chinese party showed that they had no greater enthusiasm for such plans at this time.[3]

Support for a closer linking up of the Communist parties, on the other hand, did come from Raymond Guyot, who, after a visit to Prague in February 1957, told the Central Committee of the French party:[4]

> The dissolution of the Communist International and the Information Bureau can in no wise lead to a decline in international obligations. On the contrary, it is a strengthening that is demanded. . . . We are determined to develop reciprocal relations and discussions on an intensive scale, although we realize that in the long run this will not be sufficient. Incidentally, this question has already been brought up by a number of brother parties.

The Czech and Rumanian parties strongly suggested the publication of an international theoretical-political periodical.[5]

An interesting clue is also given by the report made by John Gollan, the Secretary General of the British Communist Party,

[1] Quoted from *Ostprobleme* 1957, p. 6.

[2] See p. 224 above. Gomulka still held an unfavourable opinion of the Cominform in November 1957, as was shown on his return from the 40th anniversary celebrations of the October Revolution, when he told Warsaw activists that it was difficult to regard the results of the Cominform's work with approval. (See *Trybuna Ludu*, 29 November 1957, p. 4.)

[3] Cf. the critical article, based on a discussion in the Politbureau of the Chinese party, in *Jen Min Jih Pao*, Peking, of 29 December 1956 (reproduced in *Ostprobleme* 1957, pp. 130 ff.).

[4] *L'Humanité*, Paris, 16 February 1957, p. 4.

[5] *Ostprobleme* 1957, p. 726 and 1958, p. 4.

at the extraordinary Party Congress in April 1957. Gollan said:[1]

> However, no Communist party is suggesting the formation of a new central or other international organization. Many comrades admittedly think that in addition to bilateral discussions we can also arrange meetings of a number of Communist parties. We suggested this, and Togliatti supported the suggestion at the Italian Party Congress. At the last meeting of the French Central Committee, Guyot put forward the same view, and so did the Polish comrades in our most recent discussions.

Experience has shown that in such basic matters the German and Austrian satellites of the CPSU take no action without instructions from Moscow. Thus when both of them sent up simultaneous *ballons d'essai* at the end of November 1956, it was a sign that leading CPSU circles were themselves toying with the idea of founding a new international organization for the coordination of the diverging tendencies which had become evident in international Communism. However, in view of the refusal of such influential parties as the Polish, Italian and Yugoslav parties to entertain the thought, the Presidium of the CPSU stood no chance of bringing its wish to fruition. The old days, when Stalin could order the leaders of the Communist parties to Moscow and "persuade" them to agree to Soviet plans, were gone.

The opposition to the idea of founding a new international organization came principally from those Communists who had come to power or had maintained their leading positions against Moscow's will. As far as Tito and Gomulka were concerned, this has already been adequately demonstrated. The Chinese had also achieved power in their country without any Soviet help worthy of mention.[2]

It is quite evident that even after the 20th Party Congress the Soviet leaders still had no clear conception of how the situation

[1] *Daily Worker*, London, 20 April 1957, p. 4. In reprinting Gollan's report, the SED paper *Aus der internationalen Arbeiterbewegung* (No. 10, 25 May 1957, p. 11) left out these remarks by Gollan, which may be taken as an indication that the loyal SED Central Committee was to this extent respecting the Soviet wish for a new international organization. For a detailed description of the British Party Congress see Pelling, *op. cit.*, pp. 178 ff.

[2] See p. 306 below.

outside the Soviet Union had changed, otherwise they would have given up any idea of starting a new international organization.[1] Could they not have foreseen that neither Poland nor Yugoslavia would be interested in joining? And what position did the CPSU envisage for its own Presidium in such an organization? Did Moscow not want to admit, even to itself, that the dominant position maintained by the Soviet party in the Comintern and the Cominform had been chiefly due to Stalin's rule of terror, which alone had kept the ranks of world Communism together? If Moscow is not willing to employ the same degree of terrorism or lacks the force to do so, then the Soviets will have to forgo all claim to a correspondingly dominant position.

On this problem in the field of international collaboration, I. P. Pomelov said in *Kommunist*:[2]

> As far as the form of this collaboration is concerned—this too will be found. There are, for example, bilateral relationships and meetings between representatives of a number of parties.

For the CPSU, bilateral connections and negotiations were probably more advantageous at this time than meetings with a large number of parties in a centralized organization, in which the CPSU would have been one of a number of partners— highly respected, of course, but without any special rights. Situations might have arisen in which the majority or a considerable proportion of the members of such an international organization might have come out in opposition to the CPSU. A comparable situation did come about in Helsinki, at the meeting in November 1956 of the World Peace Council, a large-scale international organization supported by the Soviet Communists. In the course of the deliberations there were grave differences between the delegates, differences which were reflected in the communiqué issued by the World Peace Council:[3]

[1]Louis Fischer (*op. cit.*, p. 81) also points out how well the Kremlin understands Russia and how badly it understands other countries.

[2]No. 1/1957, reprinted in *Aus der internationalen Arbeiterbewegung*, E. Berlin, No. 4, 23 February 1957.

[3]Bulletin of the World Peace Council, 1 December 1956.

The Conference has considered the tragic events in Hungary. It recognizes that there are serious divergences of view in respect of this question, not only in the World Peace Council but also within national peace movements, and that the opposing views have made it impossible to formulate an evaluation acceptable to all.

Differences of opinion regarding the Soviet action in Hungary also arose in the Communist-controlled International Association of Democratic Lawyers.[1]

By contrast, in the case of bilateral discussions between the CPSU and a "brother party", the power and prestige of the Soviet Union are extremely advantageous to the CPSU. And even if no agreement is reached, there is no difficulty about keeping the unfavourable outcome secret.

Although the CPSU could not achieve the creation of an international organization, it could still make a virtue of necessity by intensifying the collaboration between Communist parties by means of bilateral discussions, and has done so since the autumn of 1956. "The maintenance of direct connection, the exchange of delegate visits and personal contacts between Party leaders, have recently become one of the acknowledged forms of intercourse between the Communist parties."[2]

At the end of the crisis which followed the events in Hungary, the Soviet Communists took an optimistic view of the situation. "Despite the blow of unparalleled violence that forces of international reaction have struck at the Communist movement", the Party Congresses of the Danish, Norwegian, American, Austrian, and Belgian parties up to the spring of 1957, together with the expressions of devotion to Moscow uttered by the SED and the Italian and French Communist parties, showed, the Russians believed, that "the unity of the Communist parties" had not been shaken.[3]

---

[1] Cf. *Die Justiz, Zeitschrift für Demokratie in Staat und Recht*, Düsseldorf, 1957, No. 1, p. 15.

[2] *Mezhdunarodnaya Zhizn*, Moscow, No. 11/1956, quoted in *Ostprobleme* 1956, p. 1572.

[3] Boris N. Ponomaryov, *The International Working-Class Movement in the present stage* (*Pravda*, 1 May 1957, reprinted in *Aus der internationalen Arbeiterbewegung*, No. 10/1957, pp. 4, 6). Ponomaryov is head of the Department of International Relations in the Central Committee of the CPSU.

The crisis in internationalism is of course not due to any blow struck at the Communist movement by the "forces of international reaction". If anything, it is the CPSU itself which, by its policies since the death of Stalin and by its intervention in Hungary, has called the crisis into being. Yet although the treachery and brutality of the Soviet intervention in Hungary are without equal in history, the functionary clique which today stands at the head of all Communist parties has been able to keep a firm grip on the majority of the membership. Twenty years of selection of Cadre personnel on Stalinist principles are bearing fruit.[1] "Stalin's guards obey without even receiving orders."

## THE FORTIETH ANNIVERSARY CELEBRATION OF THE OCTOBER REVOLUTION (NOV. 1957)

The deliberations linked with the 40th anniversary celebration of the October Revolution in Moscow highlighted the situation in international Bolshevism. The most that *all* the parties would agree to was a colourless "Peace Manifesto".[2] The more important "Declaration by Representatives of the Communist and Workers' Parties of the Socialist Countries" was signed by the representatives of only twelve of the parties.[3] The Yugoslavs refused to associate themselves with it.

The reason why the Declaration so emphatically demanded the consolidation of the unity and fraternal collaboration of the Communist parties was that this unity had been seriously imperilled since the 20th Party Congress.[4] Mao Tse-tung and Walter Ulbricht were also insistent that the "leading role" of the CPSU should be expressly acknowledged, precisely because some Communist leaders had firmly refused to accord this position to the Soviet party.[5] With the aim of countering

[1] See pp. 129 f. above and Pelling, *op. cit.*, pp. 180 ff.
[2] *Neues Deutschland*, 23 November 1957. In its efforts to prove its complete independence, the American Communist Party did not even sign this one, either. (See p. 283 above, n. 5.)
[3] The discussions took place in Moscow from 14 to 16 November 1957 (*Neues Deutschland*, 22 November 1957, p. 1). The signatories were the representatives of the parties of Albania, Bulgaria, China, East Zone of Germany, Korea, the Mongolian People's Republic, Poland, Rumania, the Soviet Union, Czechoslovakia, Hungary and Vietnam.
[4] See p. 206 above.     [5] See pp. 286 f. above.

Yugoslav tendencies towards independence, revisionism was declared to be the arch-enemy. However, this concrete background to the incipient struggle against revisionism was not clear to all the participants. The Danish delegation, for example, actually asked the question why they had now started to oppose revisionism—but received no answer. Aksel Larsen, who was still the Chairman of the Danish Communist Party at this time, told his Central Committee on 18 July 1958 that it was not true that every party in the Moscow discussions had, without any prompting, said that revisionism was a greater danger than dogmatism.[1]

The following results of the Moscow discussions were of importance to the international collaboration between the Communist parties. No new International was founded. For the foreseeable future there will be only "discussions", bilateral or multilateral, at which current problems will be discussed and experiences exchanged. The twelve parties agreed on several basic rules for the discussions, such as that the internal affairs of the individual parties must not be decided in the course of discussions between other parties and that the agenda for such discussions must be made known to all participants beforehand.[2] Some of those taking part in the Moscow discussions also reached agreement on the publication of a Marxist-Leninist periodical.[3]

[1] Aksel Larsen's statement to the Central Committee of the Danish Communist Party, 18 July 1958. On the 28 November, at a conference of Warsaw party activists, Gomulka said absolutely unequivocally that there no longer existed an "international centre of the Communist movement", and that there was no necessity to create one (*Trybuna Ludu*, 29 November 1957, p. 4). The occasionally-expressed belief that a new Comintern, "a rigidly hierarchial instrument in the hand of Moscow" (e.g. *Neue Zürcher Zeitung*, 1 December 1957, p. 3 and 8 December, p. 1), does not seem to have been confirmed, either by developments in world Communism since the death of Stalin or by the details of the Moscow deliberations which have so far reached the outside world.

[2] Cf. Gomulka's statement in *Trybuna Ludu*, 29 November 1957, p. 4. On the occasion of previous international discussions the questions to be discussed had not always been made known to the participants in advance. The Italian and French parties, for example, were taken by surprise by the attack on them at the inaugural session of the Cominform (see p. 222 above).

[3] This is shown by Friedrich Ebert's report to the 34th Meeting of the SED Central Committee (*Neues Deutschland*, 28 November 1957). Not all the representatives of the twelve parties shared in this agreement, for

Apart from the principles of equality of rights, respect for territorial integrity, sovereignty and non-intervention, the signatories of the Declaration of 14–16 November also introduced into the relations between the "Socialist" countries the element of "fraternal mutual assistance", which had been developed for the Communist parties from the slogan of the Communist Manifesto, "Workers of the world, unite!"[1] This not only had the effect of acknowledging the Soviet intervention in Hungary as justified but also meant that the CPSU will be able to appeal to this admission by the Communist parties if it should be necessary in the future.

The Declaration made it plain that the twelve parties were in agreement on certain important political and ideological questions, such as the fight against "revisionism" and the acceptance of the principle of "fraternal mutual assistance". In respect of the much larger groups of parties which signed the "Peace Manifesto", a common front could be proclaimed in certain basic questions such as "the fight against the war bloc" (NATO) and against "atomic war". To this extent the Soviet Communists had been able to bring about a certain degree of uniformity.

Nevertheless, the unity of the "Socialist camp" suffered by reason of the fact that the Yugoslavs were not included among the signatories of the Twelve-Party Declaration; that the Declaration did not include unconditional recognition of the "leading role of the CPSU" and the Soviet Union; and that the

otherwise the intention to publish a newspaper would have been included in the Declaration. On 7 and 8 March 1958 there was a meeting in Prague of "several Communist and Workers' parties", at which it was decided to publish a "theoretical and informational periodical" in Prague in the near future (*Neues Deutschland*, 11 March 1958, p. 1). The indefinite form of this announcement indicates that the parties assembled in Prague were not identical with the twelve parties whose representatives signed the Moscow Declaration. The fact that the "wish" to produce this periodical uttered in Moscow could not be realized until months later leads one to the conclusion that there must have been considerable resistance to the plan on the part of some of the Communist parties—the opponents of a new international organization.

[1]The principle of mutual assistance (solidarity) was subsequently invoked to justify the Soviet Union's intervention in Hungary (see p. 285 above). See also K. A. Asisyan, *Die Grosse Kraft des Proletarischen Internationalismus*, Berlin, 1955, p. 5.

opponents of the revival of a rigidly organized international
organization had their way.[1] These facts were indications that
the Soviet hegemony in world Communism had not been completely restored. Proletarian internationalism and the unity of
world Communism under Soviet leadership are still threatened
by the factor on which three Internationals have run aground:
nationalism.[2]

Bukharin, whom Lenin called the "best of the theoreticians",
claimed that national rivalry is impossible between Communist
states.[3] Soviet theoreticians still abide by this axiom today.[4] "In
the Socialist camp there are common interests and a common
goal; here there is not and cannot be any antagonism." These
adherents of the idea of "what is not allowed will simply not
be" were made to look fools by the policies of Yugoslavia, the
first Communist state to come into existence outside the Soviet
Union.[5]

### THE CAMPAIGN AGAINST YUGOSLAV REVISIONISM

Lenin had early on rejected as "revisionism" any "right-
wing" deviation from the classic Marxist teachings.[6] Within the
framework of "right-wing" policies belonged one of the factors
which had led to the events in Poland and the Hungarian
revolt of October and November 1956—the permissibility of
individual roads to Socialism, proclaimed at the 20th Party
Congress (although it had already been acknowledged in fact
in May 1955 by the Soviet visit to Belgrade).[7] This "right-
wing" policy was disavowed by the Soviet military intervention

---

[1]When he returned from the Moscow discussions, Gomulka said that the
Yugoslav representatives had refused to sign the Declaration because of
certain disputed points. He added that the time would come, sooner or
later, when the matters in dispute would be settled in concert with the
Yugoslav Federation of Communists (*Trybuna Ludu*, 29 November 1959,
p. 4).

[2]See p. 209 above.

[3]Armstrong, *Tito and Goliath*, *op. cit.*, p. ix.

[4]An article in *Pravda* on 9 May 1958 said, "In the unity and unanimity
of the Marxist-Leninist parties lies the guarantee of the continuing triumph
of the Socialist world-system" (*Neues Deutschland*, 11 May 1958).

[5]Louis Fischer, *Russia Revisited*, pp. 113 and 248 ff.

[6]For example in his essay *Marxism and Revisionism*, written in 1908 and
reproduced in *Collected Works*, Vol. I, pp. 67–73.

[7]See p. 251 above.

in Hungary. In the ideological sphere, too, the Soviet Communists soon encountered the dangers for the unity of world Communism which arose from the permissibility of individual roads to Socialism. Here, although they did not actually admit it, they retreated from the lessons of the 20th Party Congress. In the Declaration, the twelve parties emphatically warned against exaggerating the role of national idiosyncrasies and against deviating from the universally valid truth of Marxism-Leninism on the pretext of national idiosyncrasy. In the months that followed, revisionism, already branded as the arch-danger in the Declaration, became the target of heavy ideological and political attacks carried out by the loyal supporters of the Soviet predominance in world Communism.

To begin with, it was only revisionistic tendencies within Communist and Socialist parties which were criticized; those actually displaying these tendencies were not specifically named.[1] However, since the criticism was directed against the disavowal of the teachings of the dictatorship of the proletariat and of the leading role of the working class, and against the renunciation of the principles of proletarian internationalism and the unity of the Socialist camp, it was clear that these attacks were primarily aimed at the Yugoslav party. After all, it was the Yugoslav Communists who had persistently refused to acknowledge the supremacy of the CPSU and the Soviet Union ever since the 1948 conflict. It was also the Yugoslavs who had uncovered the crack in "the unity of the Socialist camp" when their representatives declined to append their signatures to the Declaration of the twelve parties.

The draft programme submitted by the Yugoslav party before its 7th Party Congress at the end of March 1958 brought about attacks on the Yugoslav party itself. The very fact that the Yugoslavs had issued a programme and conducted themselves in the manner of true disciples of Karl Marx may have angered Moscow, since neither the CPSU nor any other East European party had issued a programme since the end of the

[1] Cf. a leading article in *Kommunist*, Moscow, No. 2/58. Criticism of individual Polish and Yugoslav authors, such as Leszek Kolakowski, J. Kleer and Mito Hadji-Vasiliev, still contained no reproach against the Communist parties of the two countries.

war.[1] Soviet authors rejected the Yugoslav belief that there was such a thing as a non-revolutionary road to Socialism, just as they refused to accept the attempt by the author of the programme to trace proletarian internationalism back to the principles of equal rights and non-interference in the internal affairs of other Socialist countries and nothing else.[2] The critics of the Yugoslav draft wanted to see this—as they thought, one-sided—version of proletarian internationalism expanded to include "the necessity for consolidating the unity and the collaboration of the Socialist countries and of the Marxist-Leninist parties". The Soviet Union had based the justification for the military intervention in Hungary *ex post facto* on the necessity for fraternal assistance and international collaboration between Socialist countries (or international solidarity).[3] Consequently the Soviet theoreticians had a lively interest in getting this characteristic inserted into the concept of proletarian internationalism. The writers in *Kommunist* charged the authors of the Yugoslav draft programme with rejecting as "hegemonism" the efforts of the Soviet Union to play the leading role in world Communism. They added that the question of which party stood at the head of the international working-class movement depended on the location of "the centre of the world revolutionary movement".[4]

In saying this, these authors admitted something that is seldom so frankly said in Bolshevik circles nowadays—that a world revolutionary movement does exist, and that it has a

[1] It was not until some months after the Yugoslav Congress that the East German SED, at its 5th Party Congress in July 1958, decided to set up a commission to work out a new programme. The CPSU also discussed the need for a new programme at its 21st Party Congress. (Proceedings of the 5th Party Congress of the SED, E. Berlin, 1959, p. 998, and *Aus den Diskussionsreden zu Internationalen Fragen* (XXI. Parteitag), E. Berlin, 1959, p. 91 (Kuusinen's speech).)

[2] Cf. an article by R. Fedoseyev, I. P. Pomelov and W. Cheprakov in *Kommunist*, No. 6/58, which was also reprinted in the supplement to issue No. 4 of *Einheit*, the SED theoretical journal. We do not need to consider here the other points in the extensive but still "comradely" criticism contained in the article.

[3] See p. 285 above.

[4] *Kommunist*, No. 6/58, p. 35. *Einheit* reprinted this article in the supplement to No. 4 (April 1958), but amended the "centre of the world revolutionary movement" mentioned by the *Kommunist* writers to read "the centre of the international revolutionary movement".

centre. Interpreting the Twelve-Party Declaration of November 1957 in terms of Soviet desires, the *Kommunist* writers claimed that the Declaration had laid it down that "the unconquerable camp of the Socialist states is led by the Soviet Union".[1]

A considerable number of Communist parties joined in the criticism of the Yugoslav programme, their number including the Polish party, which made a restrained contribution.[2] The CPSU and the parties closely allied to it continued the campaign on the occasion of the 7th Party Congress of the Yugoslav party (22–26 April 1958). The CPSU informed the other Communist parties that contrary to its previous decision it had now decided not to send a delegation to this Party Congress and not to send any message of greeting. Accordingly, the other Communist parties—all except the Danish and Norwegian parties—ostentatiously declined to send any official delegation, too.[3]

At the congress itself all the diplomatic observers of the satellite countries except the Polish ambassador got up and left the conference hall during a speech by Alexander Rankovic. This slight alone demonstrated that matters would not rest at "comradely" criticism of the Yugoslav programme. There began to be a change in the attitude the Soviet Communists had adopted to the 1948 conflict after Stalin's death. The Soviet press campaign, supported by all the countries of the Eastern bloc, was continued after the Yugoslav Party Congress. An article in *Pravda* on 9 May 1958, giving a critical commentary on the results of the Party Congress, asserted that the Yugoslavs had committed errors of a nationalist nature in 1948 and in the following years.[4] The same line was taken in an extremely bitter attack by the Chinese, contained in an article

[1] On the real contents of this Declaration, see p. 297 above.

[2] *Trybuna Ludu*, 14 May 1958, extracts from which were reprinted in *Neues Deutschland*, 23 May 1958, p. 7.

[3] Cf. Aksel Larsen's report to the Central Committee of the Danish party on 18 July 1958 and a *Pravda* article dated 9 May 1958 on the Yugoslav Party Congress, reprinted in *Neues Deutschland* on 11 May 1958. Also the report of the SED Politbureau at the 36th meeting of the Central Committee in *Neues Deutschland* of 13 June 1958, p. 3, and *Eine offene Absage an den proletarischen Internationalismus* in the SED journal *Aus der Internationalen Arbeiterbewegung*, No. 10/1958, 24 May 1958.

[4] Cf. Section V of the *Pravda* article referred to in note 4, p. 298 above.

in *Jen Min Jih Pao* of 5 May 1958, with the title "Present-day revisionism must be condemned". The revisionism practised by the Yugoslavs, the article said, was aimed at splitting the international Communist movement and sabotaging the solidarity of the Socialist countries.

*Jen Min Jih Pao* went on:

We regard as substantially correct the criticism of the mistakes of the Yugoslav party contained in the "Resolution of the Information Bureau on the situation in the Yugoslav Communist Party" adopted on 8 June 1948, according to which the Yugoslav Communist Party has deviated from the principles of Marxism-Leninism and has gone over to the position of bourgeois nationalism.

This resumption of the Stalinist line disavowed by Khrushchev in Belgrade on 26 May 1955 was approved by the Soviet leaders. The very day after the appearance of the Chinese article it was reprinted in *Pravda*.[1] Khrushchev dispelled all doubt as to where he himself stood when he said at the 7th Party Congress of the Bulgarian Communist Party at the beginning of June 1958:

In 1948 the Conference of the Information Bureau adopted a resolution "On the Situation in the Yugoslav Communist Party", which contained justified criticism of the actions of the Yugoslav Communist Party in respect of a number of fundamental matters. In general this resolution was correct and was in accordance with the interests of the revolutionary movement. Later on, in the years from 1949 to 1953, there arose a conflict between the Yugoslav party and the other brother parties, and in the course of the struggle mistakes were made and complications ensued which did harm to our common cause.

When relations with Tito were resumed in May 1955, Khrushchev had not distinguished between the Cominform resolution of 1948 and "mistakes" made between 1949 and 1953. The statement he made at that time, that the Soviet leaders sincerely regretted everything that had happened, and were determined to sweep away everything that had piled up

[1] *Neues Deutschland* reprinted the complete text of the article on p. 4 of the issue of 13 May 1958.

during this period, had not excluded the 1948 Cominform resolution.[1] This resolution had already included the charge that the leaders of the Yugoslav party had betrayed the cause of the working class. It had included an appeal to the "sound elements" among the Yugoslav Communists to replace their incapable leaders.[2] Accordingly the Soviet offer of reconciliation in 1955 would not have been acceptable to Tito if it had not signified Soviet disavowal of the whole of the Cominform policies, including the 1948 resolution. Khrushchev, of course, had already devalued his offer of reconciliation by his assertion that the material against Yugoslavia had been fabricated by such enemies of the people as Beria, Abakumov and others, who had cheated their way into the Soviet ranks. This lie was accompanied by further examples in the declaration on the dissolution of the Cominform.[3]

The contradictions are explicable when one analyses the aim of Soviet policies towards Yugoslavia. Since Stalin's death the purpose of these policies has been to persuade Yugoslavia to return to the comity of Communist states. It was this aim which lay behind the Belgrade visit of May 1955 and behind the statements, both during the 1955 visit and at the 20th Party Congress, on the permissibility of individual roads to Socialism.[4] This policy had far-reaching consequences which had not been foreseen by the Soviet leaders—i.e. the events in Poland and Hungary in the autumn of 1956. When, at the conclusion of the 40th anniversary celebrations of the October Revolution, the Yugoslav delegates refused to sign the Twelve-Party Declaration, the Soviets probably realized once and for all that Yugoslavia could not be persuaded to become a faithful member of the East European bloc once again.[5] This fact, plus the realization that the Communist ranks might easily be weakened if the

[1]See p. 251 above. What is meant here is the resolution adopted in Bucharest at the end of June 1948, and which resulted in Yugoslavia's being expelled from the Cominform.

[2]See p. 236 above.        [3]See p. 254 above.

[4]Even though this was not the sole purpose of these declarations. (See p. 261 above.)

[5]Cf. Khrushchev's speech at the 21st Party Congress and B. N. Ponomaryov, *The International Movement at a new Stage*, *Kommunist* No. 15/1958, reprinted in *Aus der internationalen Arbeiterbewegung* No. 23/1959, 13 December 1958, p. 5.

example of independent Yugoslavia were to be tolerated any further, caused the Soviet leaders to return to a policy which comes very close to Stalinism.[1] In the battle against "revisionism", the Communist parties revile Yugoslav independence, which is just as energetically defended, ideologically as well, by the Yugoslav Federation of Communists.[2]

### THE SOVIETS AND THE CHINESE PARTY

Has Mao Tse-tung also achieved a measure of independence? In 1921 he was one of the founders of the Chinese Communist Party, and during the period of the Communists' collaboration with the Kuomintang he also belonged to the Kuomintang. In 1926–7 he organized the Hunan peasants' revolt, to which Stalin referred when he was forced to defend his China policy at the 15th Party Congress of the CPSU.[3] In the 1930s, as Ravines noted in Moscow, Mao was a devoted supporter of Stalin.[4] Stalin did not repay this devotion with any particular esteem, for at the Potsdam Conference he still felt able to say that the Kuomintang represented the only political power capable of ruling China. In 1948 Stalin admitted that he had advised the Chinese Communists against starting the battle for the possession of power in China, and would have preferred to see them find a *modus vivendi* with Chiang Kai-shek.[5] This faulty appreciation of the Chinese Communists' struggle was of a piece with such matters as Zhdanov's making little mention of the under-developed countries—and none whatever of the struggle in China—at the inauguration of the Cominform.[6]

Nor, at this time, was Mao Tse-tung himself accorded any

---

[1] The illegal executions of Nagy, Maleter and others, announced by the Hungarian Ministry of Justice on 17 June 1958, represent a return to Stalinist methods. The claim that Nagy and his supporters had continued their counter-revolutionary activities after they had taken refuge in the Yugoslav Embassy is analogous to the charges made against Yugoslavia during the Rajk trial. (See p. 240 above.)

[2] See the article by Veljko Vlahovic, *Begriff und Wesen des proletarischen Internationalismus* (*Sozialism*, Belgrade, No. 1/1958, reprinted in *Ostprobleme* No. 2/1959, p. 173).

[3] Robert Payne, *Mao Tse-tung*, London, 1951, pp. 88–101. See also p. 105 above.

[4] Ravines, *The Yenan Way*, p. 123 ff.

[5] Payne, *op. cit.*, p. 258, and Dedijer, *Tito Speaks*, p. 331.

[6] See p. 217 above.

more respect than any other leader of any other Communist party. In a report he made to the Central Committee of the Chinese Party on 25 December 1947, for example, he had suggested that not all capitalists should be treated as "reactionaries", but that the Communists should be prepared to co-operate with them, provided they were prepared to ally themselves with the anti-imperialist forces. These remarks, which were not out of consonance with the tactics Lenin had recommended for the under-developed countries, were reported on the back page of the Cominform newspaper *For Lasting Peace, For People's Democracy* of 15 January 1948, extensive portions, such as the parts dealing with cooperation with the capitalists, being either amended or cut out altogether.[1] There was, of course, nothing unusual in the Moscow censor's amending articles written by prominent Communists for the Cominform paper. In this case, however, the amendments were made because of Mao's "right-wing" tactics (e.g. co-operation with sections of the bourgeoisie) which were incompatible with the CPSU's current "left-wing line".[2]

Mao brought about a change in this treatment of himself as being on a level with any other Communist leader by the rapid and complete victory which brought him the total mastery of the whole of China (November 1949). When Mao went to Moscow in the following month he was placed at Stalin's right-hand side during the celebrations held to mark Stalin's 70th birthday, an indication that he was already regarded in Moscow as occupying second place in the hierarchy of world Communism. Stalin's death and the de-stalinization ushered in by the 20th Party Congress increased Mao's standing. During the 40th anniversary celebrations of the October Revolution he was accorded the standing of the most distinguished of all the foreign guests. At the 21st Party Congress,

---

[1] John H. Kautsky, *Moscow and the Communist Party of India*, New York and London, 1956, pp. 32 ff.

[2] See p. 245 above. It does not seem necessary to introduce the new term ("Neo-Maoist") to describe Mao's policies, as Kautsky suggests (*op. cit.*, p. 8). What Mao was doing was nothing more than a variation of the policy that the Second Comintern World Congress had, at Lenin's suggestion, approved for the colonial countries. (See p. 59 above.)

L

Chou En-lai, the representative of the Chinese Party, was the first of the delegates from the brother parties to be asked to speak.

What is the significance of the rise in the Chinese Party? Does it signify the birth of a new centre of the Communist movement in the Far East? Has Mao's party become the CPSU's rival for the title of leading power in the "peace camp"? Any attempt to answer these questions must take a number of factors in to account.

Mao cannot regard the Russian Revolution, which started as a revolt of the workers and soldiers in St Petersburg, as a model for China, since her revolution was achieved with the help of the militant peasant masses. On the other hand, barring some change in the world situation the Soviet Union is the only power which can afford to give the vast country the urgently-needed assistance she must have for her industrialization. This leads to a certain degree of dependence on the Soviet Union on China's part. This dependence is apparently unavoidable, yet it hits at Chinese pride, rooted in a culture thousands of years old and nurtured by the victory the Communists achieved over the Kuomintang, not only without assistance from any other country but indeed against Russian advice. National pride is one of the impulses behind the great Chinese expansion drive. Ten Hsiao-ping, the General Secretary of the Chinese Party, wrote in *Pravda* on 1 October 1959 that the general line of his Party was an expression of the will and determination of his 650 million countrymen to make their country mighty. Even the great numbers of Russian experts and technicians sent to China to help in her industrialization might be regarded by the Chinese as symbolizing this dependence. They certainly seem to have encountered the distrust that China has always felt for foreigners.[1] Red China is making desperate efforts to overcome her backwardness. The resolution of the Central Committee of the Chinese Communist Party of 28 August 1958 "on the formation of Communes on the land"

---

[1] During the ceremonies to mark the 10th anniversary of the Chinese People's Republic, Chou En-lai thanked the Soviet Union for having sent 10,000 experts to China in the past ten years (*Jen Min Jih Pao*, Peking, 6 October 1959, quoted from *Ostprobleme*, No. 23/59, p. 731).

is intended to accelerate the building up of Socialism and to "make active preparations for the transition to Communism".[1] The initial success of the commune policy led to optimistic prophecies in China, so enthusiastic that they were reminiscent of Zinoviev's prophecies on the imminence of world revolution in 1920:[2]

> China is advancing with lightning speed. Nowadays, even the 80-to-90-year-olds firmly and enthusiastically believe that they will live to enjoy the happiness of Communism.

This enthusiasm was not shared by the Soviet Communists, whose own experiences in the early years had taught them that the communes would fail unless they were built up on the basis of a mature economy. In the months following the establishment of the communes they were hardly mentioned in the Soviet Press or by Soviet speakers. On 1 December 1958, however, Khrushchev told an American visitor, Senator Humphrey, that the creation of communes was old-fashioned and retrograde. A similar experiment had been made in the Soviet Union after the revolution, and had failed.[3] The commune system, he said, was not as good as the Soviet *Kolkhos* and *Sovkhos* system. You could not hope for good results without some material stimulus, and this was what the communes did not offer. When the Senator interjected the remark that this view seemed pretty capitalistic to him, Khrushchev, the man who had "enriched Marxist-Leninist theory with many important thoughts and new instructive ideas",[4] replied: "Call it anything you like! It works."[5]

It is probably the unfortunate experience the Chinese underwent in putting their gigantic leap forward into practice, more than this and other critical remarks, which made them put a brake on "the over-hasty attempt to achieve Communism

---

[1] *Peking Review*, Peking, 16 September 1958, quoted in *Ostprobleme*, No. 21 of 24th October 1958, pp. 695 ff.

[2] See p. 46 above and *Jen Min Jih Pao* of 6 August 1958, quoted in *Ostprobleme*, No. 21, 24 October 1958, p. 698.

[3] Klaus Mehnert's book *Der Sowjetmensch*, Stuttgart, 1958, pp. 79 ff., gives a picture of life in Soviet youth communes.

[4] Otto Kuusinen at the 21st Party Congress.

[5] "Life" International, 12 January 1959.

under conditions of immaturity".[1] Whether these differences of opinion have led to any serious deterioration in relations between the Chinese and Soviet parties remains to be seen. At the 21st Party Congress Chou En-lai reaffirmed that the Chinese Party acknowledged its duty to strengthen the ranks of the international Communist movement, at whose head the CPSU stood—the standpoint which Mao Tse-tung had previously adopted at the 40th anniversary celebrations and which put China in the forefront of the opponents of Yugoslav revisionism.[2] It also meant that the Chinese Communists had withdrawn the cautious support for certain inclinations towards independent which had still been visible during Chou En-lai's visit to Poland in January 1957.[3]

When Chou En-lai declared at the 21st Party Congress, "the Soviet Union and China are Socialist brother countries . . . the close friendship between our countries is eternal and unbreakable", the sentiment was not based merely on his belief in "the noble principles of proletarian internationalism". It was also based on the realization that Red China was hardly in a position to push on with its industrial development without Soviet help.

Politically, on the other hand, the Chinese Party is not dependent on the CPSU to anything like the same extent. Not the least of the reasons for the immense spread of Communism in Asia has been that Stalin's successors abandoned Stalin's doctrinal views and adopted a flexible policy similar to the Chinese tactics *vis-à-vis* the national bourgeoisie. The successes that this led to for the Asian Communist parties increased Chinese prestige no less than the prestige of the Soviets, and the Chinese Party is taking advantage of this prestige to forward its own policies in Asia. Within these policies the left-wing domestic line (e.g. in the communes) parallels a radical foreign policy (e.g. in the attack on Tibet and the violation of Indian territory), which runs counter to the Soviet policy of co-exist-

---

[1] This was being said as early as 10 December 1958 by the Chinese Central Committee in the second resolution on certain questions of the communes, extracts from which were reprinted in *Ostprobleme*, No. 3/1959, pp. 71 ff. (See also Wolfgang Leonhard, *Kreml ohne Stalin*, Cologne, 1959, p. 417.)

[2] See pp. 295 and 301 f. above.      [3] See p. 282 above.

ence. During the celebrations to mark the 10th anniversary of the Chinese People's Republic, Khrushchev enjoined the Chinese to pursue a peaceful policy and on 7 November 1959 he declared in Moscow that the quarrel with India over the border area was "stupid".[1] This was unmistakable criticism of the Chinese threat to the policy of co-existence.

The aggressive behaviour of the Chinese led at the same time to differences within the Indian Communist Party, whose General Secretary, Ajoy Ghosh, tended to support Chinese claims to the border territory, while the leader of the Communist parliamentary group, Shripat Amrit Dange, backed up Nehru's standpoint. During a visit to China, Ajoy Ghosh pointed out to the Chinese leaders that their policies would only strengthen the hands of the reactionary forces in India. He failed to make any impression on the Chinese, however, and in the result the Executive Committee of the Indian Party decided to regard the Macmahon line as the frontier.[2]

The aggressive foreign policy of the Chinese leaders is paralleled by revolutionary domestic policies, as exemplified by the Communes, and, in the ideological sphere, by the "left wing" line they have been following ever since the end of the liberalization period ("Let a Hundred Flowers Blossom"). The events in Poland and Hungary obviously brought home to the Chinese the realization that when once a dictatorship starts liberalizing, it imperils its own existence. For this reason the Chinese Party has been in the forefront of the fight against revisionism ever since the November celebrations of 1957,[3] and, more recently, has included Khrushchev's policy of co-existence among the targets of its attacks on "revisionism".

In the April 1960 edition of *Red Flag*, the periodical of the Central Committee of the Chinese Communist Party, there appeared an article entitled "Long Live Leninism", in which Lenin was not only quoted to support the Chinese rejection of the "non-violent transition" and of the "parliamentary road to Socialism", but was also appealed to by the publishers—quite justifiably—to furnish proof that it is not a Leninist theory

[1] *Die Welt*, Essen, 9 November 1959, p. 3.
[2] *Neue Zürcher Zeitung*, 16 November 1959, p. 2.
[3] See p. 295 above.

that wars in the modern world are not inevitable.[1] Yet in April 1960 Otto Kuusinen, in the course of a speech in honour of the 90th anniversary of Lenin's birth, described the thesis of the non-inevitability of wars as a creation of Lenin's, the basis of "the whole of Soviet foreign policy" and the logical conclusion of the 20th and 21st Party Congresses.[2] What Kuusinen proudly described as "a new word of the Party in Marxism" is decisively rejected by the Chinese, despite the fact that they were paying lip-service to the "leading role of the CPSU" as recently as at the 21st Party Congress. Official Soviet circles continue to criticize the domestic policies and ideological and political ideas of the Chinese Communist Party. In an article published in *Pravda* on 12 June 1960, the fortieth anniversary of the publication of Lenin's book *Left-wing Communism—An Infantile Disorder*, M. Matkovski criticized the "left-wing Communists" and in particular their attempt to "leap-frog entire historical stages". By this he meant the setting up of the people's communes, which represented an attempt to move straight into a state of Communism without having first "built up" Socialism. Matkovski also attacked Communists who "mistakenly regard the efforts by states with differing political systems to achieve a state of peaceful co-existence" and consider "negotiations between leading politicians of socialist and capitalist countries" as a kind of deviation from the Marxist-Leninist position.

Matkovski did not expressly name the Chinese, but he was defending Khrushchev's policies of co-existence and diplomacy by negotiation, both of which had in fact been criticized by the Chinese.

At the Third Party Congress of the Rumanian Workers' Party, held in Bucharest in June 1960 in the presence of the entire Communist élite, including Peng Tschen, a member of the Politbureau of the Communist Party of China, Khrushchev gave a detailed exposition of his policy of co-existence. Subsequently, on 24 June 1960, twelve Communist parties published a communiqué re-affirming the principles which had been

[1] Cf. *Red Flag*, Peking, No 8/1960, English text in "Peking Review" No. 17/1960.

[2] Cf. *Pravda*, Moscow, 23 April 1960.

contained in the Moscow Declaration of November 1957[1] and which Khrushchev had proclaimed to be the basis of his policy. The validity of the Chinese standpoint was acknowledged to the extent that the communiqué contained one sentence admitting that the continued existence of imperialism provided the conditions for wars of aggression.

For the time being, therefore, the clash of views between the two greatest exponents of world Communism would appear to have been stilled. However, the Chinese have not in fact capitulated. Should they in the future feel the urge to pursue an offensive policy, they will feel themselves as little inhibited by the fact of the Bucharest compromise as they were prevented from intrusion into Indian territory by the existence of the Moscow Declaration of 1957.

The fact that the disagreements between the two great parties were made public meant more than would have been implied, for example, by differences between the British and American press over some aspect of Western foreign policy; for the Communist parties do not make a practice of airing their differences in public. This is not to say that a breach between Peking and Moscow is imminent. Nevertheless, the antagonism indicated above may lead to conflicts as soon as China can afford them, that is, as soon as she has, with Soviet help, expanded her industrial potential to the necessary degree. It is worth repeating at this point: Bukharin's statement that national rivalries are impossible between Communist states has long ago been shown to be nonsense.[2]

## PROLETARIAN INTERNATIONALISM TODAY

The movement which began after the death of Stalin has still not died away. Yugoslavia is in a position similar to that of the years of conflict, it is true, but the voices in the present "peace camp" do not speak with the degree of unanimity that Stalin was able to enforce with regard to "Titoism". The severest critics, the Chinese, are counterbalanced by the more moderate tone of the Poles. It was not until after weeks of hesitation that Gomulka finally took up a position against the present Yugoslav policies, and even then, unlike the Soviets

[1] See p. 295 above.     [2] See p. 298 above.

and the Chinese, he again rejected the whole of the Cominform policies.[1] Thus it has not proved possible to force Poland back into the condition of servility in which, like all the "people's democracies", it had been in Stalin's time.

To the Soviet leaders it must seem hopeless to try to win Yugoslavia back into the Eastern bloc at present. All the more earnestly, therefore, are they trying to patch up the cracks that first appeared in the structure of the rest of their camp in 1956 and which have repeatedly made themselves visible ever since.

Cracks and fissures appeared in various parties, yet they had no connection with each other, a sure sign of a serious crisis. In the American Party, for example, after the 20th Party Congress there arose a right-wing group, led by John Gates, the publisher of the new York *Daily Worker*, and opposed by the Moscow loyalists gathered around William Z. Foster. The pro-Soviet section of the party took advantage of the Twelve-Party Declaration of November 1957 to go into action against John Gates, who possessed a valuable means of propagating his views in the shape of the *Daily Worker*. Accordingly the Party's National Executive decided to suspend publication of the paper for a while. In January 1958 Gates left the Party and the pro-Soviet section had gained a victory.[2]

In the Canadian Labour Progressive Party (LPP),[3] the CPSU's 20th Party Congress was followed by an acute crisis, which came to a head at the 6th National Convention of the LPP (April 1957) and led to the resignation of I. B. Salsberg and other Party functionaries. Another group of independent Canadian Marxists, led by Henry Gagnon, continued the opposition to the majority of the LPP who supported Moscow. In Montreal, Gagnon's adherents founded the "Council of Socialist Clubs", the members of which were expelled from the LPP at the beginning of 1958.

[1] Speaking to Danzig shipyard workers on 28 June 1958 (extracts reprinted in *Neues Deutschland*, 29 June 1958).

[2] John Gates, *The Story of an American Communist*, New York, 1958, p. 191, and B. N. Ponomaryov, *Die Internationale Kommunistische Bewegung in einer neuen Etappe*, *Kommunist*, Moscow, 15/1958, reprinted in *Aus der internationalen Arbeiterbewegung*, 23, 13 December 1958, p. 7.

[3] In October 1959 the LPP changed its name to "Communist Party of Canada".

Among the European Party leaders, Aksel Larsen, the Chairman of the Danish Party, made a statement to his Central Committee in the summer of 1958 and revealed not only leanings towards independence but also a favourable evaluation of the Yugoslav programme.[1] He came under heavy fire not only from *Pravda* but also from such loyal supporters of the CPSU as Paul de Groot, the General Secretary of the Dutch Communist Party, and Hermann Matern, a member of the Politbureau of the SED.[2] The Danish Central Committee was unable to withstand this pressure and Larsen was duly expelled from the Danish Party on 15 November 1958. On 15 February 1959 Larsen founded the new Socialistisk Folkeparti (Socialist People's Party).

In Holland the Communist Party was split after the 20th Party Congress when an opposition section, led by the former Chairman of the Party, Gerben Wagenaar, and the trade union leader Bertus Brandsen, expressed their discontent with the General Secretary, Paul de Groot, for continuing the old course. At the beginning of 1958 Brandsen founded a new Dutch Trade Union Federation, the EVC 1958, and in April 1959 the Opposition Section formed the so-called "Brug" group, which gave rise in July 1959 to the Socialistische Werkers Partij (Socialist Labour Party).[3]

Khrushchev's reaction to this and similar cleavages was in the best Stalin style. At the 21st Party Congress he called the opposition groups "scum which polluted the pure fount of the Communist movement".[4]

This "scum" was an indication of a certain weakness which had made itself apparent in the Communist movement in the countries of the West after the death of Stalin. In the under-developed countries, and especially in those of Asia, on the other hand, things had developed differently. For one thing,

---

[1] See p. 301 above (Yugoslav programme).

[2] *Pravda*, 17 October 1958, *De Waarheid*, Amsterdam, 26 and 27 September 1958 and *Neues Deutschland*, 24 October 1958.

[3] De Groot's report on the "Brug" group to the 19th Party Congress of the Dutch Communist Party is reproduced in *Ostprobleme* No. 7, of 3 April 1959 (p. 220 ff.).

[4] N. S. Khrushchev, *Seven-Year Plan Target Figures. Report to the Special 21st Congress of the Communist Party of the Soviet Union*, London, 1959, p. 65.

Communism in Asia had achieved an accretion of strength by reason of Mao Tse-tung's victory. For another, the Asian Communist parties had profited from the fact that Stalin's successors decided to collaborate with the national bourgeoisie of the under-developed countries, for example, Egypt, India and Indonesia. The membership figure of the Indian Party rose from some 50,000 in 1953 to 230,000 in 1958.[1] The Indonesian Party claims a much greater increase, from 2,000 in 1948 to 1,500,000 in 1956.[2]

The 21st Party Congress dealt principally with economic questions, but Khrushchev and the more important guests did what they had not done at the 20th Party Congress; they gave their views on the subject of proletarian internationalism, which had in the meantime become the burning question. In the foreground of these views stood the "leading role" of the CPSU and the Soviet Union, the question which had been the subject of so much discussion following the publication of the Twelve-Party Declaration in November 1957.[3] Khrushchev rejected the Yugoslav charge that the CPSU was aiming at "hegemony" *vis-à-vis* other parties.[4] The Twelve-Party Declaration, according to which the Socialist states were led by the Soviet Union, was, he explained, merely an acknowledgment of the "historic role" of the CPSU and the Soviet Union. The other parties were not led by the CPSU and the other countries were not led by the Soviet Union.[5]

Gomulka commented that the exposition of this problem in this way was both necessary and valuable. Otto Kuusinen, a member of the Presidium, added: "Our Party makes no claim to the leading role *vis-à-vis* other Communist and Workers' Parties". Chou En-lai declared that "the consolidation of the unity of the countries of the Socialist camp, which is led by the Soviet Union" and "the consolidation of the unity of the ranks of the international Communist movement, of which the CPSU

[1]M. R. Masani, *op. cit.*, p. 221, and Overstreet and Windmiller, *op. cit.*, p. 540. Even if these figures are not absolutely accurate, the proportions they indicate are still noteworthy.

[2]*Aus der internationalen Arbeiterbewegung*, East Berlin, No. 2(88), 25 January 1958, p. 16.

[3]See pp. 286 f. above.    [4]See p. 300 above.

[5]Cf. Khrushchev, *Seven-Year Plan Target Figures*, p. 69.

is the centre" were still the sacred duty of Communists every-where.[1] We do not need to go into the nuances of meaning between these two phrases, but we can consider the changes which have taken place since the Stalin era.

In 1949 the only ones who could claim to be proletarian internationalists were those who "unconditionally supported the defence of the Soviet Union" and "unconditionally" acknowledged "the leadership of the Soviet Union and the CPSU in the peace camp".[2] Today, nothing more is demanded —at least in theory—than the recognition of the "historic role" of the CPSU and of the fact that the Soviet Union stands at the head of the "Socialist camp".

This delimitation and the cracks that have appeared in the structure make one thing definite—that the world Communist movement is no longer as unshakably united as it was under Stalin. There have been a number of regional conferences of Communist parties which, contrary to the Comintern practice, were declared permissible during the Moscow deliberations in November 1957, e.g. in March 1958 a conference of the French Party with those of the Benelux countries; in June 1958 a fifteen-party conference in Berlin; and a meeting of the West European parties in Brussels on 1 April 1959. These conferences dealt principally with the Communist opposition to German re-armament and to the European Economic Community, although there was also some discussion of the role of the national bourgeoisie in the under-developed countries.[3]

So far, no regional centres have emerged from these meetings. And yet the very spread of Communism over large parts of the earth's surface, in areas in which vastly differing conditions obtain, invites the formation of regional centres. There are Communist parties in 76 countries of the world, 13 of them being government parties. These 13 parties contain 84 per cent of the world's Communist membership (28 out of 32 million).

[1] 21st Party Congress of the CPSU, *Aus den Diskussionsreden zu internationalen Fragen*, East Berlin, 1959, p. 93 (Kuusinen), p. 116 (Chou En-lai), p. 123 (Gomulka).
[2] See p. 239 above.
[3] *Aus der internationalen Arbeiterbewegung*, No. 6/1958, p. 12, No. 13/1958, p. 3, and *Probleme des Friedens und des Sozialismus* (German edition), Prague, No. 8/1959, p. 62.

Four-fifths of the four million members living outside the Communist bloc are distributed among the Communist parties of India, France, Italy and Indonesia. The Communists can claim 26 per cent of the earth's surface, 35 per cent of the world's population and one third of the world's industrial production.[1] These impressive figures illustrate present-day world Communism. The Communist parties are numerically strong in the countries in which Communist governments have liquidated all opposition. In the countries of the Western world, on the other hand, membership figures and election successes have diminished steadily since 1945. The basic philosophy of the Communist movement has lost some of its appeal. The Communist spectre no longer haunts Europe, but is being driven on by Soviet and Chinese bayonets. In Asia, Communism has gained a considerable number of supporters through allying itself with the national bourgeoisie, but since this alliance is a purely tactical one, it is not likely to last.

In view of these developments, the relationship between the CPSU and the brother parties today is not the same as during the Comintern period. The international Apparats of the OMS no longer exist, but there has been some indication that another method is being used to maintain the links with the brother parties, namely, that of connections through members of the staffs of Soviet Embassies.[2] It has come to light that financial assistance being transmitted to the Communist parties of the free world passes through the hands of these Soviet "diplomats".[3] It is also probable that the Soviet embassies played a part in keeping the Communist parties informed on Khrushchev's conflict with Malenkov, Molotov and Shepilov. The Soviet state security service (at present called the KGB) carries out certain functions of the former OMS Section of the

---

[1]These figures, which are probably approximately correct, are taken from the central organ of the CPSU, *Partiinyaa Zhizn* No. 14/57, pp. 49 ff.

[2]The situation in West Germany is rather different. There the Communist party, banned since 17 August 1956, is not controlled directly by the CPSU, but by the "state party" of the Soviet Zone, the SED, which also provides the greater part of West German KPD's financial requirements.

[3]In October 1953, for example, a Soviet MGB official handed $25,000 to the General Secretary of the Australian Communist Party. (*Report of the Royal Commission on Espionage*, Sydney, 1955, p. 102.)

Comintern through the corresponding activities of its representatives in the Soviet Embassies.[1]

The financial dependence of the non-Russian Communist parties in the free world is not the same nowadays as it was in Comintern times.[2] The KPD once used to receive large-scale financial assistance from the Third International, whereas today its illegal work is financed by the SED. The rise of the French and Italian parties to the status of mass organizations, their consequent large income in the shape of members' subscriptions, the support given to them in certain districts of their own countries and their various business interests have furnished these parties with considerable financial resources. Things have also changed in the parties which have taken over the power in their countries, such as those in the People's Democracies and China. Wherever members' subscriptions, high as they are, do not suffice to cover material requirements, these parties simply reach into state funds.

The result is that the only parties which still depend on Soviet financial help are, in the main, those which cannot maintain themselves, for example because they form insignificant minorities in their own homeland. One instance is that of the Danish Party, which went on receiving Soviet financial assistance even after 1945. And the greater the drop in membership which a number of parties, such as the British and Italian Communist Parties, have experienced since 1956, the greater the extent to which they decline into the position of being once more dependent on financial contributions from the CPSU.

The Central Committees of the Communist parties have in a number of cases received secret circulars from the Central Committee of the CPSU informing them of certain matters or giving them the Soviet "line" on certain problems. One of these was sent out in the autumn of 1953, giving the reasons for the removal of Beria. Another, sent out in February 1955, explained why Malenkov had resigned.[3] The resolutions of the

[1]See p. 231 above. KGB is short for Komitet Gosudarstvennoi Bezopasnosti (Committee of State Security).

[2]See pp. 167 f. above, but also R. Jensen, *En Omtumlet Tilvaerelse*, pp. 99 ff.

[3]See the statement by the Polish Communist Severyn Bialer, reproduced in *Hinter dem Eisernen Vorhang*, Munich, 1956, No. 10, pp. 17 ff.

Central Committee of the CPSU condemning Malenkov, Kaganovitch and Shepilov were actually notified to the Communist parties before publication. The CPSU Central Committee also employed "confidential communications" in the spring of 1958 in order to suggest to the brother parties that they should not send delegates to the Yugoslav Party Congress.[1]

Large-scale international gatherings run by Communist-controlled organizations, e.g. congresses of the World Peace Movement or the congresses of the World Federation of Trade Unions, offer the internationally active functionaries further opportunities to meet and absorb the Moscow line away from the excitements of mass meetings.

Individual top-ranking Communists still receive invitations to visit the Soviet Union even today—for holiday trips, treatment for illnesses, etc. A large number of Communists from all over the world have attended the so-called "Central School" in the Soviet Union. In this way, ties linking Communists to the CPSU and the Soviet Union are created and represent an important factor in the control of the world Communist movement.

The necessity to "consolidate the ranks of the Communist parties" has given rise to new activity of the Central Committee of the CPSU, too. M. A. Suslov and Otto Kuusinen, both members of the Presidium and of the Secretariat, are paying closer attention to the problems of the brother parties than they did before 1956. Suslov, who attended the 14th and 15th Party Congresses of the French Party in Le Havre and Paris in 1956 and 1959, is apparently responsible for Western Europe and Kuusinen for Scandinavia and Germany. The party congresses of the smaller parties are also honoured by the visits of Soviet delegations. Thus, for the first time since 1945, a CPSU delegation including Kuusinen and Boris Ponomaryov attended the party congress of the illegal KPD held in East Germany in June 1957.[2] The British Communist Party, for the first time in its history, was honoured by the attendance of a Soviet delegation headed by Alexander Rumyantsev at its Party Congress

[1] Cf. Aksel Larsen's report to the Central Committee of the Danish Party, 18 July 1958 (see n. 3, p. 301 above).
[2] *Neues Deutschland*, 17 and 30 June 1957.

in March 1959.[1] Even Nikita Khrushchev has contributed to the consolidation of working-class unity by attending the 9th All-German Workers' Conference in Leipzig on 7 March 1959. This conference was intended to bring about unity of action between West German workers and the Communists controlling East Germany. Many were touched by his revival of a half-forgotten internationalist strain:

> But, Comrades, I want you to regard me not only as a representative of my people. Above all I am a Communist, a member of the Communist Party.[2]

In the Department of International Relations in the Central Committee of the CPSU, the affairs of the Eastern bloc Communist parties are also having more intensive attention paid to them since Yurii Antropov, who was the Soviet Ambassador in Hungary at the time of the revolt in 1956, was transferred to the Central Committee.[3]

The international theoretical periodical, *Problems of Peace and Socialism*, whose coming appearance was announced a number of times after November 1957, and which finally did appear in August 1958, will play its part in making the Moscow line known to the Communist parties. It will also have to play its part in the task which now faces the Soviet Communists, that of consolidating the unity of the "Socialist camp". In the editorial chair, Alexey Rumyantsev, formerly the editor-in-chief of *Kommunist*, represents the CPSU. The SED's representative is Lene Berg, who used to be Director of the Institute of Social Science in the SED Central Committee, and the French Party is represented by Jean Kanapa, a member of the French Central Committee.[4] The other large Communist parties have also sent representatives. To this extent the composition of the editorial staff resembles that of the Cominform paper.[5] Whether any attempt will be made to ensure Soviet control by the same practices as obtained in the Comin-

[1] *Probleme des Friedens und des Sozialismus*, Dietz-Verlag, E. Berlin, No. 6/1959, p. 68.
[2] *Neues Deutschland*, 27 March, 1959, p. 5.
[3] *Est et Ouest*, Paris, 1958, No. 197, p. 19.
[4] *Ibid.*, p. 18 and *Neuer Weg*, East Berlin, 1959, No. 14, p. 1015.
[5] See p. 230 above.

form paper (as, for example, pre-censorship of the individual items in Moscow) remains to be seen.

Unlike the Cominform paper, this one began to engage in remarkable activity soon after its first appearance. As early as October 1958 its representatives took part in a conference, held in Rome, of Communists from ten parties of Europe, America and Asia "on current forms and methods of exploitation in capitalist factories".[1]

In May 1959, A. Rumyantsev, the editor-in-chief of the paper, spoke in Leipzig at a meeting of representatives of fourteen European, Asiatic, African and South American Communist parties, on "the role of the bourgeoisie in the national liberation movement".[2] In July 1959 the editorial board sent out invitations to a "discussion on theoretical questions connected with the integration of Western Europe", for which representatives of eleven Communist parties travelled to Prague.[3] On 25 August 1959 Communist theoreticians and historians from twenty-five countries were again assembling, together with editorial representatives of the paper, this time in Bucharest, for a discussion of "the struggle of the Communist and Workers' Parties against revisionism".[4]

Meanwhile an "editorial council" has been created in Prague, the location of the paper's editorial offices, and representatives from thirty-six Communist and Workers' parties attended a meeting of the Council from 13 to 16 April 1960.[5]

The internal organization of the editorial staff, however, includes not only the editorial council but also a number of individual departments, of which the Department of the National Liberation Movement was mentioned by Radio North Korea as early as 25 September 1958, while the Home Service of Radio Moscow named a departmental head, I. T. Vinogradov, on 20 January 1960. The existence of an editorial council and various separate editorial departments, and the fact that since the birth of the paper a number of highly expensive conferences on the problems of international Communism have been held, some organized by the paper or at all events

[1] Cf. *Problems of Peace and Socialism* (German edition), No. 1/1959.
[2] Cf. *Ibid.*, 8/1959.    [3] Cf. *Ibid.*, 10/1959.    [4] Cf. *Ibid.*, 1/1960.
[5] Cf. the report in *Neues Deutschland* (East Berlin), 24 April 1960.

influenced by its representatives, show that the publishing of the paper is not the only concern of the editorial staff.

Time will tell whether this periodical—in consonance with the principles of Lenin—will step up its role as a collective organizer, that is to say as the forerunner of a new international organization.[1]

Strictly according to the text, the principles of international proletarianism have remained unchanged since the death of Stalin. However, they have had to serve purposes as far apart as justifying the steps towards reconciliation with Yugoslavia and justifying Soviet military intervention in Hungary. And now, in the name of proletarian internationalism, the devoted servants of Moscow have once more branded the Yugoslav leader as a traitor to the working class.

This means that the principles of proletarian internationalism have shown themselves to be a flexible instrument of Soviet foreign policy. The Central Committee of the CPSU will have to employ them in the future, too, if it hopes to restore the Soviet hegemony in world Communism, Gomulka having turned out to be, even during the 40th anniversary celebrations of the October Revolution, its most effective opponent within the Soviet sphere of influence.

For the future, Soviet policies will retain their characteristic feature, the effort to "consolidate the unity of the Socialist camp". Whether they will succeed in restoring the degree of uniformity in world Communism that Stalin managed to enforce is highly doubtful. The events of the years 1953 to 1956 have not been forgotten. In Eastern Europe the reestablishment of the Russian hegemony was only made possible by the intervention of the Red Army. In the West the unity of the Communist movement has been threatened with disruption. In Asia, support for Communism has shown a considerable increase, it is true, but this increase has been paralleled by the emergence of a factor which may one day menace the Soviet position in proletarian internationalism—Communist China.

[1] Lenin, *Collected Works*, Vol. 4, part 1, p. 114.

# Appendix I

## RULES AND CONSTITUTION OF THE COMMUNIST LEAGUE

*Proletarians of all lands, unite!*

### PART I. THE LEAGUE

ARTICLE 1. The aim of the League is the overthrow of the bourgeoisie, the establishment of the rule of the proletariat, the abolition of the bourgeois social order founded upon class antagonisms, and the inauguration of a new social order wherein there shall be neither classes nor private property.

Article 2. Conditions for membership are:

(a) the way of living and the activities of the members shall be consonant with these aims;

(b) the members shall be filled with revolutionary energy and with zeal for the propagation of these ideas;

(c) they shall make Communism their creed;

(d) they must abstain from participation in any other Communist, political, or nationalist society, and must inform the competent authorities of the League as to whether they are members of any other body;

(e) they shall obey the decisions of the League;

(f) they shall not disclose any matters concerning the internal life of the League;

(g) the communes shall have to be unanimous in acceptance of new members.

Those who do not observe these conditions shall be expelled. (See below, Part VIII.)

Article 3. All members are equal, are brothers, and as such they owe one another helpful service in every emergency.

Article 4. All who enter the League shall assume special membership names.

Article 5. The League is organized into communes, circles, leading circles, central committee, and Congress.

### PART II. THE COMMUNE

Article 6. The commune shall consist of not less than three and not more than twenty members.

Article 7. Each commune shall elect a chairman and an assistant. The chairman shall preside over the meetings, the assistant shall take charge of the finances and shall replace the chairman should the latter fail to appear.

Article 8. New members shall be enrolled by the chairman and the proposer, after the commune has agreed to accept him or her.

Article 9. The communes are not to know one another or to carry on any correspondence with one another.

Article 10. Each commune shall adopt a distinguishing name.

Article 11. Any member changing his dwelling place shall previously inform the chairman of his commune.

### PART III. THE CIRCLE

Article 12. The circle shall consist of not less than two and not more than ten communes.

Article 13. The chairmen and assistants of the communes shall constitute the circle committee. This shall elect a president from among its own members. Correspondence is to be maintained by the circle both with the communes and with the leading circle.

Article 14. The circle committee is the fully accredited authority for all the communes it represents.

Article 15. Isolated communes must either affiliate to the most conveniently situated circle or they must get into touch with other isolated communes so as to form a new circle.

### PART IV. THE LEADING CIRCLE

Article 16. The various circles of a land or a province are subject to a leading circle.

Article 17. The allotment of the circles of the League to province and the nomination of the leading circle is the business of the Congress acting under the advice of the central committee.

Article 18. The leading circle is the fully accredited authority for the aggregate of circles in a province. It corresponds with the circles and with the central committee.

Article 19. Newly-formed circles shall affiliate to the nearest leading circle.

Article 20. Provisionally, the leading circles are responsible to the central committee and in the last resort are answerable to Congress.

### PART V. THE CENTRAL COMMITTEE

Article 21. The central committee is the executive authority of the whole League, and as such must render account to the Congress.

Article 22. It consists of at least five members and is chosen from among the circle committees of the place where the Congress is convened.

Article 23. The central committee corresponds with the leading circles and every three months issues a report upon the condition of the League as a whole.

Article 24. The communes, the circle committees, and the central committee shall meet at least once a fortnight.

Article 25. The members of the circle committees and of the central committee are elected for one year; they are eligible for re-election; they are subject to recall at any time by those who elected them.

Article 26. The elections take place in September.

Article 27. The circle committees must guide the discussions of the communes in conformity with the aims of the League.

Should the central committee deem the discussion of certain questions to be of general interest, it shall suggest their discussion by the whole League.

Article 28. Individual members shall communicate at least once a quarter, and the individual communes at least once a month, with their respective circle committees.

Each circle shall communicate at least every two months with its leading circle; every leading circle shall send in a report to the central committee at least once a quarter.

Article 29. It is incumbent upon each committee of the League, on its own responsibility but within the limits imposed by the rules and regulations, to carry out such measures as may be needed for the safety and effective activity of the League. It must promptly report upon these matters to the higher authorities of the League.

Article 30. The Congress is the legislative authority of the League. Proposals for the alteration of the rules shall be sent in to the central committee by the leading circles. They will then be laid before the Congress.

Article 31. Each circle sends one delegate.

Article 32. A circle composed of less than 30 members shall send one delegate; of less than 60 members, two delegates; of less than 90 members, three delegates. A circle can be represented by a proxy delegate. In such a case the delegate must be given very precise instructions.

Article 33. The Congress shall assemble each year in the month of August. In case of great urgency, the central committee can summon an extraordinary Congress.

Article 34. The Congress decides the place which the central committee shall make its headquarters for the coming year. It also decides the place where the Congress shall next meet.

Article 35. The central committee takes part in the Congress in a deliberative capacity only.

Article 36. After each meeting the Congress shall issue, in addition to its circular, a manifesto in the name of the party.

## PART VIII. OFFENCES AGAINST THE LEAGUE

Article 37. Any infringement of the conditions for membership (see Article 2) shall be followed, according to circumstances, either by suspension or expulsion.

A member once expelled cannot be accepted into the League again.

Article 38. The Congress alone can decide upon expulsion.

Article 39. A member may be suspended by the circle or by the isolated commune to which he belongs, but the higher authorities must immediately be informed. The final decision rests with the Congress in such cases likewise.

Article 40. A suspended member can be reinstated by the central committee at the request of the circle concerned.

Article 41. Any act inimical to the League comes under the jurisdiction of the circle authorities, who are also responsible for enforcing whatever decision they may arrive at.

Article 42. Expelled or suspended members, and likewise all persons under suspicion, should, for the sake of the League, be supervised and rendered harmless. Any machinations on the part of such individuals are to be instantly reported to the commune concerned.

## PART IX. FINANCE

Article 43. The Congress decides the minimum amount that shall be contributed by each member of the League.

Article 44. Half of such contributions shall go to the central committee; the remaining sum shall go to the funds of the circle or the commune.

Article 45. The funds accruing to the central committee shall be utilized as follows:

1. To defray the costs of correspondence and administration;
2. To pay for printing and circulating propaganda leaflets;
3. To send out emissaries, appointed by the central committee, for the carrying out of special missions.

Article 46. The funds accruing to the local committees shall be spent as follows:

1. In paying costs of correspondence;
2. In printing and circulating propaganda leaflets;
3. In sending out special emissaries.

Article 47. Communes and circles neglecting to send in their contributions to the central committee for a period of six months shall be suspended by the central committee.

Article 48. The circle committees shall send in an account of receipts and expenditure at least every three months to their communes. The central committee shall render account to the Congress as to administrative expenditure and as to the condition of the League's finances. Any tampering with the funds belonging to the League will be rigorously dealt with.

Article 49. Extraordinary expenditure and the Congress expenses will be covered by special contributions.

PART X. NEW MEMBERS

Article 50. The chairman of the commune shall read the applicant Articles 1 to 49, shall explain their significance, and shall then in a short speech emphasize the responsibilities membership of the League entails. The aspirant shall then be asked: "Do you still wish to enter the League?" Should the answer be in the affirmative, the chairman puts the aspirant on his honour to fulfil the duties of a League member, pronounces him to be a member of the League, and takes him to the next meeting of the commune.
*London, December* 8 1847.

In the name of the Second Congress, held in the autumn of 1847,

*The Secretary—*                *The President—*
(*Signed*) ENGELS              (*Signed*) CARL SCHAPPER

## Appendix II

## GENERAL RULES OF THE INTERNATIONAL WORKING MEN'S ASSOCIATION[1]

*Considering,*

That the emancipation of the working classes must be conquered by the working classes themselves; that the struggle for the emancipation of the working classes means not a struggle for class privileges and monopolies, but for equal rights and duties, and the abolition of all class rule;

That the economical subjection of the man of labour to the monopolizer of the means of labour, that is, the sources of life, lies at the bottom of servitude in all its forms, of all social misery, mental degradation, and political dependence;

That the economical emancipation of the working classes is therefore the great end to which every political movement ought to be subordinate as a means;

That all efforts aiming at that great end have hitherto failed from the want of solidarity between the manifold divisions of labour in each country, and from the absence of a fraternal bond of union between the working classes of different countries;

That the emancipation of labour is neither a local nor a national, but a social problem, embracing all countries in which modern society exists, and depending for its solution on the concurrence, practical and theoretical, of the most advanced countries;

That the present revival of the working classes in the most industrious countries of Europe, while it raises a new hope, gives solemn warning against a relapse into the old errors, and calls for the immediate combination of the still disconnected movements;

For These Reasons—

The International Working Men's Association has been founded. It declares:

That all societies and individuals adhering to it will acknowledge truth, justice, and morality, as the basis of their conduct towards each other and towards all men, without regard to colour, creed, or nationality;

That it acknowledges *no rights without duties, no duties without rights*;

[1]These Rules were adopted in 1871 at the London Conference of the International Working Men's Association. They were based on the provisional rules drawn up by Marx in 1864 when the First International was founded.

And in this spirit the following rules have been drawn up.

1. This Association is established to afford a central medium of communication and co-operation between Working Men's Societies existing in different countries and aiming at the same end, *viz.*, the protection, advancement, and complete emancipation of the working classes.

2. The name of the Society shall be "The International Working-Men's Association".

3. There shall annually meet a General Working Men's Congress, consisting of delegates of the branches of the Association. The Congress will have to proclaim the common aspirations of the working class, take the measures required for the successful working of the International Association, and appoint the General Council of the Society.

4. Each Congress appoints the time and place of meeting for the next Congress. The delegates assemble at the appointed time and place without any special invitation. The General Council may, in case of need, change the place, but has no power to postpone the time of meeting. The Congress appoints the seat and elects the members of the General Council annually. The General Council thus elected shall have power to add to the number of its members.

On its annual meetings, the General Congress shall receive a public account of the annual transactions of the General Council. The latter may, in cases of emergency, convoke the General Congress before the regular yearly term.

5. The General Council shall consist of working men from the different countries represented in the International Association. It shall from its own members elect the officers necessary for the transaction of business, such as a treasurer, a general secretary, corresponding secretaries for the different countries, etc.

6. The General Council shall form an international agency between the different national and local groups of the Association, so that the working men in one country be constantly informed of the movements of their class in every other country; that an inquiry into the social state of the different countries of Europe be made simultaneously, and under a common direction; that the questions of general interest mooted in one society be ventilated by all; and that when immediate practical steps should be needed—as, for instance, in case of international quarrels—the action of the associated societies be simultaneous and uniform. Whenever it seems opportune, the General Council shall take the initiative of proposals to be laid before the different national or local societies.

To facilitate the communications, the General Council shall publish periodical reports.

7. Since the success of the working men's movement in each country cannot be secured but by the power of union and combination, while, on the other hand, the usefulness of the International General Council must greatly depend on the circumstance whether it has to deal with a few national centres of working men's associations, or with a great number of small and disconnected local societies; the members of the International Association shall use their utmost efforts to combine the disconnected working men's societies of their respective countries into national bodies, represented by central national organs. It is self-understood, however, that the appliance of this rule will depend upon the peculiar laws of each country, and that, apart from legal obstacles, no independent local society shall be precluded from directly corresponding with the General Council.

7a. In its struggle against the collective power of the possessing classes the proletariat can act as a class only by constituting itself a distinct political party, opposed to all the old parties formed by the possessing classes.

This constitution of the proletariat into a polical party is indispensable to ensure the triumph of the social Revolution and of its ultimate goal: the abolition of classes.

The coalition of the forces of the working class, already achieved by the economic struggle, must also serve, in the hands of this class, as a lever in its struggle against the political power of its exploiters.

As the lords of the land and of capital always make use of their political privileges to defend and perpetuate their economic monopolies and to enslave labour, the conquest of political power becomes the great duty of the proletariat.

8. Every section has the right to appoint its own secretary corresponding with the General Council.

9. Everybody who acknowledges and defends the principles of the International Working Men's Association is eligible to become a member. Every branch is responsible for the integrity of the members it admits.

10. Each member of the International Association, on removing his domicile from one country to another, will receive the fraternal support of the Associated Working Men.

11. While united in a perpetual bond of fraternal co-operation, the working men's societies joining the International Association will preserve their existent organizations intact.

12. The present rules may be revised by each Congress, provided that two-thirds of the delegates present are in favour of such revision.

13. Everything not provided for in the present rules will be supplied by special regulations, subject to the revision of every Congress.

## Appendix III

## WILHELM PIECK'S PART IN THE ARREST OF ROSA LUXEMBURG AND KARL LIEBKNECHT

FROM time to time it has been hinted that after his arrest by officers of the Dismounted Cavalry Guard (Garde-Kavallerie-Schützen-Division), Wilhelm Pieck, now President of the East German "People's Republic", gave information leading to the arrest of Liebknecht and Luxemburg.

Contrary to this belief, what actually happened was this. Hauptmann (Captain) Waldemar Pabst, at that time (1919) Senior General Staff officer of this division, had given instructions that the Einwohnerwehr (citizen guards, a kind of Home Guard) were to arrest Liebknecht and Luxemburg and to deliver them to Pabst at his headquarters in the Eden Hotel in Berlin. On 15 January 1919 Liebknecht and Luxemburg were caught and taken to the Eden Hotel, whence they were subsequently taken to meet their fate.

Hauptmann Pabst had not given instructions for the arrest of Wilhelm Pieck. In fact, Pabst did not know Pieck, who was at this time one of the leaders of the "Revolutionäre Betriebsobleute" (revolutionary factory "shop stewards"). When Pieck was brought before Pabst, he seemed to be a broken man, possibly because what he had heard from the conversation of his soldier escorts had already given him an idea of what had happened to Liebknecht and Luxemburg.

Pabst asked him if he was willing to provide information on the addresses of Communists and the location of Communist hiding places and secret weapon stores. Pieck told Pabst everything he knew and "as a reward" was set free. The information he gave was of great assistance to the soldiers of the Dismounted Cavalry Guard when they combed Berlin in the weeks following, and led to the arrest of Leo Jogiches, Rosa Luxemburg's close confidant, and the discovery of several stores of arms. Jogiches met his end shortly afterwards by "falling down a flight of stairs" in the Moabit court building in Berlin.

(The foregoing information was given to the author by Herr Waldemar Pabst, Major a.D. on 30 November 1959.)

Although Pieck's release must have seemed remarkable to everyone, and particularly to the "wide-awake" Communists, no action was ever taken against him, not even during the Moscow purges.

At this time, of course, a minute examination was being made of every detail of the past life of every Communist who happened to be in Moscow. Indeed, many of them became the objects of fictitious allegations, as Khrushchev confirmed in his secret speech. However, nothing whatever happened to Wilhelm Pieck, notwithstanding that in 1931 Kippenberger, on Thälmann's instructions, investigated the affair and assembled material bearing on the mysterious circumstances of Pieck's release. (See Wollenberg, *Der Apparat, op. cit.,* pp. 17 ff.)

Pieck had always been a submissive lackey of Stalin. He had to remain compliant in future, too, now that Stalin had up his sleeve material with which to exact loyalty to the Party—Pieck's behaviour following his arrest by the Garde-Kavallerie-Schützen-Division in 1919.

## Appendix IV

## STATUTES OF THE THIRD INTERNATIONAL

IN 1864 the International Working Men's Association, the First International, was founded in London. Its provisional rules ran as follows:

That the emancipation of the working classes must be conquered by the working classes themselves; that the struggle for the emancipation of the working classes means not a struggle for class privileges and monopolies, but for equal rights and duties, and the abolition of all class rule;

That the economical subjection of the man of labour to the monopolizer of the means of labour, that is the sources of life, lies at the bottom of servitude in all its forms, of all social misery, mental degradation, and political dependence;

That the economical emancipation of the working classes is therefore the great end to which every political movement ought to be subordinate as a means;

That all efforts aiming at that great end have hitherto failed from the want of solidarity between the manifold divisions of labour in each country, and from the absence of a fraternal bond of union between the working classes of different countries;

That the emancipation of labour is neither a local nor a national, but a social problem, embracing all countries in which modern society exists, and depending for its solution on the concurrence, practical and theoretical, of the most advanced countries;

That the present revival of the working classes in the most industrious countries of Europe, while it raises a new hope, gives solemn warning against a relapse into the old errors and calls for the immediate combination of the still disconnected movements.

The Second International, founded in Paris in 1889, undertook to carry on the work of the First International. But in 1914, at the beginning of the world slaughter, it suffered complete breakdown. Undermined by opportunism and shattered by the treachery of its leaders, who went over to the side of the bourgeoisie, the Second International collapsed.

The Communist International, founded in March 1919 in the capital of the Russian Federal Soviet Republic, Moscow, solemnly declares before the entire world that it undertakes to continue and to carry through to the end the great work begun by the First International Working Men's Association.

The Communist International was formed after the conclusion of the imperialist war of 1914–18, in which the imperialist bourgeoisie of the different countries sacrificed twenty million men.

"Remember the imperialist war!" These are the first words addressed by the Communist International to every working man and woman; wherever they live and whatever language they speak. Remember that because of the existence of capitalist society a handful of imperialists were able to force the workers of the different countries for four long years to cut each other's throats. Remember that the war of the bourgeoisie conjured up in Europe and throughout the world the most frightful famine and the most appalling misery. Remember that without the overthrow of capitalism the repetition of such robber wars is not only possible, but inevitable.

It is the aim of the Communist International to fight by all available means, including armed struggle, for the overthrow of the international bourgeoisie and for the creation of an international Soviet republic as a transitional stage to the complete abolition of the State. The Communist International considers the dictatorship of the proletariat the only possible way to liberate mankind from the horrors of capitalism. And the Communist International considers the Soviet power the historically given form of this dictatorship of the proletariat.

The imperialist war bound the destinies of the proletariat of each country very closely to the destinies of the proletariat of all other countries. The imperialist war once again confirmed what was written in the statutes of the First International: the emancipation of the workers is not a local, nor a national, but an international problem.

The Communist International breaks once and for all with the traditions of the Second International, for whom in fact only white-skinned people existed. The task of the Communist International is to liberate the working people of the entire world. In its ranks the white, the yellow, and the black-skinned peoples—the working people of the entire world—are fraternally united.

The Communist International supports to the full the conquests of the great proletarian revolution in Russia, the first victorious socialist revolution in world history, and calls on the proletariat of the entire world to take the same path. The Communist International undertakes to support every Soviet republic, wherever it may be formed.

The Communist International recognizes that in order to hasten victory, the Working Men's Association which is fighting to annihilate capitalism and create Communism must have a strongly centralized organization. The Communist International must, in fact and in deed, be a single Communist party of the entire world. The parties working in the various countries are but its separate sections. The organizational machinery of the Communist International must guarantee the workers of each country the opportunity of getting the utmost help from the organized proletariat of other countries at any given moment.

For this purpose the Communist International ratifies the following statutes:

1. The new international association of workers is established to organize joint action by the proletariat of the different countries which pursue the one goal: the overthrow of capitalism, the establishment of the dictatorship of the proletariat and of an international Soviet republic which will completely abolish all classes and realize socialism, the first stage of Communist society.

2. The new international association of workers is called "The Communist International".

3. All parties belonging to the Communist International bear the name "Communist Party of such and such a country (section of the Communist International)".

4. The supreme authority in the Communist International is the World Congress of all the parties and organizations which belong to it. The World Congress meets regularly once a year. The World Congress alone is empowered to change the programme of the Communist International. The World Congress discusses and decides the most important questions of programme and tactics connected with the activities of the Communist International. The number of votes to which each party or organization is entitled shall be fixed by special Congress decision.

5. The World Congress elects the Executive Committee of the Communist International, which is the directing body of the Communist International in the period between its World Congresses. The Executive Committee is responsible only to the World Congress.

6. The seat of the Executive Committee of the Communist International shall be determined on each occasion by the World Congress of the Communist International.

7. An extraordinary World Congress of the Communist International may be convened either by a decision of the Executive Committee or at the request of half the parties which belonged to

the Communist International at the time of its preceding World Congress.

8. The chief work of the Executive Committee falls on the party of that country where, by decision of the World Congress, the Executive Committee has its seat. The party of the country in question shall have five representatives with full voting powers on the Executive Committee. In addition the ten to thirteen most important Communist parties, the list to be ratified by the regular World Congress, shall each have one representative with full voting powers on the Executive Committee. Other organizations and parties accepted by the Communist International have the right to delegate to the Executive Committee one representative each, with consultative voice.

9. The Executive Committee conducts the entire work of the Communist International from one Congress to the next, publishes, in at least four languages, the central organ of the Communist International (the periodical *Communist International*), issues any necessary appeals in the name of the Communist International, and issues instructions which are binding on all parties and organizations belonging to the Communist International. The Executive Committee of the Communist International has the right to demand that parties belonging to the International shall expel groups or persons who offend against international discipline, and it also has the right to expel from the Communist International those parties which violate decisions of the World Congress. These parties have the right to appeal to the World Congress. Should the need arise the Executive Committee shall set up in the various countries its technical and other auxiliary bureaux, which are wholly subordinate to the Executive Committee. The representatives of the Executive Committee shall carry out their political tasks in closest contact with the party centre of the country concerned.

10. The Executive Committee of the Communist International has the right to co-opt on the committee, with consultative voice, representatives of organizations and parties which, while not belonging to the Communist International, sympathize with and stand near to it.

11. The press organs of all parties and all organizations which belong to the Communist International, and those which are recognized as sympathizing parties and organizations, are bound to publish all official decisions of the Communist International and its Executive Committee.

12. The general situation all over Europe and America compels

M

Communists throughout the world to create illegal Communist organizations side by side with the legal organization. The Executive Committee is obliged to see that this is put into effect everywhere.

13. As a rule political communication between the individual parties belonging to the Communist International will be conducted through the ECCI. In urgent cases communication may be direct, but the ECCI shall be simultaneously informed.

14. Trade unions adhering to the Communist platform and organized internationally under the leadership of the Communist International, shall form a trade union section of the Communist International. These trade unions shall send their representatives to the World Congresses of the Communist International through the Communist parties of the countries concerned. The trade union section of the Communist International shall have one representative with full voting powers on the ECCI. The ECCI has the right to send one representative with full voting powers to the trade union section of the Communist International.

15. The Communist Youth International is, like all other members of the Communist International, subordinate to the Communist International and its Executive Committee. The Executive Committee of the Communist Youth International has one representative with full voting powers on the ECCI. The ECCI has the right to send one representative with full voting powers to the Executive Committee of the Communist Youth International.

16. The ECCI confirms the appointment of the international secretary of the Communist women's movement and shall organize the women's section of the Communist International.

17. When moving from one country to another every member of the Communist International shall receive the fraternal help of the local members of the Communist International.

## Appendix V

## THE 21 CONDITIONS

THE 1st Congress of the Communist International did not draw up any precise conditions for the admission of parties to the Third International. When the 1st Congress was convened there were in the majority of countries only Communist *trends* and *groups*.

The 2nd Congress of the Communist International is meeting in different circumstances. At the present time there are in most countries not only Communist trends and tendencies, but Communist *parties* and *organizations*.

Application for admission to the Communist International is now frequently made by parties and groups which up to a short time ago still belonged to the Second International, but which have not in fact become Communist. The Second International has finally broken down. The in-between parties and the centrist groups, seeing the utter hopelessness of the Second International, are trying to find a support in the Communist International, which is growing steadily stronger. But in doing so they hope to retain enough "autonomy" to enable them to continue their former opportunist or "centrist" policy. The Communist International is becoming, to some extent, fashionable.

The desire of some leading 'centrist' groups to join the Communist International indirectly confirms that it has won the sympathies of the overwhelming majority of the class-conscious workers of the entire world and that with every day it is becoming a more powerful force.

The Communist International is threatened by the danger of dilution by unstable and irresolute elements which have not yet completely discarded the ideology of the Second International.

Moreover, in some of the larger parties (Italy, Sweden, Norway, Yugoslavia, etc.) where the majority adhere to the Communist standpoint, there still remains even today a reformist and social-pacifist wing which is only waiting a favourable moment to raise its head again and start active sabotage of the proletarian revolution and so help the bourgeoisie and the Second International.

No Communist should forget the lessons of the Hungarian revolution. The Hungarian proletariat paid a high price for the fusion of the Hungarian Communists with the so-called "left" social-democrats.

Consequently the 2nd Congress of the Communist International thinks it necessary to lay down quite precisely the conditions of admission of new parties, and to point out to those parties which have already joined the duties imposed on them.

The 2nd Congress of the Communist International puts forward the following conditions of adherence to the Communist International:

1. *All propaganda and agitation* must be of a genuinely Communist character and in conformity with the programme and decisions of the Communist International. The entire Party press must be run by reliable Communists who have proved their devotion to the cause of the proletariat. The dictatorship of the proletariat is to be treated not simply as a current formula learnt by rote; it must be advocated in a way which makes its necessity comprehensible to every ordinary working man and woman, every soldier and peasant, from the facts of their daily life, which must be systematically noted in our press and made use of every day.

The periodical press and other publications, and all Party publishing houses, must be completely subordinated to the Party Presidium, regardless of whether the Party as a whole is at the given moment legal or illegal. Publishing houses must not be allowed to abuse their independence and pursue a policy which is not wholly in accordance with the policy of the Party.

In the columns of the press, at popular meetings, in the trade unions and co-operatives, wherever the adherents of the Communist International have an entry, it is necessary to denounce systematically and unrelentingly, not only the bourgeoisie, but also their assistants, the reformists of all shades.

2. Every organization which wishes to join the Communist International must, in an orderly and planned fashion, remove reformists and centrists from all responsible positions in the workers' movement (party organizations, editorial boards, trade unions, parliamentary fractions, co-operatives, local government bodies) and replace them by tried Communists, even if, particularly at the beginning, "experienced" opportunists have to be replaced by ordinary rank-and-file workers.

3. In practically every country of Europe and America the class struggle is entering the phase of civil war. In these circumstances Communists can have no confidence in bourgeois legality. They are obliged everywhere to create a parallel illegal organization which at the decisive moment will help the Party to do its duty to the revolution. In all those countries where, because of a state of siege or of emergency laws, Communists are unable to do all their work legally, it is absolutely essential to combine legal and illegal work.

4. The obligation to spread Communist ideas includes the special obligation to carry on systematic and energetic propaganda in the Army. Where such agitation is prevented by emergency laws, it must be carried on illegally. Refusal to undertake such work would be tantamount to a dereliction of revolutionary duty and is incompatible with membership of the Communist International.

5. Systematic and well-planned agitation must be carried on in the countryside. The working class cannot consolidate its victory if it has not by its policy assured itself of the support of at least part of the rural proletariat and the poorest peasants, and of the neutrality of part of the rest of the rural population. At the present time Communist work in rural areas is acquiring first-rate importance. It should be conducted primarily with the help of revolutionary Communist urban and rural workers who have close connections with the countryside. To neglect this work, or to leave it in unreliable semi-reformist hands, is tantamount to renouncing the proletarian revolution.

6. Every party which wishes to join the Communist International is obliged to expose not only avowed social-patriotism, but also the insincerity and hypocrisy of social-pacifism; to bring home to the workers systematically that without the revolutionary overthrow of capitalism no international court of arbitration, no agreement to limit armaments, no "democratic" reorganization of the League of Nations, will be able to prevent new imperialist wars.

7. Parties which wish to join the Communist International are obliged to recognize the necessity for a complete and absolute break with reformism and with the policy of the "centre", and to advocate this break as widely as possible among their members. Without that no consistent Communist policy is possible.

The Communist International demands unconditionally and categorically that this break be effected as quickly as possible. The Communist International is unable to agree that notorious opportunists, such as Turati Modigliani, Kautsky, Hilferding, Hilquit, Longguet, MacDonald, etc., shall have the right to appear as members of the Communist International. That could only lead to the Communist International becoming in many respects similar to the Second International, which has gone to pieces.

8. A particularly explicit and clear attitude on the question of the colonies and the oppressed peoples is necessary for the parties in those countries where the bourgeoisie possess colonies and oppress other nations. Every party which wishes to join the Communist International is obliged to expose the tricks and dodges of

MX

"its" imperialists in the colonies, to support every colonial liberation movement not merely in words but in deeds, to demand the expulsion of their own imperialists from these colonies, to inculcate among the workers of their country a genuinely fraternal attitude to the working people of the colonies and the oppressed nations, and to carry on systematic agitation among the troops of their country against any oppression of the colonial peoples.

9. Every party which wishes to join the Communist International must carry on systematic and persistent Communist activity inside the trade unions, the workers' councils and factory committees, the co-operatives, and other mass workers' organizations. Within these organizations Communist cells must be organized which shall by persistent and unflagging work win the trade unions, etc., for the Communist cause. In their daily work the cells must everywhere expose the treachery of the social-patriots and the instability of the "centre". The Communist cells must be completely subordinate to the Party as a whole.

10. Every party belonging to the Communist International is obliged to wage an unyielding struggle against the Amsterdam "International" of the yellow trade unions. It must conduct the most vigorous propaganda among trade unionists for the necessity of a break with the yellow Amsterdam International. It must do all it can to support the international association of red trade unions, adhering to the Communist International, which is being formed.

11. Parties which wish to join the Communist International are obliged to review the personnel of their parliamentary fractions and remove all unreliable elements, to make these fractions not only verbally but in fact subordinate to the Party Presidium, requiring of each individual Communist member of parliament that he subordinate his entire activity to the interests of genuinely revolutionary propaganda and agitation.

12. Parties belonging to the Communist International must be based on the principle of *democratic centralism*. In the present epoch of acute civil war the Communist Party will be able to fulfil its duty only if its organization is as centralized as possible, if iron discipline prevails, and if the Party centre, upheld by the confidence of the Party membership, has strength and authority and is equipped with the most comprehensive powers.

13. Communist parties in those countries where Communists carry on their work legally must from time to time undertake cleansing (re-registration) of the membership of the Party in order to get rid of any petty-bourgeois elements which have crept in.

14. Every party which wishes to join the Communist International is obliged to give unconditional support to any Soviet republic in its struggle against counter-revolutionary forces. Communist parties must carry on unambiguous propaganda to prevent the dispatch of munitions transports to the enemies of the Soviet republics; they must also carry on propaganda by every means, legal or illegal, among the troops sent to strangle workers' republics.

15. Parties which still retain their old social-democratic programmes are obliged to revise them as quickly as possible, and to draw up, in accordance with the special conditions of their country, a new Communist programme in conformity with the decisions of the Communist International. As a rule the programme of every party belonging to the Communist International must be ratified by the regular Congress of the Communist International or by the Executive Committee. Should the programme of a party not be ratified by the ECCI, the party concerned has the right to appeal to the Congress of the Communist International.

16. All the decisions of the Congresses of the Communist International, as well as the decisions of its Executive Committee, are binding on all parties belonging to the Communist International. The Communist International, working in conditions of acute civil war, must be far more centralized in its structure than was the Second International. Consideration must of course be given by the Communist International and its Executive Committee in all their activities to the varying conditions in which the individual parties have to fight and work, and they must take decisions of general validity only when such decisions are possible.

17. In this connection, all parties which wish to join the Communist International must change their names. Every party which wishes to join the Communist International must be called: *Communist* party of such and such a country (section of the Communist International). This question of name is not merely a formal matter, but essentially a political question of great importance. The Communist International has declared war on the entire bourgeois world and on all yellow social-democratic parties. The difference between the Communist parties and the old official "social-democratic" or "socialist" parties, which have betrayed the banner of the working class, must be brought home to every ordinary worker.

18. All leading Party press organs in all countries are obliged to publish all important official documents of the Executive Committee of the Communist International.

19. All parties belonging to the Communist International, and

those which have applied for admission, are obliged to convene an extraordinary Congress as soon as possible, and in any case not later than four months after the 2nd Congress of the Communist International, to examine all these conditions of admission. In this connection all party centres must see that the decisions of the 2nd Congress of the Communist International are made known to all local organizations.

20. Those parties which now wish to join the Communist International, but which have not radically changed their former tactics, must see to it that, before entering the Communist International, not less than two-thirds of the members of their central committee and of all their leading central bodies consist of comrades who publicly and unambiguously advocated the entry of their party into the Communist International before its 2nd Congress. Exceptions can be made with the consent of the Executive Committee of the Communist International. The ECCI also has the right to make exceptions in the case of representatives of the centre mentioned in paragraph 7.

21. Those members of the party who reject in principle the conditions and these put forward by the Communist International are to be expelled from the Party.

The same applies in particular to delegates to the extraordinary Congresses.

## Appendix VI

## LETTERS OF MÜNZENBERG

(a) *To Stalin, 14 July 1937:*

"If, contrary to Party custom, I address myself to you directly and personally, I am induced to do so by my absolute and unlimited faith in you as head of the world Communist movement. . . .

The German Communist Party is perhaps the largest after the W.K.P., which you have so brilliantly and successfully led. . . .

Walter Ulbricht has said that a comrade from the SPD once declared, 'Here comes Walter to carry out Stalin's programme'. He (Ulbricht) added, 'Yes, comrades, that is what is involved. Now we are going to practise Stalinist policies.' I do not doubt, and I know, that you will refuse to allow these policies to be called 'Stalinist policies'.

This letter is intended to be a cry for help, a cry intended to draw your attention to the danger I believe I can see. Perhaps I am wrong. Perhaps I am seeing something suspicious in what are merely personal differences. If so, I shall be the first to withdraw.

Hoping to see you and to be able to carry on my work, and hoping to be given your comradely help, as in past years, I remain, etc."

(b) *To Bohumil Smeral, 23 July 1937:*

"It is the pride of my life that I am the first German Socialist to have become a comrade in the Bolshevik struggle, that I was a comrade in the difficult times and always shall be, until I die."

(c) *To Dimitroff, 14 June 1938:*

"My dear friend,

Thank you for your kind message, which was passed on to me by L.F.[1] . . .

I know that my political concepts are Communist and correct. But at the same time I also know that I have gravely offended against formal Party discipline. I told you in a previous letter that if I am measured by the normal yardstick, then I shall be condemned. . . .

I have not hitherto tried to minimize the gravity of my mistakes,

[1] "L.F." is Louis Fischer, the author of a large number of books and other writings, including *Wiedersehen mit Moskau* (Frankfurt am Main, 1957). At the date of this letter he was a journalist in Moscow and occasionally acted as a messenger between Münzenberg and Dimitroff. (Private information to the author from Mr Fischer, who now lives in New York.)

and I shall not try to do so in the future. Today, I only want to give you an explanation of my attitude, which might otherwise seem incomprehensible. I have made mistakes—especially mistakes caused by my temperament—but never in the larger political issues: neither in the question of the 1914 war nor in the question of the founding of the 'Zimmerwald Left', neither in the founding of the Third International nor in the campaign against Brandler, Ruth Fischer and the forces working against the leaders of the Comintern —nor yet again in the Trotsky affair. Following my own ideas, I was the first, with Thälmann, to declare against Zinoviev. In critical times I have spoken against Trotsky and for Stalin, against Trotsky not only in my review *Unsere Zeit* but in the whole of my political activity."

(d) *To the Comintern Secretariat for transmission to Dimitroff:*
"I am convinced that no other party than the KPD, in collaboration with the Communist International and the Soviet Union, can claim the prior right to lead the German anti-fascist movement, provided it understands its historic mission and remains true to it by relying on . . . the objective conditions, its history and the Party's traditions. I am fighting for a policy for the Party which will create and assure it prestige and authority. I have had violent battles with the Ulbricht group on account of this and many other questions to do with the strategy of our Party. I am firmly convinced that the policy I have put forward is the only correct one and that it accords with Communist ideology and with the Communist movement and its traditions.

I do not want to act against the Party and the Communist International, and I never have done, but I am today more than ever persuaded that in this fight I have been defending the interests of the KPD and of the Communist International. What has been at stake in this fight is what I treasure above all things—the fundamental principles of the Communist movement. I have always believed that the first duty that a true Communist must fulfil he owes to these principles and not to individuals. A man must obey God more than man and he must obey the Revolution and loyalty to our Russian friends more than the members of a Party organization."

# BIBLIOGRAPHY

ALEXANDER, Robert J., *Communism in Latin America*, New Brunswick, 1957.

*The Anti-Stalin Campaign and International Communism*, Oxford, 1956.

ARMSTRONG, Hamilton Fish, *Tito and Goliath*, London, 1951.

ARON, Raymond, *The Opium of the Intellectuals*, London, 1957.

BARMINE, Alexander, *Einer der entkam*, Wien, 1951.

BEDELL-SMITH, Walter, *Moscow Mission, 1946-1949*, Heinemann, 1950.

BLAGOYEVA, Stella, *Georgi Dimitroff* (Kurze Lebensbeschreibung), Deutsche Ausgabe, Berlin, 1954.

*Brief des ZK der KPJ und Briefe des ZK der KPdSU* (B), Belgrade, 1958 (mit Erklärungen).

BORKENAU, Franz, *European Communism*, Faber, 1953.

BUDENZ, Louis F., *This is My Story*, London, 1948.

CAMPESINO, El (Valentin Gonzales), *Listen, Comrades*, London, 1953.

CARR, Edward Hallett, *German-Soviet Relations between the Two World Wars*, Oxford, 1952.

CASTRO, Delgado Enrique, *J'ai perdu la foi à Moscou*, Paris, 1950.

CATTEL, David T., *Communism and the Spanish Civil War*, Berkeley and Los Angeles, 1956.

*Soviet Diplomacy and the Spanish Civil War*, Cambridge, 1958.

CHAMBERLAIN, William Henry, *The Russian Revolution 1917-1921*, London, 1935.

CHURCHILL, Sir Winston, *The Second World War* (Six Volumes), London, 1948-1954.

COLE, G. D. H., *The Second International*, London, 1956.

DALLIN, Alexander, *German Rule in Russia 1941-1945*, London, 1957.

DALLIN, David J., *Soviet Espionage*, Oxford, 1956.

*The Rise of Russia in Asia*, London, 1950.

DEDIJER, Vladimir, *Tito Speaks*, London, 1953.

DIMITROFF, Georgi, *Reichstagsbrandprozeg*, Berlin, 1946.

DJILAS, Milovan, *Lenin über die Beziehungen zwischen sozialistischen Staaten*, Belgrade, 1950.

*The New Class*, London, 1957.

DRAPER, Theodore, *The Roots of American Communism*, London, 1957.

ENGELS, Friedrich, *Zur Geschichte des Bundes der Kommunisten*, Berlin, 1949.

FISCHER, Louis, *The Soviets in World Affairs*, Princetown, 1951 (2 volumes).
*Russia Revisited*, London, 1957.

FISCHER, Ruth, *Stalin and German Communism*, Oxford, 1948.

FOSTER, William Z., *History of the Three Internationals*, New York, 1951.
*History of the Communist Party of the United States*, New York, 1952.

GATES, John, *The Story of an American Communist*, New York, 1958.

GORLITZ, Walter, *The German General Staff*, London, 1953.

HALPERIN, Ernst, *The Triumphant Heretic*, London, 1958.

HAYIT, Baymirza, *Turkestan im XX. Jahrhundert*, Darmstadt, 1956.

HOSTLER, Charles Warren, *Turkism and the Soviets*, London, 1957.

HUNT, R. N. C., *A Guide to Communist Jargon*, London, 1957.
*The Theory and Practice of Communism*, London, 1957.

HYDE, Douglas, *I Believed*, London, 1950.

ISAACS, Harold D., *The Tragedy of the Chinese Revolution*, Oxford, 1952.

JAMES, C. L. R., *World Revolution 1917-1936; The Rise and Fall of the Communist International*, London, 1937.

JOLL, James, *The Second International, 1889-1914*, London, 1955.

KHOKHLOV, Mikolai Yevgenievich, *Ich Sollte Morden*, Frankfurt, 1954.

KHRUSHCHEV, Nikita S., *Report of the Central Committee to the 20th Congress of the Communist Party of the Soviet Union*, Soviet News, 1956.

KOESTLER, Arthur, *The Invisible Writing*, London, 1954.

KOESTLER, SILONE, GIDE, WRIGHT, FISCHER and SPENDER, *The God that Failed*, London, 1950.

LAQUEUR, Walter Z., *Communism and Nationalism in the Middle East*, London, 1956.
*The Soviet Union and the Middle East*, London, 1959.

LENCZKOWSKI, George, *Russia, Iran and the West*, Ithaka (New York), 1948.

LENIN, Wladimir I., *Collected Works*, London, 1927.
*Selected Works*, London, 1955.
with SINOVIEV, *Gegen den Strom*, Hamburg, 1921.

LEONHARD, Wolfgang, *Kominform und Jugoslawien*, Belgrade, 1949.
*Child of the Revolution*, London, 1957.
*Kreml ohne Stalin*, Koln, 1959.

LOCKHART, R. B., *My Europe*, Putnam, 1952.

LUXEMBURG, Rosa, *The Russian Revolution*, Socialist Review Publishing Company, 1959.

McVICKER, Charles P., *Titoism—Pattern for International Communism*, London, 1957.

MARX/ENGELS, *Communist Party Manifesto*, London, 1948.
*Selected Correspondence*, London, 1960.
*Selected Works*, London, 1958.

MASANI, Minoo R., *The Communist Party of India*, New York, 1954.

MASSING, Hede, *This Deception*, New York, 1951.

McCARTHY, M., *Generation in Revolt*, 1953.

MEHNERT, Klaus, *Der Sovietmensch*, Stuttgart, 1958.

MIKSCHE, F. O., *Unconditional Surrender*, London, 1952.

MILLER, Harry, *The Communist Menace in Malaya*, New York, 1954.

MUENZENBERG, Willi, *Die dritte Front*, Berlin, 1930.

NAGY, Ferenc, *The Struggle behind the Iron Curtain*, London, 1948.

NAGY, Imre, *On Communism*, London, 1957.

OVERSTREET, Gene D., and WINDMILLER, Marshal, *Communism in India*, Berkeley and Los Angeles, 1959.

PAYNE, Robert, *Mao Tse-tung*, London, 1951.

PELLING, Henry, *The British Communist Party*, London, 1958.

PIJADE, M., *Das Marchen von der sovietischen Hilfe fur den Volksaufstand in Jugoslavia*, Belgrade, 1950.

RADEK, Karl, *Der Kampf der Komintern gegen Versailles*, Hamburg, 1923.

RAVINES, Eudocio, *The Yenen Way*, New York, 1951.

RECKITT, M. B., *As it Happened*, London, 1941.

REGLER, Gustav, *The Owl of Minerva*, London, 1959.

ROSMER, Alfred, *Moscou sous Lenine*, Paris, 1953.

ROTHSTEIN, Andrew, *A History of the U.S.S.R.*, London (Penguin), 1950.

SALAZAR, Sanchez, *Murder in Mexico*, London, 1950.

SCHLAMM, Willi, *Diktatur der Luge*, Zurich, 1937.

SCHMIDT, Elli, *40 Jahre Internationaler Frauentag*, Berlin, 1950.

SERGE, Victor, *The Case of Comrade Tulayev*, London, 1951.

SETON-WATSON, Hugh, *Pattern of Communist Revolution*, London, 1953.
*The East European Revolution*, London, 1957.

SHEPILOV, D. T., *Speech at the 20th Congress of the Communist Party of the Soviet Union*, Soviet News, 1956.

STALIN, Josef, *Works*, London, 1953-1955.
*Problems of Leninism*, London, 1940.
*Marxism and the National and Colonial Question*, London, 1936.

TITO, Josip Broz, *Workers Manage Factories in Yugoslavia*, Yugoslavian Embassy, London, 1951.
*Politischer Bericht des Zentralkomitees der Kommunistischen Partei Jugoslawiens* (Referat auf dem V. Kongress), Belgrade, 1948.

TROTSKI, Leo, *Die Internationale Revolution und die Kommunistische Internationale*, Berlin, 1929.
*Stalin*, London, 1947.
*The Stalin School of Falsification*, New York, 1937.
*Die Permanente Revolution*, Berlin, 1930.
*Verratene Revolution*, Zurich, 1957.

ULAM, Adam, B., *Titoism and the Cominform*, Oxford 1952.

VALTIN, Jan (Richard Krebs), *Out of the Night*, London, 1941.

WHITEHEAD, Don, *The F.B.I. Story*, London, 1957.

WHITING, Allen S., *Soviet Policies in China, 1917-1924*, New York, 1954.

WILLOUGHBY, Charles A., *Shanghai Conspiracy*, New York, 1952.

WOLFE, Bertram D., *Khrushchev and Stalin's Ghost*, London, 1957.

WOLIN, Simon, and SLUSSER, Robert M., *The Soviet Secret Police*, London, 1957.

WOLLENBERG, Erich, *Der Apparat*, Bonn, 1952.

ZELT, Johannes, *Proletarischer Internationalismus im Kampf um Sacco und Vanzett*, Ostberlin, 1958.

ZETKIN, Clara, *Zur Geschichte der proletarischen Frauenbewegung Deutschlands*, Berlin, 1958.

ZINNER, Paul (ed.), *National Communism and Popular Revolt in Eastern Europe*, Oxford, 1957.

# INDEX